How's Life?

MEASURING WELL-BEING

OECD

This work is published on the responsibility of the Secretary-General of the OECD. The opinions expressed and arguments employed herein do not necessarily reflect the official views of the Organisation or of the governments of its member countries.

Please cite this publication as:
OECD (2011), *How's Life?: Measuring well-being*, OECD Publishing.
http://dx.doi.org/10.1787/9789264121164-en

ISBN 978-92-64-11161-5 (print)
ISBN 978-92-64-12116-4 (PDF))

The statistical data for Israel are supplied by and under the responsibility of the relevant Israeli authorities. The use of such data by the OECD is without prejudice to the status of the Golan Heights, East Jerusalem and Israeli settlements in the West Bank under the terms of international law.

Corrigenda to OECD publications may be found on line at: *www.oecd.org/publishing/corrigenda*.

Foreword

This is a very special year for the OECD, as we are celebrating our 50th Anniversary. Reaching 50 is an important moment in everyone's life: you take stock of what you have achieved, you think of where you want to go next. Thinking about the future is all the more important as we are still in the aftermath of the most devastating crisis that the global economy has experienced since World War II. The hesitant recovery, high joblessness, unprecedented volatility of financial markets, and public debts that have reached levels never experienced before, make us think twice when defining the necessary policy responses in the long-run.

In this challenging environment, we are committed more than ever to our founding mission to foster economic prosperity, improve development perspectives and the well-being of our citizens. This means putting the people in the centre of economic, social and environmental policies. In short: *better policies for better lives*.

Better policies need to be based on sound evidence and a broad focus: Not only on people's income and financial conditions, but also on their health, their competencies, on the quality of the environment, where they live and work, their overall life satisfaction. Not only on the total amount of the goods and services, but also on equality and the conditions of those at the bottom of the ladder. Not only on the conditions "here and now" but also those in other parts of the world and those that are likely to prevail in the future. In summary, we need to focus on well-being and progress.

In this spirit, we launched our **Better Life Initiative**, of which this publication, *How's Life?*, is an essential part. *How's Life?* is a first attempt at the international level to present the best set of comparable and comprehensive well-being indicators for advanced and emerging economies. These indicators feed into *Your Better Life Index,* our new interactive web-based tool that allows users to choose the weights they wish to attach to various dimensions of life according to their own preferences and to compare overall well-being across countries.

Based on the experience of almost ten years of leading the reflection on better ways to measure progress, we have identified key topics which are essential to well-being in terms of material living conditions (housing, income, jobs) and quality of life (community, education, environment, governance, health, life satisfaction, safety and work-life balance). Each topic is built on specific indicators. For example, the Work-Life Balance topic is based on three separate measures: the number of employees working long hours; the percentage of working mothers; and the time people devote to leisure and personal activities.

This is published on the occasion of an international conference, organised jointly by the French Government and the OECD, to celebrate the two years since the release of the report by the *Commission on the Measurement of Economic Performance and Social Progress,* established by French President Nicolas Sarkozy and headed by Joseph Stiglitz, Amartya Sen and Jean-Paul Fitoussi. The work of the Commission has been critical in giving impetus to our path-finding work on measuring progress and to a range of initiatives around the world aimed at developing better indicators of peoples' lives. The OECD will continue to play a pivotal role in furthering the agenda of measuring well-being and progress. This includes ongoing research and analysis and high-level policy fora, such as the 4th OECD World Forum on Statistics, Knowledge and Policies, which will be held in New Delhi, India, in the autumn of 2012.

Developing better measures is not an end in itself but a means to enhance policies that improve people's lives. Statistics on critical aspects of people's lives are important, as what we measure shapes what we, collectively, strive to pursue. But statistics are obviously not enough. They need to be combined with a robust understanding and analysis of how the outcomes that these indicators measure respond to policy interventions. It is for this reason that the discussion on measuring progress and well-being needs to reach a wider audience. I hope that this publication will encourage greater discussion among policy makers and the general public about these important topics. For better policies we also need a better, broader and more inclusive measurement agenda.

Angel Gurría

Acknowledgements

This report is published under the responsibility of the Secretary General of the OECD. The opinions expressed and arguments employed herein do not necessarily reflect the official views of the Organisation or of the governments of its member countries.

The report was prepared by the Well-Being Unit of the OECD Directorate of Statistics: Carlotta Balestra (chapters 10 and 11), Romina Boarini (chapters 1 and 7), Michael de Looper and Gaetan Lafortune (chapter 5), Fabiola Riccardini (chapter 3), Nicolas Ruiz (chapter 2), Katherine Scrivens (chapters 6 and 8), Conal Smith (chapter 12), Joyce Sultan (chapters 4 and 9), under the supervision of Romina Boarini, Marco Mira d'Ercole and Martine Durand. Statistical assistance was provided by Elena Tosetto. Editorial assistance was provided by Germán Morales, Susannah Nash, Ingrid Herrbach and Sonia Primot. The report has benefited from contributions and comments from staff of other OECD Directorates and from national delegates to the OECD Committee on Statistics.

Table of Contents

This book has...

StatLinks

A service that delivers Excel® files from the printed page!

Look for the *StatLinks* at the bottom right-hand corner of the tables or graphs in this book.
To download the matching Excel® spreadsheet, just type the link into your Internet browser, starting with the *http://dx.doi.org* prefix.
If you're reading the PDF e-book edition, and your PC is connected to the Internet, simply click on the link. You'll find *StatLinks* appearing in more OECD books.

Reader's guide

Conventions

- Data shown for OECD and OECD EU are simple averages of countries displayed in each chart for the two areas.

- Each chart specifies the period covered. The mention XXXX or latest available year (where XXXX is a year or a period) means that data for later years are not taken into account.

- Each indicator is identified with a code of two letters (in either higher or lower cases) and one number (either Roman or Arabic). The two letters refer to the dimension dealt with in the chapter (e.g. IW stands for "Income and wealth"), while the number refers to the order in which the indicators are presented (e.g. I or 1 for the first indicator, II or 2 for the second indicator). Indicators are either headline indicators (identified by capital letters and Roman numbers, e.g. IW I for the first headline indicator of the dimension "Income and wealth"), or secondary indicators (coded with lowercases and an Arabic number (e.g. iw 1 for the first secondary indicator of the dimension "Income and wealth").

For all charts, ISO codes for countries are used

ARG	Argentina	FRA	France	NOR	Norway
AUS	Australia	GBR	United Kingdom	NZL	New Zealand
AUT	Austria	GRC	Greece	OECD	OECD average
BEL	Belgium	HUN	Hungary	OECD EU	OECD Europe average
BRA	Brazil	IDN	Indonesia	POL	Poland
CAN	Canada	IND	India	PRT	Portugal
CHE	Switzerland	IRL	Ireland	RUS	Russian Federation
CHL	Chile	ISL	Iceland	SAU	Saudi Arabia
CHN	China	ISR	Israel	SVK	Slovak Republic
CZE	Czech Republic	ITA	Italy	SVN	Slovenia
DEU	Germany	JPN	Japan	SWE	Sweden
DNK	Denmark	KOR	Korea	TUR	Turkey
ESP	Spain	LUX	Luxembourg	USA	United States
EST	Estonia	MEX	Mexico	ZAF	South Africa
FIN	Finland	NLD	Netherlands		

This document and any map included herein are without prejudice to the status of or sovereignty over any territory, to the delimitation of international frontiers and boundaries and to the name of any territory, city or area.

Statistics for Israel

The statistical data for Israel are supplied by and under the responsibility of the relevant Israeli authorities. The use of such data by the OECD is without prejudice to the status of the Golan Heights, East Jerusalem and Israeli settlements in the West Bank under the terms of international law.

Chapter 1

Overview

Introduction: in quest of better lives

Everyone aspires to a good life. But what does a "good" (or better) life mean? In recent years, concerns have emerged that standard macro-economic statistics, such as GDP, which for a long time had been used as proxies to measure well-being, failed to give a true account of people's current and future living conditions. The ongoing financial and economic crisis has reinforced this perception and it is now widely recognised that data on GDP provide only a partial perspective on the broad range of factors that matter to people's lives. Even during times of economic hardship, when restoring growth matters for the achievement of many well-being outcomes, such as having a good job or access to affordable housing, at the core of policy action must be the needs, concerns and aspirations of people and the sustainability of our societies.

The OECD has a long tradition of work on social indicators and quality of life.[1] More recently, the OECD has been leading the international reflection on measuring well-being and societal progress. In 2004, it held its first World Forum on "Statistics, Knowledge and Policies" in Palermo. Two more Forums have taken place, the first in Istanbul in 2007 (which led to the launch of the OECD-hosted Global Project on Measuring the Progress of Societies) and the second in Busan in 2009. Thanks to these and other efforts undertaken within the international community (Box 1.1), measuring well-being and progress is now at the forefront of national and international statistical and political agendas.

These initiatives share many important objectives. In particular, they aim to:

- Involve citizens in the discussion of what type of progress societies should strive to achieve.

- Identify a range of indicators that paint a more accurate picture of whether people's lives are getting better or worse.

- Reflect on how better measures of well-being and progress should inform public policy. Understand what drives well-being, so as to identify the range of policies needed to improve it.

On the occasion of the OECD's 50th Anniversary, held under the theme "Better Policies for Better Lives", the Organization launched the *OECD Better Life Initiative* (Box 1.2). *How's Life?*, which is part of this initiative, provides a concrete response to some of the issues mentioned above. Building on almost ten years of OECD work on progress, *How's Life?* is a first attempt at the international level to go beyond the conceptual stage and to present a large set of comparable well-being indicators for OECD countries and, to the extent possible, other major economies. This set is still exploratory and will, over the years, be improved by taking into account the outcomes of a number of methodological projects at the OECD and elsewhere as these deliver their results and lead to better measures. Nonetheless, this work is critical, as broad-based, international evidence is provided for the first time on a range of aspects of well-being. The report aims to respond to the needs of citizens for better information on well-being and to give a more accurate picture of societal progress to policy-makers.

This chapter provides an overview of the whole report. The chapter starts by first outlining the main motivations behind the quest for "going beyond GDP". The chapter then presents the main features of the framework used in this report to measure well-being, and how these translate concretely into indicators and evidence. The chapter then summarises the main findings of the report, starting from average well-being patterns in the countries analysed and then describing how well-being varies across the population. Finally, the chapter outlines the potential role of better measures of well-being for informing policy and concludes by indentifying the statistical agenda ahead for improving current indicators of well-being.

Box 1.1. **Measuring well-being: key national and international initiatives**

Today, "measuring well-being" is high on the statistical and political agendas at both the national and international level:

- Measuring well-being has been and will continue to be a key priority for the OECD, in line with its founding tradition to promote policies designed to achieve the highest living standards for all. The OECD *Better Life Initiative*, launched in May 2011, is a concrete expression of this priority.

- In 2008, French President Nicolas Sarkozy established the *Commission on the Measurement of Economic Performance and Social Progress*, chaired and coordinated by Joseph Stiglitz, Amartya Sen and Jean-Paul Fitoussi. In September 2009, the Commission published a report that included around 30 recommendations on how to improve measures of well-being and progress (Stiglitz *et al.*, 2009). Many of these recommendations are followed-up in *How's life?*.

- At the European level, the European Commission issued a communication on "GDP and beyond" in September 2009, identifying key actions to improve current metrics of progress (EC, 2009). Some of the themes of this Communication have found an echo in the five key targets (with supporting indicators) set by the European Commission to guide its policies in the EU 2020 Strategy. To support these processes, the statistical office of the European Community (Eurostat) and the French national statistical office (INSEE) initiated a process (the INSEE/Eurostat Sponsorship Group) to develop recommendations in line with the Stiglitz report, to be implemented within the European Statistical System. The OECD is contributing to this Sponsorship.

- The United Nations Economic Commission for Europe, in co-operation with the OECD and Eurostat, are pursuing work on measuring sustainable development, aiming to develop better metrics for human well-being and sustainability.

- Several countries have launched progress and well-being-related initiatives in the form of public national consultations (Australia, the United Kingdom), Parliamentary Commissions (Germany, Norway), National Roundtables (Italy, Spain, Slovenia), projects for integrating and disseminating statistics on a jurisdiction's economic, social and environmental conditions (the United States), dedicated statistical reports (Australia, Austria and Ireland) and a range of other initiatives (France, Japan, Korea, Luxembourg, Switzerland and China).

Box 1.2. **The OECD Better Life Initiative**

The OECD Better Life Initiative combines various streams of OECD work on well-being, including *How's Life?*, a Compendium of OECD Well-Being Indicators (OECD, 2011a) released during the OECD's 50th Anniversary celebration in May 2011, and the interactive, web-based tool *Your Better Life Index* (www.oecdbetterlifeindex. org). The Compendium of OECD Well-Being Indicators presented a preliminary, synthetic version of some of the indicators considered in *How's Life?*. All the indicators shown in the Compendium are included in *How's Life?* as headline indicators. *How's Life?* extends the analysis carried out in the Compendium, by enlarging the set of indicators and by looking at inequalities in well-being across the population. The *Your Better Life Index* aims to reach out to citizens, who are the ultimate beneficiaries of research and work on well-being: the voice of the public is critical in the debate on what matters most for the progress of societies.

Since its creation in 1961, the OECD has worked to help governments of member countries deliver good policies and improve the economic and social well-being of nations. The health of economies is of fundamental importance. But what ultimately matters is the well-being of citizens. The 50th Anniversary offers the opportunity to reaffirm the OECD's commitment to contribute to people's well-being through "Better Policies for Better Lives".

Where do we come from: GDP and beyond

Discussions about whether GDP is an accurate proxy of people's well-being predate the System of National Accounts on which GDP is based. Clearly, policy-makers have never focused single-mindedly on GDP growth as the single metric for measuring well-being. They have often tried to enhance the overall well-being of citizens, today and in the future, by taking into account a range of factors that reach beyond the total value of the goods and services produced by a country in a given year, to include distributional concerns and environmental quality. Nevertheless, standard measures of economic performance such as GDP continue to be widely used as general proxies of well-being, despite their well-known limitations in this regard (Box 1.3).

Box 1.3. **GDP is not an accurate measure of people's well-being**

GDP is a measure of the value of final goods and services produced within a country in a given time-period. Although the inventors of GDP never intended to use it as a measure of social welfare, in the absence of better measures of well-being, many (including the OECD) have used GDP as the main metric for gauging whether societies were prospering. However, from the perspective of assessing people's well-being, GDP has some important shortcomings:

- Since GDP includes income paid to non-residents and excludes residents' income from production in other countries, it does not provide a good measure of residents' income.

- Since GDP makes no allowance for the consumption of capital goods in the production process, it overestimates the value of output that might be consumed in a given period with an unchanged stock of capital.

- While GDP can be adjusted for "net income from abroad" and for capital depreciation to arrive respectively at the concept of gross national income (GNI) and net national income (NNI), even per-capita NNI is an imperfect approximation of the economic resources actually enjoyed by individuals and households, as shown by the differences between changes in NNI and changes in Household Net Disposable Adjusted Income over time (Figure 1.1).

● An important additional limitation of GDP and of other economic aggregates based on national accounts is that they do not provide information on how economic resources are shared across individuals.

● Further, GDP does not measure some factors that contribute to households' material well-being, such as own-produced household services – *e.g.* child care and parenting.

● Some of the activities included in GDP actually correspond to a reduction in people's well-being (as in the case of higher transport costs due to increased congestion and longer commuting) or to activities aimed at remedying some of the social and environmental costs associated with production (as in the case of spending on pollution abatement). These "regrettables" contribute to high economic activity but they obviously do not add to people's well-being.

● Importantly, a range of key attributes of individuals and communities are not captured by GDP and the system of economic accounts. These attributes include people's health status, their happiness, their personal security and their social connections, all of which matter to people independently of their effect on people's consumption possibilities. A common attribute of these factors is that they are not mediated and exchanged through markets, hence their evaluation needs to rely on non-monetary measures.

● Finally, GDP cannot show whether well-being can be kept up over time because it only partially integrates information on how the various types of capital that sustain well-being are changing over time.

Figure 1.1. **Net national income and household net adjusted disposable income in real terms**

Average annual growth in percentage, 1995-2009 or latest available period

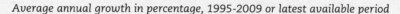

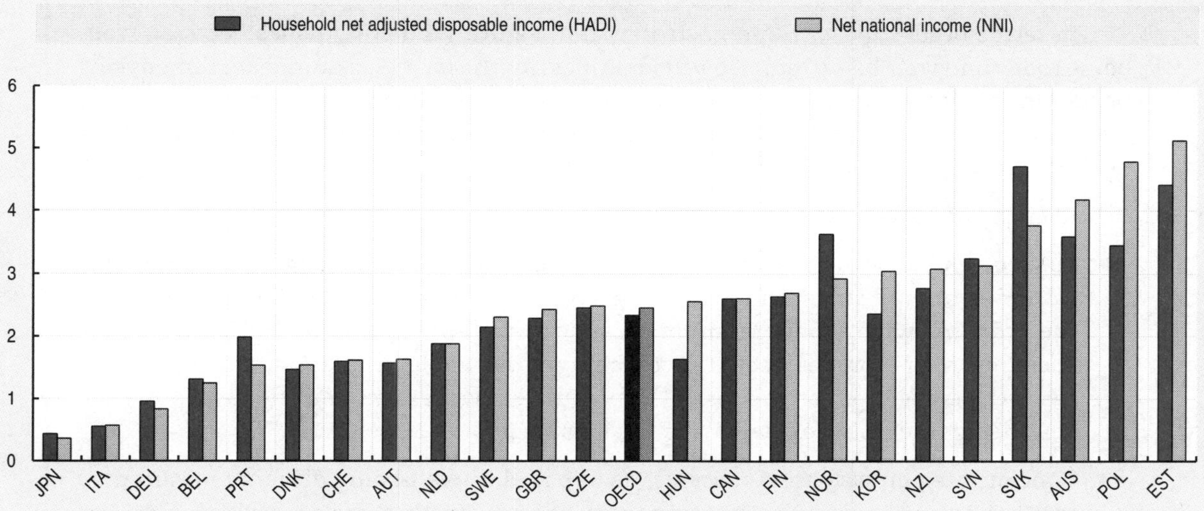

Note: The *annualized growth rate refers to 1995-08 for Australia and Switzerland; 1995-10 for Finland, Portugal (only for the HADI) and Sweden; and 1996-08 for Japan. The net national income growth rate refers to 1995-06 for the Slovak Republic.*
Sources: OECD, National Accounts data; Statistics New Zealand.

StatLink ᴍˢᴘ http://dx.doi.org/10.1787/888932491846

Many alternative approaches to measuring well-being have been suggested to overcome some of these limitations (for a review, see Boarini *et al.*, 2006; Stiglitz *et al.*, 2009; Fleurbaey, 2009). All these approaches recommend extending the scope of measurement to include a broader range of well-being components.[2] Putting together these indicators in a consistent framework is indeed one of the objectives of this report. This framework is presented in the next section.

A framework for measuring well-being

Defining well-being is challenging because it requires looking at many aspects of people's lives, as well as understanding their relative importance. Although there is no single definition of well-being, most experts and ordinary people around the world would agree that it requires meeting various human needs, some of which are essential (*e.g.* being in good health), as well as the ability to pursue one's goals, to thrive and feel satisfied with their life.

Since well-being is a complex phenomenon and many of its determinants are strongly correlated with each other, assessing well-being requires a comprehensive framework that includes a large number of components and that, ideally, allows gauging how their interrelations shape people's lives.

The framework underpinning *How's Life?* identifies three pillars for understanding and measuring people's well-being: i) material living conditions; ii) quality of life; iii) and sustainability (Figure 1.2). This approach draws closely on that proposed by Stiglitz *et al.*, (2009) by previous OECD work[3] and by measurement practices around the world.[4]

In terms of its *scope*, the approach shown in Figure 1.2 distinguishes between well-being today and well-being tomorrow. It identifies, for the former, a number of dimensions pertaining to either material living conditions or quality of life that are critical to people's lives; and, for the latter, a number of conditions that have to be met to preserve the well-being of future generations.

In terms of its *focus*, the approach:

- Puts the emphasis on *households and individuals*, rather than on aggregate conditions for the economy since, as discussed above, there may be a discrepancy between the economy-wide economic situation and the well-being of households.[5] Generally speaking, the report assesses the well-being of the whole population, though in some cases the focus is put on groups of the population who are more likely to face specific well-being trade-offs (*e.g.* work and life balance).

- Concentrates on *well-being outcomes*, as opposed to well-being drivers measured by input or output indicators. Outcomes may be imperfectly correlated with inputs (*e.g.* health expenditure may be a poor predictor of health status if the health care system is inefficient) or outputs (*e.g.* the number of surgical interventions performed may say little about people's health conditions).

- Looks at the *distribution of well-being* across individuals. This is especially important when there are disparities in achievements across population groups and when these are correlated across dimensions (*e.g.* when the likelihood of earning a low income is correlated with low educational achievement, poor health status, poor housing, etc.). In particular, *How's Life?* looks at disparities across age groups, gender, income or socio-economic background.

● Considers both *objective and subjective aspects of well-being*. Objective components of well-being are essential to assess people's living conditions and quality of life, but information on people's evaluations and feelings about their own lives is also important for capturing the psychological aspects of people's "beings and doings" (*e.g.* feelings of insecurity) and understanding the relationship between objective and subjective components of well-being.

Figure 1.2. **The "How's Life?" framework for measuring well-being and progress**

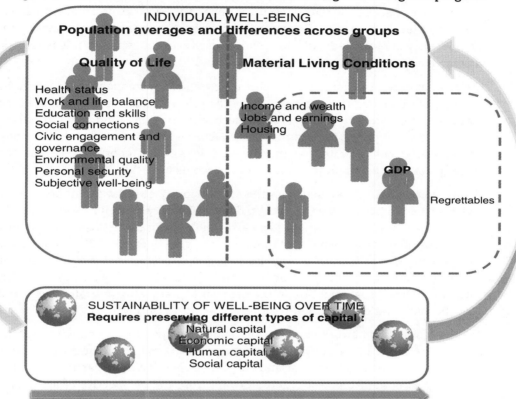

Source: OECD.

In terms of current well-being, *How's Life?* considers the following dimensions:[6]

● *Under material living conditions*: i) *Income and wealth*; ii) *Jobs and earnings*; and iii) *Housing*. Income and wealth capture people's current and future consumption possibilities. Both the availability of jobs and their quality are relevant for material well-being, not only because they increase command over resources but also because having a job provides the opportunity to fulfil one's own ambitions and build self-esteem. Finally, housing and its quality are essential not only to meet basic needs but also to have a sense of personal security, privacy and personal space.

● *Under quality of life*: i) *Health status*; ii) *Work and life balance*; iii) *Education and skills*; iv) *Civic engagement and governance*; v) *Social connections*; vi) *Environmental quality*; vii) *Personal security*; and viii) *Subjective well-being*.[7] Being healthy is important in itself but also for performing a range of activities relevant to well-being, including work. Similarly, everyone aspires to becoming educated, but it is also a great asset for raising the living standards of individuals and society as a whole. Being able to reconcile work and life is important for the well-being of those who value having both a job and a family while, more generally, being able to spend time on non-remunerated activities helps individuals to remain healthy and productive. Civic engagement and quality of governance matter for well-being, as they allow people to have more control of their lives. Social connectedness is a basic human need that also helps fulfil many other important goals (*e.g.* finding a job). The quality of the environment where people live affects their health and their ability to do a number of essential activities. Likewise, an environment where people can feel secure is important to a good life. Finally, considering how people feel in terms of their own evaluations and emotions is important for seeing whether they are satisfied with their lives as a whole, and whether this is the result of objective living circumstances or other factors.[8]

This thematic structure for current well-being covers many components, reflecting both *individual* capabilities (conditions in which some choices are made, and peoples' abilities to transform resources into given ends, for instance, health; Sen, 1998) and material outcomes (*e.g.* income or consumption). Important *social* capabilities are not considered in this report or are considered to only a limited extent. Future editions of this report will integrate these aspects to the extent that appropriate indicators become available.

Ideally, comprehensive evidence on the sustainability of today's well-being should have been included in this report. However, data availability as well as well unresolved conceptual issues (Box 1.4) have imposed a narrower focus for the first issue of the report, namely, a focus on environmental sustainability (drawing upon the OECD Green Growth Strategy Indicators, see Chapter 10, Annex A10.1) and selected aspects of human capital sustainability (Chapter 7, Box 7.7). Future editions of *How's Life?* will more systematically integrate indicators of sustainability in the core set of well-being indicators, as suitable indicators become available (Box 1.4).

The conceptual framework used in this report has been discussed with high-level representatives of National Statistical Offices of OECD member countries. There is nevertheless scope for improvement and further development, in particular with the objective of making the framework more relevant from the perspective of all countries covered by the analysis.[9]

Box 1.4. **Measuring whether well-being can be sustained over time**

One critical issue in a report of this type is whether current well-being can be sustained in the future. This refers to the capacity of societies to achieve well-being outcomes that can last over time. If future achievements could be observed (or accurately predicted) today, the measurement of sustainability would be conceptually similar to the measurement of current well-being. This is, however, not the case for most outcomes of interest. Hence, the measurement of sustainability has to follow a different track.

The approach taken in this report, which is in line with the one pursued by other international initiatives in this field (such as the UNECE-OECD-Eurostat Taskforce on Sustainable Development) is that the measurement of sustainability requires looking at the evolution over time of the different stocks of capital (economic, environmental, human and social) that sustain the various dimensions of well-being, and in particular at how decisions taken today affect these stocks.

Non-sustainable patterns of development may reflect excessive consumption of today's resources and inadequate investments (implying that overall stocks of various types of capital in per capita terms may be declining over time), as well as imbalances in the composition and distribution of the various stocks. A further important distinction between the measurement of current and future well-being is that the former focuses on the conditions of individuals and households, while the latter requires looking at the conditions of systems (economic, social and ecological) of which individuals are part. This makes the measurement of sustainability significantly more challenging than the measurement of current well-being.

Selecting indicators

Measuring well-being requires choosing indicators that suitably capture the dimensions and domains of well-being presented in the previous section. A great effort has been put into choosing *available* indicators that are conceptually sound as well as relevant to measuring well-being across the population from the perspective of informing policy. To that end, *How's Life?* distinguishes between *headline indicators*, i.e. indicators that are deemed to be of sufficiently good quality (see below) and can be used for monitoring well-being over time and across countries, and *secondary indicators* that provide complementary evidence (*e.g.* indicators covering more specific aspects of the dimension at hand, with more limited country coverage, or based on sources that were deemed to be less robust than in the case of headline indicators).

The selection of indicators presented in *How's Life?* has relied on international standards on measurement, including: *i)* policy relevance; *ii)* quality of the underlying data; *iii)* comparability of the concepts and survey questions used; and *iv)* frequency of compilation (see Box 1.5). The selection has been made in consultation with OECD experts and National Statistical Offices of OECD member countries. While the chosen set of indicators represents the best available proxies for outcomes in the different dimensions of well-being, these indicators do not meet all the criteria required by an ideal set. In this respect, the indicators presented in this report should be understood as being experimental and evolutionary. This implies that they will change in the future as better measures are developed and as countries reach agreement on indicators that are more apt to summarise the state of the various dimensions of people's lives.

An ideal set of well-being indicators should come from an internationally harmonised data collection based on common definitions and survey practices, and collected as part of the official statistical system of member countries. While current OECD work aims at developing guidelines for the collection of more comparable statistics for some of the dimensions included in Figure 1.2 (*e.g.* household wealth, subjective well-being), for the time being it is impossible to collect all the relevant information on the basis of available official data. As a pragmatic solution, in the few instances where the existing official data are not fully comparable across countries, this report makes use of data from non-official sources (in particular from the *Gallup World Poll*).[10] While these non-official sources have well-known limits in terms of sample size, sampling frames, mode of data collection, etc., they cover a wide range of countries and rely on a harmonised questionnaire around the world. The indicators based on non-official sources are included in this report as "place holders", until better and more comparable official statistics in these fields are developed.[11] Results based on these non-official data have to be interpreted with great caution.

Box 1.5. **The choice of How's Life? indicators**

The *How's Life?* framework shown in Figure 1.2 has guided the selection of indicators. Critical criteria for selection have been that indicators: capture well-being achievements at the individual or household level; measure well-being outcomes; allow disaggregation, so as to assess the well-being of different population groups; and gauge the joint distributions of achievements, *e.g.* whether a person with a disadvantage in one dimension also experiences poor outcomes in another. The indicators have also been chosen so as to fulfill standard statistical requirements, such as that they:

- *Have face validity, i. e.* the capacity to capture what is intended to be measured. Face validity is defined with respect to the target concept that one seeks to measure, *i.e.* substantive interpretations of the dimensions of well-being that matter to people's lives, according to a large body of evidence and practices.

- *Focus on summary outcomes, i.e.* on relatively broad achievements (such as "good health status") that can be easily understood (*e.g.* displaying no ambiguity in interpretation, showing either good/bad performance or progress/regress when looking at changes over time).

- *Are amenable to change and sensitive to policy interventions,* which is important from the perspective of improving the design of policies that bear on well-being and, ultimately, on people's lives.

- *Are commonly used and accepted* as well-being indicators within the statistical and academic communities. This is more often the case for indicators relying on statistical instruments developed within the official statistical system but it can also be the case for indicators based on surveys conducted by other institutions.

- *Ensure comparability across countries.* Comparability is ensured when concepts and definitions follow internationally agreed standards and the surveys/instruments from which data are collected are based on a harmonised questionnaire and similar implementation design. However, comparability can also be achieved by putting together broadly comparable instruments *ex post*; this latter approach is used by the OECD in a number of fields (*e.g. Health at a Glance*).

- *Ensure maximum country coverage:* strictly speaking, this is not a data quality criterion but a working constraint given the aim of producing comparable evidence for OECD and some of other major economies.

- *Are collected through a recurrent instrument,* which is important for monitoring changes in well-being over time.

These criteria define the "ideal" set of indicators for monitoring well-being across countries and over time. In practice, finding indicators that meet all these criteria equally well is challenging and will remain so for quite some time. Against this background, the criteria above have been mapped against existing indicators. This mapping has led to the identification of the indicators shown in this report, most of which meet most of these criteria. For instance, all indicators focus on summary outcomes that can be easily understood and interpreted. A majority of indicators have full face-validity, while a few others meet this criterion only partially. Most indicators can be influenced by policies and all of them change over time, although to different degrees. Almost all the indicators rely on definitions that are comparable across countries. Country coverage is very large for all the indicators retained and data are collected on a recurrent basis, though not necessarily in a timely way.

While the current choice of indicators represents a good approximation of the ideal concepts, the selection will be improved in the future as better statistics become available.

Main findings of *How's Life?*

Average patterns of well-being across dimensions

The following main patterns emerge from this report:

- In most OECD countries, average measures of household income and wealth have increased over the past fifteen years. Alternative indicators of the material resources enjoyed and consumed by households point in the same direction, despite some differences between objective and subjective indicators.

- There are large differences in employment rates across OECD countries, with evidence of a general rise in most countries. Long-term unemployment is low in most OECD countries and has generally declined since the mid-1990s. The importance of both temporary work and involunatry part-time work has, however, increased slightly during the past fifteen years.

- Housing conditions are good in the majority of OECD countries, though housing costs constitute a major concern for households in many OECD countries.

- In most OECD countries, people can expect to live a long life, and great progress has been accomplished in emerging countries in reducing infant and adult mortality rates. However, a significant share of the OECD population reports chronic health problems, and the number of those who suffer from serious disabilities is significant.

- The balance of work and non-work activities has changed considerably in recent decades, with overall gains in leisure and reductions in hours worked. These trends, however, mask the increased complexity of people's lives, with both men and women taking on a wider variety of tasks in the workplace and at home.

- Educational attainment has increased substantially over the past decades, with countries converging towards similar levels of education. However, the quality of educational outcomes, as measured by the reading skills of 15 year-old students, varies greatly across countries – though this variance has fallen over the past ten years.

- Social connections are relatively strong in all OECD countries, with the majority of people seeing friends and/or relatives on a regular basis, and reporting that they have someone to count on in times of need. There are wider cross-country variations in levels of interpersonal trust.

- In all OECD countries people enjoy a high level of political rights but they do not necessarily exert them effectively. Low trust in public institutions and declining levels of civic engagement point to a growing gap between how citizens and elites perceive the functioning of democratic systems.

- In most OECD countries the concentration of particulate matter in the air has dropped in the last twenty years, while remaining well above target levels. People living in emerging countries are exposed to much higher concentrations of pollutants and often live without basic services such as access to safe drinking water and sanitation.

- The number of homicides is low in most OECD countries, although with striking variations across countries. Assaults have decreased in most OECD countries, while they are still common in some emerging countries. The large majority of OECD residents feel safe when walking alone in their neighbourhood at night, even though there are significant differences across countries.

● For most countries average levels of subjective well-being are high. However, there are significant differences across OECD countries, with some reporting lower average levels of subjective well-being than many middle-income and developing countries, regardless of the measure used. While there is only limited information available on how subjective well-being has changed over time, it appears to have risen in some countries and stagnated in others.

Well-being at a glance: summarising average patterns

The above findings provide a first answer to the question "how's life?" in the various dimensions analysed in this report. However, well-being results from the complex interaction of multiple factors and depends on the relative importance that each person or society attaches to them. It is therefore useful to get a summary picture, as well as an understanding of how achievements in the various dimensions are correlated with each other.

Table 1.1 provides a birds-eye view of average well-being outcomes across countries by showing OECD countries according to whether they are top performers, bottom performers or average performer for all the headline indicators included in *How's Life?*. The table shows that no country ranks consistently at the top or bottom of the distribution, although life is generally quite good in countries like Australia, Canada, Sweden, New Zealand, Norway and Denmark, while it is much less so in Turkey, Mexico, Chile, Estonia, Portugal and Hungary. However, in some of the latter group of countries, life has become considerably better in the past decade or so, for example in Chile and Estonia. Most of the emerging countries tend to score relatively poorly in most dimensions, but the information available for these countries is currently very limited. One advantage of the "traffic-lights" used in Table 1.1 is that they help to identify easily the domains and dimensions where countries could improve their performance. While traffic lights are useful to signal areas where policies should concentrate in the future, they are not informative of the policy impact on observed outcomes. Indeed, drawing policy lessons from such an exercise would require identifying causal relationships between policies and outcomes, as well as understanding how the various dimensions of well-being are intertwined.

Table 1.1. An overview of headline well-being indicators in OECD countries

"Circles" denotes OECD countries in the top two deciles, "diamonds" those in the bottom two deciles, "triangles" those in the six intermediate deciles

The table presents, for each OECD country (Australia, Austria, Belgium, Canada, Chile, Czech Republic, Denmark, Estonia, Finland, France, Germany, Greece, Hungary, Iceland, Ireland, Israel, Italy, Japan, Korea, Luxembourg, Mexico, Netherlands, New Zealand, Norway, Poland, Portugal, Slovak Republic, Slovenia, Spain, Sweden, Switzerland, Turkey, United Kingdom, United States), a symbol (circle, diamond or triangle) for each headline well-being indicator, grouped as follows:

Material Living Conditions
- Income and Wealth — IW I: Household net adjusted disposable income per person (2009); IW II: Household financial net wealth per person (2009)
- Jobs and Earnings — JE I: Employment rate (2010); JE II: Long-term unemployment rate (2010); JE III: Average annual earnings per employee (2009)
- Housing — HG I: Number of rooms per person (2009); HG II: Dwelling without basic facilities (2009)

Quality of Life
- Health Status — HS I: Life-expectancy at birth (2009); HS II: Self-reported health status (2009)
- Work and Life — WL I: Employees working very long hours (2009); WL II: Time devoted to leisure and personal care (2000); WL III: Employment rate of women with children of compulsory school age (2008)
- Education and Skills — ES I: Educational attainment (2009); ES II: Students' cognitive skills (2009)
- Social Connections — SC I: Social network support (2010)
- Civic Engagement and Governance — CG I: Voter turn-out (2007); CG II: Consultation on rule-making (2008)
- Environmental Quality — EQ I: Air quality (2008)
- Personal Security — PS I: Intentional homicides (2008); PS II: Self-reported victimisation (2010)

Subjective Well-being
- SW I: Life-satisfaction (2010); SW II: Affect balance (2010)

Note: In this table the indicator "Dwelling with basic facilities" considers only data referring to dwellings without indoor flushing toilet. "Dwelling without basic facilities" considers only data referring to dwellings without indoor flushing toilet.

Source: OECD's calculations based on the indicators shown in this publication.

StatLink ⟲ http://dx.doi.org/10.1787/888932493746

A second way of responding to the demand for a concise picture of overall well-being across countries is to construct a composite indicator (OECD, 2008). Because the weights assigned to the various well-being dimensions vary across countries and people, the OECD has designed *Your Better Life Index (www.oecdbetterlifeindex.org)*, an interactive composite index of well-being that combines information on the eleven dimensions of well-being listed in Table 1.1, and which allow users to rate these dimensions according to their own preferences.[12] The tool also shows how changing the weights assigned to the various dimensions affects the overall picture.

For illustrative purposes, Figure 1.3 shows the scores of *Your Better Life Index* that are obtained when the weights are set equally across the eleven dimensions of well-being, when they are set equally across the two broad domains of well-being (*i.e.* material living conditions and quality of life), and when they are set according to BLI users' own weights (based on the around 4 000 choices made by users up to now).[13] The results are broadly in line with those highlighted in Table 1.1, regardless of the set of weights used. While the robustness of the Index to the weights used is partly due to the correlation of many components of well-being, it also suggests that well-designed composite indices are useful for sending a simple message that is not unduly affected by the weights assigned to the various components of the index.[14] However, composite indices have limitations and cannot be used for policy evaluation.

Figure 1.3. **"Your Better Life Index": country scores**

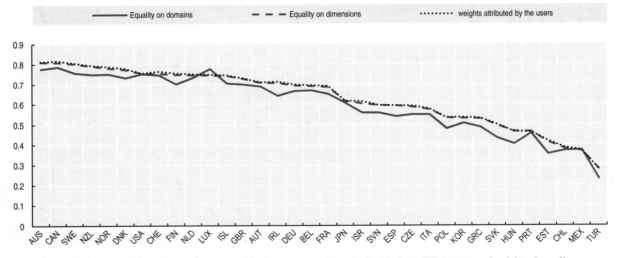

Note: The graph shows the country scores of the "Your Better Life Index" with three different sets of weights: "equality on domains" refers to equal weight given to material living conditions and quality of life (i.e. 1/6 to the three dimensions under material living conditions and 1/16 to the eight dimensions under quality of life), "equality on dimensions" refers to equal weight given to each dimension (e.g. 1/11), "weights attributed by the users" refer to the average of weights given by real users of the "Your Better Life Index" so far.
Source: Boarini R., G. Cohen, V. Denis and N. Ruiz (2011), "Designing Your Better Life Index: methodology and results", Statistics Directorate Working Paper, (forthcoming), OECD Paris.

StatLink ⧉ *http://dx.doi.org/10.1787/888932491865*

This broad analysis does not provide definitive conclusions as to the exact mechanisms at play that result in the good performance of some countries as compared to others. This would require examining the joint distribution of well-being outcomes, as well as their possible interaction, at the individual level (as opposed to the country level) so as to shed light on the causality links between well-being components. Despite this limitation, this analysis highlights two important results (see also Annex 1.A1): first, some well-being indicators and dimensions are well correlated to each other, indicating broad consistency in the aspects measured; second, the lack of perfect correlation indicates that, in order to understand people's well-being, it is important to consider all of the aspects at the same time.

Well-being across different groups of the population

Some of the important findings in this report concern the extent to which well-being outcomes vary across the population within each country. The report shows that the distribution of achievements is very uneven in all the dimensions analysed, though there are some countries where inequalities are consistently smaller (*e.g.* the Nordic countries). Another common pattern is that certain population groups, in particular people with lower incomes and less education, experience the largest disadvantages. Patterns by age and gender are in general more complex and differentiated across domains.

Some of the detailed patterns of inequality in well-being include the following:

- Compared to the OECD average, income inequality remains high in a few OECD countries and in emerging countries, and there is evidence that income is increasingly concentrated at the very top of the distribution. The number of income-poor people has increased in many OECD countries.

- There are large health disparities across income groups, part of which can be attributed to life-style and environmental factors. Furthermore, women tend to live longer than men, but they also report a lower health status as well as higher disability.

- The distribution of family chores is still strongly influenced by gender: men are more likely to work longer hours in paid work than women, while women spend longer hours in unpaid domestic work than men. Better-educated individuals are more likely to work longer hours than less-educated individuals, and better-educated women to be in employment in comparison with less-educated women. Time crunches are particularly sharp for parents.

- The elderly, the poor and the less-educated tend to have weaker networks of social support, in comparison with other population groups. Trust in others generally rises with people's education, age and income, though it tapers off at the high end of the age and income distributions.

- The poor, the less-educated and young people tend to participate less in political life. Trust in the judicial system and in the functioning of national government also tends to rise with people's education and income.

- Men are more likely to be the victim of crime, though women have the strongest feelings of insecurity. People living in large urban areas or their suburbs are more likely to be the victim of an assault and to fear crime. Social ties increase the feeling of security.

- Young people, the elderly and people from poor socio-economic backgrounds are the most vulnerable to pollution. In OECD countries, populations living in large cities or their suburbs are significantly less satisfied with their local environment than people living in rural areas or small towns.

- Women report slightly higher average life satisfaction than men, so do higher-income people and better educated individuals. Life satisfaction is also higher among those who have friends to count on and those who volunteer. Life satisfaction is lower for the unemployed and those with health problems.

The existence of large inequalities across all the dimensions of people's life implies that an overall assessment of countries' performance (such as the one provide in Table 1.1 and Figure 1.3) would differ significantly if it were to account of both average achievements and inequalities across countries. More work will be needed to integrate these inequalities into an overall assessment of people's life.[15]

Better policies for better lives: how better measures of well-being may inform policy-making

Developing better measures of well-being brings to the fore the question of how to design policies and processes that best support these goals. While the OECD has developed, over the years, a rich set of recommendations on how various policies can best support countries' economic growth, the extent of knowledge about the policies that "work best" in enhancing other dimensions of people's well-being is more scant.

Developing such an understanding is challenging, as broad measures of well-being outcomes will reflect several factors. For example, in the case of health outcomes, some of the relevant drivers may pertain to the characteristics of individuals (*i.e.* patients), others to the programmes for service delivery and implementation (*e.g.* the health care system), and still others to the environment where people live (*e.g.* environmental and working conditions, immigration, income and other inequalities). Some of these factors may not necessarily be directly amenable to policy interventions, while other measures of societal progress (*e.g.* measures of social connections or subjective well-being) may be just too general to identify a causal link to government interventions in specific fields. While indicators such as those in this report are better suited to monitor well-being than to evaluate the impact of specific policy measures, it is nevertheless important to take into account how the outcomes that these indicators measure respond to policy intervention.[16] As mentioned above, policy relevance is one of the criteria involved in the choice of the *How's Life?* indicators. However, further analysis of the links between well-being and policy will be necessary to fine-tune the choice of the indicators from the policy perspective.

This report does not explicitly look at the link between well-being and policy, although various chapters discuss some of the policy drivers in areas where there is adequate understanding of how policy impacts on specific well-being outcomes (*e.g.* education, employment). This limited evidence will have to be complemented with in-depth studies of the policy determinants of well-being in each country and, in particular, of the coherence of the various policy instruments and their competing or reinforcing effects on overall well-being.

A final important question that is relevant for policy is how well-being indicators should be interpreted and used in connection with standard measures of economic performance. Well-being indicators are meant to complement measures of economic performance rather than to supplant them. Measures of economic performance are important not only to assess the health of economies and contributing factors, but also to inform about the policy and institutional settings that shape people's well-being. This is true, in particular, for factors that affect the sustainability of well-being over time. For instance, high productivity growth may benefit citizens directly, by increasing earnings, and indirectly, *e.g.* by increasing profits and investment. Similarly, high trade competitiveness may influence people's well-being through job creation and favourable terms of trade that increase residents' purchasing power. Another example is public finances, whose sustainability is essential for ensuring services to citizens and for implementing other policies that have a direct bearing on people's lives. These economic considerations are critical when assessing people's current and future well-being.

The statistical agenda ahead

One important objective of this report is to take stock of the quality and comprehensiveness of existing well-being statistics. Such an assessment is critical in order to move the statistical agenda forward and to ensure that statistics evolve in line with the needs of policy-makers and the general public.

To that end, each chapter of this report discusses the validity of existing measures in the various well-being dimensions and provides a roadmap of the statistical developments needed in each field. The general message from this exercise is that a great deal of effort still needs to be made to improve existing measures for most of the well-being dimensions analysed in this report. In particular, there are still several gaps between the target and the actual concepts that existing indicators measure. Another problem, which is particularly serious for the quality of life domain, is that some of the relevant official statistics are not directly comparable across countries. As a second-best solution, this report has relied on statistics produced by non-official sources, despite their lower quality.

Some of the priorities for future work in this field are:

- The development of an integrated framework for measuring household income, consumption expenditures and wealth at the micro-level.

- The introduction of disparities between households with different characteristics into the national accounts framework.

- Better measures of the quality of employment, in particular measures of work safety and ethics, of workplace relationship and work motivation, as well as better measures of earnings inequality.

- Better measures of the quality of housing services beyond the availability of basic amenities, of housing costs and affordability.

- Better measures of morbidity, as well as of mental health and disability in particular, along with better measures of risk factors and drivers of different health outcomes.

- Better measures of non-cognitive skills, such as social and personality skills, as well as measures of the cognitive development of young children and of the adult population.

- More harmonised and recurrent measures of time use, as well as of time crunches and time stress.

- Better measures of social connections, social network support, interpersonal trust and other dimensions of social capital.

- Better methodologies and concepts for civic engagement indicators, in particular regarding how people perceive the quality of democratic institutions of the country where they live, so as to complement expert's assessments of specific practices within the public sector.

- Broader and more consistent measures of environmental quality, *e.g.* by moving from data on the concentration of various pollutants to information on the number of people exposed to them.

- More harmonised and complete measures of personal security and of various types of crimes, as well as of violence against women and children.

- A robust set of comparable measures of subjective well-being in its different aspects, as well as greater coverage by these measures across countries and over time.

Together with Eurostat and other international experts, the OECD has started to work on some of these issues, notably on the framework for the joint measurement of income, consumption and wealth; on the introduction of disparities within the household account of the SNA; and on the definition of guidelines for measuring subjective well-being (see Chapters 2 and 11 for further details). The Eurostat/INSEE Sponsorship Group is also developing recommendations to fill in some of the statistical gaps identified above for EU countries. The OECD stands ready to help countries producing official statistics on well-being and progress and envisages setting up new expert groups for defining guidelines for measuring well-being.

It is important for the international statistical community to ensure that the specific actions outlined above will be conducted in a consistent and coherent manner in order to avoid duplication of efforts and ensure cross-country comparability. Priorities will have to be set, also in line with national policy strategies that may focus on specific well-being areas and make use of a broader set of indicators, reflecting country-specific characteristics and the national political and social context. From this perspective, the statistical agenda described above should be seen as a working framework that could serve countries' priorities and particular needs. As implementing this measurement agenda will involve costs for national and international statistical systems, efforts should be made to adapt and streamline existing instruments, such as general social surveys, which do not always have a coherent framework of analysis.[17] Another advantage of using this type of surveys is that the individual-level information that these collect in many facets of people's lives would allow the simultaneous measurement of many dimensions of well-being, which is fundamental to understand and enhance the well-being of the most disadvantaged.

Conclusion

While this report presents a range of well-being indicators, which can be used to paint a broad picture of people's lives, the measurement of well-being remains challenging. Future OECD work will aim to consolidate this effort, in particular by selecting better indicators. It will also be important to extend the scope of this report by better integrating sustainability considerations into the analysis, and by focusing on some groups of the population who have been largely ignored in this first edition (*e.g.* immigrants, people with disabilities). While national statistical offices have a critical role to play in developing better indicators in many fields, this report also aims to encourage greater discussion by policy makers and the general public about the best way to measure and contribute to better lives.

Notes

1. OECD and United Nations guidelines on social indicators developed in the 1970s were critical to the development of internationally harmonised social statistics.

2. The approaches include: i) extending national account aggregates to a range of other dimensions that have value for individuals and communities, and which could be valued under different assumptions in monetary terms; ii) using a broad range of indicators (both monetary and non-monetary) so as to combine the many different facets of well-being into a summary scoreboard; iii) aggregating indicators into a composite index of well-being, following the normalisation and (arbitrary) weighting of individual components; iv) looking at some summary measures, such as life satisfaction or happiness, which are supposed to reflect the importance of different determinants of well-being.

3. See, in particular Hall *et al.* (2010), which suggests a framework for measuring progress in societies. While the domains covered by Hall *et al.* are broadly consistent with those used in *How's Life?*, the main difference is that the former develops a conceptual framework irrespective of the actual availability of indicators that are needed to assess well-being. *How's Life?* goes beyond the conceptual stage, and its underlying framework reflects the availability of existing indicators for the countries covered in this report, among other considerations.

4. See, for example, reports by Australia (*Measures of Australia's Progress*), Finland (*Findicator – Set of Indicators for Social Progress*), Germany (*Sustainable Development Report*) and New Zealand (*Measuring New Zealand's Progress Using a Sustainable Development Approach*).

5. While the indicators of *How's Life?* capture the well-being of households and individuals, some of the underlying sources are not based on individual-level data. This is notably the case of the indicators of income and wealth, earnings, governance and quality of air, which rely on either national accounts or other types of aggregate-level data.

6. These dimensions closely match those proposed in the Stiglitz-Sen-Fitoussi Commission's report (with some change in the terminology); their selection has been carried out in consultation with OECD countries' National Statistical Offices.

7. The Stiglitz-Sen-Fitoussi Commission's report contains one dimension of quality of life that is not listed in Figure 1.2: this pertains to "economic insecurity", which captures a broad range of risks (*e.g.* of losing one's job, of becoming sick or developing a permanent invalidity) over the course of one's life. This dimension has been excluded here because of a lack of suitable indicators, although the chapter on Jobs and Earnings consider some of the risks associated with economic insecurity, namely job insecurity. A broader analysis of economic insecurity as well as of other dimensions of quality of life, might be included in future issues of *How's Life?* as better measures and indicators become available.

8. Welfare theories take two positions with respect to subjective well-being. Welfarist theories, and in particular the "new utilitarian" approach proposed by Layard (2005), identify subjective well-being as a measure of overall well-being, for which the various dimensions of material living conditions and quality of life are simple drivers. Conversely, non-welfarist theories (so-called "resourcist theories", Fleurbaey, 1996) argue that subjective well-being represents one independent aspect of well-being alongside other dimensions, such as material living conditions, health status, human contact, etc. This report follows the latter approach.

9. For instance, some national statistical offices suggested that families should have a more prominent role in this framework, and be considered as a stand-alone dimension, while others favoured using a life-course perspective.

10. The Gallup World Poll is conducted in approximately 140 countries around the world based on a common questionnaire, translated into the predominant languages of each country. With few exceptions, all samples are nationally representative of the resident population aged 15 and over in the entire country, including rural areas. While this assures a good degree of comparability across countries, results may be affected by sampling and non-sampling errors. Sample sizes are limited to around 1000 persons in each country, with larger samples for some of the major countries. Micro-data based on the Gallup World Poll have been made available courtesy of the

Gallup Organisation. Robert Manchin and Femke De Keulenaer are kindly acknowledged for their help and advice in processing the data.

11. To ensure minimum quality standards, quality checks were conducted to establish whether Gallup World Poll indicators are reliable and relevant. This analysis suggests that these indicators correlate well with similar indicators from other international surveys and datasets. These indicators are also strongly correlated with other objective indicators of well-being at both the country and the individual level (although correlations are much weaker for the latter).

12. *Your Better Life Index* gathers indicators expressed in different units (dollars, years, etc). To compare and aggregate values expressed in different units, values are normalised. Normalisation is done according to a standard formula that converts the value of the original indicator into a number ranging between 0 (for the worst possible outcome) and 1 (for the best possible outcome). To choose weights, users have to rate each dimension from 0 (*i.e.* "this dimension does not matter to me") to 5 (*i.e.* "this dimension is very important to me"). The scores given to each dimension are converted into weights by dividing the score given to each dimension by the sum of the scores given to all dimensions. *Your Better Life Index* was designed to meet specific statistical properties, such as robustness with respect to the structure, to the imputation of missing data, to the weights assigned and to the method of aggregation (Boarini *et al.*, 2011).

13. By the end of july 2011, the *Your Better Life Index* website attracted over half a million visitors and over a million web page visits from 214 countries; each visitor stayed on the website for a little less than five minutes on average.

14. One reason behind the low sensitivity of the composite indices to the weights used is the fact that many indicators of well-being are well correlated with each other. Table 1.A1.1., in the annex to this chapter, shows that countries that tend to perform well in one indicator or dimension are more likely to perform well in others. This may be due to positive spill-over across well-being dimensions, but also to complex causal pathways between components of well-being. Some of these interactions are well-known: for instance, countries with better education are more likely to have a lower unemployment rate, thanks to better skills matching; similarly, individuals with higher levels of education are more likely to live longer and be in better health. This may also result from successful policy strategies that pursue a number of concurrent objectives (*e.g.* "flexicurity" in Scandinavian countries).

15. Evidence on the impact of deprivation on the *Your Better Life Index* is provided in Boarini *et al.*, 2011.

16. See Barca and McCann (2011) for a discussion of how outcome indicators could be used in the context of monitoring and evaluating regional policies.

17. Together with European countries, Eurostat is already exploring the potential for harmonising existing social surveys across EU countries with the technical, human and material resources currently available.

References

Barca F and P. McCann (2011), "Outcome Indicators and Targets - Towards a Performance-Oriented EU Cohesion Policy", http://ec.europa.eu/regional_policy/sources/docgener/evaluation/performance_en.htm

Boarini R., A. Johansson and M. Mira d'Ercole (2006), "Alternative Measures of Well-being", *OECD Social, Employment and Migration Working Papers No. 33*, OECD, Paris.

Boarini R., G. Cohen, V. Denis and N. Ruiz (2011) "Designing the "*Your Better Life Index*": Methodology and results", *OECD Statistics Directorate Working Paper* (forthcoming), OECD, Paris.

European Commission (2009), "GDP and beyond: Measuring progress in a changing world", *Communication from the Commission to the Council and the European Parliament*, Brussels.

Fleurbaey M. (1996), *Theories Economiques de la Justice*, Economica, Paris.

Fleurbaey M. (2009), "Beyond GDP: The Quest for a Measure of Social Welfare", *Journal of Economic Literature*, Vol. 47, Issue 4, pp. 1029-47.

Hall J., E. Giovannini, A. Morrone and G. Ranuzzi (2010), "A Framework to Measure the Progress of Societies", *OECD Statistics Directorate Working Paper No. 34*, OECD, Paris.

Layard R. (2005), *Happiness: Lessons from a New Science*, Penguin Press, London.

OECD (2008), *Handbook on Constructing Composite Indicators – Methodology and User Guide*, Report jointly prepared by the OECD and the Joint Research Centre of the European Commission, OECD Publishing, Paris.

OECD (2010), *National Accounts at a Glance 2010*, OECD Publishing, Paris.

OECD (2011a), *Compendium of OECD well-being indicators*, OECD Publishing, Paris.

OECD (2011b), *Towards Green Growth: Monitoring Progress: OECD Indicators*, OECD Green Growth Studies, OECD Publishing, Paris.

Sen A. (1998), *Development as Freedom*, Oxford University Press 1999

Stiglitz, J.E., A. Sen and J.-P. Fitoussi (2009), *Report by the Commission on the Measurement of Economic Performance and Social Progress*, http://www.stiglitz-sen-fitoussi.fr/documents/rapport_anglais.pdf.

ANNEX 1.A

Cross-country correlations between different well-being indicators

Well-being is multidimensional, as a good life depends on many factors. An interesting question is whether and to what extent these factors tend to be correlated, that is, if high achievement in one dimension of well-being is associated with high achievement in another dimension. Table 1.A.1 provides a general answer to this question, as it looks at the correlations existing between the various dimensions and indicators of well-being analysed in this report. Correlations are calculated at country level; therefore they have to be interpreted as evidence of a statistically significant association between countries' performance in the various dimensions of good living.

Table 1.A.1 shows that most well-being indicators are correlated with each other (at the 1% level of significance). Employment rate, household net adjusted disposable income and social network support are the indicators that are mostly correlated with the other indicators (in the sense that they are correlated with many other indicators, and the strength of this relationship is relatively high). The two housing indicators and life-satisfaction also display a quite strong correlation with many of the headline indicators of *How's Life?*. While none of the indicators is perfectly correlated with any other, most indicators paint a consistent image of well-being in OECD countries, suggesting that interrelationships among dimensions of well-being are high.

Table 1.A.1. Correlations between the headline indicators included in "How's Life?"

	Household net adj. disposable income	Household net financial wealth per capita	Employment rate	Long-term unemployment rate	Average annual earnings per employee	Number of rooms per person	Dwelling without basic facilities	Life-expectancy at birth	Self-reported health status	Employees working very long hours	Time devoted to leisure and personal care	Employment rate of women with children of compulsory school age	Educational attainment	Students' cognitive skills	Social network support	Voter turnout	Consultation on rule-making	Air quality	Intentional homicides	Self-reported victimisation	Life-satisfaction	Affect balance
INCOME AND WEALTH Household net adj. disposable income	1.00	0.69	0.54	-0.33	0.88	0.69	-0.70	0.63	0.68	-0.21	0.29	0.10	0.21	0.31	0.63	0.50	0.14	-0.48	-0.46	-0.41	0.63	0.38
Household net financial wealth per capita		1.00	0.39	-0.34	0.68	0.48	-0.34	0.53	0.45	0.09	-0.08	0.22	0.13	0.16	0.33	0.27	-0.13	-0.05	-0.11	-0.17	0.46	0.24
JOBS AND EARNINGS Employment rate			1.00	-0.55	0.62	0.57	-0.57	0.62	0.39	-0.47	0.17	0.85	0.38	0.45	0.65	0.11	0.30	-0.39	-0.36	-0.29	0.64	0.48
Long-term unemployment rate				1.00	-0.49	-0.33	0.10	-0.33	-0.38	-0.17	-0.10	-0.40	-0.14	-0.19	-0.25	-0.20	-0.33	-0.09	-0.02	0.12	-0.60	-0.56
Average annual earnings per employee					1.00	0.81	-0.50	0.61	0.73	0.03	0.28	0.33	0.09	0.17	0.59	0.51	0.07	-0.23	0.15	-0.01	0.81	0.63
HOUSING Number of rooms per person						1.00	-0.55	0.60	0.61	-0.24	0.30	0.34	0.00	0.47	0.64	0.40	0.27	-0.41	-0.26	-0.12	0.70	0.49
Dwelling without basic facilities							1.00	-0.61	-0.52	0.54	-0.56	-0.45	-0.25	-0.20	-0.74	-0.17	-0.24	0.47	0.54	0.32	-0.61	-0.19
HEALTH STATUS Life-expectancy at birth								1.00	0.40	-0.35	0.20	0.35	0.08	0.40	0.50	0.26	0.07	-0.18	-0.50	-0.30	0.57	0.22
Self-reported health status									1.00	0.15	0.30	0.20	0.03	0.12	0.62	0.37	0.23	-0.29	-0.14	-0.20	0.68	0.25
WORK AND LIFE BALANCE Employees working very long hours										1.00	-0.39	-0.62	-0.50	-0.45	-0.43	0.04	-0.08	0.34	0.33	0.12	-0.14	0.10
Time devoted to leisure and personal care											1.00	-0.05	-0.06	-0.13	0.33	0.51	-0.28	-0.32	-0.25	0.46	0.45	0.15
Employment rate of women with children of compulsory school age												1.00	0.57	0.54	0.61	-0.08	0.24	-0.47	-0.08	-0.25	0.47	0.25
EDUCATION AND SKILLS Educational attainment													1.00	0.43	0.41	-0.16	0.15	-0.32	-0.25	-0.53	0.30	-0.02
Students' cognitive skills														1.00	0.25	0.00	0.37	-0.45	-0.52	-0.65	0.18	0.21
SOCIAL CONNECTIONS Social network support															1.00	0.23	0.25	-0.52	-0.39	-0.36	0.73	0.36
CIVIC ENGAGEMENT AND GOVERNANCE Voter turnout																1.00	-0.29	-0.01	-0.07	0.14	0.34	0.21
Consultation on rule-making																	1.00	-0.27	-0.18	-0.40	0.20	0.30
ENVIRONMENTAL QUALITY Air quality																		1.00	0.40	0.44	-0.23	0.00
PERSONAL SECURITY Intentional homicides																			1.00	0.64	-0.10	-0.09
Self-reported victimisation																				1.00	-0.17	-0.14
SUBJECTIVE WELL-BEING Life-satisfaction																					1.00	0.47
Affect balance																						1.00

Note: Correlation coefficients shaded in blue are not statistically significant at 5% level. Correlation coefficients are calculated at country level.
Source: OECD calculations.

StatLink http://dx.doi.org/10.1787/88892493765

Chapter 2

Income and Wealth

Income and wealth are essential components of individual well-being. Income allows people to satisfy their needs and pursue many other goals that they deem important to their lives, while wealth makes it possible to sustain these choices over time. Both income and wealth enhance individuals' freedom to choose the lives that they want to live, though there are some aspects of their lives that cannot be bought by money. This chapter presents a set of indicators that aims to provide a coherent, but non-exhaustive, picture of the economic conditions of people and households. The indicators measure the principal components that shape material conditions, their dynamics and how they are distributed within each country. This chapter finds that income and wealth have been substantially enhanced during the last fifteen years. However, this rise did not lift all boats: income inequality has been rising in many countries, and some groups have been left behind. This suggests that growth-oriented policies need to be designed to take into account distributional considerations.

Why do income and wealth matter for well-being?

Household income and wealth are essential components of individual well-being. The ability to command resources allows people to satisfy basic needs and pursue many other goals that they deem important to their lives. Economic resources enhance individuals' freedom to choose the lives that they want to live and protect them against economic and personal risks. At the society-wide level, economic resources allow countries to invest in education, health, security, etc. Indeed, even if income alone is insufficient to assess a country's welfare, it is often a necessary condition for the country's overall development.

Household wealth, which derives from the accumulation of personal savings as well as from transfers between generations, also contributes in an important way to individual well-being, *e.g.* by protecting people from unexpected shocks and allowing them to smooth consumption over time. Preserving people's wealth also ensures that their material living standards can be sustained over time.

It is not enough to look simply at average levels of both household income and wealth. It is also critical to assess how economic resources are shared across individuals and population groups. Information on the distribution of household income and wealth, and how these are correlated, is therefore central for designing policies to improve people's material well-being. In addition, policies have to take into consideration distributional impacts to assess a possible trade-off between equity and efficiency and to consider whether some groups of the population will be left behind, with the potential drag on future growth that this implies.

Measuring income and wealth

The measure and analysis of economic resources available to the population has a longstanding tradition. Economic statistics were among the first statistics ever to be produced,[1] and this long tradition has led to consistent, harmonised and regularly updated measures of economic resources.[2] In this respect, existing indicators of household economic resources are closer to ideal indicators than most other indicators of well-being shown in this report.

Economic statistics are compiled at an aggregate level through the national accounts system and at an individual level through household surveys and administrative records. The former have the advantage of being fully consistent with economy-wide measures such as GDP and productivity, while the latter make it possible to look at the distribution of economic resources within a country.

In general, income statistics at both the aggregate and individual levels are available with a greater degree of harmonisation than wealth statistics. Indeed, internationally comparable income indicators cover a large range of revenues, while wealth indicators tend to focus on a relatively narrow set of assets and liabilities. The collection of income indicators is also timelier than wealth indicators, especially at the individual level.

Despite the good quality of measures of economic resources, these indicators can be improved in several ways. First, it will be important to increase the consistency of the definitions and coverage between national accounts and household surveys.[3] Secondly, existing measures of household economic resources are often developed through separate instruments, making it impossible to analyse their "joint distribution" at the individual level (*i.e.* to indentify people who combine low income and adequate wealth, or vice versa). Some of these limits are addressed by a number of OECD ongoing projects that are discussed in more detail at the end of this chapter.

Selected indicators

Household net adjusted disposable income (IW I)

Household net adjusted disposable income is the best measure of people's economic resources that is available from the national accounts, as it combines information on a large number of market and non-market resources. Household net adjusted disposable income is obtained by adding to the flows that make up people's gross income (earnings, self-employment and capital income, as well as current monetary transfers received from other sectors) the social transfers in-kind that households receive from governments (such as education and health care services), and then subtracting the taxes on income and wealth, the social security contributions paid by households as well as the depreciation of capital goods consumed by households. The resulting aggregate can be viewed as the maximum amount that a household can afford to consume without having to reduce its assets or to increase its liabilities.[4]

Measures of average household net adjusted disposable income per capita are available within the system of national accounts (SNA) based on well-established standards for all OECD countries (OECD, 2010).[5] The concept hence meets a number of the criteria characterising "ideal" indicators (Table 2.1). Its main drawback is a lack of information at a disaggregated level (e.g. for different types of households). Household net adjusted disposable income is expressed in purchasing power parities for private consumption in the year 2000 (US dollars PPPs), so as to allow meaningful cross-country comparisons over time.[6]

Table 2.1. **The quality of income and wealth indicators**

		Target concept	INDICATORS								
			Relevance to measure and monitor well-being				Statistical quality			
			Face validity	Unambiguous interpretation (good/bad)	Policy amenable outcomes	Can be disaggregated	Well-established instrument collected	Comparable definition	Country coverage	Recurrent data collection
Income and wealth										
IW I	Household Net Adjusted Disposable Income	Current and future consumption possibilities	√	√	~	x	√	√	√	√
IW II	Household Net Financial Wealth		~	√	~	x	√	√	√	√
iw 1	Household Final consumption	Realised material well-being	√	√	~	x	√	√	√	√
iw 2	Household Total consumption		~	~	~	x	~	~	~	~
iw 3	Subjective evaluation of material well-being	Satisfaction with material conditions	~	√	~	√	~	~	√	√

Note: The symbol √ shows that the indicator selected largely meets the criterion shown in the table; the symbol ~ that the indicator meets the criterion to a large extent; the symbol x that the indicator does not meet the criterion or it meets it only to a limited extent.

Household net financial wealth (IW II)

Net financial wealth is important to protect households from economic hardship and vulnerability. Based on national accounts definitions, this aggregate includes a number of assets (*e.g.* gold, currency and deposits, shares, securities other than shares, loans, insurance technical reserves and other accounts receivable or payable owned by households) net of their financial liabilities. While this measure is available for most OECD countries, its obvious limitation is that it excludes households' non-financial assets (*i.e.* land and dwellings) which, in most countries, represent the largest component of households' overall net wealth. For example, it is estimated that on average in the OECD countries 67% of the population are homeowners (OECD, 2007). Comparable SNA information on land and dwellings is currently available only for a small number of OECD countries.

Household final consumption (iw 1)

Material well-being can also be evaluated by looking at household consumption expenditures. While adjusted net disposable income describes the consumption and saving *possibilities* available to households, it is ultimately consumption that informs about their *"achieved"* or *"realised"* material conditions. Household final consumption covers all purchases made by resident households to meet their everyday needs. It is shown here as a secondary indicator, as consumption informs on current material well-being, but may not necessarily reflect life-long well-being possibilities.

Subjective evaluation of material well-being (iw 2)

The indicators discussed so far are objective indicators. However, self-perceived evaluations of material living conditions offer a useful complement. Several recent analyses have drawn attention to the increasing gap between the evolution of objective measures of people's economic situation and people's own appreciation of this (Stiglitz *et al.*, 2009). The many factors that account for this gap (*e.g.* differences in the concepts measured, scope of measurement, limited validity of either type of indicator, different needs of households with the same amount of economic resources) underscore the importance of relying on both types of measures to assess people's material living conditions.

The indicator shown here is based on the European Union Statistics on Income and Living Conditions (EU-SILC). It refers to the share of the population who declare that they are "having great difficulty or difficulty to make their ends meet". The indicator relies on the same question across countries and is thus broadly comparable, although contextual factors and cultural effects may affect comparisons. It is also timely, as it is part of the core EU-SILC modules produced every year. However, this indicator is available only for European countries, which is why it is included here as a secondary indicator.

Measuring inequalities and poverty

Indicators of average material well-being need to be supplemented with information on how this is distributed across the population. Looking at the distribution is important not only for getting a more accurate picture of the actual living conditions of different types of households and individuals, but also for designing tax and social policies.

As discussed above, it is not possible to assess income distribution through national accounts. Therefore indicators on the distribution of household economic resources refer to the concept of household disposable income, as measured through a combination of household surveys and administrative records. The distributional indicators used in this chapter refer to the concept of "equivalised" [7] household disposable income, based on micro sources, as opposed to household net adjusted disposable income, drawn from the national accounts.[8] The income data necessary to calculate measures of inequalities are typically collected less frequently and require more time to compute than national accounts data; this implies that information on the distribution of household income presented in this chapter is less timely than that on average conditions. Two types of inequality measures are presented here:

- The Gini index, a summary measure of income dispersion in the population.[9] This measure is easy to understand, and has a number of appealing properties, such as summarising in a single number the income differences between each pair of people, rather than measuring distances relative to an arbitrary reference point such as the mean. This measure does nevertheless have some shortcomings (e.g. it can exhibit some inconsistency between measures at the national and sub-national levels; and it cannot be interpreted for variables with negative values, such as net wealth); for a discussion of the properties of the Gini index, see Sen and Foster, 1998.

- Measures of low income are also important, as low-income people typically experience deprivations in several domains, not just material ones. Indicators of low income usually look at its prevalence (i.e. headcount measures of the share of the population falling below a given income threshold) and intensity (i.e. gap measures of the average income shortfall of the poor expressed as a percentage of the income threshold). Both of the indicators shown in this chapter rely on a low-income threshold defined as 50% or 60% of the median income in each country.

Average patterns

Households have enjoyed higher income on average over the past fifteen years

Cross-country differences in household net adjusted disposable income *per capita* are large (Figure 2.1). For the countries analysed, household net adjusted disposable income is highest in Luxembourg, about six times as high as in Chile, the OECD country with the lowest level. In all these countries, the main component of household net adjusted disposable income is compensation of employees, followed by income from unincorporated enterprises and transfers in-kind provided by the public sector (Figure 2.2). Social security contributions and other taxes paid by households, net of the current monetary transfers that they receive, represent around 10% of household net adjusted disposable income. The structure of household net adjusted disposable income is relatively homogeneous across countries, with the exception of property income and of net contributions and taxes paid by households, which vary quite substantially across the countries considered.

Household net adjusted disposable income increased during the past decade or so in all OECD countries, with the largest rises recorded in Slovenia, the Slovak Republic, Estonia, Norway and the Russian Federation, while it has remained broadly stable in Japan, Italy and Mexico. Cross-country differences have changed little over the period. Overall, household income and GDP have not always moved in parallel during this period (Box 2.1). While numerous factors affect trends in household income, and disentangling their effects is difficult, Figure 2.3 shows that most changes in household net adjusted disposable income are due to movements in primary income. However, in most countries household net adjusted disposable income grew at a faster pace than gross income, indicating that redistributive policies have enhanced households' well-being.

Figure 2.1. **Household net adjusted disposable income per capita, 2009**

US dollars at 2000 PPPs

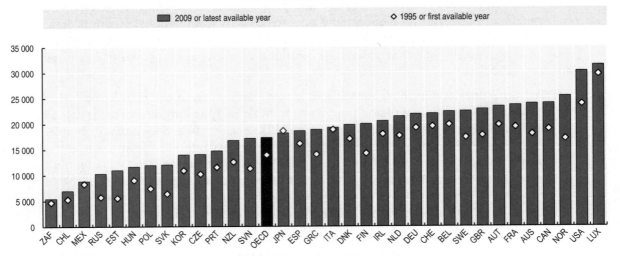

Note: Households include non-profit institutions serving households, except for New Zealand. Purchasing Power Parities are those for actual individual consumption of households. The latest available year is 2008 for Australia, Japan, Switzerland and the Russian Federation; and 2010 for Finland, Portugal and Sweden. The first available year is 2000 for Greece and Spain; 2002 for Ireland and the Russian Federation; 2003 for Chile, Mexico and South Africa; and 2006 for Luxembourg. Purchasing Power Parities for South Africa are OECD estimates.

Sources: OECD, National Accounts data; Statistics New Zealand; OECD estimates.

StatLink ᯆᏕ *http://dx.doi.org/10.1787/888932491884*

Figure 2.2. **From gross income to net adjusted disposable income of households per capita, 2009**

US dollars at 2000 PPPs per capita

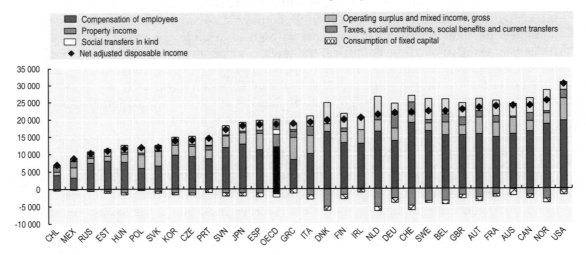

Note: The latest available year is 2008 for Australia, Japan, Switzerland and the Russian Federation; and 2010 for Finland, Portugal and Sweden. The sum of compensation of employees, property income and operating surplus is the primary income (also called market income). Taxes, social and in-kind benefits and various other transfers from the public sector represent the secondary income (*i.e.* income that the government redistributes to households directly or indirectly). Purchasing Power Parities are those for actual individual consumption of households.

Source: OECD, National Accounts data; Statistics New Zealand.

StatLink ᯆᏕ *http://dx.doi.org/10.1787/888932491903*

Figure 2.3. **Real annual growth rates of various households income measures**

Growth rates in percentages, period 1995-2009

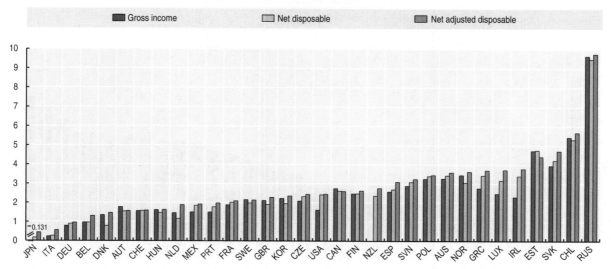

Note: Households include non-profit institutions serving households, except for New Zealand. The annualized growth rate refers to 1995-2008 for Australia and Switzerland; 1995-2010 for Finland, Portugal and Sweden; 1996-2008 for Japan; 1998-2009 for the United States; 2000-09 for Greece and Spain; 2002-08 for the Russian Federation; 2002-09 for Ireland; 2003-09 for Chile and Mexico; and 2006-09 for Luxembourg. Data are deflated using actual individual consumption. Gross income data is not available for New Zealand.

Source: OECD, National Accounts data; Statistics New Zealand.

StatLink ᴍꜱᴸ *http://dx.doi.org/10.1787/888932491922*

Box 2.1. **Discrepancies between GDP and household net adjusted disposable income**

Country-wide measures of economic production such as GDP cannot be considered as satisfactory proxies of households' material conditions, as shown by Figure 2.4. First, in around half of the countries household net adjusted disposable income represents only two-thirds of GDP, with a share lower than 60% in Luxembourg, Slovenia, Sweden and Korea. Second, in many OECD countries, these gaps have increased considerably in the past fifteen years. Such gaps highlight the discrepancy between a country's economic performance and the economic situation of households.

Many factors underlie these differences, including a faster rise in company re-invested profits than in employee compensation – resulting in a lower share of primary income accruing to households; changes in redistribution policies through taxes and social benefits; changes in firms' practices on the distribution of company profits and profits transferred abroad; and a faster rise in consumer prices than in the GDP deflator. However, discrepancies between GDP and household net adjusted disposable income may also be reflective of resources that will increase household living standards in the future (*e.g.* re-invested profits generate economic activity and thus income for households) or diminish it (*e.g.* higher public expenditure today financed through public debt may imply lower public expenditure tomorrow). Overall, it remains challenging to assess the impact of current redistribution of resources across the sectors of the economy on households' future well-being.

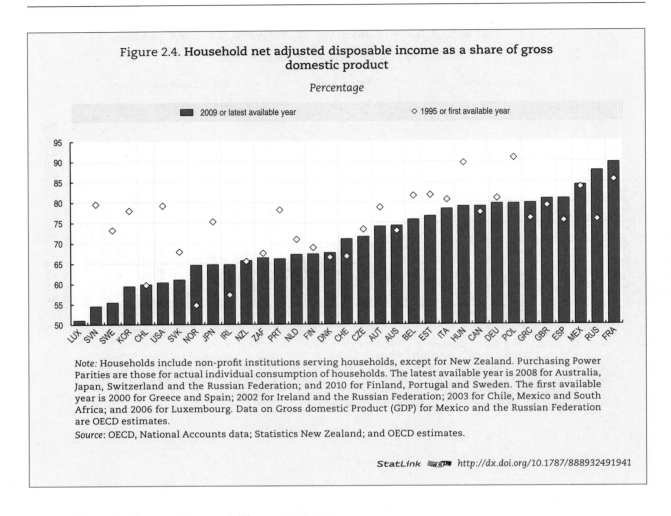

Figure 2.4. Household net adjusted disposable income as a share of gross domestic product

Percentage

■ 2009 or latest available year   ◇ 1995 or first available year

Note: Households include non-profit institutions serving households, except for New Zealand. Purchasing Power Parities are those for actual individual consumption of households. The latest available year is 2008 for Australia, Japan, Switzerland and the Russian Federation; and 2010 for Finland, Portugal and Sweden. The first available year is 2000 for Greece and Spain; 2002 for Ireland and the Russian Federation; 2003 for Chile, Mexico and South Africa; and 2006 for Luxembourg. Data on Gross domestic Product (GDP) for Mexico and the Russian Federation are OECD estimates.

Source: OECD, National Accounts data; Statistics New Zealand; and OECD estimates.

StatLink ᵐˢ￫ http://dx.doi.org/10.1787/888932491941

Households are also wealthier on average

Household net financial wealth per capita differs across countries to a larger extent than does household income per capita (Figure 2.5). Household net financial wealth per capita is highest in the United States (with an average financial wealth nearly three times as large as income) and the lowest in the Slovak Republic, Norway and Poland.[10] Over the past fifteen years, net financial wealth has increased in most OECD countries, most notably in Israel, Germany and Sweden. Falls were, however, recorded in Ireland, Greece and Switzerland. The bulk of household net financial wealth reflects net equity in life insurance and pension reserves, shares and, for some countries, currency and deposits (Figure 2.6).

As mentioned above, non-financial assets account for a large share of households' total wealth, with land and dwellings owned by households accounting for the largest part. Unfortunately, statistical information on these assets is sparse and often not comparable across OECD countries.[11] Looking at countries where data are available, net financial wealth accounts for around one-third of total net wealth in Australia, Hungary and the Czech Republic, 80% in Japan and 60% in Canada.

Figure 2.5. **Household net financial wealth per capita**

US dollars at 2000 PPPs

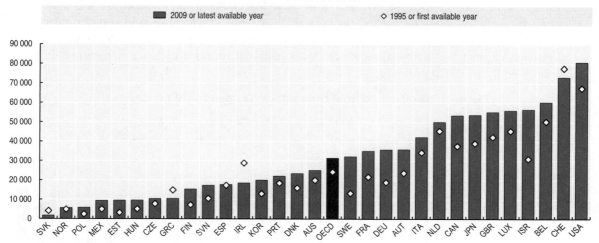

Note: Households include non-profit institutions serving households. Purchasing Power Parities are those for private consumption of households. The latest available year is 2010 for Belgium, Greece, Hungary, Norway, Slovenia and the United Kingdom. The first available year is 1997 for Mexico; 1999 for Switzerland; 2001 for Ireland, Israel and Slovenia; 2002 for Korea; and 2006 for Luxembourg.

Sources: OECD, National Accounts data; Statistics New Zealand.

StatLink http://dx.doi.org/10.1787/888932491960

Figure 2.6 **Decomposition of household financial wealth of households by type of assets**

Percentage, 2009

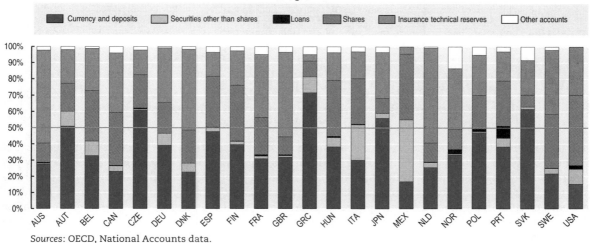

Sources: OECD, National Accounts data.

StatLink http://dx.doi.org/10.1787/888932491979

Consumption expenditure increased at a slower pace than household income

Like income and wealth, household final consumption expenditure per capita varies across countries. It is highest in Luxembourg and the United States and lowest in Mexico, the Russian Federation, Chile and Estonia (Figure 2.7). Over the past fifteen years, household consumption expenditure per capita has increased in all countries but at a slower pace than household income. The strongest increases have been recorded in the United States, the

United Kingdom, Australia, Canada, Finland, the Slovak Republic, Poland, Estonia and the Russian Federation. By contrast, in Ireland, Spain and Mexico the level of final consumption remained broadly unchanged. Growth of household consumption expenditures is lower when households' pre-committed outlays, such as rent, utility bills and repayment of the principal residence through household loans and mortgages, are excluded. Box 2.2 discusses experimental measures of non-market consumption, which are currently being developed by an OECD project.

Figure 2.7. **Household final consumption expenditure per capita**

US dollars at 2000 PPPs

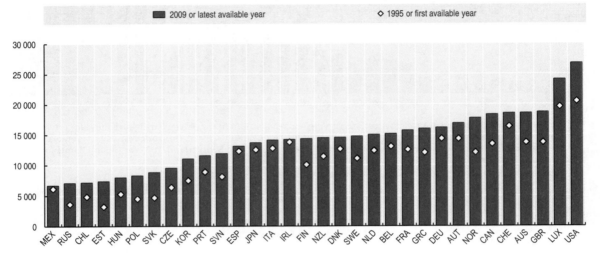

Note: Households include non-profit institutions serving households. Data are in US dollars at 2000 PPPs using the deflator of private consumption of households. The latest available year is 2007 for New Zealand; 2008 for Australia, Chile, Greece, Japan, Switzerland and the Russian Federation; and 2010 for Finland. The first available year is 1996 for Chile and Japan; 2000 for Greece and Spain; 2002 for Ireland and the Russian Federation; and 2003 for Mexico.
Source: OECD, National Accounts data.

StatLink ᗢᔕᐤ *http://dx.doi.org/10.1787/888932491998*

Box 2.2. **Accounting for non-market production of household services enhances material well-being**

Final consumption, as defined and measured in the national accounts, focuses on marketable goods and services bought by households. While there is widespread agreement that many non-marketable services (such as own-produced meals, child care, etc.) contribute to people's material well-being, most of these services fall outside the production boundary of the national accounts and do not enter into the standard measurement of living standards – the only exceptions being dwelling services that benefit home-owners. To remedy this deficiency, the OECD has recently developed experimental measures of the monetary value of own-account production of services by households (Ahmad et Koh, 2011).

The evaluation of own-account production of household services is performed in two steps: first, the amount of time allocated to household production (on items such cooking, cleaning, child-care, shopping, etc.) is computed, using information from Time Use Surveys; second, this number of hours is converted into a monetary aggregate by considering either the average wage prevailing on the labour market (as an approximation of the opportunity cost) or the typical wage of a worker performing housework (replacement cost).

Estimates of the non-market consumption of household services highlight two main results (Figure 2.8). First, the value of own-account services of households is significant but varies across countries and according to the method used to value the time that households devote to produce these services. Second, including own-account services produced by households in measures of consumption per capita does not fundamentally change the position of countries in international comparisons, although all countries improve their position relative to the United States (the country where household final consumption expenditure per capita is the highest). This "catching up" effect is largest for lower income countries such as Mexico or Poland, where the "marketisation" of the production of household services is less developed. Differences across countries may reflect involuntary choices, for example when unemployment obliges labour force participants to "produce at home" while, unconstrained, they would have chosen to have a paid job and to purchase on the market a greater share of the services that they consume.

While providing interesting insights, these estimates are only a very first step towards the production of satellite accounts for the household sector. Much more work is needed to consolidate the methodology and produce these on a more systematic basis, as for instance suggested in Eurostat (2003). Interesting examples of comprehensive accounts for the production of the household sector can be found in Landefeld *et al.* (2009) for the United States and in Ruger and Varjonen (2008) for Finland and Germany.

Figure 2.8. **Household total consumption, including non-market services, 2008**

US dollars per capita at 2008 PPPs, USA=100

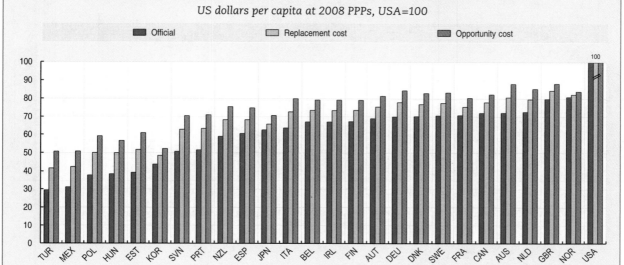

Note: "Official" refers to consumption as it is measured in the National Accounts. The second and third bars refer to measures of total consumption where non-market services have been included using two types of valuation for the labour used in household production: "replacement cost" values time spent using the wage of a household worker while "opportunity cost" uses the average wage prevailing on the labour market.

Source: OECD (2011), "Incorporating Household Production into International Comparisons of Material Well-Being", OECD Statistics Directorate Working paper (forthcoming).

StatLink ⟲ http://dx.doi.org/10.1787/888932492017

Comparing income and consumption provides an indication of the sustainability of household living standards. In 2009, households in Greece, New Zealand and Denmark recorded negative household saving rates, indicating that average current household consumption was higher than the current income received during the same year. By contrast, household net saving rates were positive and relatively high in many continental European countries. Saving rates started to decline towards the end of the 1990s in many OECD countries, notably Korea, Japan and the United Kingdom, while they remained more stable in the euro area and in the United States. These trends have been reversed following the recent financial crisis, as many households strived to repair the losses to their assets. The drivers of these trends are essentially related to institutional, demographic and socio-demographic factors at the country level, while real interest rates, credit conditions and inflation influence household savings at the macroeconomic level (Hüfner and Koske, 2010).

In European countries many households find it difficult to make ends meet

The share of households in European countries who declare that they are having difficulty making ends meet is around 15% on average, with 10% reporting that they are having strong difficulty (Figure 2.9). Over 40% of households report strong or some inability to make ends meet in Greece, Hungary and Portugal, as compared to only 8% in Germany and Norway.

Figure 2.9. **Population unable to make ends meet, 2008**

Percentage of the population

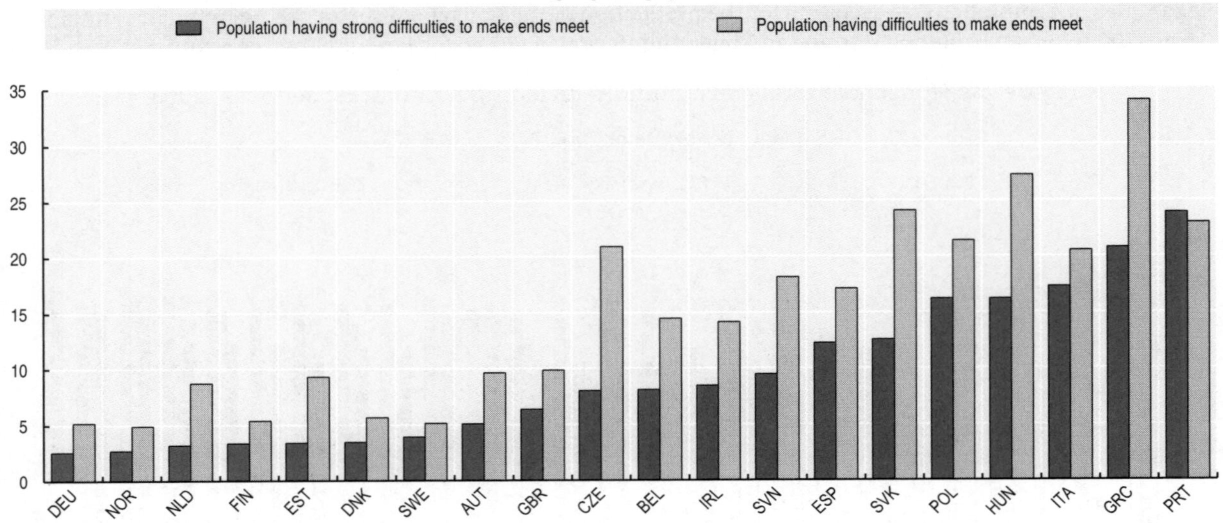

Source: OECD Secretariat calculations based on data from the European Union Statistics on Income and Living Conditions (EU-SILC).

StatLink ☜ http://dx.doi.org/10.1787/888932492036

There is a relatively strong correlation between the various measures of income and wealth

While the various indicators discussed so far measure different components of households' material well-being, it is interesting to see whether they provide a consistent picture. Per capita levels of household income and wealth are significantly correlated across countries, though to a lower extent than household income and consumption expenditures (Table 2.2).

The correlation between household adjusted disposable income per capita and measures of how households perceive the state of their material conditions is also interesting (Stiglitz et al., 2009). Across OECD countries, higher average household income per capita is associated with lower reported inability to make ends meet, but this relationship tends to flatten out along the income ladder (not shown here). Economic insecurity (e.g. having a precarious job) and higher levels of certain types of household expenditures that weigh heaviest on people's budget (e.g. housing) are possible reasons for the discrepancy between objective measures of household living conditions and the subjective appreciation of them reported by people.

Table 2.2. **Correlation between different indicators of income and wealth**

		IW I Household net adjusted disposable income	IW II Household net financial wealth	iw 1 Household final consumption	iw 2 Household total consumption	iw 3 Share of households having strong difficulties to make ends meet
IW I	Household net adjusted disposable income	1 (31)	0.70 (28)	0.95 (31)	0.96 (25)	-0.52 (20)
IW II	Household net financial wealth		1 (28)	0.73 (28)	0.66 (25)	-0.24 (20)
iw 1	Household final consumption			1 (28)	0.66 (25)	-0.35 (20)
iw 2	Household total consumption				1 (25)	-0.55 (17)
iw 3	Share of households having strong difficulties to make ends meet					1 (20)

Note: Values in parenthesis refer to the number of observations. All correlations are significant at the 1% level. As the two different measures of household total consumption are almost perfectly correlated with each other (correlation of 0.99), only one is represented here (opportunity cost).
Source: OECD's calculations.

StatLink http://dx.doi.org/10.1787/888932493803

Inequalities

The shape of the income distribution differs significantly across countries...

Despite the substantial increase in average living standards experienced during the past fifteen years, not all people have benefited from this to the same extent. There are indeed large differences in how household disposable income is distributed within countries (Figure 2.10). Some OECD countries such as Chile and Mexico, but also Turkey, the United States and Israel, have a much more unequal income distribution than others. By contrast, the Nordic and Eastern European countries are characterised by lower income inequalities.

Figure 2.10 **Gini index of income inequalities.**

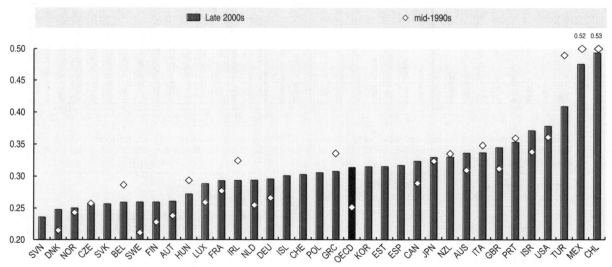

Note: Data refer to mid-2000s instead of late 2000s for Greece and Switzerland. For Austria, Belgium, the Czech Republic, Estonia, Finland, Iceland, Luxembourg, Poland, Portugal, the Slovak Republic, Slovenia, Spain and Switzerland the values are provisional.
Source: OECD Income distribution and poverty database.

StatLink http://dx.doi.org/10.1787/888932492055

...and across time

Figure 2.10 also shows how the Gini index has changed relative to the mid-1990s (OECD, 2011b). Over this long time period, income inequality increased in most OECD countries, especially in Sweden, Netherlands and Denmark, while it fell in a few, such as Turkey, Ireland, Belgium, Greece, and Chile. While it is challenging to assess the driving forces of income inequality, some key factors are described in Box 2.3.

Box 2.3. **What drives income disparities?**

The income distribution in OECD countries depends on many factors. First, changes in demographic patterns and household structures may increase inequality: for example, the recent increase in the share of people living alone have decreased households' economies of scale for consumption, putting specific population groups such as single parents, young persons and elderly living alone at greater risk of poverty. Population ageing combined with the increasing economic insecurity of youth reinforces this risk. Second, labour market trends may contribute to higher income inequality (figure 2.11); earnings account for a large share of household disposable income and earnings disparities have increased rapidly over the past two decades (chapter 3 on "Jobs and earnings"); another trend is the increased incidence of atypical work such as part-time and temporary jobs. Third, the degree of redistribution achieved by policies, through cash benefits and taxes, may have changed over time. On average, redistribution schemes in OECD countries reduce income inequality by around one-third, with cash benefits having the greatest impact; over the last decade, tax systems have became less progressive, notably so in the case of income taxes. A detailed analysis of policy and non-policy drivers of income disparities is presented in (OECD, 2011b).

Figure 2.11. **Inequality in market and disposable income, among the entire population, 2008**

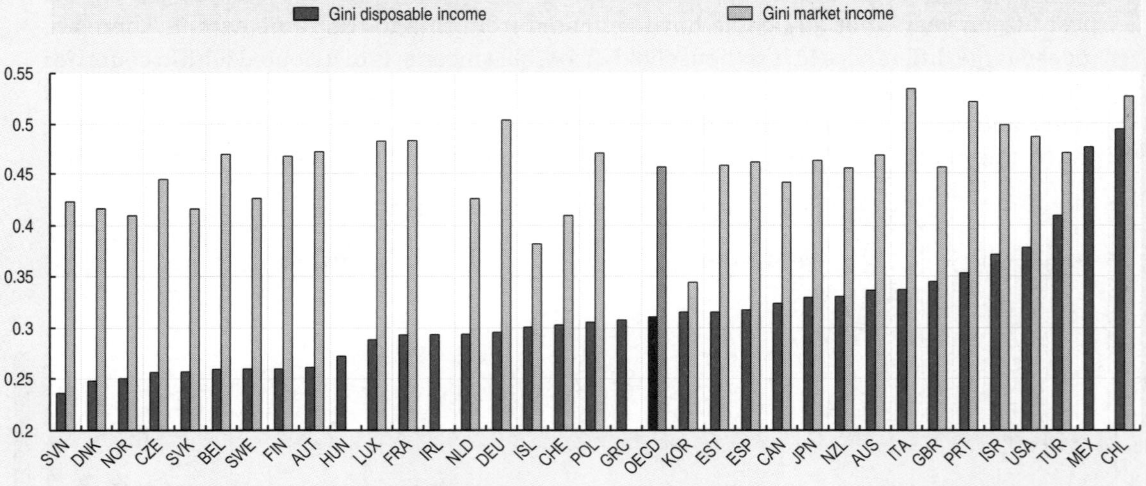

Note: OECD average excludes Greece, Hungary, Ireland and Mexico, as no data on market incomes are available for these countries. Data refer to 2006 for Japan; 2007 for Denmark, Hungary and Turkey and 2009 for Chile. For Austria, Belgium, the Czech Republic, Estonia, Finland, Iceland, Luxembourg, Poland, Portugal, the Slovak Republic, Slovenia, Spain and Switzerland the values are provisional. Countries are ranked in increasing order of disposable income inequality.
Source: Adapted from OECD (2011b) Income distribution and poverty database.

StatLink ᴹˢ⁵ᴾ http://dx.doi.org/10.1787/888932492074

Cross-countries differences in low income levels are also large

As in the case of overall income inequality, the number of low-income people varies significantly across OECD countries (Figure 2.12). In Mexico and Israel, at least 25% of the population is below the low-income threshold of 60% of median income, compared to only

10% in the Czech Republic. The low-income headcount is below 20% in all OECD European countries, with the exception of Italy, Spain and Estonia, where it is above, on average. These general patterns are consistent for a lower poverty threshold (*i.e.* 50% of median income, Figure 2.12 second panel. However, the number of low-income people changes substantially across the two poverty measures, particularly so for the Czech Republic, Denmark, Finland, France, Hungary, Israel, Netherlands and Sweden. This suggests that many of the policies targeted towards low-income people succeed in fighting poverty only to a limited extent. As poverty is defined in relative terms (*i.e.* with respect to the median), the observed patterns tend to reflect inequality at the lower end of the income distribution, rather than absolute living standards.

Figure 2.12. **Incidence of income poverty**

Percentage of low-income people over the total population

Poverty threshold at 60% of the median income

Poverty threshold at 50% of the median income

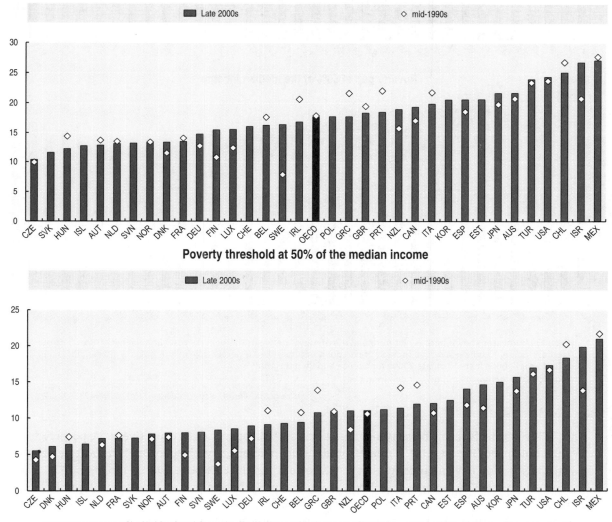

Note: Percentage of individuals with equivalised disposable income of less than 60% or 50 % of the median income of the entire population. Data refer to mid-2000s instead of late 2000s for Greece and Switzerland. Data for mid-1990s are not available for Estonia, Island, Korea, Poland, the Slovak Republic, Slovenia and Switzerland.

Source: OECD Income distribution and poverty database.

StatLink ⟶ http://dx.doi.org/10.1787/888932492093

Figure 2.13. **Depth of income poverty, late 2000s**

Income of the low-income people as percentage of the poverty threshold

Poverty gap at 60% of the median income

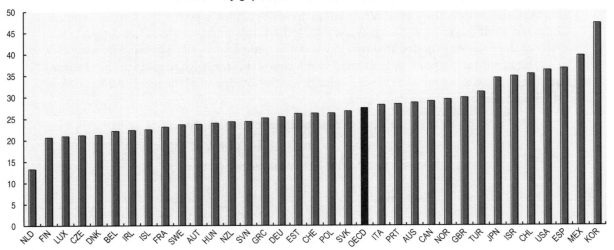

Poverty gap at 50% of the median income

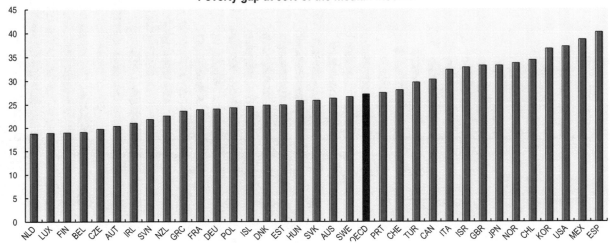

Note: The indicator shown here is computed as the distance between the poverty threshold (set at 60% or 50% of median income) and the average income of the poor, expressed as a percentage of the poverty threshold. Data refer to mid-2000s instead of late 2000s for Greece and Switzerland.

Source: OECD Income distribution questionnaire.

StatLink ⟦⟧ *http://dx.doi.org/10.1787/888932492112*

The depth of income poverty also varies across OECD countries, irrespective of the poverty threshold used (Figure 2.13). Korea records the deepest poverty: the people at the bottom of the distribution have an income that is 47% lower than the 60% poverty threshold (and 37% lower than the 50% poverty threshold). Conversely, Netherlands, Canada, Czeck Republic, Finland and Luxembourg have poverty gaps well below the OECD average. Across countries, there is a strong correlation between the prevalence of low income and its depth, with countries recording the largest number of low-income people also being those where these people are the furthest away from the poverty threshold. Some countries, however, have both a low prevalence of low income and a large poverty gap.

The two indicators presented here refer to what is conventionally referred to as "income poverty". This reflects the view that income is essential to exit poverty. Nonetheless, low income is only one aspect of material deprivation, and dimensions other than economic resources are also important (OECD, 2008; Alkire and Foster, 2011).

What about wealth inequality and how does it relate to income distribution?

The empirical analysis of wealth distribution is severely constrained by weaknesses in available data. Ongoing international initiatives aim to address these weaknesses, but currently the state of knowledge on wealth inequality is far more uncertain than for income inequality. The analysis of the joint distribution of income and wealth faces similar challenges. The Luxembourg Wealth Study (LWS), an international research project, provides data on wealth and income through a coherent and harmonised framework. For the countries covered by the LWS[12] it appears that:

- Although there are significant cross-country differences in the distribution of household wealth, these differences are on average more pronounced than those for income. Within countries, wealth inequalities (as measured by quartile ratios) are on average twice as large as for income.

- Net wealth and income are highly, but not perfectly, correlated. For example, many of the households classified as income poor do own some assets (Sierminska et al., 2006).

The statistical agenda ahead

Despite the rich amount of statistical information available in this field (compared to other dimension of people's well-being) data gaps remain significant, requiring action in a number of fields:

- First, the availability of data on average economic conditions needs to be improved, in line with the recommendations of the last editions of the system of national accounts. Not all OECD countries currently compile detailed household sector accounts, and even when they do practices differ in terms of household sector definition (e.g. including or excluding non-profit institutions serving households, treatment of unincorporated enterprises) and the range of transactions included (e.g. whether measures include or exclude capital depreciation or social transfers in kind provided by governments). There is a need for a more accurate decomposition of the household sector where households ought to be clearly isolated from the other components of the sector.

- Second, to enhance the availability of comparable data, especially for measures of the household balance sheet, action should be taken to expand the coverage of assets to dwellings and land, so as to better monitor how household net worth changes with developments in the housing market, and to improve the timeliness of the compilation of household balance sheets.[13]

- Third, it would be important to develop better measures of non-market household services, in particular by improving the comparability and the timeliness of Time Use Surveys (see also Chapter 6 on the Work and Life Balance).

- Fourth, the availability, timeliness and comparability of micro data on household economic conditions need to be improved. This applies in particular to micro data on household wealth, an area where no international standards currently exist and where few countries undertake regular compilations. Steps also need to be taken to develop instruments that would allow understanding the relationship between income and other dimensions of people's material conditions, for example, joint surveys on household income, consumption and wealth, or matching of individual records. To address this issue, the OECD has set up an expert group whose mandate is to develop guidelines to measure income, consumption and wealth in a fully integrated framework.

- Fifth, there needs to be better reconciliation of macro (national accounts) and micro measures (*e.g.* survey-based) of household economic conditions, in order to achieve greater comparability between them. This would allow considering average achievements and their distribution simultaneously. To that end, the OECD and EUROSTAT have set up an expert group whose mandate is to compare both sources in order to measure disparities within the national accounts framework, using a common methodological basis across OECD countries.

Conclusion

This chapter has discussed material conditions in OECD countries on the basis of some well-established measures of household income and wealth. In most OECD countries, judged on these grounds, life has been getting better, as average measures of household income and wealth have risen over the last fifteen years. Alternative indicators considered in this chapter point toward the same conclusion, despite some differences between objective and subjective indicators. But life is not equally good for everybody, as not all households have experienced an equally good rise in living standards. Within-country inequalities remain high in many countries, as does the number of low-income people. This suggests a strong role for policies that specifically address distributional concerns.

Notes

1. At the microeconomic level, the first household survey on material conditions took place in the United Kingdom in 1795; at the macroeconomic level a first quantitative framework for measuring national income can be traced back to 1665 in the United Kingdom.

2. See the second edition of the Canberra Group Handbook on Household Income Statistics (UN, 2011) and the System of National Accounts 2008 for the latest updates on the underlying framework.

3. Discrepancies reflect differences in terms of both population coverage and practical definitions of several elements included in survey data on household economic resources. For example, national accounts have a broader definition of the household sector, including non-profit institutions serving households and unincorporated enterprises, and also exhaustive population coverage while surveys typically exclude some specific groups (*e.g.* people living in institutions or in remote and sparsely populated areas).

4. All the data shown in this chapter refer to the aggregate of households (which includes unincorporated enterprises) and non-profit institutions serving households. SNA data referring to the sector of households alone are available for only 22 of the 32 OECD countries that regularly compile household accounts.

5. Ideally, average household net adjusted disposable income should be expressed on an equivalised basis (*i.e.* adjusted by the possible economies of scales enjoyed by households in sharing the income of their members) and not *per capita*. This would increase comparability with the income indicators used for assessing inequality, which are typically expressed in equivalised terms. However, carrying out a similar adjustment for aggregate income indicators, such as those derived from national accounts, would require annual data on the number of both people and households, which are not available within the SNA (EU countries are planning to make increasing use of aggregates "per consumption unit" in the future). Measures of income and consumption per consumption unit typically rise at a slower pace than per capita measures, reflecting trends

towards smaller families, the greater frequency of divorce and separations and the increase in people living alone. This mechanism is also one of the drivers of greater income inequality.

6. For comparison at one point in time current PPPs are preferred over constant PPPs since they capture both volume and price changes. However, when combining cross-country comparisons and time-series analysis, constant PPP series are considered best-practices. A caveat on the use of constant PPPs is that they do not fully take into account shift in prices and price structures; this may be problematic if the analysis is carried out over a long period of time (Bournot *et al.*, 2011).

7. The notion of "equivalisation" implies that the income attributed to each person in a household reflects income sharing within the household and adjusts for household needs. All the distributional indicators shown in this chapter assume that these needs increase with household size, but less than proportionally (total household income is divided by the square root of household size).

8. In addition to the differences discussed above, further discrepancies between the two approaches arise as the macro-economic definition focuses on the type of transaction from which incomes are generated while it disregards the medium of payment. Conversely the micro-economic definition relies on the medium of payment as the main factor for classifying incomes in various typologies.

9. The Gini index is defined as the area between the Lorenz curve, which plots cumulative shares of the population from the poorest to the richest, against the cumulative share of income that they receive) and the 45° line, taken as a ratio of the whole triangle. It ranges between zero (everybody has the mean income) and one (all income goes to the richest individual).

10. These differences may partly reflect the varying importance of household non-financial assets in total net wealth across countries.

11. See OECD *National Accounts at a Glance (2010)* for additional developments.

12. Austria, Canada, Cyprus, Finland, Germany, Italy, Japan, Luxembourg, Norway, Sweden, United Kingdom, United States.

13. These recommendations are contained in the Report *"Emphasize the Household Perspective"*, from the Eurostat Taskforce on Household Perspective and Distributional Aspects of Income, Consumption and Wealth established as part of the Eurostat/Insee Sponsorship, which follows-up Stiglitz *et al.*, (2009).

References

Ahmad N. and S.-H. Koh(2011), "Incorporating Household Production into International Comparisons of Material Well-Being", OECD Statistics Directorate Working Paper (forthcoming), Paris.

Alkire, S. and J. Foster (2011), "Counting and multidimensional poverty", *Journal of Public Economics*, Vol. 95, No. 7-8, pp. 476-487.

Bournot S., F. Koechlin and P. Shreyer (2011), "2008 Benchmark PPP Measurement and Uses", OECD Statistical Brief, March, No. 17.

Chakravarty, S. R. (2009), *Inequality, Polarization and Poverty: Advances in Distributional Analysis*, Springer-Verlag, Heidelberg.

Eurostat (2003), *Household Production and Consumption, Proposal for a Methodology of Household Satellite Accounts*, Luxembourg.

Hüfner, F. and I. Koske (2010), "Explaining Households Saving Rates in G7 Countries: Implications for Germany", *OECD Economics Department Working Paper*, No. 754.

Landefeld J.S., B.M. Fraumeni and C.M. Vojtech (2009), "Accounting for household production: A prototype satellite account using the American Time-Use Survey", *Review of Income and Wealth*, Series 55, No. 2.

OECD (2007), *Regions at a Glance*, OECD Publishing, Paris.

OECD (2008), *Growing Unequal? Income Inequality and Poverty in OECD Countries*, OECD Publishing, Paris.

OECD (2010), *National Accounts at a Glance*, OECD Publishing, Paris.

OECD (2011) *The Causes of Growing Inequality in OECD Countries,* OECD Publishing, Paris.

Ruger Y. and J. Varjonen (2008), "Value of Household Production in Finland and Germany, Analysis and Recalculation of the Household Satellite Account System in Both Countries", *National Consumer Research Center Working Paper* No. 112.

Sen, A. (1999), *Development as Freedom*, Oxford, Oxford University Press.

Sen, A. and J. E. Foster (1998), *On Economic Inequality*, Oxford University Press.

Sierminska, E., A. Brandolini and T.M. Smeeding (2006), "Comparing Wealth Distributions across Rich Countries: First Results from the Luxembourg Wealth Study", *Luxembourg Wealth Study Working Paper No.1.*

Stiglitz, J.E., A. Sen and J.-P. Fitoussi (2009), Report by the Commission on the Measurement of Economic Performance and Social Progress, http://www.stiglitz-sen-fitoussi.fr/documents/rapport_anglais.pdf

United Nations (2011), *The Camberra Group Handbook on Household Income Statistics*, forthcoming, Geneva.

Chapter 3

Jobs and Earnings

Having a job that matches one's aspirations and competencies and that pays adequate earnings is a universal aspiration of people around the globe. In general, the economic growth of the past fifteen years has gone in hand with an increase in employment and earnings in most OECD and other major economies, but these accomplishments are being put to a serious test by the ongoing economic crisis. Further, earnings inequalities have increased in most OECD countries, some aspects of working conditions (e.g. involuntary part-time) have worsened, and having a job seems to provide less of a shield against the risk of poverty than in the past. Women, youth and older workers face relatively high job insecurity and weaker ties with the labour market. Even though employment statistics generally meet high statistical standards, there is scope for improvement in several domains, as in the case of data on hours worked, earnings disparities and measurement of the quality of employment. While many international organisations have been active in defining a measurement framework for assessing job quality, information gaps in this field are still very large, especially as far as official statistics are concerned.

Why do jobs and earnings matter for well-being?

The availability of jobs and the earnings they pay are essential to individual well-being. Not only do good jobs increase people's command over resources, but they also provide people with a chance to fulfil their own ambitions, to develop skills and abilities, to feel useful in society and to build self-esteem. Jobs shape personal identity and create opportunities for social relationships.

Research has also shown that being unemployed has a large negative effect on physical and mental health (Wilson and Walker, 1993) and on subjective well-being (Clark and Oswald, 1994); this suggests that the negative effect of joblessness on well-being goes well beyond the income loss that unemployment brings. There is also evidence that this impact is persistent over time and that psychological resilience to unemployment is low (Dolan et al., 2008).

Working conditions can be as important as job availability in terms of their consequences on people's lives, as people spend a considerable amount of time at work. Work represents many people's main recognised contribution to the community where they live, and it is a source of pride and dignity; the quality of their jobs is therefore fundamental for them.[1]

The quality of jobs, and how to measure this, has attracted increased interest among the international community (Economic and Social Council, 2010). The International Labour Organisation (ILO) developed the concept of "decent work" in the early 1990s (Box 3.1), and, more recently, other initiatives to measure the quality of jobs have been undertaken by the UNECE and Eurostat (UNECE, 2010). These initiatives highlight that job quality depends on certain critical factors such as job safety and the ethics in the work-place, the income and benefits from employment, job security and social protection, social dialogue, workplace relationships and job motivation. This chapter considers some indicators of job quality, in addition to standard indicators measuring the availability of jobs.

This chapter should be read in connection with Chapter 2 on "Income and Wealth" and Chapter 6 on "Work and Life Balance", as earnings represent the main component of household income and are shaped by, among other factors, hours worked and the balance between paid work and other activities.

Box 3.1. **The ILO's definition of decent work**

The concept of "decent work" was introduced in 1999 by the International Labour Organisation (ILO) and defined as :"opportunities for women and men to obtain decent and productive work in conditions of freedom, equity, security and human dignity" (ILO, 2003).

This definition is based on a broad concept of work encompassing all forms of economic activity (Anker et al., 2003; Ghai, 2003; and UNECE, 2010). It has six dimensions: the notion of "opportunities for work", which refers to the ability of every man and woman who wants to work to be able to find work; the notion of productive work, which refers to work that ensures sustainable development and provides acceptable livelihoods for workers and their families; the fact that work should be freely chosen and not forced; that workers should be free to join workers' organizations; that work should be characterised by the absence of discrimination and the equitable treatment of workers; that the health of workers and their families should be safeguarded, with adequate protection provided in the event of illness or other contingencies; and, finally, that workers should be treated with respect at work.

The ILO has made "decent work" the organising principle for its activities, and has set an agenda for incorporating the goal of decent work for all into national strategic planning objectives. The ILO decent work agenda is based on four strategic objectives: i) fundamental principles and rights at work; ii) employment creation; iii) social protection; and iv) social dialogue.

Source: ILO (2011a, 2011b).

Measuring jobs and earnings

An ideal set of indicators of jobs and earnings will inform on both quantity and quality of jobs, as well as the extent to which working conditions meet people's expectations and allow them to earn a good living.

Concerning the *quantity* of jobs, ideal indicators should measure the availability of jobs for those who want to work but also the actual intensity of labour market participation in relation to the desired number of working hours. Employment and unemployment indicators are conventional measures of labour market participation; yet employment ratios convey a relatively rough picture of actual work intensity, as they provide no indication of whether people are under-employed (*i.e.* work less than they would like to).[2]

Concerning the *quality* of jobs, the UNECE-ILO-Eurostat Taskforce on this subject recommends including:[3]

- Measures of job safety and employment, workplace injuries, unacceptable forms of labour (*e.g.* child labour) as well as unfair treatment, such as discriminatory work situations.

- Measures of earnings and benefits from employment, which indicate whether jobs are paid reasonably and fairly with respect to the labour inputs provided, but which also gauge whether financial rewards from work provide people with sufficient resources to enjoy good living standards.

- Measures of security of employment and social protection that inform about whether workers can count on stable and regular employment and whether, when they are out of work, they can rely on adequate social protection and avoid poverty.

- Measures of social dialogue, capturing the freedom of workers to organise and bargain with employers about their working conditions.

- Measures of workplace relationships and work motivation that inform about the social characteristics of work (*e.g.* whether there is a productive, friendly and cooperative working atmosphere) and about people's work satisfaction in a broader sense (*e.g.* fulfilling one's own expectations, allowing the development of skills and abilities, etc.)

In practice, many of these aspects of the quality of employment are not adequately covered by existing indicators available at the international level, and the above concepts only provide broad guidance for measurement. Indeed, while indicators on jobs are robust and based on harmonised international definitions (*e.g.* ILO and SNA), many indicators of job quality are affected by the small scale of existing surveys on the subject, and often rely either on official surveys that are not harmonised across countries or on surveys conducted outside the boundaries of the official statistical system.

Moreover, some traditional labour-market indicators, such as earnings and hours worked, suffer from a serious lack of harmonisation at the cross-national level (for instance, in terms of concepts, universe, timing, etc.), which severely limits cross-country comparative analysis in this area.

Therefore, the evidence discussed in this chapter provides a relatively good picture of the quantity of jobs, assessed through standard employment and unemployment indicators, but only an imperfect one of job quality, as apprehended through indicators of earnings, occupational injuries, as well as temporary and part-time jobs.

Table 3.1 **The quality of job and earnings indicators**

		Target concept	INDICATORS							
			Relevance to measure and monitor well-being				Statistical quality			
			Face validity	Unambiguous interpretation (good/bad)	Amenable to policy changes	Can be disaggregated	Collected through a well-established instrument	Comparable definition	Country coverage	Recurrent data collection
	Jobs and Earnings									
JE I	Employment rate		√	√	√	√	√	√	√	√
JE II	Long-term unemployment	Quantity of jobs	√	√	√	√	√	√	√	√
je 1	Involuntary part-time employment		√	√	√	√	√	~	√	√
JE III	Average annual earnings per employee		~	√	√	x	~	~	√	√
je 2	Employees working on temporary contracts	Quality of jobs	√	√	√	√	√	~	√	√
je 3	Work accidents: fatal and non fatal injuries		√	√	√	~	~	~	~	√

Note: The symbol √ shows that the indicator selected largely meets the criteria shown in the table; the symbol ~ that the indicator meets the criteria to a large extent; the symbol x that the indicator does not meet the criterion or it meets it only to a limited extent.

Selected indicators

Employment rate (JE I)

This indicator refers to the share of the working-age population (aged 15 to 64 in most OECD countries) that declare having worked in gainful employment for at least one hour in the previous week. According to the ILO definition, this also comprises persons who, having already worked in their present job, were temporarily not at work during the reference period and had a formal attachment to their job (*e.g.* due to parental leave, sickness, annual leave, strike or lock-out).

Data on employment rates come from the national Labour Force Surveys (LFSs), and are consistent with ILO recommendations. LFSs are regularly compiled and revised, which allows monitoring changes in labour market conditions. However, differences across countries in questionnaire wording and design, survey timing, and the age groups covered mean that some care is required in interpreting cross-country differences in indicator levels.

One obvious shortcoming of the employment rate indicator as a measure of well-being is the fact that some people may be out of paid work by choice (*e.g.* to stay with their children, to study or to perform other valued activities). A second shortcoming is that the employment rate is affected by the structure of the population (e.g. a higher share of the school-age population will lower the employment rate). In these circumstances, a lower employment rate in one country will not imply lower well-being than in a country where the employment rate is higher. Conversely, people may be employed but working less than they would wish, a limitation that is partly addressed by the underemployment indicator discussed below. Finally, it should be noted that country comparisons of changes in employment rates (as well as changes in other labour market indicators shown in this chapter) are affected by differences in the cyclical positions of various countries (EC, 2010).

Long-term unemployment rate (JE II)

Long-term unemployment places people at risk of social exclusion, poverty and deprivation. This indicator refers to the number of persons who have been unemployed for one year or more as a percentage of the active labour force (the sum of employed and unemployed persons). According to the ILO definition, the unemployed comprise all persons of working age who, during the reference period of the survey, were: i) without work, i.e. not in paid employment or self-employment during the reference period, ii) available for work, and iii) actively seeking work, i.e. had taken specific steps in the previous four weeks to seek paid employment or self-employment, where the specific steps may include registration at a public or private employment office, application to employers, checking at worksites or farms, placing or answering newspaper advertisements, seeking assistance from friends or relatives, looking for land, building, machinery or equipment to establish their own enterprise, arranging for financial resources, applying for permits and licences, etc.

Data are drawn from LFSs, and the methodoligical caveats mentioned above apply. In addition, one limitation of the unemployment indicator from the perspective of assessing well-being is that it excludes people who wish to work but feel discouraged about actively seeking a job, because they deem their probability of finding one to be very low. The international definition of unemployment used here is not linked to any institutional or legal provisions (such as the receipt of unemployment benefits or registration as a job seeker with a public employment office) and is intended to refer exclusively to a person's particular activities during a specified reference period. As a result, unemployment statistics based on the international definition used here may differ from the national statistics on registered unemployment that are used in some countries.

Involuntary part-time employment (je 1)

Part-time workers may be disadvantaged as compared to full-time workers in terms of pay, job security, training, promotion, risk of poverty (Box 3.2) and access to unemployment benefits or re-employment assistance when becoming unemployed. However, people may also choose to work part-time because they prefer to spend more time with their family or to have a lower professional responsibility (OECD, 2010b). What counts the most for people's well-being is whether part-time work is voluntary or involuntary.

Box 3.2. **Is work the best antidote to poverty?**

Employment considerably reduces the risk of poverty, but does not necessarily eliminate it:

- Having a job is a major factor limiting the risk of poverty faced by households with a head of working age. In virtually all countries, the (income) poverty rate among jobless households (i.e. those where no member is gainfully employed) is more than double the rate observed among working households.

- In-work poverty is significant almost everywhere. On average 7% of individuals living in households with at least one worker are poor in the OECD area. Consequently, this group accounts for more than 60% of all the poor of working age.

- For most of the working poor, underemployment is a major problem. The average intensity of work among the working poor differs sharply from that observed among the rest of the employed population. On average over 21 European countries, only slightly more than 20% of the working poor work full-time for a full year, and almost 70% of this group work six months or less during the year (in full-time equivalent months). By contrast, more than half of individuals living in a non-poor household work full-time over the full year.

- For families with children and low earnings potential, even full-time employment may not completely secure economic self-sufficiency. On average, working full-time at the bottom of the wage ladder (i.e. at around 40% of the average wage) brings the disposable incomes of two-earner couples with children to only 65% of the median income, while the incomes of lone parents in low-paid work remain at the poverty threshold (or even below it) in most countries.

Source: OECD (2008b).

Involuntary part-time workers are defined here as those who usually work less than 30 hours per week either because they were unable to find a full-time job or declaring they would prefer to work more hours. The indicator used here shows the prevalence of involuntary part-time workers on total employment. Data come from the OECD Employment Database, and cover all OECD countries. However, definitions of involuntary part-time workers are not fully harmonised, which may hamper cross-country comparisons. For these reasons, this indicator is considered as secondary.

Average gross annual earnings of full-time employee (JE III)

An important aspect of job quality is the wage and other monetary benefits that originate from employment. Earnings represent the main source of most households' income. In addition, an indicator on earnings may also inform on the extent to which work is remunerated fairly and is treated with respect and dignity.

The earnings indicator used here shows the average annual earnings per full-time employee, covering all sectors of the economy and all types of dependent employment. The indicator is given by the total wage bill divided by the number of full-time equivalent employees in the total economy and expressed in PPP rates. The number of full-time equivalent employees is obtained by multiplying data on the number of employees by the ratio of hours worked by all employees and by those working full-time,[4] in order to correct for the prevalence of part-time work, which varies considerably across countries.

Data come from the OECD National Accounts, and cover all sectors of the economy and all types of dependent employment. This enables international comparisons of the levels and trends of average annual earnings. Compared to alternative earnings series, the OECD National Accounts series have the advantage of covering both full-time and part-time workers. National Accounts data also include undeclared earnings (as part of the so-called "non-observed" economy), although differences in methodologies may affect international comparability.[5]

An additional limitation of this indicator is that it does not measure the earnings gained per hour worked and thus the opportunity cost of spending time out of work. Another weakness is that it refers to an average concept and thus does not inform about earnings inequality within the population; the survey data on earnings inequality presented later in this chapter are hence not directly comparable to the national accounts data on average earnings described above.

Employees working on temporary contracts (je 2)

Another essential factor in the quality of employment is job security. Employees working on temporary contracts often face a higher risk of job losses than do permanent workers, and are therefore more vulnerable than workers with an open-ended contract, especially in countries with smaller social safety nets (OECD, 2010b).

This indicator refers to temporary workers as a share of total employees. Temporary employment includes "fixed-term contracts", employment by "temporary employment agencies" and "seasonal workers". Data come from the OECD Employment Database. Although the quality of the data is good, cross-country comparisons should be made with caution, due to some differences in the definition of temporary workers. Moreover, as temporary employment includes all types of temporary employment, this indicator does not provide information on individuals' reasons for choosing or accepting this type of work arrangement. For these reasons, this indicator is presented as a secondary indicator.

Work accidents (je 3)

This indicator is a standard measure of safety at work, and shows the frequency of fatal and non-fatal injuries, which is expressed as the number of work accidents during 12 consecutive months per 100 000 workers. Data come from the ILO LABORSTA database, the Eurostat New Cronos database and the Injuries, Illnesses and Fatalities (IIF) database of the US Bureau of Labor Statistics (BLS).

International comparisons of work accidents are difficult because of differences in both record-keeping (e.g. statistics sometimes only record compensated accidents in workplaces of a sufficient size and exclude minor injuries) and data sources (e.g. insurance companies, social security registers, labour inspectorates, establishment censuses and special surveys). Moreover, employers may underreport work accidents in countries where the social security contributions that they pay depend on the frequency of accidents (i.e. experience-rating). Comparability is generally higher in the case of fatal injuries, as country definitions differ in terms of the length of absences from work considered (OECD, 2007). Data for some countries may exclude accidents affecting the self-employed or those working in small firms, may refer to compensated rather than reported injuries, and may express accidents relative to the insured rather than to all workers. However, comparability has improved since the adoption in 1998 of an ILO Resolution that sets out standards for data collection and presentation. Since the quality of this indicator does not meet high statistical standards, it is presented here as a secondary indicator.

Average patterns

Employment rates have increased but large differences across OECD countries remain

Compared with other OECD countries, employment rates in 2010 were low in Turkey, where less than one in two persons aged 15-64 is employed (Figure 3.1). Broadly speaking, employment is relatively low in Southern European countries and high in Switzerland and in the Nordic countries. Since the mid-1990s, there is evidence of a general increase in employment, although there is large variation across OECD countries. Employment has also considerably increased in the Russian Federation, the only emerging country with available information. Countries where the employment rate has increased the most in the past fifteen years or so are Spain and the Netherlands. Conversely, employment rates have declined considerably in Turkey and, to a lesser extent, in the United States, Estonia and the Czech Republic (Figure 3.1). Cross-country differences in employment as well as the trends over time are affected by the economic cycle and the resilience of labour markets to macroeconomic shocks, which may differ considerably across countries.

Figure 3.1. **Employment rate**

Percentage of employed 15-64 aged over the population of the same age

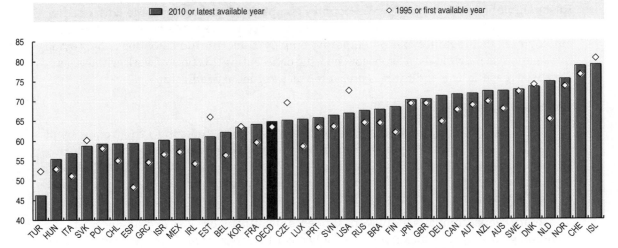

Note: The first available year is 2001 for Brazil and 2002 for Slovenia. The latest available year is 2009 for Brazil.
Source: OECD, Labour Force Statistics database.

StatLink 🔗 *http://dx.doi.org/10.1787/888932492131*

In most OECD countries long-term unemployment rates are low

In 2010, long-term unemployment rates were below 4% in most OECD countries. They are virtually nil in Korea, Mexico and Norway, while they are almost three times as high as the OECD average (3%) in Estonia, the Slovak Republic and Spain. Since the mid-1990s, long-term unemployment rates have declined in many OECD countries, particularly in Spain, the Russian Federation, Italy and Finland. Exceptions to this trend are the United States, Portugal and Estonia (Figure 3.2). These contrasting trends may partly reflect the different timing and impacts of the recent financial crisis.

Figure 3.2. **Long-term unemployment rate**

Percentage of people aged 15-64 who have been unemployed for one year or more over the labour force of the same age

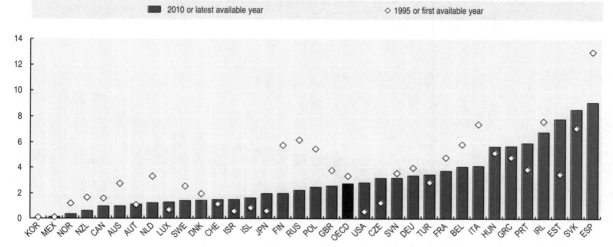

Note: The first available year is 1999 for the Russian Federation and 2002 for Slovenia. The latest available year is 2008 for the Russian Federation.

Source: OECD, Labour Force Statistics database.

StatLink ⟡ *http://dx.doi.org/10.1787/888932492150*

The incidence of involuntary part-time work has increased in many countries

Involuntary part-time employment represents less than 3% of total employment in many OECD countries, although this share is much higher in Japan and Australia (Figure 3.3). In the past fifteen years, involuntary part-time work has increased considerably in Japan, Spain, Italy and Germany. Conversely, other countries, such as Norway, Finland and Sweden, show a strong decrease in the percentage of involuntary part-time workers. In the Czech Republic, Hungary, Ireland and the Netherlands, involuntary part-time employment has remained fairly stable.

Figure 3.3. **Incidence of involuntary part-time employment**

Percentage of total employment

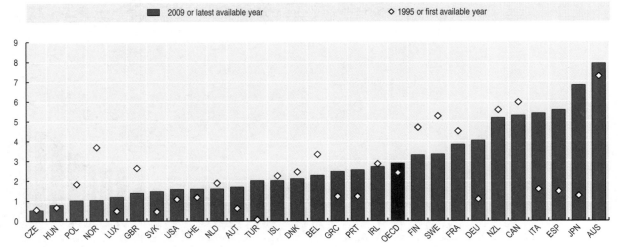

Note: The first available year is 1996 for Finland; 1998 for the Czech Republic and the United States; and 2001 for Australia and Poland. The latest available year is 2002 for Iceland; and 2004 for Turkey. In 1995, the incidence of part-time employment was virtually nil (0.06) in Turkey.

Source: OECD, Labour Force Statistics database.

StatLink ⬛⬛⬛ http://dx.doi.org/10.1787/888932492169

Average gross annual earnings have increased in all OECD countries

Average gross annual earnings per employee in the OECD area differ significantly across OECD countries. In the United States and Luxembourg, average gross annual earnings are more than three times higher than in the Eastern European countries. Between 1995 and 2009, annual gross wages per employee have increased in all OECD countries (Figure 3.4), though their growth has slowed in more recent years due to the financial crisis. Earnings increases have been particularly strong in Eastern European countries but also in Norway and Ireland. Gross annual earnings have been fairly stable over the past fifteen years in Spain, Japan, Italy and Germany.

Figure 3.4. **Average gross annual earnings of full-time employees in the total economy**

US dollars at 2008 PPPs

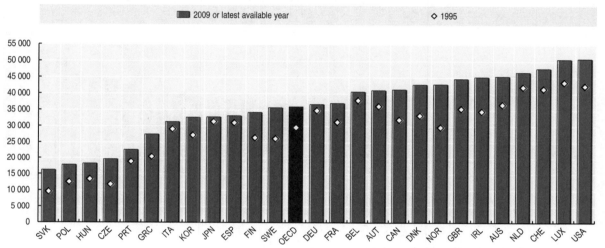

Note: The average annual earnings of per full-time employees are obtained by dividing the National Accounts based total wage bill by the number of employees in the total economy, multiplied by the ratio of weekly usual hours worked per full-time employee related to those worked by all employees. Average annual earnings are calculated with a deflator for private final consumption expenditures in 2008 prices. The latest data refer to 2007-08 for Greece.
Source: OECD estimates based on OECD National Accounts Database and OECD (2010), OECD Economic Outlook, No. 87

StatLink ∎∎∎⬛ *http://dx.doi.org/10.1787/888932492188*

More than one-fifth of all employees work on temporary contracts in some OECD countries

In most OECD countries, fewer than 15% of total employees work on temporary contracts. In Spain and Poland, however, one employee out of four works on a temporary contract (Figure 3.5). Over time, the percentage of temporary workers has decreased in Spain and Turkey, while it has increased substantially in Poland, Portugal and the Russian Federation. Some subjective measures of job insecurity as perceived by workers are presented in Box 3.3.

Figure 3.5 **Employees working on temporary contracts**

Percentage of total employees

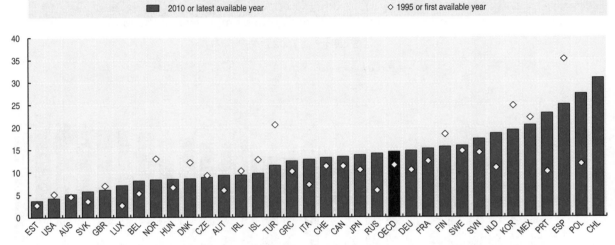

Note: The first available year is 1996 for Luxembourg and Norway; 1997 for Canada, Finland, Hungary and Sweden; 1998 for Australia and Switzerland; 1999 for the Russian Federation; 2001 for Poland; 2002 for Estonia and Slovenia; and 2004 for Korea. The latest available year is 2004 for Mexico; 2005 for the United States; 2006 for Australia; 2008 for the Russian Federation; and 2009 for Hungary and Iceland.

Source: OECD, Labour Force Statistics database.

StatLink ⟪⟫ http://dx.doi.org/10.1787/888932492207

Box 3.3. **Perceived job insecurity in European countries**

Information on job insecurity as perceived by workers is provided by the European Working Conditions Survey (EWCS), which is conducted every five years by the European Foundation for Improvement of Living and Working Conditions, based on a representative sample of European employees and self-employed people on different work-related dimensions (EFILWC, 2006). In 2005, in OECD Europe about 15% of workers declared that they might lose their job in the next six months (Figure 3.6). Although differences in perceived job security may reflect differences in labour market policies and institutions among countries, there is evidence that employees on temporary contracts feel less secure than do permanent workers. Similarly, lower-skilled manual workers feel less secure in their job than clerical workers (EWCS, 2006).

Figure 3.6. **Perceptions of job insecurity**

Percentage of employees and self-employed over age 15 declaring they might lose their job in the next six months, 2005

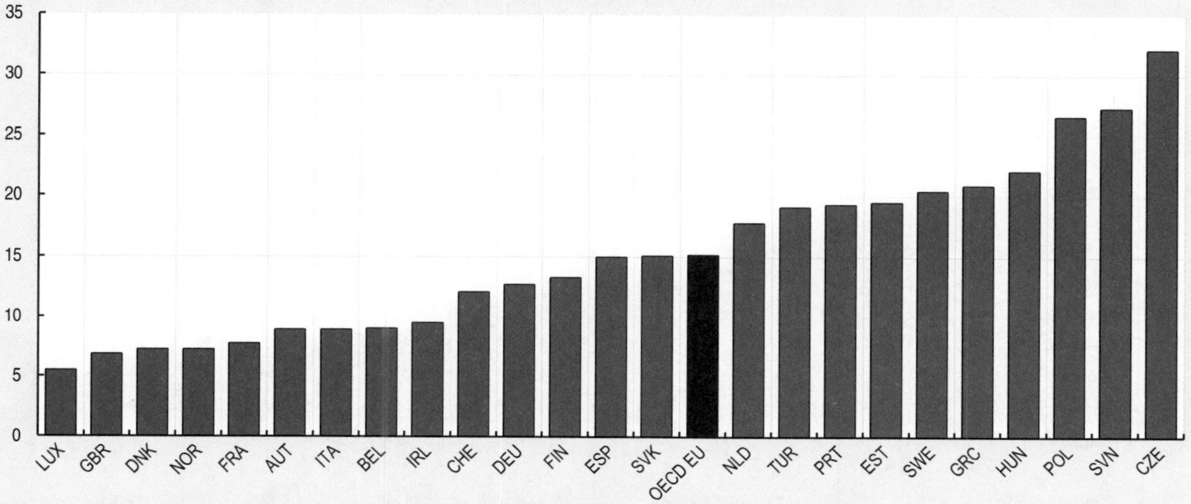

Source: The European Foundation for the Improvement of Living and Working Conditions, 2006.

StatLink ⬛📈 http://dx.doi.org/10.1787/888932492226

Work accidents in some OECD countries still are not insignificant, in particular fatal injuries.

In 2003, there were fewer than six fatal accidents per 100 000 workers in most OECD countries. This figure was higher in Mexico and Turkey (Table 3.2). While strict national legislation and strong safety cultures and partnerships can lower injuries at work, some occupational sectors remain more dangerous than others (OECD, 2007). In most OECD countries, non-fatal injuries were more frequent in the agricultural and/or the construction sector, while they were also particularly high in the manufacturing sector in countries such as Spain, Portugal, Norway, Canada and Hungary. Comparability is, however, especially limited in the case of non-fatal injuries.

Table 3.2. **Work accidents in selected OECD countries.**

Fatal and non-fatal accidents in 2003 per 100 000 workers, and lost workdays per worker involved in 2001

	Work accidents			Non-fatal work accidents by industry			
	Fatal	Non-fatal	Days lost per worker involved	Agriculture	Manufacturing	Construction	Transport
Compensated injuries							
Australia	2.0	1,230	6.0	2,561	2,070	2,201	2,056
Finland	2.7	2,847	5.7	5,226	3,339	5,908	3,534
Germany	3.5	3,674	4.3	12,160	3,432	7,029	3,702
Luxembourg	3.6	5,033	..	9,795	4,887	10,812	4,415
Belgium	3.9	3,456	5.7	5,387	3,572	6,398	3,898
Greece	3.9	2,090	..	1,265	3,226	4,519	1,820
New Zealand	5.2	1,605	..	4,992	2,456	3,781	2,104
France	5.4	4,689	5.9	4,778	4,232	10,066	6,123
Canada	6.1	2,227	5.7	2,212	3,914	3,428	2,650
Reported injuries							
United Kingdom	1.0	1,614	..	2,139	1,519	2,493	1,868
Sweden	1.6	1,252	5.3	1,355	1,717	2,090	1,583
Netherlands	1.8	1,188	..	..	..	..	..
Denmark	2.4	2,443	..	1,284	4,141	3,773	2,991
Japan	3.1	233	..	1,028	287	584	440
Norway	3.1	3,325	..	3,161	5,563	5,835	4,448
Hungary	3.4	656	..	748	1,235	469	960
Ireland	3.9	1,262	..	..	..	..	..
Czech Republic	4.5	1,872	6.4	3,947	3,256	3,429	1,966
Slovak Republic	4.7	801	5.1	2,720	1,601	2,049	882
Poland	4.9		5.0	..	..	..	..
Italy	5.6	3,267	..	..	..	..	..
Spain	6.0	6,520	7.7	2,401	8,820	13,651	6,526
Austria	6.6	2,629	..	..	..	..	..
United States	8.0	1,626	6.0	..	..	..	..
Portugal	8.4	4,054	..	880	5,773	6,851	3,624
Mexico	12.0	2,968	..	..	..	..	..
Turkey (2001)	20.6	..	..	..	..	..	..

Note: Countries in each panel are ranked in increasing order of fatal accidents. Data on the frequencies of fatal and non-fatal injuries for the EU-15 and Norway are weighted based on the EU-15 employment structure (by industry).

Source: ILO Laborsta database; Eurostat New Cronos database; and US Bureau of Labour Statistics website on fatal work accidents and occupational injuries (www.bls.gov/iif).

StatLink ᵐᵐˢ᪲ *http://dx.doi.org/10.1787/888932493841*

The various indicators capture different dimensions of the quantity and quality of jobs and earnings

The set of indicators presented in this chapter summarises information about selected characteristics of jobs, working conditions and earnings. It is important to assess whether these indicators are interlinked (Table 3.3). In general:

- The ratio of employment to the working-age population is strongly and negatively correlated with both long-term unemployment and fatal work accidents. By contrast, it is strongly and positively correlated with annual earnings per employee.

- Long-term unemployment is strongly and negatively correlated with annual earnings per employee.

- The share of employees working on temporary contracts correlates positively with the number of non-fatal work accidents.

The absence of strong correlations between the other indicators underscores the importance of looking at a range of measures to obtain a good appreciation of jobs and earnings.

Table 3.3. **Correlation between different indicators of jobs and earnings**

		JE I Employment rate	je 1 Involuntary part-time employment	JE II Long-term unemployment rate	je 2 Employees working on temporary contracts	JE III Annual earnings per employees	je 3 Fatal work accidents	je 3 Non-fatal work accidents
JE I	Employment rate	1 (36)	0.10 (29)	-0.55*** (35)	-0.08 (33)	0.61*** (26)	-0.66*** (18)	-0.16 (16)
je 1	Involuntary part-time employment		1 (29)	-0.03 (29)	0.17 (28)	0.12 (25)	-0.02 (17)	0.27 (15)
JE II	Long-term unemployment rate			1 (35)	-0.08 (33)	-0.49** (26)	0.02 (18)	0.24 (16)
je 2	Employees working on temporary contracts				1 (33)	-0.33 (26)	0.12 (18)	0.62** (16)
JE III	Annual wages per employees					1 (26)	-0.21 (16)	0.01 (15)
je 3	Fatal work accidents						1 (18)	0.43 (16)
je 3	Non-fatal work accidents							1 (16)

Note: Values in parenthesis refer to the number of observations. ** Indicates that correlations are significant at the 5% level; while *** indicates that they are significant at the 1% level.

Source: OECD's calculations.

StatLink ⇲ http://dx.doi.org/10.1787/888932493860

Inequalities

Employment rates are lower for women, the youth and the elderly

Employment rates for women are lower than for men in all OECD countries except Estonia (Figure 3.7, Panel a). The gender difference is particularly high in Turkey and Mexico, and relatively small in Canada, Estonia and the Nordic countries. Over the past 15 years, female employment rates have increased in most OECD countries, although there are large variations across countries (OECD, 2010b). In Spain, Ireland and the Netherlands, the female employment rate has increased by more than 15 percentage points, while in the Slovak Republic, Poland, Sweden and Iceland, it has remained fairly stable, and it has decreased in Turkey and the Czech Republic. The increase in employment rates for women may be explained by cyclical factors but also by improvements in the provision of childcare facilities, which have made it easier for mothers with young children to return to work.

The experience of workers when entering the labour market has a profound influence on their later working life. Getting off to a good start facilitates the integration of youth into the world of work and lays the foundation for a good career, while it can be difficult to catch up after an initial failure (OECD, 2010c). Youth have the lowest employment rate of all age groups, and the employment gap with prime-age workers is very large, especially in Hungary, the Slovak Republic, Greece and Italy (Figure 3.7, Panel b). In addition, the average employment rate for 15 to 24 year-olds in the OECD area has tended to decline between 1995 and 2009, with marked falls in Eastern European countries and the United States. In other countries, such as France, Iceland and the Netherlands, youth employment has increased, while it has remained steady in Australia and Estonia (OECD, 2010b). Alongside the decline in youth employment rates, there has been an increase in share of youth who are not in employment, education or training.

Employment rates are also lower among older people (55 to 64 years old) than among the prime-age population, though these differences vary greatly across countries. For instance, employment rates of people aged 55-64 are very low in Turkey, Hungary and Poland and very high in Iceland, New Zealand and Sweden (Figure 3.7, Panel b). Employment rates for older people have increased sharply in the Netherlands, New Zealand, Germany, the Slovak Republic and Finland, while they have remained fairly stable in Poland, Japan and Greece, and decreased by more than 13 percentage points in Turkey (OECD, 2010b)

Figure 3.7. **Inequalities in employment rates by gender and age, 2010**
Panel a: Employment rates by gender

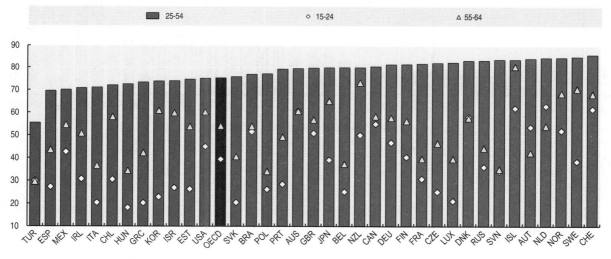

Panel b: Employment rates by age

Note: The latest available year is 2009 for Brazil.
Source: OECD, Labour Force Statistics database.

StatLink ⟦▤⟧ http://dx.doi.org/10.1787/888932492245

Employment increases with educational attainment

In all OECD countries, a higher proportion of 25 to 64 year-olds with a tertiary level of education are employed than those with only an upper secondary degree. Likewise, those with an upper secondary qualification are generally more likely to have a job than those with a lower educational level. The gender gap diminishes as the level of education rises (OECD, 2011b).

Long-term unemployment rates are high for women and youth

Average long-term unemployment in the OECD area is higher among women than men, though the difference is small on average (Figure 3.8, Panel a). This gender gap is particularly high in Greece, while in Ireland long-term unemployment is much greater among men. Over the past 15 years, long-term unemployment rates for women have decreased in almost all OECD countries (OECD 2010b). A sharp decrease has been observed in Spain, Italy and Ireland. By contrast, Turkey and the Czech Republic have experienced a moderate increase in women's long-term unemployment rates.

Figure 3.8. Inequalities in long-term unemployment rate, by gender and age, 2010

Panel a: Long-term unemployment rates by gender

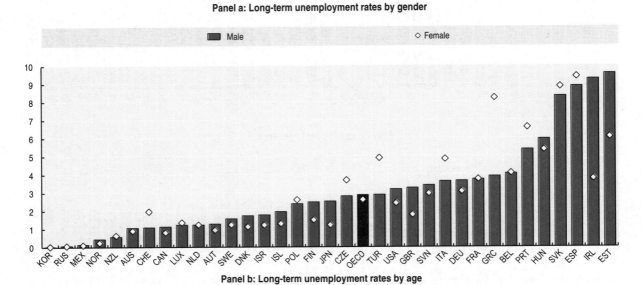

Panel b: Long-term unemployment rates by age

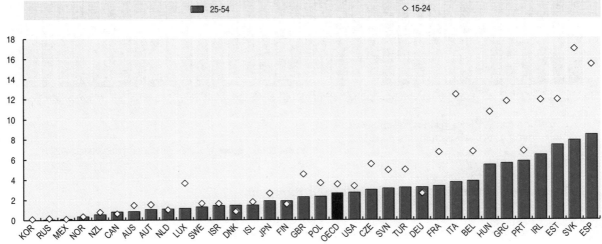

Source: OECD, Labour Force Statistics database.

StatLink ᴍꜱ𝗹 http://dx.doi.org/10.1787/888932492264

3. JOBS AND EARNINGS

In 2010, the youth long-term unemployment rate was 3.5% on average for the OECD, i.e. about 1 percentage point higher than for prime-age workers. Youth long-term unemployment rates are particularly high in the Slovak Republic, Spain and Italy (Figure 3.8, Panel b).

For low-educated people (those below upper secondary education), long-term unemployment rates remained fairly stable at around 10% in 2010 (down from 11% in 1995), with two notable exceptions: Estonia, where the rate has decreased sharply, and the Slovak Republic, where the rate has reached high levels (OECD, 2011b). Available data (not shown here) also show that, for middle and high-educated people, long-term unemployment rates declined slightly between 1995 and 2009.

Earnings disparities have grown sharply in many OECD countries

The measures of earnings inequalities presented in this section are based on the OECD Earnings Database, which draws from different sources such as surveys of individuals and firms, administrative registers and tax records.[6] The data refer to working-age individuals holding a full-time job. While full-time jobs account for the largest share of total employment in all OECD countries, the exact definition used in the different sources of earnings data may differ from that used in Labour Force Surveys. The data also refer to different earnings concepts (hourly and weekly earnings in most cases, annual and monthly earnings for some countries) and may include different elements of the employee remuneration packages. Because of these differences, this indicator is better suited for assessing changes in earning distributions over time than for comparing levels of earnings inequality across countries (Atkinson, 2007; OECD, 2008a).

Evidence based on these measures for selected OECD countries show an increase in earnings disparities in the OECD area (Figure 3.9), though large differences exist across the analysed countries. The incidence of low-paid work has also risen substantially in Australia and Germany and to a lesser extent in Korea. The number of low-paid workers has remained broadly stable in Japan, New Zealand, the United States and the United Kingdom. Earnings disparities between the extremes of the distribution (9th decile and 1st decile) have increased in New Zealand, Korea, Australia and Hungary, but declined in France. Similar trends are observed when comparing the highest earnings to the median ones (OECD, 2011a).

Earning disparities are much wider when looking at the personal earnings of all workers (i.e. both full-time and part-time workers, OECD, 2008). This reflects differences in working hours and in the wage rates of various types of workers, as workers in non-standard jobs (e.g. temporary contracts) are typically paid less per hour than other workers (OECD, 2008).[7] This suggests that people working a low number of hours and in non-standard jobs are typically at the bottom of the distribution of annual earnings (Burniaux, 2007; OECD, 2008).

While there are large gender gaps in earnings (Strauss and de la Maisonneuve, 2007; OECD, 2011a), within-gender disparities are significantly different (OECD, 2008). Earnings vary substantially also across groups defined by occupation, education, experience and other individual traits (Strauss and de la Maisonneuve, 2007; OECD, 2008b).

HOW'S LIFE? MEASURING WELL-BEING ©OECD 2011   **75**

Figure 3.9. **Trends in earnings inequality for full-time employees**

Index 1995=100

Low Pay Incidence

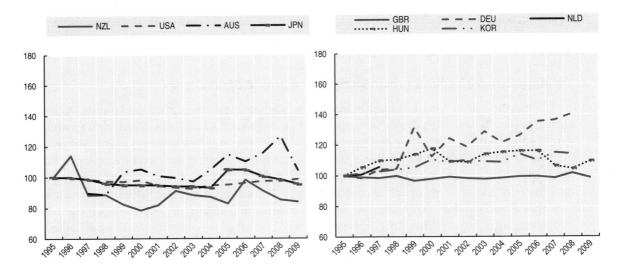

Decile9/Decile 1

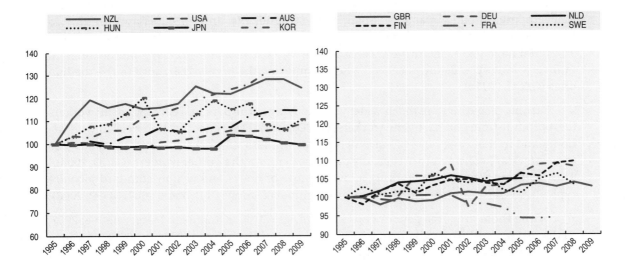

Decile 9/Decile 5

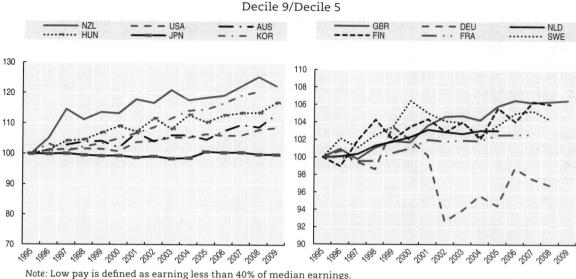

Note: Low pay is defined as earning less than 40% of median earnings.
Source: OECD Earnings database.

StatLink ⟨⟨⟩⟩ *http://dx.doi.org/10.1787/888932492283*

The statistical agenda ahead

Even though employment statistics generally meet high statistical standards, this chapter has stressed the need of improving labour market indicators, as in the case of data on hours worked and earnings. The ongoing Eurostat initiative represents an important step forward for developing new indicators for under-employment and for the potential unused labour supply in European countries.[8] Concerning hours worked, a greater effort should be made to harmonise existing surveys and collection methodologies, in particular with respect to the categories of workers, types of contracts and types of jobs. Likewise, more systematic and comprehensive collections of earnings data at the micro-level, based on comparable definitions, are needed.

Another important area for future statistical work is the measurement of the quality of employment. While many international organisations have been active in defining a measurement framework for assessing decent work and the quality of work, the information gap in this field is still very large, especially as far as official statistics are concerned. It would be desirable that National Statistical Offices increase their efforts to produce more comprehensive and comparable objective and subjective indicators on:

- *Job security and ethical behaviour at work, e.g.* indicators on the number of employees declaring that they are exposed to dangers and physical risks in their workplace or reporting being exposed to psychological risks (harassment, discrimination, etc.), as well as work accidents.

- *Social dialogue,* for example by including information on the share of workers covered by national contracts or who are unionised, but also broader information on workers' capacity to influence their working conditions.

- *Additional indicators of job quality*: for instance, information on the quality of the working environment and on individual satisfaction with the job. An indicator of job satisfaction from a non-official survey is discussed in Box 3.4 to convey the potential interest of including similar types of questions in surveys conducted by National Statistical Offices.

Box 3.4. **Satisfaction with working conditions in selected European countries**

Subjective measures of satisfaction with working conditions are useful to shed light on how jobs are perceived to meet workers' professional, social and individual needs. According to the European Working Conditions Observatory (EFILWC, 2006), workers generally report high levels of satisfaction with their working conditions (Figure 3.10). In 2005, around 83% of workers in OECD-Europe declared being satisfied or very satisfied with their working conditions. In Denmark, Norway, the United Kingdom, Switzerland, Austria, Belgium, the Netherlands and Germany, over nine persons in ten expressed contentment with their work. By contrast, only one person out of two in Turkey, and two out of three in Greece was satisfied with his/her working conditions. While this survey provides interesting insights on workers' satisfaction with their work, the results should be taken with care, as they are based on surveys conducted on small samples.

Figure 3.10. **Satisfaction with working conditions in European countries**

Percentage of workers aged 15-64 satisfied or very satisfied with their working conditions, 2005

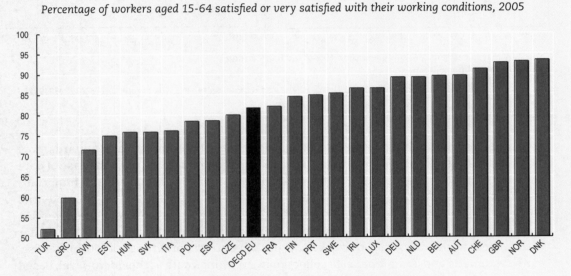

Source: The European Foundation for the Improvement of Living and Working Conditions

StatLink 🔗 *http://dx.doi.org/10.1787/888932492302*

Conclusion

The economic growth of the past fifteen years has gone hand-in-hand with a general increase in employment and in average earnings. Nevertheless, large differences remain across OECD countries in both employment rates and annual earnings levels. Average annual hours worked per person in employment have also fallen slightly in most OECD countries over the past twenty years (OECD, 2010). At the same time, earnings inequalities have increased, some aspects of working conditions (*e.g.* involuntary part-time, temporary jobs) have worsened, and having a job is not always an adequate protection from the risk of poverty. In addition, women, youths and older workers face relatively high job insecurity and weaker ties with the labour market. Lastly, the economic crisis that is still affecting OECD countries has weighed heavily on jobs and earnings, lowering the material living standards of millions of workers around the globe.

Notes

1. People care about "jobs and justice, bread and dignity, freedom to voice people's needs, their hopes and their dreams" (Somavia, 2011).

2. To address this issue, Eurostat is currently leading a project aimed at developing a "volume" indicator of the potential or unused labour supply, expressed as the number of hours that workers are willing to offer on the labour market. Similar work is ongoing in other OECD countries (e.g. Australia). For a discussion of these issues see Elliot and Dockery (2006).

3. The UNECE-ILO-Eurostat framework also includes two additional components: "skills development and training" and "working hours and balancing work and non-working life". These two aspects are dealt with in the chapters on "Education and Skills" and "Work and Life Balance" respectively and are thus not considered in this chapter.

4. This ratio is computed based on data on usual weekly hours worked by full-time employees and by all employees in their main jobs.

5. The National Accounts aggregate for wages and salaries include the social security contributions paid by workers while excluding those paid by firms. This implies that differences across countries in the financing of social security affect the earnings comparisons shown here.

6. Measures refer to the distribution of personal earnings among workers, differently from measures of income inequalities (described in the chapter on Income and Wealth), which refer to the household as the basic unit within which income is pooled and shared among its members.

7. Since part-time jobs and temporary workers have increased recently and these types of workers work fewer hours than full-time and permanent workers, the inclusion of non-standard workers significantly widens the distribution of annual earnings among all employees.

8. It would also be important to understand better the links between labour market participation decisions (in particular the fact of being active, partly active or inactive) and well-being, as inactive people may derive considerable well-being from the non-work activities they perform, when they have voluntarily chosen to be out of the labour market.

References

Anker R., I. Chernyshev, P. Egger and F. Mehran (2003), "Measuring decent work with statistical indicators", *International Labour Review*, Issue 142, No. 2.

Atkinson, A.B. (2007), "The Long Run Earnings Distribution in Five Countries: 'Remarkable Stability', U, V, or W?", *Review of Income and Wealth*, Vol. 53, No. 1, pp. 1-24.

Clark, A.E. and A.J. Oswald (1994), "Subjective well-being and unemployment", *Economic Journal*, Vol. 104, pp. 648–659.

Dolan P., T. Peasgood and M. White (2008), "Do we really know what makes us happy? A review of the economic literature on the factors associated with subjective well-being", *Journal of Economic Psychology*, Vol. 29, pp 94-122.

Economic and Social Council (2010), *Potential indicators for measuring of quality of employment*, Conference of European Statisticians Manuals, guidelines and recommendations, Paris, 8-10 June, United Nations.

EFILWC - European Foundation for Improvement of Living and Working Conditions (2006), *European Working Conditions Survey*, EFILWC, Dublin, http://www.eurofound.europa.eu/surveys/ewcs/index.htm

EFILWC (2011), *European Working Conditions Survey*, EFILWC, Dublin, http://www.eurofound.europa.eu/surveys/ewcs/index.htm

Elliot, L. and A. Dockery (2006), "Are the 'Hidden Unemployed' Unemployed?", *Centre for Labour Market Research, Discussion Paper Series*, no. 2, http://www.business.curtin.edu.au/files/06.2.pdf

European Commission (2010), "Short time working arrangements as response to cyclical fluctuations", *European Economy, Occasional Papers*, no. 64, Brussels, http://ec.europa.eu/economy_finance/publications/occasional_paper/2010/op64_en.htm

Ghai D. (2003), "Decent work: Concept and Indicators", *International Labour Review*, Issue 142, No. 2.

ILO (2003), *Safety Culture at Work. Safety in numbers - Pointers for a global safety culture at work*, Geneva.

ILO – International Labour Organisation (2011a), *Measuring decent work*, http://www.ilo.org/integration/themes/mdw/lang--en/index.htm

ILO (2011b), "Regulating for Decent Work: New Directions" in Sangheon Lee and Deirdre McCann (eds.), Labour Market Regulation, forthcoming, http://bravo.ilo.org/global/publications/books/forthcoming-publications/WCMS_153548/lang--en/index.htm

OECD (2007), *Society at a Glance 2006: OECD Social Indicators*, OECD Publishing, Paris.

OECD (2008a), *Growing Unequal? Income Distribution and Poverty in OECD Countries*, OECD Publishing, Paris.

OECD (2008b), *Employment Outlook*, OECD Publishing, Paris.

OECD (2010a), *Economic Outlook no. 87*, OECD Publishing, Paris. http://stats.oecd.org/Index.aspx?DataSetCode=EO87_FLASHFILE_EO87

OECD (2010b), *Employment Outlook. Moving Beyond the Crisis*, OECD Publishing, Paris.

OECD (2010c), *Off to a Good Start? Jobs for Youth*, OECD Publishing, Paris.

OECD (2011a), "Growing Income Inequality in OECD Countries: What Drives it and How Can Policy Tackle it?", OECD Forum on Tackling Inequality, 2 May, Paris.

OECD (2011b), *Education at a Glance*, OECD Publishing, Paris.

Saint-Martin A. (2009), "Is Work the Best Antidote to Poverty?", in *OECD Employment Outlook*, 2009.

Somavia, J. (2011), "A new era of social justice based on decent work", *Education for Development*, Vol.10, No. 2 March-April.

Stiglitz, J.E., A. Sen and J.-P. Fitoussi (2009), Report by the Commission on the Measurement of Economic Performance and Social Progress, http://www.stiglitz-sen-fitoussi.fr/documents/rapport_anglais.pdf.

Strauss H. and C. de la Maisonneuve (2007), "The Wage Premium on Tertiary Education: New Estimates for 21 OECD Countries", *OECD Economics Department Working Paper*, No. 589, Paris.

UNECE (2010), *Measuring Quality of Employment - Country Pilot Reports*, United Nations.

Wilson, S.H. and G.M. Walker (1993), "Unemployment and Health: A Review", *Public Health*, Vol. 107, pp. 153-162.

Chapter 4

Housing conditions

Housing is a major element of people's material living standards. It is essential to meet basic needs, such as for shelter from weather conditions, and to offer a sense of personal security, privacy and personal space. Good housing conditions are also essential for people's health and affect childhood development. Further, housing costs make up a large share of the household budget and constitute the main component of household wealth. This chapter describes housing conditions through indicators of the living space available, access to basic sanitary facilities, the weight of housing costs on household income and people's satisfaction with their housing. No core set of housing indicators currently exists, which underscores the need for more comparable data in this field. Overall, housing conditions seem good in most OECD countries although, in terms of living space, the results are less satisfactory when household composition is taken into consideration. On average, almost all household dwellings in OECD countries have access to basic sanitary facilities, although important differences remain across countries, and a non-negligible share of people in OECD countries live in overcrowded dwellings. Housing costs are a major concern for households' finances, and income is an essential driver of housing conditions.

Why do housing conditions matter for well-being?

Everyone has the right to adequate housing, which means more than just four walls and a roof over one's head.[1] Housing is essential to meet basic needs, such as being sheltered from extreme weather and climate conditions. Housing should offer people a suitable place to sleep and rest, where they are free of risks and hazards. In addition, housing should give a sense of personal security, privacy and personal space. Finally, housing is important to satisfy other essential needs, such as having a family.[2] All these elements make a "house" a "home" and are intrinsically valuable to people.

Besides their intrinsic value, housing conditions may affect a wide range of other outcomes. As housing costs make up a large share of the household budget (OECD, 2007b), people, particularly those on low incomes, are often constrained by the level of resources left for other essential expenditures, such as food, healthcare and education. High housing costs can thus threaten households' material well-being and economic security. They may also generate forms of housing stress[3] that may seriously hamper relations between households' members and impair the development of children (see Box 4.4).[4]

Poor housing quality (*e.g.* lack of access to basic sanitation and functional utilities, overcrowding, etc.) is also a major driver of health status, with effects on both physical and mental health (OECD, 2008a, 2009 and 2011b). It can lead to domestic violence and to children's low school performance (OECD, 2009). The capacity to engage in basic social activities, such as inviting people at home, may also be threatened by poor housing conditions. Research has shown that poor housing quality is associated with lower levels of democratic participation and, more generally, with lower levels of social capital (Glaeser and Sacerdote, 2000).

Housing is also the largest component of households' net worth, and changes in housing markets in terms of the conditions and availability of credit or changes in housing prices may have a disproportionate effect on households' material well-being (OECD, 2007b and 2011a). Besides the economic rationale for investing in housing, home ownership offers a sense of control and security that tenants do not have, and it allows households to decide about the appearance of their home (Foley, 1980).

Measuring housing conditions and their effects on people's well-being is a complex task because there are very few comparable indicators and no harmonised housing surveys across countries; while all countries conduct decennial housing censuses, these differ widely in terms of the comparable information that they provide on housing. Therefore, the evidence presented in this chapter is limited in two important ways. First, it relies mainly on data for European countries only.[5] Second, due to the lack of an internationally agreed definition, this chapter does not take into account those who experience the most extreme form of housing deprivation, *i.e.* the homeless (Box 4.1). It is thus paramount to enhance international statistical standards on housing conditions. Such measures would allow designing better housing policies, particularly in favour of the most deprived.

Measuring housing conditions

An ideal set of indicators to measure housing conditions would inform about both the physical characteristics of the dwelling (*e.g.* availability of electricity, water supply, indoor flushing toilets, bathroom requirements, cooking facilities, the quality of materials and construction and whether parts of the dwelling are deteriorated or damaged) and the broader environmental characteristics of the areas where the dwellings are located (*e.g.* exposure to noise, indoor pollution, etc.).[6] The broader residential setting may be especially

> ## Box 4.1. **The difficult measurement of homelessness**
>
> Homelessness is one of the most acute forms of material deprivation. Homelessness refers to the inability of people to enjoy a permanent accommodation. Being homeless increases the likelihood of lacking other basic human rights (such as the rights to work, to health-care and social security, to privacy and education) because having a permanent address is typically a prerequisite for exercising a number of these rights. Many homeless people have to "share" their living area with other people and to change their shelter very often, thus hampering their dignity.
>
> There is no international agreement on how to define and measure homelessness. Homelessness can include many conditions, ranging from "rough sleepers" (*i.e.* people sleeping rough on the street) to living in inadequate or insufficient housing (*e.g.* in tents, caravans, etc.). The "rough sleeper" definition has been strongly criticised because it is too stereotypical and misses an important number of homeless people (Ryabchuk, 2007).
>
> Standard household surveys may not provide an adequate measure of the number of homeless in individual countries. The "hidden" homeless (those sleeping rough in less visible areas or those with extremely poor housing conditions) may not self-report themselves as homeless for reasons of stigma or may simply not be surveyed. In addition, different definitions of homelessness apply across the OECD. For instance, Australia employs an extended definition of homelessness that includes, beyond people sleeping rough in the street ("absolute homelessness"), those living in transitional housing programmes, using emergency shelters or staying temporarily with friends, family or in lodging ("relative homelessness"). Conversely, Japan counts as homeless only rough sleepers and people in emergency shelters.
>
> There are also differences in definitions in other countries. Southern European countries (Portugal, Spain and Italy) use narrower definitions of homelessness (*e.g.* only people sleeping rough on the street) than Northern European countries (Denmark, Norway, Sweden and Finland), which include people staying temporarily with friends or family.
>
> *Source:* Adapted from Richardson (2009).

important for satisfying socially-perceived necessities, while difficulty in access to the dwelling (absence of public transport or a lift) can make housing very unsatisfactory for the elderly, disabled people and mothers with young children.[7] The set of indicators would also inform about the tenure status of households and the impact of this on psychological and material well-being.

In practice, it is difficult to measure housing conditions and their effect on people's well-being not only because no international statistical standards are available but also because the factors shaping people's housing conditions are heterogeneous, often interrelated and frequently amplified by coincident factors (Saegert and Evans, 2003). Being ill-housed may depend on a variety of factors, ranging from the residence's physical attributes to characteristics related to the presence of socially-perceived necessities. Consequently, views about what basic needs should be satisfied may vary across and within countries.

This chapter provides information on housing conditions related to living space requirements and to access to basic sanitary facilities (indoor flushing toilets and the presence of a bathroom) that can be considered critical for people's comfort and basic needs – at least from the perspective of OECD households. These indicators are complemented with an objective indicator of the pressure of home costs on income and a subjective indicator based on people's satisfaction of their housing conditions. A summary assessment of the quality of the indicators of housing conditions used in this chapter is provided in Table 4.1.

Table 4.1. **The quality of housing indicators**

	Target concept	INDICATORS							
		Relevance to measure and monitor well-being				Statistical quality			
		Face validity	Unambiguous interpretation (good/bad)	Amenable to policy changes	Can be disaggregated	Well-established instrument collected	Comparable definition	Country coverage	Recurrent data collection
Housing									
HO I Number of rooms per person in a dwellin	Quality of housing	~	√	√	x	√	~	~	~
ho 1 Housing cost overburden rate	Housing affordability	√	√	√	√	x	√	√	x
HO II Lack of access to basic sanitary facilities: abscence of indoor flushing toilets and/or a bathroom (bath or shower)	Quality of housing	~	√	~	x	√	~	~	~
ho 2 Satisfaction with housing	Satisfaction with housing	√	~	~	√	x	√	√	x

Note: The symbol √ shows that the indicator selected largely meets the criteria shown in the table; the symbol ~ that the indicator meets the criteria to a large extent; the symbol x that the indicator does not meet the criterion or it meets it only to a limited extent.

Selected indicators

Number of rooms per person (HO I)

This indicator provides information on housing overcrowding, which has long been identified as a major housing problem (Myers *et al.*, 1996). Having sufficient space is essential to meet people's basic need for privacy and for making home a pleasant place to be. Too many tenants in a dwelling may also have a negative impact on children's health or school performance.

Housing overcrowding is measured as the number of rooms in a dwelling (including living rooms but excluding kitchen and bathrooms) divided by the number of persons living in the same dwelling. For European OECD countries, data come from the European Union Statistics on Income and Living Conditions (EU-SILC), an official statistical instrument aimed at collecting timely and comparable cross-sectional and longitudinal data on living conditions. Data are thus of good quality and can easily be compared across the countries covered by the survey. As for other OECD countries, data come from National Statistical Offices. Since, in general, the source of data for non-European countries is the Population Census, they are only broadly comparable with those from EU-SILC for European countries.

This indicator suffers from a number of limitations. First, it does not take into account the possible trade-off between the size of the dwelling and its location; this is important as the accommodation environment (*e.g.* exposure to specific hazards, the proximity of public services such as schools and hospitals) also matters to people's well-being; indeed, some households choose to live in smaller houses or apartments located in better serviced areas, rather than in larger homes located in poorer neighbourhoods. Second, an ideal indicator of the available space per person in a dwelling would refer not just to the number of rooms available but also to their overall size (*e.g.* the number of square meters per person). For instance, the size of accommodation is generally smaller in urban areas relative to rural ones; hence, the distribution of the population on the territory has potential implications for international comparisons of this indicator. Lastly, the notion of sufficient space per person is largely influenced by the age and gender composition of the household; for example, a couple with two teenage children of different gender will have different needs in terms of available space than a couple with two young kids of around the same age. Eurostat has developed an indicator of overcrowded conditions that tries to overcome some of these shortcomings (Box 4.2).

Housing cost overburden rate (ho 1)

The housing cost overburden rate shown here is an indicator of housing affordability. It is measured as the percentage of the population living in households where the total housing costs (net of housing allowances) represent 40% or more of their equivalised disposable income.[8] This indicator is thus a measure of the housing costs effectively supported by households. This indicator is limited to European countries and relies on data from the EU-SILC survey. Housing costs, in the EU-SILC definition, refer to monthly costs and include actual rents paid, the costs of utilities (water, gas, electricity and heating), housing taxes and compulsory insurance, as well mortgage interest payments and regular maintenance and repairs by home owners while excluding the repayments of principal on mortgages. The section below describing the evidence for this indicator also provides information on housing affordability for a few non-European countries (Australia, Canada and the United States), but based on a different income threshold.[9]

This indicator is an imperfect proxy of the pressure of housing costs on the household budget: indeed, some middle- and high-income households can decide to spend a large amount (40% or more) of their disposable equivalised income for housing, without incurring any form of material deprivation.

Lack of access to basic sanitary facilities (HO II)

This indicator provides an assessment of selected housing deficiencies. The focus is on the lack of facilities for personal hygiene, as this is clearly detrimental to individuals' health and dignity. This indicator sheds light on the quality of the accommodation and provides a proxy measure of the notion of "decent housing".

Two basic facilities are considered here: indoor flushing toilets (measured as the percentage of people not having an indoor flushing toilet for the sole use of the household) and bathrooms (measured as the percentage of people having neither a bath nor a shower). Data are shown for European countries, based on the EU-SILC survey, complemented with data for other countries based on nationally representative surveys conducted by National Statistical Offices. As for other indicators, the comparability of data across countries is limited due to the different sources used.

The notion of "decent housing" includes other basic aspects of housing conditions, such as the quality of the roofs, floors, doors and window frames, which may also have adverse effects on people's health conditions and comfort.[10] For capturing these notions, an indicator of "deficit in other basic aspects of housing conditions" is presented in Box 4.3.

Satisfaction with housing (ho 3)

Housing satisfaction may be defined as the "perceived gap between a respondent's needs and aspirations and the reality of the current residential context" (Galster, 1987). There is evidence that people evaluate their satisfaction with housing relative to other persons, their own past experience and expectations for the future. This subjective indicator is therefore useful for capturing possible discontent with housing conditions in relation to unobservable circumstances that are not captured by the previous objective indicators. This indicator captures the extent to which people's perceived needs for housing services are met in practice.

This indicator relies on the following question: "Are you satisfied or dissatisfied with your current housing, dwelling, or place you live?" with responses grouped into two categories (satisfied or dissatisfied). Data come from the Gallup World Poll. Reported individual housing satisfaction can be used as an ordinal measure of true housing satisfaction (Vera-Toscano and Ateca-Amestoy, 2008), although cultural norms may influence people's perception of satisfactory housing. While these data are available for all OECD countries, the small samples and other methodological shortcomings of the Gallup World Poll survey imply that results based on this indicator have to be taken with caution.

Average patterns

Living space requirements are met in most OECD countries

Living space requirements, i.e. in terms of having one's own room, are fulfilled in all OECD countries on average. However, there are significant differences in the number of rooms per person across OECD countries. The worst conditions in terms of living space requirements appear to exist in the Eastern European countries and in Israel (where respondents claim that they have no more than 1.2 rooms per person) while respondents in Australia, Belgium, Canada and New Zealand have, on average, more than 2 rooms per person (Figure 4.1). The indicator of overcrowding developed for European countries by Eurostat (which takes into consideration the household composition) also shows that an important share of people in Eastern European countries live in overcrowded conditions (Box 4.2).

Figure 4.1. **Rooms per person**

Average number, 2009 or latest available year

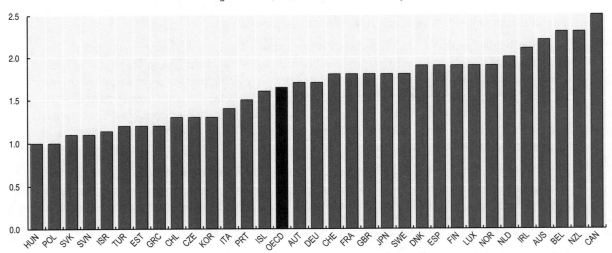

Note: Data refer to 2001 for Chile; 2005 for Korea; 2006 for Australia, Canada, and New Zealand; and 2008 for Israel and Japan. Data for Australia refer to the number of bedrooms (*i.e.* excluding the living room) per person. Data for Australia, Canada, Israel and New Zealand are OECD's calculations based on national data.

Sources: European Union Statistics on Income and Living Conditions (EU-SILC), National Statistical Offices and OECD's calculations.

StatLink ⬛🖿 http://dx.doi.org/10.1787/888932492321

The American Housing Survey conducted by the US Census Bureau uses a different reporting for overcrowding, which cannot directly be compared with the data in Figure 4.2. This survey reports the share of people ving in housing where the number of persons per room is 0.50 or less, from 0.51 to 1, from 1.01 to 1.50, or above 1.51: the standard of "one person per room" is thus met when people live in dwellings where the number of persons per room is equal or less than one. This standard appears to be generally fulfilled as 70% of US respondents lived in households where there was less than one person per room in 2007, which corresponds to having at least one room per person. The percentage of people that can be considered as living in overcrowded conditions is around 2% in the United States, a share that has been falling over time.

Box 4.2. **Eurostat's measure of overcrowding**

The notion of "sufficient" living space depends on the household composition. According to Eurostat, a person is considered as living in an overcrowded dwelling if the number of rooms available is less than: one room for the household; one room per couple in the household; one room for each single person aged 18 or more; one room per pair of single people of the same gender between 12 and 17 years of age; one room for each single person between 12 and 17 years of age and not included in the previous category; one room per pair of children under 12 years of age.

The overcrowding rate is defined as the percentage of the population living in an "overcrowded dwelling".

According to this definition, about 55% of people live in overcrowded dwellings in Hungary, while this share is below 2% in the Netherlands. The indicator correlates well with the indicator of rooms per person presented in Figure 4.1.

Figure 4.2. **People living in overcrowded dwelling in European countries**

Percentage of total population, 2009

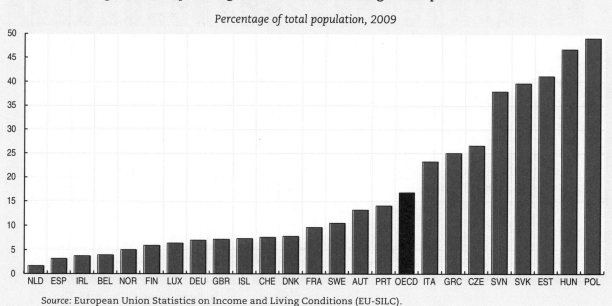

Source: European Union Statistics on Income and Living Conditions (EU-SILC).

StatLink 🔗 http://dx.doi.org/10.1787/888932492340

Many European households spend a substantial share of their income on housing

Housing represents the largest component of expenditures for many households in Europe. In 2009, about 10% of the population in the 24 OECD countries surveyed by EU-SILC lived in households that spent 40% or more of their equivalised disposable income on housing (Figure 4.3). There are, however, large cross-country differences. The share of the population where housing costs are equal to or greater than 40% of their equivalised disposable income is small in France, Luxembourg, Slovenia and Ireland but very high in Denmark and Greece. To some extent, this may reflect public housing policies and in particular social housing or housing subsidies provided by governments. However, this indicator has to be interpreted with caution because it does not factor in essential housing allowances (such as tax benefits for renters or investment grants for owners).[11]

Figure 4.3. **Housing cost overburden rate in European countries**

Percentage, 2009

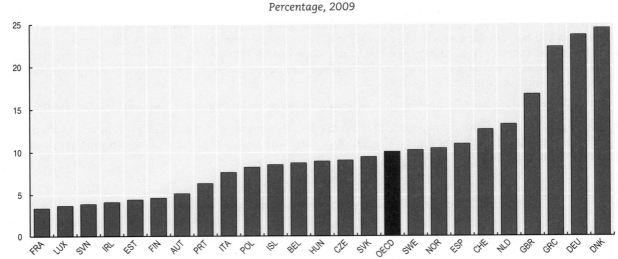

Note: Data refer to people living in households where the total housing costs ("net" of housing allowances) represent 40 % or more of their disposable income.

Source: European Union Statistics on Income and Living Conditions (EU-SILC).

StatLink ᵃᵐˢᵖ *http://dx.doi.org/10.1787/888932492359*

Housing affordability is evaluated according to other standards in Australia, Canada and the United States. In 2009, more than 38% of households in the United States spent 30% of their current income on housing costs, while this share was around 25% in Canada in 2006. In 2008, 36% of low income renter households in Australia were classified as being in condition of rental stress.

The housing cost overburden rate varies widely, depending on the tenure status, across European countries (Table 4.2). In general, tenants are more likely to experience financial difficulties than owners. However, home-owners with a mortgage (or a loan) can face large housing costs that impose an unreasonable burden on their income. Among tenants, those paying reduced rent or with rent-free accommodation are more likely to enjoy affordable housing than those paying a market rent. The only exception to this pattern is Sweden where the housing cost overburden rate is higher for tenants paying reduced prices (or nothing) than for tenants paying market prices.

Table 4.2. **Housing cost overburden rate in European countries by tenure status**

Percentage of total population, 2009

Countries	Total	Owner occupied		Tenant	
		With mortgage or housing loan	With no outstanding mortgage or housing loan	At a market price	At a reduced price or free
Austria	5.1	1.2	1.4	12.4	6.4
Belgium	8.7	2.5	2.9	30.6	12.7
Czech Republic	9	10.1	6.1	23.2	14.0
Denmark	24.4	23.1	16.8	29.7	
Estonia	4.4	11.4	1.9	20.9	6.3
Finland	4.6	3.2	2.5	11.6	7.5
France	3.4	1.2	0.5	10.0	5.0
Germany	23.6				
Greece	22.2	10.5	13.6	67.1	3.6
Hungary	8.9	16.4	5.2	44.0	14.5
Iceland	8.5	9.0	4.9	13.3	5.8
Ireland	4.1	2.3	1.3	21.9	1.9
Italy	7.6	7.7	2.6	27.4	8.9
Luxembourg	3.7	0.8	0.2	13.3	4.6
Netherlands	13.2	12.2	4.7	17.7	5.9
Norway	10.4	9.8	5.9	28.2	14.6
Poland	8.2	6.0	7.3	32.8	8.7
Portugal	6.3	8.2	2.3	19.9	4.7
Slovak Republic	9.4	32.3	6.9	13.4	9.6
Slovenia	3.9	9.3	2.6	13.1	5.4
Spain	10.9	14.7	3.3	40.8	10.3
Sweden	10.2	4.3	10.9	20.6	31.5
Switzerland	12.6	7.8		17.0	11.9
United Kingdom	16.7	10.3	9.4	40.7	26.6
OECD	10	9.3	5.1	24.8	10.0

Note: Data refer to people living in households where the total housing costs ("net" of housing allowances) represent 40 % or more of their disposable income.

Source: European Union Statistics on Income and Living Conditions (EU-SILC).

StatLink 🔗 *http://dx.doi.org/10.1787/888932493898*

Access to basic facilities is high in OECD countries on average but with large disparities across countries

The lack of basic facilities such as a bath, shower and indoor flushing toilets is almost non-existent in the majority of OECD countries (with only 1 or 2% of the population reporting this problem, Fig. 4.4). However, in some countries, a substantial share of the population lack basic facilities. A higher share of European households experience other housing inconveniences such as a leaking roof; damp walls, floors or foundation; or rot in window frames or the floor (Box 4.3). The poorest dwelling conditions are recorded in Eastern European countries (Hungary, Poland), in Asian countries (Japan, Korea), in Mexico and, especially, in Estonia and Turkey, where almost 13% of households live without an indoor flushing toilet.

Figure 4.4. **People living in dwellings without basic sanitary facilities**

Percentage of total population, 2009 or latest available year

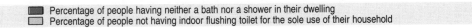

■ Percentage of people having neither a bath nor a shower in their dwelling
□ Percentage of people not having indoor flushing toilet for the sole use of their household

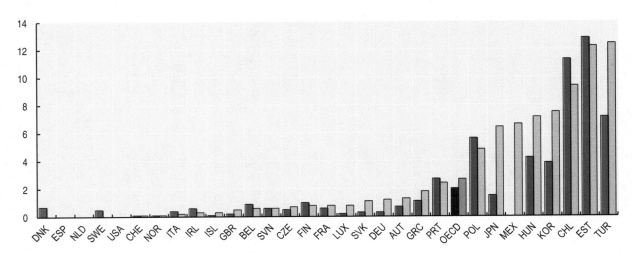

Note: Data refer to 2001 for Chile; to 2005 for Korea and Mexico; and to 2008 for Japan. The first indicator refers to dwellings without a shower in the case of Chile; to dwellings without a bathroom (but with a bathtub on the premises) in the case of Japan; to dwellings without a place surrounded by walls with a separate door and used for bathing in the case of Turkey; to total occupied dwellings with no bathtub nor shower in the case of the United States. The second indicator refers to the absence of a toilet in the dwelling in the case of Chile; to absence of a toilet in inhabited private dwellings in the case of Mexico; to lack of toilets inside the housing unit in the case of Turkey; and to occupied dwellings without a flushing toilet in the case of the United States. Countries are ranked (from left to right) in increasing of the series referring to lack of an "indoor flushing toilet".

Source: European Union Statistics on Income and Living Conditions (EU-SILC) and national statistical offices of Chile, Japan, Mexico, Turkey and the United States.

StatLink ⟋⟋⟋ *http://dx.doi.org/10.1787/888932492378*

Box 4.3. **Deficits in other basic housing conditions in Europe**

This indicator refines the notion of "decent housing". It is measured as the share of the total population living in a dwelling with either a leaking roof, or damp walls, or damp floors and foundation, or rot in window frames or floor. In 2009, one in four households living in European countries reported at least one of these problems with their accommodation (Figure 4.5). However, this average figure hides wide differences among European countries: households in the Nordic countries are less likely to report poor housing conditions (albeit this share is above 10% in Iceland) than those in Eastern European countries, where about one household in three experienced this type of housing deficit. Based on this indicator, 42% of surveyed households in Turkey suffer from poor housing conditions.

Figure 4.5. **Deficits in other basic housing conditions in European countries**

Percentage of total population, 2009

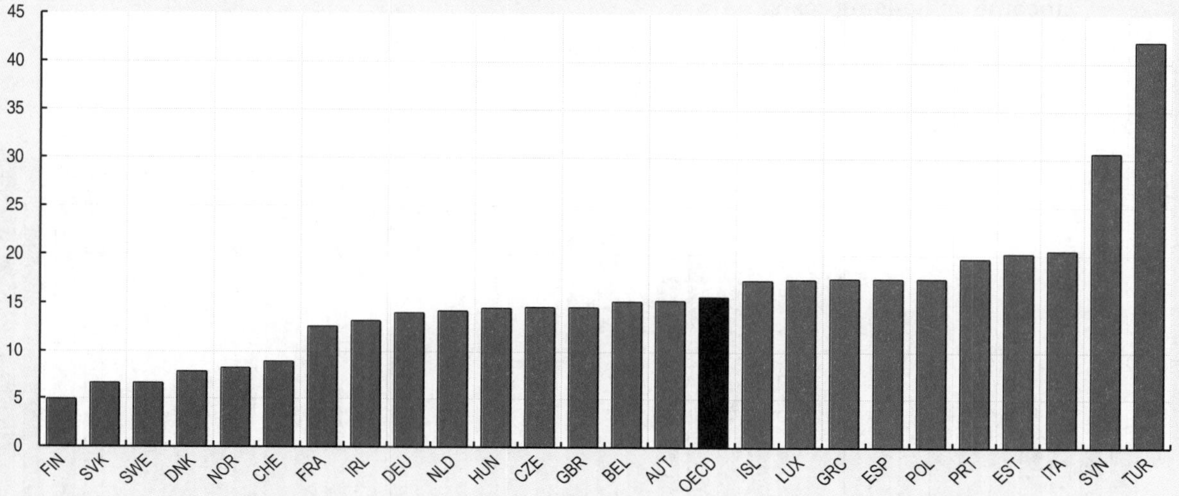

Note: Data refer to people living in a dwelling with either a leaking roof; or damp walls, floors or foundation; or rot in window frames or floor.
Source: European Union Statistics on Income and Living Conditions (EU-SILC).

StatLink ⟶ http://dx.doi.org/10.1787/888932492397

Satisfaction with housing differs widely between OECD countries and emerging countries

The majority of OECD respondents surveyed by the Gallup World Poll declared that they were satisfied with the housing, dwelling or place where they live (Figure 4.6). In Germany, Ireland, Spain and Belgium more than 90% of households express satisfaction with housing while in Turkey this share is close to 65%. The share of the population declaring satisfaction with their housing is significantly lower in emerging countries, especially in South Africa, the Russian Federation and, to a lesser extent, Indonesia.

Objective and subjective indicators of housing conditions paint a consistent picture

The indicators presented in this chapter provide information about certain dimensions of housing conditions. Table 4.3 reports correlation coefficients between these indicators and highlights the following patterns:

- Subjective satisfaction with housing is strongly correlated with all of the objective indicators of housing conditions. There is a very high negative correlation between the lack of indoor flushing toilets and housing satisfaction. The number of rooms per person, a proxy for the available space per person, is also positively associated with levels of satisfaction with housing.

- Various objective indicators of housing quality are also well correlated, suggesting a coherent picture of housing conditions in the countries analysed. For instance, the number of rooms per person is negatively correlated with lack of access to basic facilities.

- Conversely, the indicator of housing costs does not correlate well with other housing indicators. This is not very surprising due to the way the indicator is constructed, and this suggests that financial factors related to housing do capture a different dimension of housing conditions. The absence of correlation underscores the need to look at other measures of the pressure of housing costs so as to separate out households that suffer from financial constraints and those that choose to spend a large share of their income on housing costs.

Figure 4.6. **Satisfaction with housing**

Percentage, 2007 or latest available year

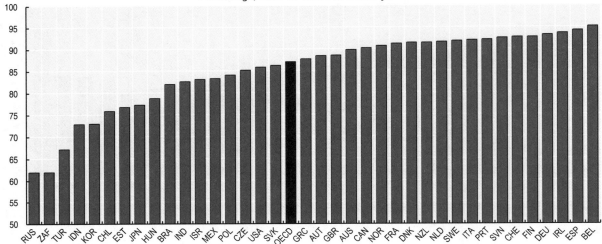

Note: Data refer to people satisfied with the current housing, dwelling or place where they live. Data refer to 2009 for Turkey; to 2006 for Austria, Finland, Ireland, Norway, Portugal, the Slovak Republic, Slovenia, Switzerland and the United States; and to 2005 for Canada.
Source: Gallup World Poll.

StatLink 🔗 *http://dx.doi.org/10.1787/888932492416*

Table 4.3. **Correlations between different indicators of housing conditions**

| | HO I
Number of rooms per person | ho 1
Housing cost overburden rate | HO II
Lack of access to basic sanitary facilities: | | ho 2
Satisfaction with housing |
			Absence of indoor flushing toilets	Absence of a bathroom (bath or shower)	
HO I Number of rooms per person	1 (33)	0.07 (25)	-0.64*** (29)	-0.53*** (29)	0.65*** (31)
ho 1 Housing cost overburden rate		1 (25)	-0.20 (25)	-0.23 (25)	0.13 (23)
HO II Lack of access to basic sanitary facilities					
Absence of indoor flushing toilets			1 (31)	0.83*** (30)	-0.91*** (29)
Absence of a bathroom (bath or shower)				1 (30)	-0.7*** (28)
ho 2 Satisfaction with housing					1 (33)

Note: Values in parenthesis refer to the number of observations. ** Indicates that correlations are significant at the 5% level; *** indicates that they are significant at the 1% level. Regarding the indicator of "Housing costs", data for Australia, Canada and the United States are not considered here as the thresholds defining housing affordability differ from the one used in European countries.
Source: OECD's calculations.

StatLink 🔗 *http://dx.doi.org/10.1787/888932493917*

Inequalities

Income and age are major drivers of inequalities in housing conditions in European countries

From a policy perspective, understanding which groups of the population are more likely to suffer from poor housing conditions is essential for designing effective housing policies. In Europe, the elderly are the most likely to report a lack of access to basic sanitary facilities such as baths, showers and indoor flushing toilets (with the exception of Hungary), probably because they live in older dwellings. However, in countries that spend an important part of their GDP on long-term care programmes, such as the Netherlands, Sweden and Switzerland (Colombo *et al.*, 2011), the elderly do not lack such basic facilities much more than other age groups due to the important role of residential homes and specific policy interventions aimed at the frail elderly. On the other hand, poor housing conditions are known to be especially detrimental to children (Box 4.4).

Table 4.4. **Lack of access to basic sanitary facilities in European countries, by age group**

Percentage of total population, 2009

Countries	Absence of indoor flushing toilets			Absence of bath or shower		
	Less than 18 years	From 18 to 64 years	65 years or over	Less than 18 years	From 18 to 64 years	65 years or over
Austria	0.9	1.4	1.8	0.4	0.5	1.8
Belgium	0.3	0.6	1.4	0.3	0.6	2.6
Czech Republic	0.3	0.7	1.5	0.2	0.5	1.2
Denmark	0.0	0.0	0.0	0.3	1.0	0.4
Estonia	9.8	10.8	20.2	10.4	11.2	21.5
Finland	0.4	0.7	1.3	0.4	1.0	1.5
France	0.5	0.7	1.2	0.2	0.4	1.7
Germany	1.0	1.4	0.8	0.0	0.1	0.2
Greece	1.1	1.4	3.7	0.8	0.8	2.4
Hungary	8.8	6.4	7.8	5.4	3.7	4.9
Iceland	0.0	0.4	0.5	0.0	0.0	0.2
Ireland	0.0	0.3	0.6	0.3	0.6	1.2
Italy	0.2	0.2	0.4	0.2	0.3	0.9
Luxembourg	0.9	0.9	0.0	0.0	0.2	0.3
Netherlands	0.0	0.1	0.0	0.0	0.0	0.0
Norway	0.1	0.1	0.0	0.1	0.1	0.2
Poland	4.3	4.2	8.5	5.2	4.9	9.7
Portugal	1.5	2.0	4.6	1.7	2.2	5.6
Slovak Republic	1.2	0.9	2.0	0.2	0.2	0.6
Slovenia	0.3	0.5	1.3	0.3	0.6	1.4
Spain	0.0	0.0	0.0	0.0	0.0	0.0
Sweden	0.0	0.0	0.0	0.2	0.6	0.7
Switzerland	0.0	0.0	0.2	0.1	0.1	0.2
United Kingdom	0.6	0.5	0.5	0.1	0.2	0.3
OECD	1.3	1.4	2.4	1.1	1.2	2.5

Source: European Union Statistics on Income and Living Conditions (EU-SILC).

StatLink ᴍⴱ *http://dx.doi.org/10.1787/888932493936*

Box 4.4. **The impact of poor housing conditions on children**

Housing conditions and child development outcomes are strongly linked, as children spend most of their time indoors. The factors shaping children's well-being are complex, interrelated and difficult to untangle. For instance, the effects of housing characteristics may vary at different stages of a child's life-course. Problems due to the lack of affordable housing may affect children during early childhood (due to their adverse impacts on the family's ability to meet basic needs) while neighborhood effects have a strong impacts on adolescents. Further, the causality between poor housing conditions and the development and well-being of children is probably multidimensional and hard to identify, as common variables may influence housing conditions and children's development simultaneously (*e.g.* parents' income, employment status, educational background etc.).

However, evidence suggests that three types of factors have a significant effect on children's well-being:

- The home environment (cleanliness, lack of repair, safety, indoor air pollution) has an important effect on children's health status and may affect the cognitive development of young children. Cleanliness has also been related to later educational attainment (even after controlling for income). Children living in housing environments containing potential hazards are more likely to refrain from their inclination to explore and learn.

- The lack of living space that some children experience leads to a lower sense of autonomy and poorer cognitive development. Children interacting in crowded conditions display increased levels of social withdrawal (Loo, 1972) even during the first few weeks at nursery school (Lidell and Krueger, 1989). Overcrowding may cause psychological distress and poorer behavioral adjustment at home. Parke (1978) has shown the importance of providing a stimulus shelter such as a private bedroom, which provides children a secure space to be and to play.

- High housing costs have consequences for the allocation of the households' budget (less material goods for children) and increase parents' stress, which may be transmitted to their offspring. Evidence suggests that exposure to stressful life-events in the family, such as economic hardship, can adversely impact children's development and well-being.

Research has also shown that linkages between poor housing conditions and child development are often irreversible and transmit to adulthood, and that interventions are more effective if implemented early in life (Shonkoff *et al.*, 2009). There are large differences among OECD countries in terms of the housing conditions faced by children (Figure 4.7), with younger children generally more disadvantaged than older ones.

Figure 4.7. **Children living in overcrowded conditions**

Percentage of children living in overcrowded homes, by age of the youngest child, 2006

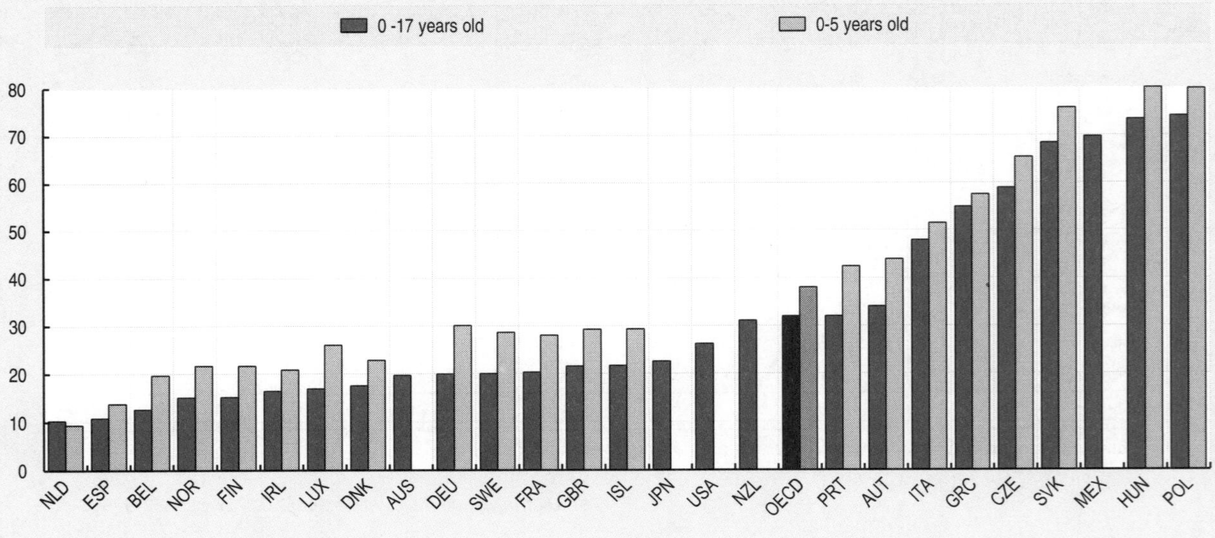

Note: Overcrowding is assessed through questions on "number of rooms available to the household" for European countries; on the "number of bedrooms" in Australia; on whether the household "cannot afford more than one bedroom" or "cannot afford to have a bedroom separate from eating room" in Japan; and on the "number of rooms with kitchen and without bath" in the United States. Overcrowding conditions refer to cases when the number of household members exceeds the number of rooms (*i.e.* a family of four is considered as living in an overcrowded accommodation when there are only three rooms – excluding kitchen and bath but including a living room). Information is not available for children aged 0-5 for Australia, Japan, Mexico, New Zealand and the United States.

Source: Data are taken from EU-SILC (2006) for 22 European countries; from the survey Household Income and Labour Dynamics in Australia (HILDA) 2005 for Australia; from the Shakai Seikatsu Chousa (Survey of Living Conditions) 2003 for Japan; from the Survey of Income and Program Participation (SIPP) 2003 for the United States. Data for Mexico were provided by the Mexican authorities.

Source: Adapted from OECD (2009).

StatLink ⧉ *http://dx.doi.org/10.1787/888932492435*

The higher the household's income, the lower is the probability that people will face housing cost problems (Figure 4.8). However, the relationship between household income and the share of people reporting high housing costs varies considerably across countries. In Greece and Denmark, more than half of low-income people declared spending 40% or more of their equivalised disposable income on housing, while in France this was the case for only 10% of low-income people. People with lower incomes are also more likely to face poorer basic housing conditions and to be less satisfied with their housing (Box 4.5). The lack of standard facilities for the sole use of the household is always more prevalent among lower-income people.

Figure 4.8. **Housing cost overburden rate by income quintile in European countries**

Percentage of total population, 2009

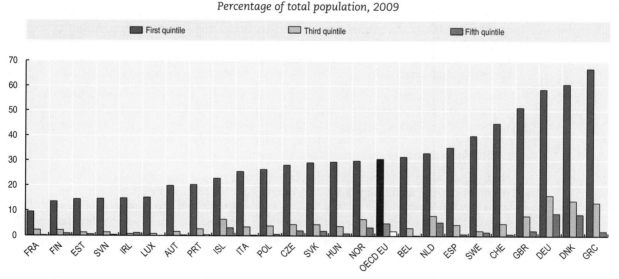

Note: Data refer to people living in households where the total housing costs ("net" of housing allowances) represent 40 % or more of their disposable income.
Source: European Union Statistics on Income and Living Conditions (EU-SILC).

StatLink ⧉ *http://dx.doi.org/10.1787/888932492454*

Box 4.5. **Drivers of housing satisfaction**

Housing satisfaction is an important component of the quality of life, as housing represents the largest consumption item and investment in an individual's lifetime. Satisfaction with housing can be accounted for by several factors. Three types of determinants have been identified in the literature as major influences on housing satisfaction: 1) individual characteristics (socio-economic determinants) and household attributes, 2) housing characteristics (basic facilities, overcrowding) and 3) social interactions originating in one's residential neighbourhood.

Table 4.5 reports the results of a multivariate analysis of housing satisfaction based on a selection of socio-economic and environmental variables available in the Gallup World Poll (see Balestra and Sultan, 2012 for more details on the analysis). The results are shown separately for OECD and emerging countries. The main results are:

- In OECD countries, women are more likely to express high levels of housing satisfaction than men, while no gender pattern is visible in non-OECD countries.

- In neither the OECD area nor emerging countries does marital status seem to affect levels of housing satisfaction.

- In both OECD and non-OECD countries, housing satisfaction increases with people's age, which may be explained by the fact that home ownership rises with age (Andrews and Caldera Sánchez, 2011). The effect of age on housing satisfaction is "U-shaped", in line with previous research (Van Praag *et al.*, 2003).

- Housing satisfaction increases with educational level in both OECD and emerging countries, but the effect is only significant for people with tertiary education in OECD countries.

- Having children under 15 years of age is associated with lower levels of housing satisfaction in OECD and emerging countries (though the effect is only significant for people declaring at least three children under 15 in OECD countries). In emerging countries, having at least one child under 15 years old is a greater predictor of housing satisfaction than income and the fact of holding a secondary education.

- Both "affordable housing" (based on the question "In your city or area where you live, are you satisfied or dissatisfied with the availability of good affordable housing?") and "beauty setting" (based on the question "In your city or area where you live, are you satisfied or dissatisfied with the beauty or physical setting?") are positively and strongly associated with housing satisfaction.

- Housing satisfaction increases with income, though the impact is weaker in OECD member countries in comparison to emerging countries. When removing the variables "affordable housing" and "beauty setting", the effect of income on housing satisfaction increases (*i.e.* the coefficient associated with income becomes larger) in both OECD and non-OECD countries. This suggests that the effect of income is partly captured by environmental variables related to housing (*e.g.* the presence of "affordable housing" and the "beauty setting" of the area where people live) presented in Table 4.5.

Table 4.5. **The determinants of housing satisfaction**

Marginal effects of explanatory variables on satisfaction with housing

Explanatory variables	Satisfaction with housing	
	OECD countries only	Other major economies only
Female	0.0241**	-0.001
Married	0.002	-0.033
Age 25-34	-0.0373*	-0.045
Age 35-54	-0.023	-0.001
Age 55-64	0.017	0.0923**
Age 65+	0.0663**	0.0927**
Secondary education	0.004	0.0642***
Tertiary education	0.0577***	0.0607**
One child under 15	-0.004	-0.0709***
Two children under 15	-0.017	-0.0572**
Three children under 15	-0.0459*	-0.022
Four children or more under 15	0.026	-0.062
Household income	0.0166***	0.0447***
Affordable housing	0.1607***	0.1719***
Beauty setting	0.0790***	0.0549***
Observations	13,005	4,330

Note: Probit analysis includes all OECD countries (except Turkey), Brazil, China, India, Indonesia, the Russian Federation and South Africa. * indicates that values are significant at 10% confidence level; ** indicates that they are significant at 5% confidence level; and *** indicates that they are significant at 1% confidence level. The variable "household income" refers to the natural logarithm of the household disposable income.
Source: OECD's calculations based on data from the Gallup World Poll, 2005, 2006 and 2007.

StatLink ⬛🖼️⬛ *http://dx.doi.org/10.1787/888932493955*

This analysis has some limitations, notably the fact that it does not include other explanatory variables that are usually found to be meaningful for explaining housing satisfaction (*e.g.* access to basic facilities, see *e.g.* Vera-Toscano and Ateca-Amestoy, 2008). The tenure status of the household could also be added to the list of variables, even though research has produced mixed results. The household composition (weakly proxied by two binary variables – "children" – and marital status – "married") could be refined. Finally, neighborhood features are absent from the analysis despite their substantial influence on housing satisfaction (Manski, 1993; Galster, 1987; Cornwell and Sirgy, 2002; Vera-Toscano and Ateca-Amestoy, 2008).

The statistical agenda ahead

Indicators of housing conditions are correlated with almost all other dimensions of people's well-being presented in this report because housing conditions are so essential to people's well-being. However, housing conditions are not satisfactorily measured at the international level, and no core sets of comparable housing indicators exist at this stage. At least four areas for improvement can be identified:

- In general, survey questions on housing conditions, such as those included in the European Union Statistics on Income and Living Conditions, could be included in large sample surveys of all OECD countries through a harmonised questionnaire based on comparable definitions. In particular, data on the number of bedrooms per person (instead of the number of rooms per person) are needed because they better measure the available personal living space, which is an essential component of personal well-being.

- Many of the existing survey questions on housing focus on aspects of deprivation but fail to provide a broader picture of the quality of housing services for average households. For instance, information should be collected on the perception of indoor quality of the dwellings, such as thermal insulation (essential to maintain adequate indoor temperatures), dampness and mould (causing asthma problems), exposure to noise, and global indoor air quality. These indicators could be usefully complemented by objective information on the quality of dwellings obtained through physical inspections of the dwelling organised by appropriate institutions.

- Additional statistical gaps concern the residential setting of dwellings and the neighbourhood (*e.g.* the natural lighting of the dwelling, the exposure to noise, or the access to green areas, satisfaction with the area of living). In this regard, the Survey of Income and Housing collected by the Australian Bureau of Statistics contains a number of relevant indicators of dwelling conditions, and in particular indicators of satisfaction with the dwelling and its environment that may be interesting to include in a harmonised questionnaire.[12] Further, a disaggregation of the indicators by tenure status and geography would be important steps forward for the comprehension of satisfaction with housing and housing territorial inequalities.

- Finally, better and more comparable data are necessary to assess the financial aspects of housing, through the development of better measures of housing costs, financial stress due to housing, and housing affordability. In particular, it would be important to adopt a common definition of housing financial overburden. Issues to be addressed in this respect would include the range of items to include in housing costs, the threshold over which a share of income spent on housing cost could be objectively considered unbearable and whether this threshold should vary with household income.

Conclusion

This chapter has provided a general picture of housing conditions and of how these impact on people's well-being. The concept of housing conditions is a broad one, encompassing both the dwelling's physical attributes and symbolic characteristics. The chapter has focused on selected basic physical characteristics of the dwelling, as reported by individuals, as well as on measures of satisfaction with housing. Overall, the evidence provided in this chapter shows that housing conditions are good in a majority of OECD countries. On the other hand, high housing costs constitute a major concern for households in many OECD countries.

Having satisfactory accommodation is one of the most valuable aspects of people's lives. In the future, it will be essential to better document housing conditions in general and for the most vulnerable in particular, *e.g.* the homeless and people living in emergency shelters, whose numbers appear to be rising in many countries.

Notes

1. The human right to adequate housing is recognised under international law and codified in the Universal Declaration of Human Rights (1948, article 25(1)) and in other major international human rights treaties (*e.g.* in the International Covenant on Economic, Social and Cultural Rights, 1966, which considers the protection of the right to adequate housing as central). Several non-binding declarations, resolutions and recommendations by the United Nations and its specialised agencies regard housing as a human right. Some are of a general application for every human being; others focus on the right of disabled persons, women and children to secure adequate accommodation (United Nations High Commissioner for Human Rights, 2009).

2. High housing costs may partly explain why women are having fewer children than desired (OECD, 2007a), which may in turn impact fertility rates (D'Addio and Mira d'Ercole, 2005a and 2005b).

3. Housing stress is a generic term to denote the negative impact on households straining to secure adequate housing (see Arthurson *et al.*, 2006 for literature on the subject).

4. Conger *et al.* (1994) have shown that financial difficulties increases parental stress, which raises the likelihood of inconsistent or punitive behaviour by parents towards their children. Harkness and Newman (2005) observed that unaffordable housing impacts children's well-being and development. Overall, economic distress can lead to intimate violence and family stress (Fox *et al.*, 2002).

5. The Integrated Public Use Microdata Series (IPUMS) provides access to census records from around the world that contain information on housing conditions. However, these data are often not comparable, despite the existance of United Nations guidelines on population and housing censuses.

6. As noted by Pynoos *et al.* (1973): "When households consume 'housing', they purchase or rent more than the dwelling unit and its characteristics; they are also concerned with such diverse factors as health, security, privacy, neighbourhood and social relations, status, community facilities and services, access to jobs, and control over the environment. Being ill-housed can mean deprivation along any of these dimensions."

7. Conley (2001) has shown that housing plays a key role in social stratification. The existence of financial constraints for low-income people and, at the opposite end, the wish of higher-income people to signal their status may lead to housing segregation, sometimes reinforced by segregation between different ethnic groups or races. Housing conditions also affect children's educational outcomes. Housing segregation tends to reproduce from one generation to the next.

8. "Housing allowances" refers to interventions by public authorities to help households to meet the cost of housing. This definition excludes tax benefits related to housing and all capital transfers (in particular investment grants). This may restrict the comparability of the housing cost overburden rate in European countries.

9. For instance, Australian households are assessed as being in stress if they are in the bottom 40% of equivalised disposable household income and if their housing costs exceed 30% of gross income. Housing costs in Australia do not include electricity, or other heating costs. Harding *et al.* (2004) classify Australian households as experiencing "extreme" housing stress if housing costs exceed 50% of their income. Canada measures the affordability with the percentage of households that spend 30% or more of their household total income on housing costs. Besides the different threshold used in Canada, the affordability indicator is calculated using income before taxes and deductions, rather than disposable income, as in the EU-SILC based indicator. US households are considered in housing stress when housing costs represent 30% or more of the household current income. For these countries, data are based on the 2006 American Housing Survey, conducted by the U.S. Census Bureau, for the Unites States; on the 2006 Census for Canada; and on the Survey of Income and Housing (2007-2008) conducted by the Australian Bureau of Statistics for Australia.

10. Additional aspects of housing conditions, such as the healthiness of the environment and adequate heating, should also be considered, but this is not possible due to the lack of relevant indicators (Boarini and Mira d'Ercole, 2006; Andrews *et al.*, 2011). Further, indicators on indoor air quality are needed since a low quality can be very dangerous for health (in 2009, the WHO attributed

2.7% of the global burden of disease to selected elements of indoor air pollution (WHO, 2009)) and because this is a major source of dissatisfaction with housing (at least at the European level, where 10% of respondents in eight European cities claimed to be dissatisfied with this aspect, WHO, 2007). As a large share of households declared to be exposed to noise (OECD, 2008a), this type of indicator must account for measuring people's comfort with their housing environment.

11. This may artificially increase the value of the indicator and thus not reflect the reality of the housing costs effectively supported by households. For instance, the payment of accommodation and heating costs are essential allowances granted to about 10% of households in Germany (but not taken into consideration here).

12. The Survey of Income and Housing conducted by the Australian Bureau of Statistics covers three domains related to housing satisfaction (using a 5-point scale): i) satisfaction with the location of the dwelling; ii) satisfaction with the block of land on which the dwelling is built; and iii) satisfaction with the dwelling itself.

References

Andrews, D. and A. Caldera Sánchez (2011), "Drivers of Homeownership Rates in Selected OECD Countries", *OECD Economics Department Working Papers*, No. 849.

Andrews, D., A. Caldera Sánchez and Å. Johansson (2011), "Housing Markets and Structural Policies in OECD Countries", *OECD Economics Department Working Papers,* No. 836, OECD Publishing.

Arthurson, K., T. Burke, M. Gabriel, K. Jacobs and J. Yates (2006), "Conceptualising and measuring the housing affordability problem", National Research Venture 3: Housing Affordability for Lower Income Australians, Research Paper 1.

Balestra, C. and J. Sultan (2012), "Home Sweet Home: the determinants of residential satisfaction and its relation with well-being", OECD Statistics Directorate Working Paper (forthcoming).

Boarini, R. and M. Mira d'Ercole (2006), "Measures of Material Deprivation in OECD Countries", *OECD Social, Employment and Migration Working Papers*, No. 37, OECD Publishing, Paris.

Chamberlain, C. and D. Mackenzie (2008), "Australian Census Analytic Program: Counting the Homeless, 2006", ABS Catalogue No. 2050.0.

Colombo, F., A. Llena-Nozal, J. Mercier and F. Tjadens (2011), *Help Wanted?: Providing and Paying for Long-Term Care*, OECD Health Policy Studies, OECD Publishing, Paris.

Conger, R. D., X. Ge, G. H. Elder, F. O. Lorenz and R. L. Simons (1994), "Economic Stress, Coercive Family Process, and Developmental Problems of Adolescents", *Child Development*, Vol. 65, No. 2, Children and Poverty, pp. 541-561.

Conley D. (2001), "A Room with a View or a Room of One's Own? Housing and Social Stratification", *Sociological Forum*, Vol. 16, No. 2, pp. 263-280.

Cornwell, T. and J. M. Sirgy (2002), "How Neighborhood Features Affect Quality of Life", *Social Indicators Research*, Vol. 59, No. 1, pp. 79-114.

D'Addio, A.C. and M. Mira d'Ercole (2005a), "Trends and Determinants of Fertility Rates in OECD Countries: The Role of Policies", *OECD Social Employment and Migration Working Papers*, No. 15, OECD Publishing, Paris.

D'Addio, A.C. and M. Mira d'Ercole (2005b), "Policies, Institutions and Fertility Rates: A Panel Data Analysis for OECD countries", *OECD Economic Studies*, No. 41, OECD Publishing, Paris.

Foley, D. L. (1980), "The sociology of housing", *Annual Review of Sociology*, Vol. 6, pp. 457-478.

Fox, G. L., M. L. Benson, A. A. DeMaris and J. Van Wyk (2002), "Economic Distress and Intimate Violence: Testing Family Stress and Resources Theories", *Journal of Marriage and Family*, Vol. 64, No. 3, pp. 793-807.

Galster, G. C. (1987), "Identifying the correlates of dwelling satisfaction: An empirical critique", *Environment and Behaviour,* Vol. 19, No. 5, pp. 539-568.

Galster G. C. (1987), *Homeowners and Neighbourhood Reinvestment,* Duke University Press, Durham, NC.

Glaeser, E. L. and B. Sacerdote (2000), "The Social Consequences of Housing", *NBER Working Papers,* No. 8034, National Bureau of Economic Research, Inc.

Harding, A., S. Kelly and B. Phillips (2004), "Trends in Housing Stress", National Centre for Social and Economic Modelling (NATSEM), University of Canberra, Paper presented at the "National Summit on Housing Affordability", Canberra.

Harkness, J. and S. J. Newman (2005), "Housing Affordability and Children's Well-Being: Evidence from the National Survey of America's Families", *Housing Policy Debate,* Vol. 16, No. 2, pp. 635-666.

Liddell, C. and Kruger, P. (1989), "Activity and social behaviour in a crowded South African township nursery: A follow-up study on the effects of crowding at home", *Merrill-Palmer Quarterly,* Vol. 35, No. 2, pp. 209-226.

Loo, C. (1972), "The effects of spatial density on the social behavior of children", *Journal of Applied Social Psychology,* Vol. 2, No. 4, pp. 372-381.

Manski, C. F. (1993), "Identification of endogenous social effects: The reflection problem", *The Review of Economic Studies,* Vol. 60, No. 3, pp. 531-542.

Ministry of Health, Labour and Welfare (2009), "Nationwide Survey on the Homeless Situation", www.mhlw.go.jp/bunya/seikatsuhogo/homeless06.

Myers, D., W. C. Baer and S.-Y. Choi, (1996), "The Changing Problem of Overcrowded Housing", *Journal of the American Planning Association,* Vol. 62, No. 1, pp. 66-84.

OECD (2007a), *Babies and Bosses - Reconciling Work and Family Life: A Synthesis of Findings for OECD Countries,* OECD Publishing, Paris.

OECD (2007b), *Society at a Glance 2006: OECD Social Indicators,* OECD Publishing, Paris.

OECD (2008a), "Non-income Poverty: What Can we Learn from Indicators of Material Deprivation?", in *Growing Unequal?: Income Distribution and Poverty in OECD Countries,* OECD Publishing, Paris.

OECD (2008b), *Statistics, Knowledge and Policy 2007: Measuring and Fostering the Progress of Societies,* OECD Publishing, Paris.

OECD (2009), "Comparative Child Well-being across the OECD", in *Doing Better for Children,* OECD Publishing, Paris.

OECD (2011a), "Housing and the Economy: Policies for Renovation", in *Economic Policy Reforms 2011: Going for Growth,* OECD Publishing.

OECD (2011b), *Society at a Glance 2011: OECD Social Indicators,* OECD Publishing, Paris.

Parke, R.D. (1978), "Children's Home Environments: Social and Cognitive Effects", in I. Altman and J.F. Wohlwill (eds.), *Children and the Environment,* Second Edition, New York: Plenum Press, pp. 33–81.

Pynoos, J., R. Schafer and C. Hartman, eds. (1973), *Housing Urban America,* Chicago, Aldine, pp. 597

Ryabchuk, A. (2007), "In the Shadow: Experiences of Homelessness among Casual Workers in Construction Industry in Post-Soviet Ukraine", www.nbuv.gov.va/portal/soc-gum/maukma/soe/2007-70/12-ryabchyk-a.pdf

Richardson, D. (2009), "Extreme Poverty and Vulnerability in OECD countries: A Scoping review", Paper presented at the Working Party on Social Policy, mimeo, Paris.

Saegert, S. and G. W. Evans (2003), "Poverty, Housing Niches, and Health in the United States", *Journal of Social Issues,* Vol. 59, No. 3, pp. 569-589.

Shonkoff, J.P., W.T. Boyce and B.S. McEwen (2009), "Neuroscience, Molecular Biology, and the Childhood Roots of Health Disparities: Building a New Framework for Health Promotion and Disease Prevention", *Journal of the American Medical Association*, Vol. 301, No. 21, pp. 2252-2259.

Taylor, M. P., D. J. Pevalin and J. Todd (2007), "The psychological costs of unsustainable housing commitments", *Psychological Medicine,* Vol. 37, pp. 1027-1036.

United Nations High Commissioner for Human Rights (2009), "The Human Right to Adequate Housing", *Fact Sheet* No. 21 (Rev. 1).

Van Praag, B. M. S., P. Frijters, and A. Ferrer-i-Carbonell (2003), "The anatomy of subjective well-being", *Journal of Economic Behavior & Organization*, Elsevier, Vol. 51, No. 1, pp. 29.

Vera-Toscano, E. and V. Ateca-Amestoy (2008), "The relevance of social interactions on housing satisfaction", *Social Indicators Research*, Vol. 86, No. 2, pp. 257-274.

WHO (2007), *Large analysis and review of European housing and health status (LARES) – Preliminary Overview*, World Health Organisation Regional Office for Europe, Copenhagen.

WHO (2009), *Global Health Risks: Mortality and burden of disease attributable to selected major risks*, World Health Organisation, Geneva.

Yates, J. and M. Gabriel (2006), "Housing affordability in Australia", National Research Venture 3: Housing Affordability for Lower Income Australians (Research Paper 3).

Chapter 5

Health status

Being healthy is one of the most valued aspects of people's lives, and one that affects the probability of having a job, earning an adequate income, and actively participating in a range of valued social activities. People's health status is, however, difficult to measure, as it encompasses a variety of dimensions, such as the length of people's lives, the presence and severity of chronic conditions, and the many aspects of physical morbidity and mental health. This chapter describes people's health status through some well-established indicators of mortality and morbidity. In most OECD countries, people can expect to live long lives and report good or very good health. However, a large proportion of the population report chronic health conditions, and the number of those who are limited in some way in their daily activities is also significant. Inequalities in health status are also pervasive, with women and older people reporting lower satisfaction with their health status, and with large health disparities across income groups. Comparative information on people's health status remains limited in important ways, and the same applies to our understanding of the interplay of the various factors that determine health outcomes.

Why does health status matter for well-being?

The length of life and whether it is lived free of illness and disability both have intrinsic value for people. In fact, health status is consistently ranked as one of the most valued aspects in people's lives, together with having a job, in surveys conducted in OECD countries. Health status also has instrumental value because it enhances people's opportunities to participate in education and training programmes and in the labour market as well as to have good social relationships. At the societal level, countries with better overall health outcomes also display higher average income and wealth, higher employment rates, higher rates of participation in political activities, higher social network support and higher overall life satisfaction.

Many factors affect how healthy we are. Individual characteristics such as genetic makeup, whether we drink alcohol or smoke, are overweight, or have high cholesterol, are important. So are the conditions in which we live and work, our income and the amount of money that is spent on health-care and prevention. Health status depends on the interaction of these societal, environmental, socioeconomic, biological and lifestyle factors, most of which can be modified by health-care and other policies. Taken together, these influences can determine whether we stay healthy or become ill.

But what does it mean to be healthy? In its broadest sense: "health is a state of complete physical, mental and social well-being and not merely the absence of disease or infirmity" (WHO 1948).[1] While this definition does not lend itself naturally to measurement, it illustrates well that the concept of health is a broad and overarching one, and that health affects many aspects of life. This definition also highlights that objective health conditions and subjective aspects of health are important for everyone.

However, several aspects of health status, such as chronic conditions, mental states and the prevalence and intensity of disability, remain challenging to measure. Developing better measures would help not only to better assess people's health status, but also to gauge the performance of health systems in preventing or treating ill health, and to design more effective policies. Indeed, measuring and monitoring some of the key determinants of health outcomes (e.g. risky behaviours) is fundamental to implementing the right policies. In particular, it is important to understand why some population groups have poorer health than others, and to develop and evaluate policies and interventions to prevent disease and promote health for these groups.

Measuring health status

Measuring health status is complex, since many factors contribute to good health. An ideal set of indicators would provide information about the most important diseases and conditions causing poor health, disability or death as well as the various risk factors that lead to poor health. Ideal indicators would also inform on the linkages between the various health components and how, for instance, physical and psychological aspects of health are related, as functioning across multiple domains is a critical aspect of health. In practice the picture of health status provided by existing indicators is incomplete (Table 5.1).

In OECD countries at least, mortality indicators rely on well-established reporting standards, based on internationally harmonised sources and collection methods (Mathers et al., 2005). However, they refer only to the length of people's lives, rather than to the health conditions of the living.

Measures of morbidity are inherently more difficult to construct, as morbidity (or illness) is multidimensional (one may suffer from various diseases), not always measurable through objective measures (*e.g.* pain), and may require a longitudinal follow-up to assess whether conditions are temporary or chronic. The severity of illness conditions may also vary considerably across diseases. As a result, comparative indicators of physical morbidity are much less satisfactory than those measuring mortality. The current statistical system for collecting information on morbidity is also unevenly developed across OECD countries. Usually there is no requirement for the compulsory registration of diseases, and thus no easy way of recording their occurrence. In some countries, registers are kept for certain diseases such as cancer and diabetes, or doctor visits and hospitalisations are recorded, but summarising information on the prevalence and incidence of diseases is challenging. Where they exist, health examinations of the population provide the most reliable data, although these are expensive to carry out on large numbers of people. Surveys based on health interviews are another method for collecting information on illnesses, disabilities, risk factors and general health status. However, these surveys also differ across countries and may also suffer from various biases or not cover the entire population (*e.g.* children or elderly people living in institutions).

In line with the framework used in this publication, this chapter studies selected *outcome* indicators of health, *i.e.* indicators that inform on selected aspects of health status (*i.e.* mortality and morbidity). The choice of indicators has closely followed some of the health measures considered by the Framework on Health Statistics developed by the Inter-Secretariat on Health Statistics (Box 5.1), though this framework is not yet wide-spread and would benefit from further use and development. The chapter does not deal with indicators of health input (*e.g.* health expenditure), output (*e.g.* number of interventions) or drivers (*e.g.* life style behaviour). The role of risk factors, such as smoking and alcohol use, is also not explicitly considered or is considered only to a limited extent (*e.g.* obesity).

Selected indicators

Life expectancy at birth (HS I)

Life expectancy is a summary measure of mortality rates by age groups. It is relevant for measuring the average longevity of the population as a whole and is collected using well-established standards. Life expectancy can be measured at birth and at various ages. All life expectancies measure how long on average people could expect to live based on the age-specific death rates currently prevailing. Life expectancy at birth is, however, only an estimate of the expected life span of a given cohort, as the actual age-specific death rates of any particular birth cohort cannot be known in advance. Measures of life expectancy at birth refer to people born today and are computed by the OECD as the unweighted average of life expectancy for men and women.

Measures of life expectancy are based on data of good quality for all OECD countries, while there is scope for improvement in other major economies. Life expectancy indicators meet a number of criteria characterising "ideal" indicators (Table 5.1), with the exception of the availability of disaggregated information across various population groups. Indeed, life expectancy measures available for international comparisons can be broken down only by gender, and few countries are able to provide information on life expectancy by educational attainment and income, as these measures require either linking mortality to records from census population or one-off surveys.

> ### Box 5.1. **The Framework on Health Statistics developed by the Inter-secretariat on Health Statistics - UN Statistical Commission**
>
> The Inter-secretariat Working Group reports on work by the Washington Group on Disability Statistics and the Budapest Initiative on health statistics, both of which are aimed at developing modules of health survey questions that can be used to generate comparable data across countries (see the final section on the Statistical Agenda for more details on these initiatives). The Working Group has also developed a framework to organise the various dimensions of health that need to be addressed by the statistical system. The framework looks at both general and specific measures of health and identifies the various relationships between measures of health. In particular, it includes:
>
> - **General measures of health status.** These measures are generally considered to be the core health indicators that are needed to monitor the overall health status of a population. The levels and changes in these measures result from a variety of factors that are captured by other measures in the Framework. General health measures include: life expectancy; infant mortality; self-rated health and summary measures (*e.g.* health-adjusted life expectancy).
>
> - **Measures of the functional status of the population.** Functioning can be measured across a range of domains, including sensory, mobility, cognition, psychological, communication and the upper body. Disability measures are also included in this level, as they combine functioning with information about the environment to describe the extent to which all citizens can fully participate in society. The Budapest Initiative and the Washington Group are developing measures of functional status.
>
> - **Biological measures, including physiological characteristics, pathologies and diseases.** Diseases or conditions are defined by a range of pathological characteristics that themselves relate to biological structure and function. These physiological characteristics can be complex and measured at the level of the organ (or multiorgans) or they can be more targeted, such as genetic abnormalities or predispositions. Measures of disease states are common, and there are many examples of disease-specific measures available. Cause-of-death measures would be included here. Also included in this set of measures would be characteristics such as pain or fatigue.
>
> - **Risk factors.** This set of measures includes factors that either increase or decrease the risk of developing pathologies and diseases and that therefore affect functional levels and general measures of health. Specific examples are diet and nutrition, smoking and physical activity.
>
> - **Related factors** include measures related to health care, including supply, access, utilisation, expenditures and health system characteristics.

Infant mortality rate (hs 1)

While life expectancy at birth is the best summary measure of mortality, it is also important to know whether death occurs at early or later ages. To capture this, infant mortality rates are also presented here. However, since these refer to a very narrow age group, they cannot be considered as a measure expressing the health status of the population as a whole. They are thus considered as a secondary indicator, providing additional evidence on mortality and health status. Data on infant mortality are broadly comparable across countries, although there may be slight differences in the way that premature deaths are recorded.

Table 5.1. **The quality of health status indicators**

Target concept		INDICATORS								
		Relevance to measure and monitor well-being				Statistical quality				
		Face validity	Unambiguous interpretation (good/bad)	Amenable to policy changes	Can be disaggregated	Well-established instrument collected	Comparable definition	Country coverage	Recurrent data collection	
Health status										
HS I Life expectancy at birth	Length of life	√	√	√	~	√	√	√	√	
hs 1 Infant mortality		√	√	√	~	√	√	√	√	
HS II Self-reported health status	Morbidity in its different dimensions	√	√	√	√	√	~	~	√	
hs 2 Self-reported longstanding illness		√	√	√	√	√	~	~	~	
hs 3 Self-reported limitations in daily activities		√	√	√	√	√	~	~	~	
hs 4 Overweight and obesity		~	√	√	√	√	~	√	√	

Note: The symbol √ shows that the indicator selected largely meets the criteria shown in the table; the symbol ~ that the indicator meets the criteria to a large extent; the symbol x that the indicator does not meet the criterion or it meets it only to a limited extent

Self-reported health status (HS II)

Indicators of self-perceived general health status are one of the few morbidity indicators that are available for all OECD countries on a broadly comparable basis. They have the advantage of summarising in a single measure a broad range of dimensions of health, since they refer to the overall health status of the respondent. The indicator is based on questions such as: "How is your health in general?", with answers classified in different categories, usually "very good, good, not very good, poor". Data are based on general household surveys or on more detailed health interviews undertaken as part of countries' official statistical systems.

Although the questions used to collect this information are harmonised across European countries, they are worded slightly differently (and have different response scales) in some non-European OECD countries. Since self-reported health status relies on the subjective views of the respondents, it may reflect cultural biases or other contextual factors, especially in some Asian countries. Since the elderly generally report poorer health, countries with a larger proportion of aged persons will also have a lower proportion reporting good or very good health, unless the data are age-standardised. However, there is evidence that these indicators are a relatively good predictor of future health care use and mortality (Miilunpalo *et al.*, 1997).[2]

Self-reported longstanding illness (hs 2)

Official health interviews and general household surveys collect other measures of self-reported health conditions. The first refers to the prevalence of chronic illnesses. This indicator is phrased in more objective terms than for self-rated health, with questions such as: "Do you have any long-standing illness or health problem which has lasted, or is expected to last for six months or more?". However, the measure is dependent on whether people are diagnosed and can report their diagnosis, and it says little about the severity of the condition and its impact upon people's functioning.

Since the indicator is based on a strictly comparable format, it is currently limited to European countries. Many non-European OECD countries, such as the United States and Australia, also collect this type of information, although in a different fashion, which makes comparisons difficult. For this reason, this indicator is included in the analysis as a secondary indicator.

Self-reported limitations in daily activities (hs 3)

The other self-reported health status indicator refers to the experience of disabilities resulting from a severe health problem. The indicator shown here is based on the following question: "For at least the past six months, have you been hampered because of a health problem in activities people usually do?", with answers classified as "yes, strongly limited/yes, limited/no, not limited". As in the case of the previous indicator, strictly harmonised information on self-reported limitations is currently available only for European countries, and for this reason it is shown here as a secondary indicator.

Overweight and obesity (hs 4)

In addition to general measures of health status, anthropometric measures also provide information on people's health status. One such measure relates people's weight and height to derive an indicator of overweight and obesity. Both conditions matter for current health status and, even more, as predictors of medical conditions in the future. Overweight and obesity were not retained as primary indicators since they refer to health outcomes that are not necessarily severe, but since they are known to be important risk factors for serious illnesses, including hypertension, high cholesterol, diabetes, cardiovascular diseases, respiratory problems (asthma), musculoskeletal diseases (arthritis) and many others, they were retained as secondary indicators. A caveat on the use of indicators of overweight and obesity is that the associations between these indicators, the percentages of body fat and health risks may differ for some ethnic groups and populations.

The indicators of overweight and obesity are defined as the share of the population whose Body Mass Index (BMI=kg/m2) is, respectively, from 25 to 30 and over 30, in line with the World Health Organization classifications. The data on weights and heights are collected either through health interview surveys, which ask persons to report their own height and weight, or through health examinations that record objective information on people's height and weight. The latter method provides more reliable information and in general higher estimates of overweight/obesity than do self-reports.

Average patterns

Life expectancy has increased strongly, both in OECD and emerging countries

Life expectancy at birth differs significantly among OECD and other major economies (Figure 5.1). Japan leads a large group of countries (including more than half of the OECD countries) in which total life expectancy at birth currently exceeds 80 years. A second group, including the United States, China, Brazil and a number of central and eastern European countries, have a life expectancy of between 70 and 80 years. Life expectancy is much lower in some emerging countries, particularly South Africa and India, where it is less than 65 years.

In nearly all OECD and emerging countries, there have been large gains in life expectancy over the past few decades. Chile, China, Indonesia, Turkey, India, Korea, Brazil and Mexico have moved rapidly towards the OECD average. However, other countries are still characterised by high mortality rates and, in terms of length of life, they are well below the OECD average. There are many factors underlying changes in life expectancy, and identifying their separate effects is often difficult (Box 5.2). While in some countries gains in life expectancy have outpaced gains in living standards, in others the reverse has been observed. The Russian Federation saw life expectancy decline in the 1990s, due largely to societal changes, increases in external causes of death and other risk factors such as excess consumption of alcohol; there is evidence that this trend is now reversing and life expectancy has started to increase again (Popov, 2011). In South Africa, life expectancy has also fallen recently because of the devastating HIV/AIDS epidemic.

Figure 5.1. **Life expectancy at birth and years gained since 1960**

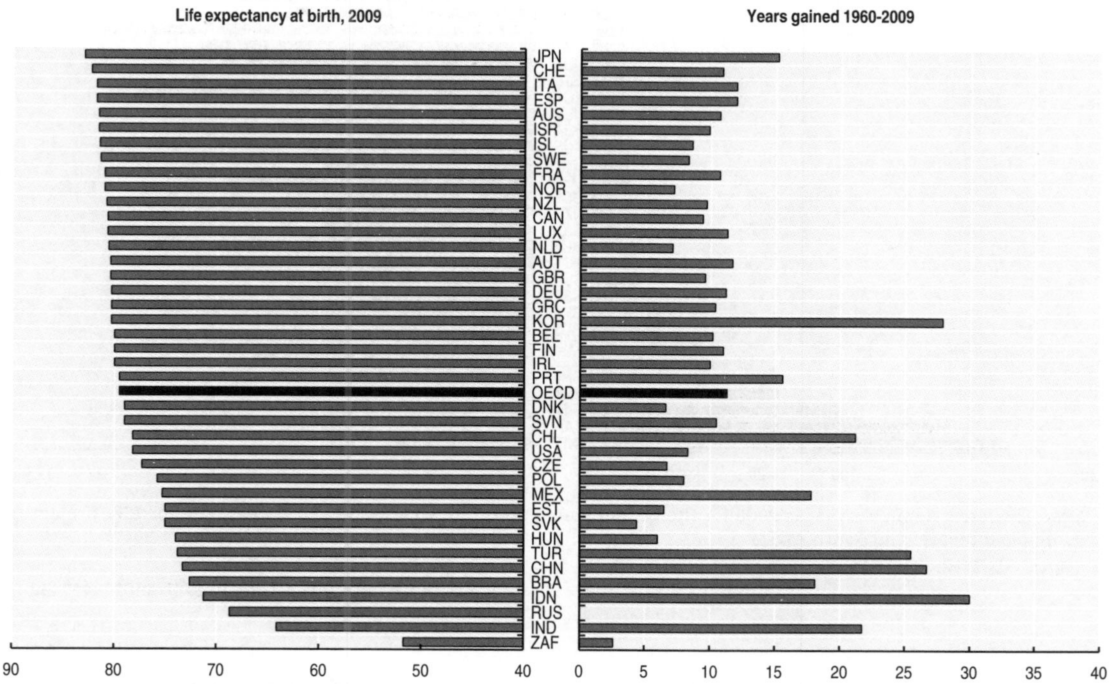

Note: The latest available year is 2008 for Italy; and 2007 for Canada. Years gained are calculated starting from 1961 for Canada, New Zealand and Italy. For the Russian Federation the gain is nil.
Source: OECD Health Data.

StatLink ⧉ http://dx.doi.org/10.1787/888932492473

Infant mortality has declined everywhere, but remains a serious issue in some emerging countries

Infant mortality is affected by the economic and social conditions in which mothers and babies live, as well as by the effectiveness of health-care systems. In most OECD countries, infant mortality is low and there is little difference in rates (Figure 5.2). A small group of OECD and emerging countries, however, have infant mortality rates over 10 deaths per 1 000 live births. In India, South Africa and Indonesia, rates are 30 or above.

The annual rate of decline in infant mortality across all OECD countries since 1970 averages almost 5 per cent, with Portugal, Korea and Turkey exhibiting the most substantial falls. The reduction of infant mortality has been slower in India, the Russian Federation and the United States. The infant mortality rate in the United States used to be well below the

OECD average, but is now above average. Significant differences are also evident in infant mortality rates among various racial groups in the United States, with African-American women more likely to give birth to high-risk, low birth-weight infants (NCHS, 2011).

Figure 5.2. **Infant mortality 2009 and its decline since 1970**

Deaths per 100,000 live births   *Average annual rate of decline (%)*

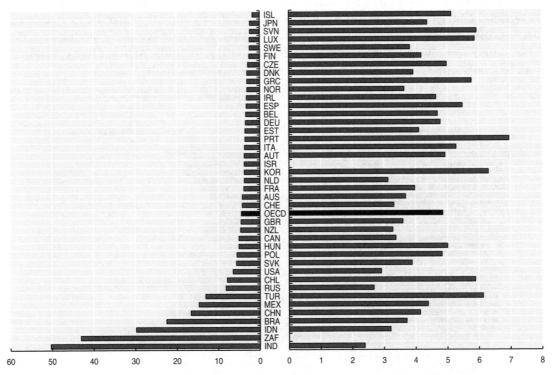

Note: The latest available year is 2008 for the United States; and 2007 for Canada and Korea. Data for 1970 are not available for Israel and South Africa.
Source: OECD Health Data.

StatLink ⟡ *http://dx.doi.org/10.1787/888932492492*

Box 5.2. **Many factors account for the increase in life expectancy**

Increases in life expectancy reflect, to a significant extent, higher living standards, improved life-styles and better education, as well as greater access to quality health services. Other factors such as better nutrition, sanitation and housing also play a role, particularly in countries with developing economies.

In OECD countries higher economic prosperity, measured by GDP per capita, is generally associated with higher life expectancy at birth, although the relationship is less pronounced at higher levels of income (Figure 5.3). There are also notable differences in life expectancy between OECD countries with similar incomes per capita, such as Japan and Denmark. Such a relationship also exists between life expectancy and health expenditure. The United States stands out as having both high GDP and health expenditure per capita, but a lower level of overall life expectancy than might be expected. High rates of mortality for some diseases at older ages, the legacy of smoking, and other factors such as obesity and economic inequality have been suggested as possible reasons for the United States' poorer performance (Crimmins *et al.*, 2010). One recent study found that high rates of obesity, tobacco use and other preventable risk factors for an early death are important drivers of the gap between life expectancy in the United States and that in other countries (Kulkarni *et al.*, 2011).

Figure 5.3. **Life expectancy, GDP and health spending per capita**

Life expectancy at birth and GDP per capita

Life expectancy at birth and health spending per capita

2009 (or latest year available)

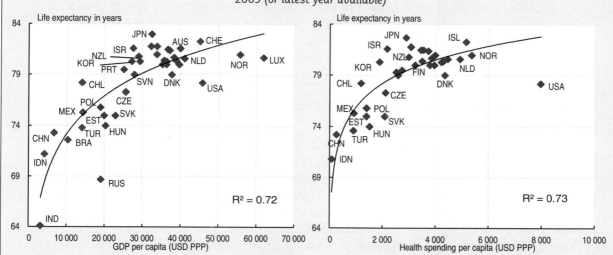

Note: Data refer to 2008 for Italy; and 2007 for Canada. In the right-hand panel, data refer to 2008 for Australia, Japan, Luxembourg, Portugal, Turkey, China, India and Indonesia; and to 2007 for Greece.

Source: OECD (2010), *Health at a Glance: Asia/Pacific 2010*, OECD Publishing; and OECD Health Data, Paris.

StatLink ᴍᴸᴸ http://dx.doi.org/10.1787/888932492511

Multivariate analysis also suggests that while health care spending accounts for much of the improvement in life expectancy over the past 15 years, other determinants such as GDP growth, environmental improvements and education are also important drivers. Taken together, these explain much of the cross-country differences in life expectancy, as well as of their changes over time (Table 5.2).

Table 5.2. **Contributions of main explanatory variables to changes in health status 1991-2003**

	GAINS IN LIFE EXPECTANCY				DECLINE IN INFANT MORTALITY RATE
	At birth		At age 65		
	Women	Men	Women	Men	
Explained by	Years				Deaths per 1 000 live births
Health care spending	1.14	1.34	0.38	0.37	-2.53
Smoking	0.00	0.12	0.09	0.21	-0.21
Alcohol	0.06	0.07	0.02	0.00	-0.24
Diet	0.02	0.02	0.02	0.03	0.03
Pollution	0.15	0.29	0.15	0.22	-0.75
Education	0.50	0.49	0.26	0.14	-0.89
GDP	0.11	0.63	0.20	0.39	-1.01
Observed changes	2.49	3.45	1.40	1.63	-4.67

Note: Contributions of health status determinants are calculated using panel data regressions on a sample of countries for which data were available. Observed changes in health status are calculated for the OECD area. The sum of identified contributions may thus differ from the actual change in life-expectancy.

Source: OECD (2010b), *Health Care Systems: Efficiency and Policy Settings*, OECD, Paris.

StatLink ᴍᴸᴸ http://dx.doi.org/10.1787/888932493993

In OECD countries, the majority of the population reports being in good health....

Although there have been remarkable gains in life expectancy in most OECD countries in recent decades, it matters whether these extra years of life are lived in good health or with increased chronic disease and disability. On average, around 70% of the OECD population report good or very good health, although there is a large variation across countries (Figure 5.4). Respondents from the United States, New Zealand, Canada and Australia report good or very good health most often, compared with lower levels in the Slovak Republic, Japan and Portugal[3].

...but in European countries around one-third of the population suffer from chronic diseases...

Three-in-ten adults who were surveyed in European countries report having a long-standing illness or health problem, with a higher prevalence in Finland, Estonia and France, and a lower prevalence in Italy and Luxembourg (Figure 5.5). Examples of long-standing illnesses include arthritis and back pain, asthma, anxiety/depression, cancer, diabetes, heart attack and stroke. These chronic illnesses represent a growing burden in all OECD countries, and their increased prevalence has been attributed to a range of causes, including the ageing of populations and lifestyle factors such as smoking, physical inactivity and excessive alcohol intake.

Figure 5.4. **Adults reporting good or very good health**

Percentage, 2009

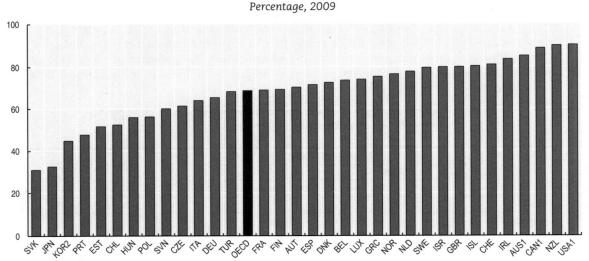

Note: Adults are generally defined as individuals aged 15 years and over. Data refer to 2008 for Turkey; and 2007 for Australia, Japan and New Zealand. Results for countries marked with a "1" are not directly comparable with those for other countries, due to differences in reporting scales, which may lead to an upward bias in the reported estimates. The result for Korea (marked with a "2") is not directly comparable due to differences in reporting scales, which may lead to a downward bias in the reported estimates.

Sources: OECD Health Data; and European Union Statistics on Income and Living Conditions (EU-SILC).

StatLink ⟹ *http://dx.doi.org/10.1787/888932492530*

Figure 5.5. **Adults reporting a long-standing illness or health problem in European countries**

Percentage, 2009

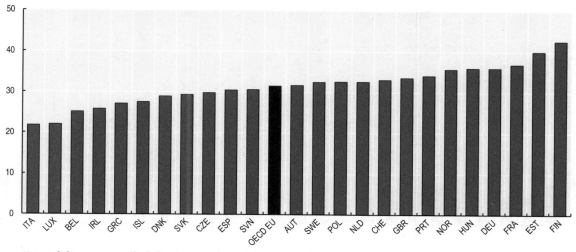

Note: Adults are generally defined as people aged 15 years and over
Source: OECD Health Data; and European Union Statistics on Income and Living Conditions (EU-SILC).

StatLink ⬛⬛ *http://dx.doi.org/10.1787/888932492549*

....and about one-quarter of the population are limited in some way in their daily activities

The same survey asks European respondents to assess whether they have any health problems that limit their ability to perform normal daily activities. Around one-in-four respondents across Europe reported having such limitations, with 8% "strongly limited" and 17% "limited to some extent" (Figure 5.6). There are, however, large differences across countries. More than one-third of respondents in the Slovak Republic reported an activity limitation induced by health problems, compared with only 15% in Iceland and Sweden.

Overweight and obesity affect a large share of the population in some OECD countries

In many OECD countries, large proportions of the population are overweight or obese. On average, 17% of the population is obese in the OECD (Figure 5.7). The proportion of obese people varies from about one-third in the United States and Mexico, to around one-in-four in New Zealand, Chile, Australia and Canada, to less than 5% in a number of Asian countries including India, Indonesia, China, Japan and Korea. Rates of obesity have risen rapidly in recent decades, affecting all population groups to varying extents, with more educated and higher socio-economic status women displaying substantially lower rates, and mixed patterns being observed for men (Sassi, 2010).

The various indicators capture different dimensions of health status

While the various indicators of health status presented here measure different aspects of health, it is important to assess whether they convey a consistent picture. In general:

● The two mortality indicators are well correlated with each other, indicating that countries with higher life expectancy at birth also experience low infant mortality rates (Table 5.3).

Figure 5.6. **Adults reporting a limitation in usual activities owing to health problems in European countries**

Percentage, 2009

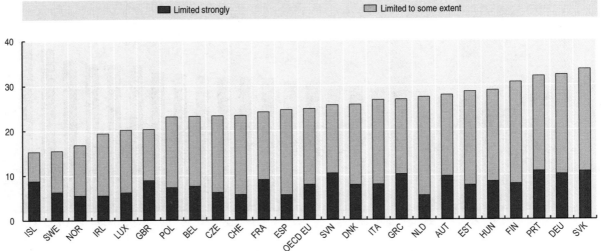

Note: Adults are generally defined as individuals aged 15 years and over.

Sources: European Union Statistics on Income and Living Conditions (EU-SILC); Swiss Federal Statistical Office.

StatLink *http://dx.doi.org/10.1787/888932492568*

- Correlations are weaker when looking at the various morbidity indicators. Countries where a higher share of the population report positive evaluations of their health status also feature a lower prevalence of self-reported limitations in daily activities but also a higher prevalence of obesity. Overall, these patterns suggest that these indicators capture distinct elements of overall morbidity.

- There is a weak positive correlation between life expectancy at birth and self-reported health (a correlation that becomes more significant when excluding Japan, a country that combines the highest life expectancy at birth and the second-lowest self-reported health). The dispersion of country outcomes between these two measures remains high, however, suggesting that these indicators capture separate dimensions of health status that do not necessarily move in tandem.

Table 5.3. **Correlation between different indicators of health status**

	HS I Life-expectancy at birth		hs 1 Infant mortality		HS II Self-reported health status		hs 2 Self-reported longstanding illness		hs 3 Self-reported limitations in daily activities		hs 4 Overweight and obesity	
HS I Life expectancy at birth	1	(41)	-0.86***	(41)	0.39**	(35)	-0.26	(25)	-0.42**	(25)	0.06	(41)
hs 1 Infant mortality			1	(41)	-0.04	(35)	0.18	(25)	0.42**	(25)	-0.24	(41)
HS II Self-reported health status					1	(35)	-0.19	(25)	-0.69***	(25)	0.45***	(35)
hs 2 Self-reported longstanding illness							1	(25)	0.31	(25)	-0.08	(25)
hs 3 Self-reported limitations in daily activities									1	(25)	-0.02	(25)
hs 4 Overweight and obesity											1	(41)

Note: Values in parenthesis refer to the number of observations. ** Indicates that correlations are significant at the 5% level; *** indicates that they are significant at the 1% level.

Source: OECD's calculations.

StatLink *http://dx.doi.org/10.1787/888932494012*

Figure 5.7. **Obesity among adults**

Percentage, 2009 or latest available year

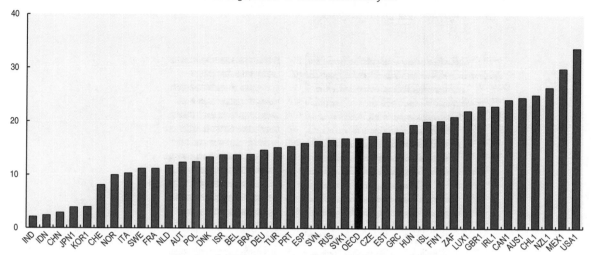

Note: The latest available year is 2010 for Denmark; 2008 for Belgium, Canada, the Czech Republic, Estonia, France, Greece, Israel, Norway, the Slovak Republic, Turkey, and the United States; 2007 for Australia, Finland, Iceland, Ireland, New Zealand, Slovenia and Switzerland; 2006 for Austria, Mexico, Portugal and India; 2005 for the Russian Federation and South Africa; 2004 for Poland; 2002 for China and 2001 for Indonesia. Data for countries marked with a "1" are based on health examination rather than health interview surveys. Adults are generally defined as individual over 15 years old.

Sources: OECD Health Data; WHO Global Infobase.

StatLink ⬛ᴵˢᴸ *http://dx.doi.org/10.1787/888932492587*

The absence of very strong correlations between the various indicators underscores the importance of looking at a range of measures to gain a better appreciation of people's health status.

Inequalities

Despite substantial improvements in health status in OECD countries over the past 50 years, differences in mortality and morbidity continue to exist not only between countries but also within countries. These health inequalities are apparent across many population groups, including as broken down by age, gender, race or ethnicity, geographic area or socioeconomic status.

Men and youth report being healthier

Self-reported measures of morbidity worsen steadily with people's age (Boarini *et al.*, 2011). The elderly are the least satisfied with their health as it is they who most often experience health problems that limit their daily activities. Women also tend to be less satisfied with their health than men and suffer more frequently from health problems, a pattern that contrasts with their higher life expectancy. These findings, which are based on a large sample of countries, including OECD and emerging countries, are corroborated by previous research reviewed in de Looper and Lafortune, 2009.

Figure 5.8. **Adults reporting good or very good health, by income quintile**

Percentage and ratio of highest to lowest quintile, 2009 or latest available year

Highest income quintile ■ Lowest income quintile

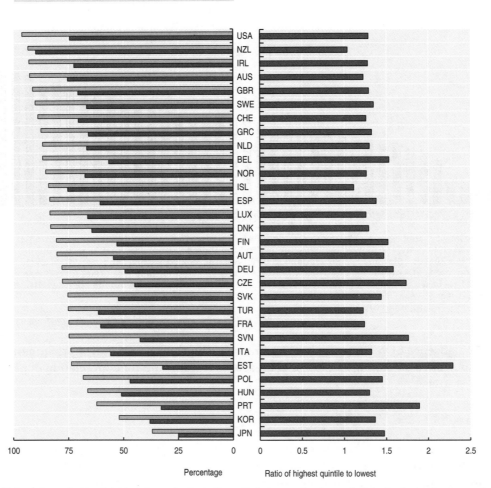

Percentage   Ratio of highest quintile to lowest

Note: Values shown in the right-hand panel refer to the ratio between the share of adults in the top income quintile reporting good or very good health to the corresponding share of adults in the bottom income quintile. Data refer to 2008 for Turkey; and 2007 for Australia, Japan and New Zealand. Adults are generally defined as individuals over 15 years old.

Sources: OECD Health Data; European Union Statistics on Income and Living Conditions (EU-SILC).

StatLink ᘕᘊᕱ *http://dx.doi.org/10.1787/888932492606*

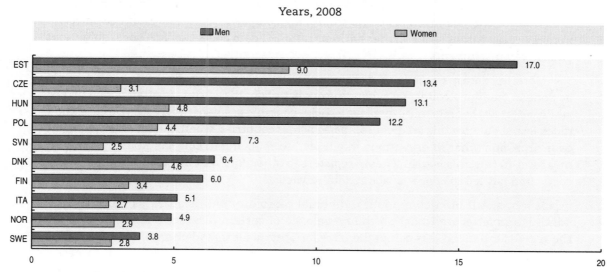

Figure 5.9. **Gaps in life expectancy between persons with high and low educational attainment at age 30 in selected EU countries**

Years, 2008

Note: Data for Italy refer to 2007.

Sources: Eurostat (2010), "Highly Educated Men and Women Likely to Live Longer", Eurostat Statistics in Focus, 24/2010.

StatLink ⌇⌇⌇ http://dx.doi.org/10.1787/888932492625

Income and education play a key role in shaping both mortality and morbidity

Socio-economic background also has a large influence on health status in all countries, regardless of their political structures or health-care systems. As socioeconomic disadvantage grows, people live and work in more difficult circumstances, with harmful effects on their health. In addition, behaviours that are detrimental to health, such as smoking, excess drinking and poor nutrition, also tend to increase with greater socioeconomic disadvantage. Finally, disadvantaged persons often have greater problems in accessing appropriate health care and make use of available services to a lesser extent or devote a high share of their income to out-of-pocket health spending. The result is that economically worse-off people are ill more often and die earlier.

Despite extensive evidence regarding socio-economic influences on health outcomes, evidence that would allow comparing the size of these inequalities across countries, and how they have evolved over time remains scant. In all countries for which evidence is available, people in higher income groups report better health status than those in lower income groups (Figure 5.8), although this difference varies greatly across countries: in Estonia people in the highest income quintile are more than twice as likely to report good health as those in the lowest quintile, whereas in New Zealand the proportions are similar.

Comparing inequalities in health status across countries using more objective measures than self-reports remains challenging.[4] However, some estimates of life expectancy by educational status in Europe show that, for both men and women, highly educated people are likely to live longer (Figure 5.9). Differences in life expectancy are particularly large in Eastern European countries, and more pronounced for men than for women. In Estonia, 30-year-old men with a high level of education can expect to live 17 years longer than men of the same age with a low educational level. Bulgaria, the Czech Republic, Hungary and Poland show a similar pattern.

The statistical agenda ahead

This chapter noted that some aspects of health status are more difficult to measure than others. There is much scope for improving comparative measures of health status in many areas through the further harmonisation of data collection methods, definitions and survey instruments.

Mortality data in OECD countries are generally of good quality, but more work needs to be done in emerging countries, where the quality of death registers is often poor. Further, while we know that mortality displays a socioeconomic gradient in all countries, we know much less about how this gradient compares across countries, whether it has been changing over time, and what interventions might lead to reducing it. One method of improving measures in this area is to link death registers to other data sets, although this has proved costly and has led to concerns about data privacy.

Much is still unknown about individual morbidity and health risk factors. Good administrative records exist on the prevalence of certain diseases such as cancer, but the records are much less comprehensive for other widespread chronic conditions such as cardiovascular disease, obesity and other biomedical risk factors. Health examination surveys can help address this, although these too are costly.

Comparative data on morbidity, based on population censuses and household surveys, also remain sparse. There are ongoing international efforts to develop more comparable measures of population health status. At the European level, for instance, Euro Reves 2 has proposed a minimum European Module (MEHM) to monitor health across Europe.[5] At a more global level, the Budapest Initiative aims to develop a new common instrument for measuring health status, suitable for inclusion in national interview surveys.[6] Similarly, the Washington Group on Disability Statistics coordinates international efforts to develop disability measures for inclusion in censuses and national surveys.[7]

These efforts have led to the development and field-testing of modules that would allow for more robust international comparisons of health status and disability, but have not yet been implemented consistently. Beyond measures of physical morbidity, there is little comparative information on mental health. The limited information that exists suggests that a large proportion of the population is affected at some point in their lives with some mental health problems, but there are few reliable measures to compare mental health across large numbers of countries (Box 5.3).

Finally, further progress is needed in two areas:

● Developing summary measures of health status that combine morbidity and mortality in a single statistic (Box 5.4). The debate about which summary measure to use, and how this measure should be constructed, is still ongoing. At the European level, Disability Free Life Expectancy (also known as Healthy Life Years) is widely used as a "structural indicator" and is computed regularly by Eurostat. At the global level, WHO favours a more complex and data-intensive indicator of Health Adjusted Life Expectancy. Any summary measure of health status raises issues about the weight that should be attached to various conditions. Regardless of the type of summary measure selected, it will be important to harmonise the underlying national data if internationally comparable data are to be produced.

● A greater understanding of the interactions of the various factors that determine health outcomes, including characteristics of the individual, the health care system and the care paths followed by patients (i.e. who gets treated, and what kind of interventions they receive). A concise picture of health performance requires developing better measures of progress in health care to understand how and why the quality of care varies across patients' needs for care. The OECD has begun to address these data gaps through the OECD Health Care Quality Indicators Project (OECD, 2010c).

Box 5.3. **Measuring the prevalence and intensity of mental health problems**

Measuring mental health requires multi-question surveys that look at the prevalence, severity and treatment of different mental health problems. While no common instrument to measure mental health has been implemented on an ongoing basis in OECD countries, some comparative evidence is available through surveys undertaken in the early 2000s as part of the WHO Mental Health Consortium. In countries where this type of surveys is available, there is evidence that common mental health problems (i.e. anxiety, mood disorders, disorders linked to impulse control or the use of alcohol or drugs) affect around 14% of the population on average in any given year (Table 5.4). While in China, Israel, Italy, Japan and Spain 10% or less of respondents reported a mental health problem at some point during the previous year, this share reached 19% in France and 27% in the United States.

Most of these cases are classified as "mild" or "moderate", and are often left untreated. Around one-quarter of these cases are, however, serious, even though a significant proportion of these respondents declared that they did not use any mental health services in the prior 12 months (Kessler and Üstün, 2008).

Table 5.4. **Prevalence and severity of mental health problems in selected countries, around 2005**

	Prevalence in the preceding 12-months, share of total population					Severity, share of those experiencing such problems		
	Type of disorder					Level of severity		
	Anxiety	Mood	Impulse	Substance	Any	Serious	Moderate	Mild
Belgium	8	5	2	2	13	32	38	30
China	3	2	3	2	7	14	32	54
France	14	7	2	1	19	19	43	39
Germany	8	3	1	1	11	21	43	36
Israel	4	6	..	1	10	37	35	28
Italy	7	3	0	0	9	16	48	37
Japan	4	3	0	1	7	13	46	41
Mexico	8	5	2	2	13	26	34	41
Netherlands	9	5	2	2	14	31	31	38
New Zealand	15	8	..	4	21	25	41	34
South Africa	8	5	2	6	17	26	32	43
Spain	7	4	1	1	10	19	42	38
United States	19	10	11	4	27	25	39	36
Average	9	5	2	2	14	23	39	38

Source: Kessler, R. C. and T. B. Üstün, eds. (2008), The WHO World Mental Health Surveys: Global Perspectives on the Epidemiology of Mental Disorders, Cambridge University Press, New York.

StatLink ᴍˢᴾ http://dx.doi.org/10.1787/888932494031

Conclusion

This chapter has discussed health status in OECD countries and in other major economies on the basis of some well-established measures of mortality and morbidity. In many of these countries, people can expect to live a long life, and great progress has been accomplished in low-income countries to reduce infant and adult mortality rates. However, a significant proportion of the population reports chronic health problems, and the number of those who suffer from serious disabilities is not negligible, especially among the elderly and less wealthy individuals. This holds true irrespective of the economic development of the country. Although income and wealth bring health, other factors such as life-styles and the environment in which people live, grow and work also play a role. Large health disparities remain across income groups; these should be targeted by specific policy interventions aimed at improving healthy behaviour and helping the most disadvantaged groups of the population access health care.

Box 5.4. **Summary measures of population health**

The different dimensions of people's health have led to the development of new types of indicators over the past few decades that seek to combine mortality and morbidity into a single measure of health status, allowing better quantification of health-related quality of life. All of these measures aim to calculate the average number of years that are spent in good health, after adjusting for years lived with some form of illness or disability. Although the calculation of these measures is complex, they are easy to interpret, and all rely on value judgements about living in different states of health. The harmonisation of underlying data sources and methods is still an issue.

One of these measures is Disability Free Life Expectancy (DFLE), which in Europe is also known as Healthy Life Years (HLY). DFLE calculates the number of remaining years that a person of a certain age can expect to live without disability, using mortality data from life tables and estimates of the prevalence of disability among population groups. Disability estimates are obtained as a self-reported measure of long-term activity limitation, based on a simple dichotomous variable of whether a person is moderately/severely disabled, or not disabled.

A number of other countries calculate similar measures, although their methods and concepts may differ slightly. Japan has made calculations of disease-free life expectancy (Cabinet Office, Government of Japan, 2006), and the United States has calculated years free from activity limitation (U.S. Department of Health and Human Services, 2006).

Another summary measure of population health is Health-Adjusted Life Expectancy (HALE), which is regularly calculated by a number of OECD countries (*e.g.* Australia and Canada) as well as by the World Health Organisation. This measures the number of years that a person can expect to live in full health, free from disability or disease, if current morbidity and mortality conditions continue. HALE adjusts life expectancy by subtracting the average number of years spent in unhealthy states from the overall life expectancy, taking into account the relative severity of such states. The measures of health status usually come from questions asked in health surveys about key dimensions of physical and mental functioning. The weighting of years of life depends on how different combinations of health status are valued, and they range from 0 (in case of death) to 1 (in case of full health).

Notes

1. "Social" here refers to the impact of health on social functioning and the physical and mental capacity of individuals to participate in society.

2. Another limitation of these indicators is that, since, the institutionalised population is not surveyed, they underestimate the true morbidity rates. Indicators of self-reported longstanding illness and daily limitations suffer from a similar problem.

3. When calculating the indicator over three response items (*i.e.* the percentage of adults with "very good, good or fair" health status), the values for Korea are significantly higher.

4. In the case of mortality, such comparisons would typically require linking a registry of individual deaths with census data providing information on people's income, education or occupation. To get internationally comparable data, this resource-intensive process would also need to be handled in a uniform manner across countries, with due regard to privacy issues.

5. The minimum European Health Module (MEHM) is a set of three global questions on general perceived health, chronic health problems and global activity limitation. In 2007, Eurostat provided new guidelines for these questions to the Member States, in order to improve data comparability from 2008 onwards. Since 2008, national version of the EU-SILC use the questions of the MEHM, translated with well-defined and common standards. Further improvements are ongoing.

6. In 2007, the Joint UNECE/WHO/Eurostat Task Force on measuring health status (also known as "the Budapest initiative") approved a survey module to produce internationally comparable estimates of health status (the Budapest Initiative Mark 1 module, BI-M1). The Task Force is currently working towards an improved module (BI-M2); the field-testing of this improved module includes questions on walking, cognition (*i.e.* difficulty in concentrating, remembering or making decisions), affect, pain and fatigue.

7. In 2006, the Washington Group on Disability Statistics approved a "short set" of six disability questions for use in population censuses, covering the domains of seeing, hearing, walking, cognition, self-care and communication. The Group is currently pursuing the field-testing of an "enlarged set" of questions for use in household surveys, covering the 10 domains of vision, hearing, upper body, learning, cognition, affect, pain, fatigue and communication (United Nations, 2010).

References

Boarini R., M. Comola F. De Keulenauer, R.Manchin and C. Smith (2011), "Well-being patterns around the world: New evidence from the Gallup World Poll", OECD Statistics Directorate Working Paper, OECD Publishing, Paris.

Cabinet Office, Government of Japan (2006), *White Paper on the National Lifestyle 2006*, Tokyo.

Crimmins, E. M., S. H. Preston and B. Cohen eds. (2010), *Explaining Divergent Levels of Longevity in High-Income Countries*, National Academies Press, Washington, D.C.

Eurostat (2010), "Highly Educated Men and Women Likely to Live Longer", Eurostat Statistics in Focus, 24/2010.

Kessler, R. C. and T. B. Üstün, eds. (2008), *The WHO World Mental Health Surveys: Global Perspectives on the Epidemiology of Mental Disorders*, Cambridge University Press, New York.

Kulkarni S. C., A. Levin-Rector, M. Ezzati and C. Murray (2011), "Falling behind: Life Expectancy in US counties from 2000 to 2007 in an International Context", *Population Health Metrics*, Vol. 9, No. 16.

Looper de, M. and G. Lafortune (2009), "Measuring Disparities in Health Status and in Access and Use of Health Care in OECD Countries", OECD Health Working Papers No. 43, OECD Publishing, Paris.

Mathers, C., D. Ma Fat, M. Inoue, C. Rao and A. D. Lopez (2005), "Counting the Dead and What They Died From: An Assessment of the Global Status of Cause of Death Data", *Bulletin of the World Health Organization*, Vol. 83, No. 3, pp. 171-177.

Miilunpalo, S., I. Vuori, P. Oja, M. Pasanen and H. Urponen (1997), "Self-rated Health Status as a Health Measure: The Predictive Value of Self-reported Health Status on the Use of Physician Services and on Mortality in the Working-age Population", *Journal of Clinical Epidemiology*, Vol. 50, pp. 90-93.

NCHS (National Center for Health Statistics) (2011), *Health, United States, 2010: With Special Feature on Death and Dying*, NCHS, Hyattsville, MD.

OECD (2009), *Health at a Glance 2009, OECD Indicators*, OECD Publishing, Paris.

OECD (2010a), *OECD Health Data 2010, Statistics and Indicators*, online and on CD-ROM, OECD Publishing, Paris.

OECD (2010b), *Health Care Systems: Efficiency and Policy Settings*, OECD Publishing, Paris.

OECD (2010c), *Improving Value in Health Care: Measuring Quality*, OECD Health Policy Studies, OECD Publishing, Paris.

OECD (2010d), *Health at a Glance: Asia/Pacific 2010*, OECD Publishing, Paris.

Popov, V. (2011), "Mortality Crisis in Russia Revisited: Evidence From Cross-Regional Comparison", CEFIR/NES Working Paper No. 157, Centre for Economic and Financial Research at New Economic School, Moscow.

Sassi, F. (2010), *Obesity and the Economics of Prevention: Fit Not Fat*, OECD Publishing, Paris.

United Nations (2011), Washington Group on Disability Statistics, unstats.un.org/unsd/methods/citygroup/washington.htm, Accessed 8 March 2011.

U.S. Department of Health and Human Services (2006), Healthy People 2010 Midcourse Review, U.S. Government Printing Office, Washington, D.C.

World Health Organization (1948), "Constitution of the World Health Organization", Geneva, apps.who.int/gb/bd/PDF/bd47/EN/constitution-en.pdf

Chapter 6

Work and life balance

The ability to combine work, family commitments and personal life is important for the well-being of all household members. It is also important for society as a whole, as it ensures that people have sufficient time to socialise and participate in the life of the community. This chapter presents a selection of indicators that describe the distribution of people's time between paid work, time with family, commuting, leisure and personal care. The balance of work and non-work activities has changed considerably in recent decades, with overall gains in leisure and reductions in hours worked. However, these trends conceal the increased complexity of people's lives, with both men and women taking on a wider variety of tasks in the workplace and at home. The distribution of tasks within the family is still influenced by gender roles: men are more likely to work longer hours of paid work, while women spend longer hours in unpaid domestic work. While gender imbalances are shaped by culture, policy makers can help to address the issue by encouraging supportive and flexible working practices, thereby making it easier for parents to strike a better balance between work and home life.

Why does work-life balance matter for well-being?

Young or old, rich or poor, one thing that every person has in common is the number of hours they have in a day. The way those 24 hours are divided between different activities is a key determinant of well-being. The work-life balance refers to "a state of equilibrium between an individual's work and personal life".[1] Obtaining such a balance is central to people's well-being: too little work can prevent people from earning enough income to attain desired standards of living, and may reduce their sense of purpose in life; but too much work can also have a negative impact on people's well-being if their health or personal lives suffer as a consequence.

An individual's ability to satisfactorily combine work, family commitments and personal life is important not only for the well-being of the person but also for that of the whole household. In particular, the well-being of children is strongly affected by the capacity of parents to both work and spend an adequate amount of time with them. Parental nurturing is crucial for child development, especially in the early years and prime age adults (typically women) also play a critical (and increasingly important) role for the care of their elderly parents. A balanced allocation of time between work and personal life is also important at a society-wide level, as it ensures that people have sufficient time to socialise and participate in the life of the community.

Measuring work and life balance requires looking at various objective and subjective dimensions, and identifying areas of possible conflicts between different activities that people want or have to perform in their daily lives. However, only a few surveys measure conflicts between work, family and other areas of personal life as perceived by people, and these surveys have a very uneven geographic and time coverage. Developing better measures of work-life balance is important from a policy perspective, as working conditions, the provision of childcare facilities and various other family policies strongly affect people's capacity to reconcile work and life (OECD, 2011b).

Measuring work and life balance

Measuring work-life balance is challenging. Firstly, because the cut-off point between "too much" and "too little" will differ depending on each person's preferences, priorities and household circumstances. For instance, two persons working the same number of hours may experience very different levels of well-being depending on how much they enjoy their job or whether or not they have children to raise; similarly, it also matters whether these two people are free to choose their time use allocation or instead are constrained from doing so. Second, besides the objective allocation of time across various activities and its determinants, it is important to look at whether people experience a "time crunch" – i.e. the stressful feeling that there simply is not enough time in the day to get everything done. While this is a subjective perception, and people with very different schedules may in fact share the same time crunch, its consideration matters for assessing well-being. Hence, an ideal set of indicators for work-life balance would include indicators that measure the occurrence of objective conflicts between daily activities, people's personal enjoyment of these activities, and their perceived time stress.

The majority of available indicators on work-life balance come from time use surveys. These surveys give a detailed picture of how people spend their time in different activities. Data from these surveys highlight the extent or degree to which individuals can balance their work and personal lives. One limitation of time use surveys, however, is that they neither record whether people enjoy these activities, nor whether they are free to choose how they organise their time. Similarly, these surveys do not allow for an assessment of whether people feel overwhelmed, under pressure, or relaxed about their schedule. The very few international surveys containing the latter type of information cover a small number of countries and are often one-off in nature. Some of their findings are included in this chapter for illustrative purposes, but they will need to be developed and improved significantly before becoming a regular and trustworthy instrument for monitoring well-being. Finally, because women with children typically face different challenges than men in reconciling their work and personal life (Hill, 2005), the chapter considers one indicator that focuses only on women and which provides an indirect proxy of their ability to reconcile family and work. Table 6.1 assesses the quality of the indicators used in this chapter.

Selected indicators

Long working hours (WL I)

Paid work is an essential part of life for many people. While longer working hours do not necessarily negatively impact well-being (*e.g.* if the worker gains a high degree of job satisfaction from the time spent at work), there is evidence to suggest that very long working hours can impair personal health, jeopardise safety and increase stress (Spurgeon *et al.*, 1997). The indicator used here refers to the proportion of employees usually working long hours on their main job; the self-employed are excluded, as many of them are likely to regularly work much longer hours than other workers out of a deliberate choice.[2] This indicator is based on data from Labour Force Surveys; it is thus broadly comparable across OECD countries and of high quality.

Choosing a threshold for long working hours is to some extent arbitrary. Here the threshold has been set at 50 hours usually worked per week for several reasons. First, when considering the amount of time that each person devotes to commuting, to unpaid work and to satisfy their basic needs (such as sleeping and eating), workers usually working more than 50 hours per week are likely to be left with only very few hours for other activities (one or two hours per day). Second, in countries where there is a regulation on maximum working time, this is generally limited to 48 hours per week.

Time for leisure and personal care (WL II)

Leisure and personal care are both essential for individuals' physical and mental well-being. Leisure activities such as socialising and watching TV, as well as personal care activities such as eating and sleeping, tend to bring more intrinsic enjoyment than activities related to paid and unpaid work (Krueger *et al.*, 2009). Furthermore, having time to rest and recuperate away from work is important for health, productivity and stress reduction. Since the perspective of this chapter is that of work-life balance, the population group chosen for expressing this indicator is that of all workers (including both employees and self-employed).

The boundary between leisure and personal care can sometimes be blurry. Leisure generally includes activities that people choose to do for their own pleasure, such as seeing friends, going to the cinema, playing sports and pursuing hobbies. Personal care tends to include necessities such as sleeping, eating, hygiene and grooming, as well as time needed for other personal, medical and household services. However, many personal care activities can also be undertaken for pleasure rather than necessity. Because the distinction between personal care and leisure is not always well-defined, and because both matter to individual well-being, the indicator used here refers to the amount of time that full-time workers devote to the sum of these two activities.

Data on time spent in leisure and personal care come from national time use surveys (Box 6.1). For some countries and some very specific items of time allocation, the comparability of these surveys may be an issue; the data shown here have, however, been harmonised *ex post* by the OECD and are deemed to be broadly comparable. Time use surveys are not available for all OECD countries, however, and are typically carried out with a very low frequency.

Box 6.1. **Time use surveys: some methodological issues**

Over 60 countries around the world collect time use data, providing a rich source of critical information on work-life balance. However, a range of methodological issues provide a challenge for international comparisons. Data on time use are collected through the use of diaries, where respondents record their activities during short (around 10 minute) intervals for a continuous period of 24 hours (or 1440 minutes). Respondents use their own words to describe their activities, either by writing their own diaries, or by verbally reporting their activities by telephone, which are then re-coded according to the country's classification system. The level of detail in the classification system used varies widely between countries, from around 400 items in Austria and the United States, to only 21 in Hungary. This implies that, in order to harmonise national data, important information may be lost. The most detailed surveys tend to collect information on:

- Simultaneous activities. For example, cooking a meal while looking after the children, or eating while watching TV. However, not all surveys collect data on secondary activities.

- Purpose of activity. For example, rather than "travel", most surveys will distinguish between travel for work and travel for leisure. This level of detail is especially important in determining work-life balance issues.

- With whom the activity was performed. It can be interesting to know whether an activity is being undertaken alone or with others, and if so, with whom. However, not all surveys collect this information.

National Time Use surveys also differ in regard to other methodological issues, such as sample design and the period over which the survey is conducted. Most countries spread the data collection over an entire year, although some cover shorter periods, which may not give as accurate a picture of time use patterns in a typical day. In Europe, Eurostat has developed guidelines on "Harmonised European Time Use surveys" (HETUS), giving recommendations on sample design, data collection and coding issues. However, the time use data of European member states are still not fully comparable. The United Nations Statistics Division (UNSD) has also published classification guidelines for time use statistics, which are, however, mainly geared to less-developed countries.

National time use surveys are usually conducted around once every 10 years, but with higher frequency in some countries (*e.g.* every year in the United States). In order to improve the timeliness of data, some countries are experimenting with "light" versions of a time-diary to be conducted at more frequent intervals.

Source : UNECE, 2010; Miranda, 2011.

Commuting time (wl 1)

For people with jobs outside of the home, travel to and from the workplace can significantly extend the working day and eat into leisure and family time. Furthermore, commuting does not just take up time; it can also be stressful, tiring and expensive. Indeed, it seems that commuting to work is the daily activity that gives the least amount of enjoyment, with commuting home from work only marginally more enjoyable (Krueger et al., 2009).[3] It is unsurprising therefore that people with longer commuting times tend to report lower subjective well-being (Stutzer and Frey, 2008). Since commuting is detrimental to well-being on many accounts, it is included here as a secondary indicator. This indicator refers to the number of minutes spent commuting on a typical day by all workers. The indicator is also based on time use surveys and thus shares the same limitations of the previous indicator.

Satisfaction with allocation of time (wl 2)

As a proxy of the capacity to reconcile work and life, as perceived by individuals, the chapter presents an indicator on people's satisfaction with their time balance, which is suggestive of the time crunches experienced by individuals. This indicator relies on the question: "Could you tell me if you think you spend too much, too little or just about the right amount of time" in four areas: i) my job/paid work; ii) contact with family members living in this household or elsewhere; iii) other social contact (not family); iv) own hobbies/interests.[4] The results are shown as the percentage of people replying "just the right amount of time" in various areas. The data are collected through the European Quality of Life Survey. The main limitations of this survey are that the sample is small, the responses can be affected by cultural factors, and the results are available for European countries only.[5] For these reasons, this indicator is included in the analysis as a secondary indicator.

Employment rate of mothers with children of compulsory school age (WL III)

Women are more likely than men to be prevented from entering the workforce because of family commitments. The employment rate of mothers with children of compulsory school age is an indirect measure of the ability of mothers to combine paid work and family responsibilities. When children are very young, many mothers may prefer to be with them, as this is a critical period for child development. However, as children attain school age, many mothers may wish to return (or enter) the labour market but be hindered from doing so by many factors, such as inflexible school schedules that are not necessarily in tune with parents' work commitments. If policies to support work-life balance, such as flexible working time arrangements, are inadequate, mothers may be forced to choose between family and paid work, thereby negatively impacting their employment rates. Comparing employment rates of mothers with school-age children and rates of all women (in the 25-54 age range) hence provides information on the extent of work-life imbalances.

The indicator shown here excludes mothers with very young children because these mothers may have a stronger personal preference to stay at home in these early years. This indicator relies on data collected through national Labour Force Surveys. Its statistical quality is therefore high. Table 6.1 gives an overview of the quality and relevance of the indicators chosen.

Table 6.1. **The quality of work-life balance indicators**

		INDICATORS							
	Target concept	Relevance to measure and monitor well-being				Statistical quality			
		Face validity	Unambiguous interpretation (good/bad)	Policies amenable outcome	Can be disaggregated	Well-established instrument collected	Comparable definition	Country coverage	Recurrent data collection
Work-Life Balance									
WL I Employees working more than 50 hours per week	Work-life time balance	√	√	√	√	√	√	√	√
WL II Time in leisure and personal care		√	√	~	~	√	~	~	~
wl 1 Commuting time		√	√	~	~	√	~	~	~
wl 2 Satisfaction with work-life time allocation	Satisfaction with work-life time balance	√	√	~	√	~	√	~	~
WL III Employment rate of mothers with school-age children	Ability to reconcile family and work	~	√	√	~	√	√	√	√

Note. The symbol √ shows that the indicator selected largely meets the criterion shown in the table; the symbol ~ that the indicator meets the criterion to a large extent; the symbol x that the indicator does not meet the criterion or it meets it only to a limited extent.

Average patterns

Only a small proportion of employees work excessively long hours in most countries

While the proportion of employees regularly working over 40 hours a week is significant (the greatest incidence of working hours being in the band 35-44 hours), the share of those working more than 50 hours is not very large (Figure 6.1). Turkey is by far the country with the highest proportion of people working very long hours, with almost half of all employees regularly working over 50 hours a week, followed by Mexico and Israel with a fifth of employees. In Australia, New Zealand, the United Kingdom and the United States over 1 in 10 employees regularly work 50-plus hours per week. At the other end of the scale, in the Netherlands, Sweden, the Russian Federation and Denmark, very long working hours are rare, with only around 1-2% of employees working over 50 hours on a regular basis. Unfortunately, employee-only data on usual working hours are not available for Japan and Korea – two countries with very high annual and weekly working hours for all workers.

In around half of the countries for which data are available, there has been relatively little change since 1995 in the proportion of employees working very long hours. However, Belgium, Italy, Germany, Spain, France, Austria and Turkey have all seen an increase. On the other hand, Denmark, Estonia, Hungary, Ireland, Canada, Portugal, the Slovakian Republic, the United States, the United Kingdom, New Zealand, Australia and Mexico have all seen a reduction in the proportion of employees working very long hours. In Ireland and Canada, this proportion more than halved. However, some caution is needed when interpreting these trends, as they may partly reflect the strong negative impact of the financial crisis on the number of hours worked. Box 6.2 gives an overview of some determinants of long working hours.

Figure 6.1. **Employees usually working very long hours**

Percentage of employees working 50 hours or more per week

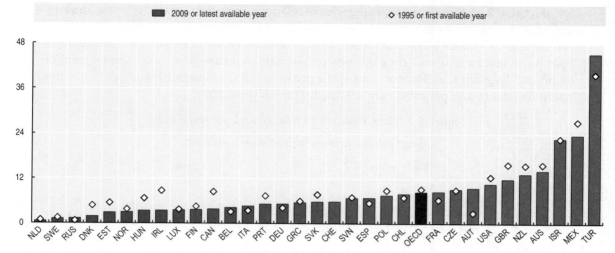

Note: Data refer to employees usually working 50 hours or more per week, except for the Russian Federation for which data refer to people who worked 51 hours and more. Jobs covered are the main job for Austria, Canada, the Czech Republic, Finland, Hungary, Mexico, Poland, the Slovak Republic, Sweden, Turkey and the United States; and all jobs for Australia, Iceland, New Zealand and Norway. The latest available year is 2007 for Israel and the Netherlands; and 2008 for Chile and the Russian Federation. The first available year is 1996 for Chile; 1998 for Hungary; 2001 for Austria; 2002 for Estonia, Norway, Poland, Slovenia and Sweden; and 2004 for the Czech Republic and Finland. There is a break in the series in 1998/1999 for Belgium, in 2002/2003 for France and in 2004 for Austria as a continuous survey has been introduced. In the case of Austria, employees whose working time varies considerably are not included from 2004. Starting from 2002 the number of hours worked excludes the main meal breaks for the Slovak Republic.

Sources: OECD Labour Force Statistics database; and Swiss Federal Statistical Office.

StatLink ᴍ🔍ᴘ *http://dx.doi.org/10.1787/888932494050*

Box 6.2. **Main determinants of working hours**

Working long hours on a regular basis reduces the amount of time for leisure and personal care, can lead to stress and health problems and can negatively affect family relations (Ganster and Schaubroeck, 1991; Major *et al.*, 2002). So, why do people choose to allocate more time to paid work than to leisure or family? Higher income is a principal reason. Men tend to increase their working hours after marriage and children (whereas women tend to decrease their working hours) so as to assure a sufficient income for the whole household. Some people are obliged to take on multiple jobs, or work overtime just in order to meet higher household needs. Beyond the necessity to meet basic needs, the desire to improve material living standards and emulate the better-off can also be important factors in increased work hours. This is suggested by the fact that working hours tend to be longer in countries with high levels of income inequality (Bowles and Park, 2005). Longer hours can also be encouraged by the prevailing culture and norms within an organisation or across a whole society.

Policy can have an important impact on working hours. For example, regulations limiting working time, such as the "European Union Working Time Directive", have a direct impact on hours worked.[6] Legal entitlements to paid vacation, sick leave and maternity and paternity leave are also important. Finally, taxation policy shapes financial incentives for working longer hours. High marginal taxes tend to lower the hours worked, especially for second earners (OECD, 2008). For example, whereas Europeans work around 38 hours per week and take around 4 weeks of paid leave per year, US employees typically work an additional 3 hours (at 41 hours per week) on average and have only 2 weeks of annual leave.

In OECD countries, workers spend just under 15 hours per day on leisure and personal care

Figure 6.2 presents the two categories of leisure and personal care together, ranking countries by the combined total.[7] Across the OECD, on average, workers spend 4.3 hours on leisure and 10.5 hours on personal care, with a combined total of 14.8 hours. The Japanese spend the least amount of time on leisure and personal care, with a combined total of 14 hours.[8] Belgium and Denmark are at the other end of the scale with around 15.8 hours spent on leisure and personal care (OECD, 2011a; Miranda, 2011).

Figure 6.2. **Time devoted to leisure and personal care**

Hours per day, persons in full-time employment

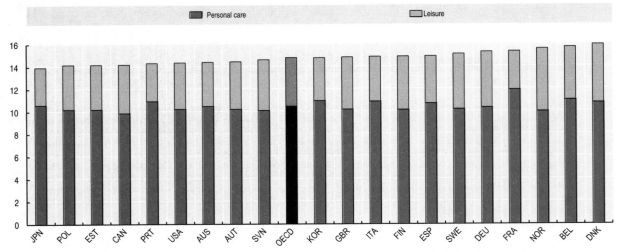

Note: Data refer to 1998-99 for France; 1999 for Portugal; 1999-2000 for Estonia and Finland; 2000-01 for Norway, Slovenia, Sweden, and the United Kingdom; 2001 for Denmark; 2001-02 for Germany; 2002-03 for Italy and Spain; 2003-4 for Poland; 2005 for Belgium and Canada; 2006 for Japan; 2008 for the United States; 2008-09 for Austria; and 2009 for Korea. Data have been normalised to 1440 minutes per day: in other words, for those countries for which the time use did not sum up to 1440 minutes, the missing or extra minutes (around 30-40 minutes usually) were equally distributed across all activities. Data for Hungary, Ireland, Portugal, Turkey and South Africa were excluded as they also include part-time employed. Data generally refer to people aged 15 and more, except for Austria, for which no age limit is defined.
Source: OECD Time Use Survey database.

StatLink ⟐ *http://dx.doi.org/10.1787/888932492644*

In all countries, a larger share of time is spent on personal care than on leisure. This is not surprising, as sleeping and eating alone tend to take up around 8 hours and 1-2 hours per day, respectively (OECD, 2009). Canadian and Norwegian full-time workers spend the least time on personal care at around 10 hours per day, whereas French workers spend the most time, at over 12 hours per day. However, French workers, alongside Portuguese and Japanese workers, spend the least time on leisure, at only 3.4 hours per day. Turkish, Korean and Australian workers also devote relatively low amounts of time to leisure, at around 3.8 hours per day, as compared to over 5 hours in Norway and Denmark.[9] Changes in time use and leisure in the last half-century are discussed in Box 6.3.

Box 6.3. **Trends in time use in the last half-century**

In the last half-century, patterns of work-life balance have changed significantly in all OECD countries. Overall, there has been a general decline in annual hours worked per worker, from around 2100 hours in 1960 on average across the OECD, down to below 1600 hours in 2005. A significant part of this decline has reflected an increase in the share of workers working part-time. Over the same period, time spent in leisure and personal care also increased. In the United States, between 1965 and 2003, weekly leisure time increased by over 5 hours per person and weekly personal time increased by approximately 30 minutes per person (Aguiar and Hurst, 2006). These changes have largely been driven by increases in paid annual leave and by improvements in household technology, meaning that time previously spent on housework and cooking is freed up for leisure.

Patterns in time use over the life course have also changed. As people live longer, and in some countries, retire at earlier ages, the proportion of time devoted to paid work in a lifetime has decreased. A study of time use patterns among older adults in the United States, the United Kingdom and the Netherlands from the 1960s to the 1990s showed that while older women's time in paid work has increased, older men have reallocated time previously spent in paid work to housework, leisure (especially passive activities such as watching TV and reading), sports and fitness, and recreational travel, while time devoted to volunteering has remained broadly stable (Gauthier and Smeeding, 2010). As many countries are now actively pursuing policies to delay the age of retirement, these patterns may well be set to change in the coming decades.

One of the most striking changes in time use in the past five decades is the rise in the amount of time that women devote to paid work. Up until the second half of the twentieth century, the roles of married men and women tended to be clearly defined: men went out to earn a wage while women stayed at home to care for children and elderly relatives, as well as to take care of cooking, cleaning and other unpaid household tasks. This gender-based division of labour between paid and unpaid work – known as the "male breadwinner model" – has become increasingly outmoded, as reflected in the dramatic rise in the share of women who hold a paid job. For example, European employment rates for prime-aged women (aged 25-54) rose from an average of 11% in the early 1960s to over 70% in 2009, with this rate well over 80% in several countries including Austria, Canada, Denmark, Finland, France, the Netherlands, Slovenia and Sweden. There are a number of cultural, economic and technological reasons for this change, not least the increase in positive social attitudes towards women working after marriage and after motherhood. In a 2009 Eurobarometer survey, 81% of European respondents agreed with the statement that "it is indispensable for a woman to have her own pay" (EC, 2010a).

In OECD countries workers spend on average 38 minutes per day commuting

Figure 6.3 shows the average amount of time spent travelling to and from paid work by full-time workers. On average, across the OECD countries included in the analysis, workers spend 38 minutes per day commuting. Workers in the United Kingdom, Spain, Italy, Japan, Turkey, Korea and South Africa have relatively lengthy commutes, with 40 minutes or more per day being taken up with travel to and from work, on average. Ireland, Denmark, Sweden, the United States and Finland, on the other hand, have relatively low commuting averages, at below 30 minutes.

Figure 6.3. **Commuting time**

Minutes per day, persons in full-time employment

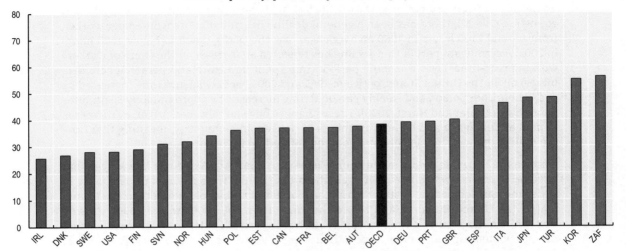

Note: Data refer to 1998-99 for France; 1999 for Portugal and India; 1999-2000 for Estonia, Finland and Hungary; 2000 for South Africa; 2000-01 for Norway, Slovenia, Sweden, United Kingdom; 2001 for Denmark; 2001-02 for Germany; 2002-03 for Italy and Spain; 2003-4 for Poland; 2005 for Belgium, Canada and Ireland; 2006 for Japan and Turkey; 2008 for United States; 2008-09 for Austria; and 2009 for Korea. Data have been normalised to 1440 minutes per day: in other words, for those countries for which the time use did not sum up to 1440 minutes, the missing or extra minutes (around 30-40 minutes usually) were equally distributed/subtracted across all activities. Employed refers to full-time employed except for Hungary, Ireland, Portugal, Turkey and South Africa, for which they refer to all employed (e.g, part-time employed are included). Data refer to people aged 15 or more, except for Austria, where no limit of age is defined, and for Hungary (people aged 15-74 are considered).
Source: OECD Time Use Survey database.

StatLink ⧉ *http://dx.doi.org/10.1787/888932492663*

In European countries, over three-quarters of workers are not satisfied with some aspect of their work-life balance

To assess to what extent people are satisfied with their work-life balance, an indicator available only for European countries is included here (Figure 6.4). It is based on questions asking whether respondents are satisfied with the amount of time spent in four areas: family, social contact, paid work and hobbies. Fewer than 25% of European workers responded that they felt the amount of time they spent in each of the four areas was "just right", varying from a low of 13% in Norway to a high of 34% in Germany. In general, the perceived imbalance mainly affects people's feeling that they spend too much time in paid work and not enough in the other three areas. However, this is not always the case. For example, in Greece, 12% of workers feel that they spend too much time with family. In Austria, 7% of workers feel that they spend too little time in work.

Figure 6.4. **European workers satisfied with their work-life time balance**

Percentage, 2007

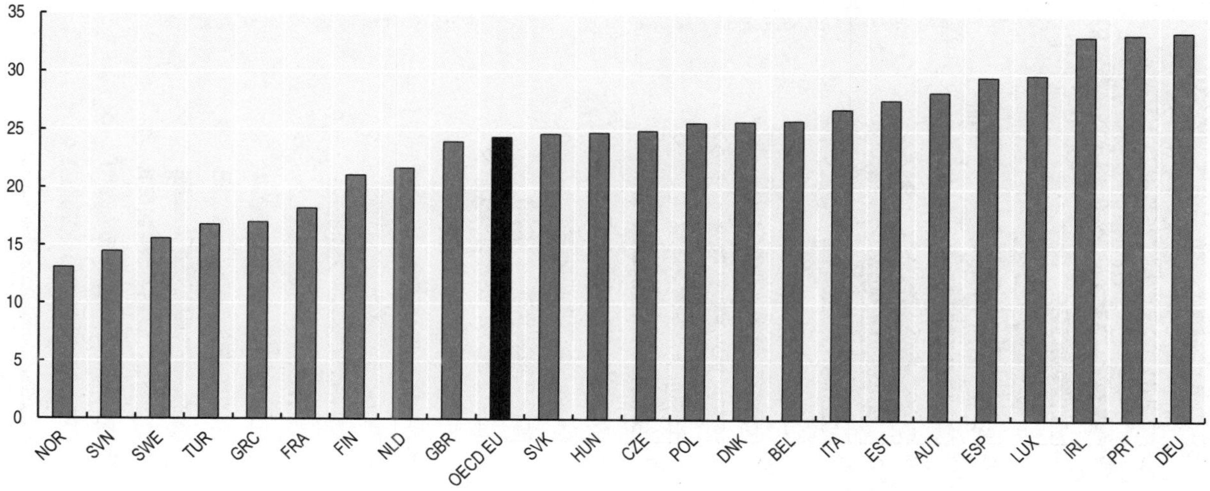

Note: The figure shows the proportion of people feeling that they spend "just the right amount" of time in each of the following areas: job/paid work; contact with family members living in this household or elsewhere; other social contact (not family); and own hobbies/interests.
Sources: Second European Quality of Life Survey.

StatLink ⟐⟐⟐ http://dx.doi.org/10.1787/888932492682

Two-thirds of women with school-age children work in some capacity

Figure 6.5 shows the employment rate for women with children of compulsory school age (aged around 6-14 years). On average, across the OECD, 66% of mothers with children of compulsory school age are working in some capacity, compared with an average female (25-54 years) employment rate of 71%. The maternal employment rate varies, however, from a high of just under 87% in Iceland, to a low of 24% in Turkey. Maternal employment of women with children aged 6-14 is also low in Italy, Greece and Ireland.

There are still significant gaps between the desired level and actual level of women's labour force participation, with family responsibilities explaining a large part of these gaps (see Box 6.4 for a discussion of the determinants of maternal employment).

Figure 6.5. **Employment rate of women with children of compulsory school age**

2008 or latest available year

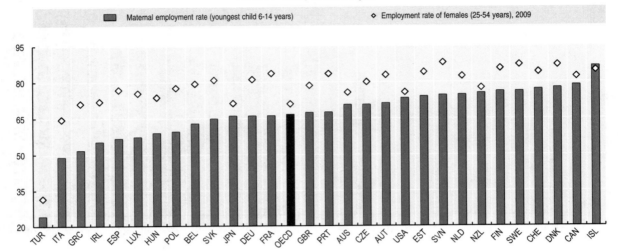

Note: Maternal employment rates refer to mothers with a child aged between 6 and 14 in Australia, Denmark, Iceland, Japan, New Zealand, Sweden, Switzerland and the United States; and to mothers with the youngest child aged 6-15 years in Canada. Data refer to 2010 for Canada; 2007 for Sweden; 2006 for Mexico and Switzerland; 2005 for Australia, Japan, New Zealand and the United States; 2002 for Iceland; and 1999 for Denmark.

Sources: Maternal employment rate: OECD Family Database based on data from European Labour Force Surveys (2007-08) for EU countries, Iceland, Norway and Turkey; Australian Bureau of Statistics for Australia; Labour Force Survey (2010) for Canada; Statistics Denmark for Denmark; Statistics Iceland for Iceland; Japanese national census (2005) for Japan; Encuesta Nacional de la Dinamica Demográfica (2006) for Mexico; Swiss Labour Force Survey (2009) for Switzerland; US Current Population Survey (2005) for the United States. Employment rate of females: OECD Labour Force Survey database.

StatLink ᵐˢᵖ *http://dx.doi.org/10.1787/888932492701*

Box 6.4. **Factors influencing maternal employment rates**

Paid employment of women is an important goal for gender equity, material well-being and poverty reduction, in particular for single mothers and their children. Nonetheless, there are still gaps between actual and desired employment rates for women. One of the main reasons is that, despite changing attitudes to the gender division of paid and unpaid work in the household, women remain primarily responsible for childcare and family responsibilities. A recent OECD study of unpaid work using time use survey data for 21 countries showed that mothers spend more than twice as much time as fathers taking care of children – a pattern seen in all countries (Miranda, 2011). As a consequence, many women find it difficult to combine work and motherhood. In Europe, for example, women are twenty times more likely than men to be prevented from working because of family responsibilities. In addition, more and more women, especially highly-educated women, are delaying having children or foregoing motherhood entirely in order to pursue careers, leading to patterns of declining fertility rates, postponement of childbearing, and an increase in childless households.

Balancing work and life is simply more challenging for women as they have to manage their time across an expanding range of activities. While women represent an increasing share of the labour force, they have also retained the bulk of domestic responsibilities. The increasing complexity of women's lives over the past half-century is a potential source of stress and life dissatisfaction, as evidenced by the fact that, in several countries, women's subjective well-being relative to men has declined since 1970 (Stevenson and Wolfers, 2009). However, patterns of maternal employment are not uniform across countries, and indeed countries with the highest employment rates of women today are also experiencing relatively high fertility rates, suggesting that policies can facilitate the combination of work and family responsibilities (OECD, 2011b). A multitude of factors influence maternal employment including: child-related leave; availability of high-quality and affordable childcare; tax treatment of second earners and childcare subsidies; flexible working arrangements; cultural preferences; and education. The section on inequalities in this chapter looks at the impact of education on the employment of mothers with school-age chlidren.

Source: OECD, 2011b.

Some, but not all, indicators of work-life balance are correlated across countries

Work-life balance captures a variety of dimensions, and the indicators shown here measure different aspects. Cross-country correlations between the different indicators highlight a number of patterns (Table 6.2):

- There is a strong negative correlation between the indicator on long working hours and the indicator measuring satisfaction with elements of work-life balance. In countries where large proportions of employed people work very long hours, a smaller percentage of people are satisfied with the amount of time they spend at their jobs and with the amount of time available for personal interests and hobbies. However, correlations with the other two dimensions of work-life satisfaction measured here (family and social contact time) are not statistically significant.

- There is a strong positive correlation between commuting time and the proportion of employees working long hours. However, when Turkey is excluded from the analysis, the correlation loses its statistical significance.

- The four sub-indicators measuring satisfaction with time allocation in different areas (paid work, family, social contact and hobbies) are generally weakly correlated, suggesting that it is important to address multiple dimensions of work-life balance rather than focusing on a single area (*e.g.* paid work). There is, however, a strong positive relationship between social contact and family (*i.e.* people who are satisfied with the amount of time they spend socialising also tend to be satisfied with the amount of time spent with family), and between paid work and hobbies (*i.e.* people who are satisfied with the amount of time spent in paid work also tend to feel they spend the right amount of time on personal hobbies).

- There is a strong negative correlation between the proportion of employed people working long hours and the employment rate of women with school-age children. This may reflect the fact that in families where only the father works, they are likely to work longer hours, or that women find it harder to find a job in countries where long work days are more prevalent.

- The employment rate of women with school-age children tends to be lower in countries with longer commuting times. This may be because long commutes reduce the capacity of women to combine work and family schedules and, hence, deter maternal employment.

- Finally, there is a strong positive correlation between the employment rate of women with school-age children and satisfaction with time spent in employment. This suggests that working time conditions are more favourable for all workers in countries where women find it easier to combine family and work, for example, by working part-time.

Table 6.2. **Correlation between different indicators of work-life balance**

		WL I Employees working more than 50 hours per week	WL II Time in leisure and personal care	wl 1 Commuting time	wl 2 Satisfaction with work-life time allocation				WL III Employment rate of mothers with school-age children
					Job	Family	Social contacts	Hobby	
WL I	Employees working more than 50 hours per week	1 (32)	-0.28 (21)	-0.52** (20)	-0.63*** (23)	-0.07 (23)	0.20 (23)	-0.54*** (23)	-0.61*** (27)
WL2	Time in leisure and personal care		1 (24)	-0.20 (23)	0.45 (17)	-0.05 (17)	-0.22 (17)	0.19 (17)	0.07 (21)
wl 1	Commuting time			1 (23)	-0.32 (16)	0.11 (16)	0.40 (16)	-0.24 (16)	-0.59*** (20)
wl 2	Satisfaction with work-life time allocation								
	- Job				1 (23)	0.28 (23)	0.18 (23)	0.65*** (23)	0.51** (21)
	- Family					1 (23)	0.52** (23)	0.28 (23)	-0.18 (21)
	- Social contacts						1 (23)	0.28 (23)	-0.22 (21)
	- Hobby							1 (23)	0.55** (21)
WL III	Employment rate of mothers with school-age children								1 (29)

Note: Values in parenthesis refer to the number of observations. ** Indicates that correlations are significant at the 5% level; *** indicates that they are significant at the 1% level.

Source: OECD's calculations.

StatLink ⟐ http://dx.doi.org/10.1787/888932494088

Inequalities

Gender is a key determinant of inequalities in work-life balance

Overall, men spend longer hours in paid work. Figure 6.6 shows the average usual weekly working hours on the main job for men and women. On average across the OECD, men spend around 5 hours more than women in paid work per week (with men working 40 hours per week compared to 35 hours for women). In Australia, Austria, Iceland, the Netherlands, Switzerland and the United Kingdom, the difference in working hours doubles to around 10 hours more for men. In general, men spend over 50% more time than women commuting to work, with an average of 36 minutes per day, compared with 23 minutes for women.

Figure 6.6. **Hours worked per week on the main job by gender**
Usual working hours, 2009 or latest available year

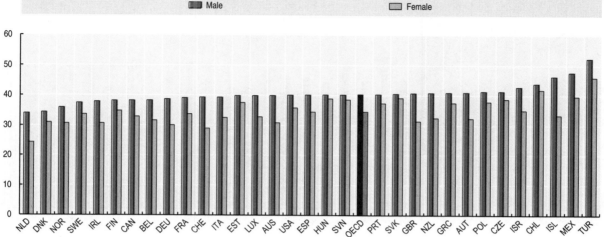

Note: Data refer to 2006 for Canada; 2002 for Iceland; 2004 for Mexico; and 2007 for Israel.
Source: OECD Labour Force Statistics database.

StatLink ⟨⟩ *http://dx.doi.org/10.1787/888932492720*

However, fewer hours in paid work for women do not result in greater leisure time; on the contrary, women tend to have less leisure time than men (Figure 6.7). On average, across the 29 OECD countries presented here, men have around half an hour more leisure time than women per day. While this may not seem like much of a difference, over a year, this adds up to around 180 hours, or the equivalent of an additional four-and-a-half weeks of vacation (assuming a 40-hour work week) for men. The gender difference is greatest in Portugal and Italy, and in India and South Africa, where men have around 1-1.5 hours more for leisure per day.

Women tend to have less leisure time than men because they spend more time in unpaid activities at home (*e.g.* housework, childcare and looking after elderly relatives). Women spend an average of two-and-a-half hours more per day than men in unpaid work across the OECD. Further, the unpaid tasks women perform are sometimes more taxing and less enjoyable than those performed by men. For example, while both men and women participate in childcare, women tend to spend more time in physical routine tasks like changing diapers, feeding and bathing, while men, on the other hand, tend to take on more pleasurable tasks such as reading and playing (OECD, 2011b; Miranda, 2011).

Figure 6.7. **Time devoted to leisure per day, by gender**

Hours per day, persons in full-time employment

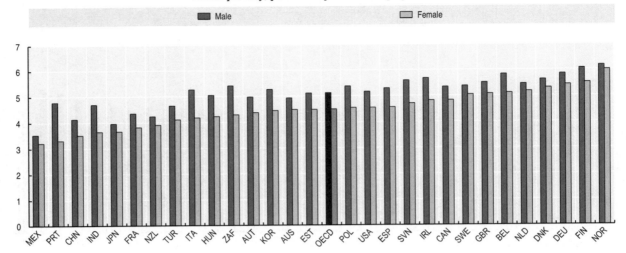

Note: Data refer to 1998-99 for France and New Zealand; 1999 for Portugal and India; 1999-2000 for Estonia, Finland and Hungary; 2000 for South Africa; 2000-01 for Norway, Slovenia, Sweden and the United Kingdom; 2001 for Denmark; 2001-02 for Germany; 2002-03 for Italy and Spain; 2003-4 for Poland; 2005 for Belgium, Canada and Ireland; 2005-06 for the Netherlands; 2006 for Australia, Japan and Turkey; 2008 for the United States and China; 2008-09 for Austria; and 2009 for Korea and Mexico. The indicator refers to people aged 20-59 for Hungary and 30-59 for Korea. Data have been normalised to 1440 minutes per day: in other words, for those countries for which the time use did not sum up to 1440 minutes, the missing or extra minutes (around 30-40 minutes usually) were equally distributed across all activities.

Source: OECD Time Use Survey database.

StatLink 🔢 *http://dx.doi.org/10.1787/888932492739*

Income and education influence longer working hours, but their effect differs across countries

Socio-economic factors such as income and educational attainment also impact work-life balance, although patterns vary across countries. A study examining the "time crunch" by income level for two-earner parent couples in Canada, Germany, Sweden, the United Kingdom and the United States showed that there is a general tendency for working hours to increase as income increases (Burton and Phipps, 2007). For example, in the United Kingdom, 31% of working-parent couples in the top income decile worked a combined total of over 90 hours per week in 2007, compared to fewer than 7% in the bottom decile.[10] The other countries showed similar patterns, with the exception of Sweden, where very long working hours were low across the board and especially among the poor.

The working hours of both men and women also tend to increase by level of education. In the United States, the gap in average weekly working hours between highly-educated men and less-educated men is about 3.7 hours, which is nearly as large as the difference in working hours between highly-educated men and highly-educated women (Frase and Gornick, 2009).[11]

Similar patterns of working hours that increase along with educational level can be seen in Austria, Belgium, France, Germany, the Netherlands, Luxembourg and Switzerland. However, the reverse is the case (*i.e.* the less-educated work longer hours) in Mexico, Hungary, the Russian Federation, Greece and Italy. Finally, in Ireland, Spain and Israel the relation between usual working hours and education differs between men and women, with hours of paid work increasing with education for women, but decreasing for men (Frase and Gornick, 2009).

Education also impacts maternal employment in European countries: better-educated mothers are more likely to work

Figure 6.8 shows the employment rate for women with school-age children (6-11 years of age) in selected European countries by level of educational attainment. Women who have school children and who have achieved tertiary education are much more likely to work than those with at most upper secondary education who, in turn, are more likely to have a job than those with less than upper secondary education. On average, across the European countries, only 50% of mothers of school-age children with less than upper secondary education are employed, compared to 73% of those with upper secondary and 87% of those with tertiary education. Better-educated women are also more likely to be better paid, and therefore to be more able to afford childcare or housekeeping services.

Figure 6.8. Employment rate of women with school-age children, by level of educational attainment

2009

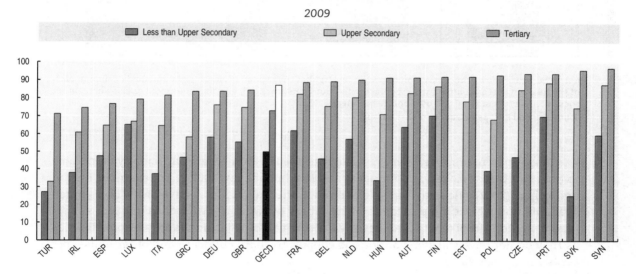

Note: Data on women with less than upper secondary education are not available for Estonia. The data refer to children aged 6-11.
Source: Eurostat, European Labour Force Surveys.

StatLink ᘎᓀᔲᓀ *http://dx.doi.org/10.1787/888932492758*

Parents are more likely to experience a time crunch, with sole parents being particularly vulnerable

Parenthood is probably the single factor that has the most direct impact on work-life balance. Data available for European countries show that while people without children can also have difficulties reconciling work demands and personal life, parents are more likely to experience a "time crunch" (Figure 6.9). While 29% of childless men and 28% of childless women are satisfied with their "time balance", this share drops as the number of children increases, especially for women: for example, only 20% of women with three or more children are satisfied with their time balance.

Figure 6.9. **In Europe, workers' satisfaction with work-life time balance decreases with the number of children living at home**

Percentage of workers, 2007

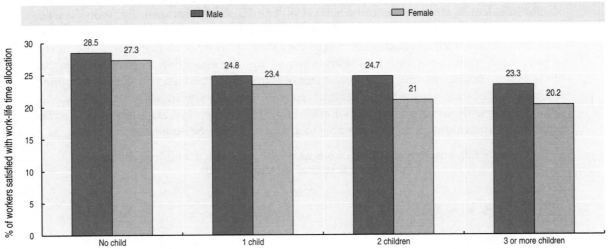

Note: The figure shows the proportion of people feeling that they spend "just the right amount" of time in each of the following areas: job/paid work; contact with family members living in this household or elsewhere; other social contact (not family); and own hobbies/interests.
Source: Second European Quality of Life Survey.

StatLink ⬛🖘 *http://dx.doi.org/10.1787/888932492777*

Single-parent families, overwhelmingly headed by women, are particularly vulnerable to time shortages (Vickery, 1977; Harvey and Mukhopadhyay, 2007).[12] For example, Burton and Phipps (2007) calculate that sole parents in the United States have only 71% as much available non-work time per capita as members of two-parent families. Indeed, single-parent workers are likely to find it even harder to combine job and family responsibilities as they do not have the same options as couples to share childcare and other household tasks when necessary.

The statistical agenda ahead

Measuring the amount of time that people devote to the various activities that make up their work and life, and how these contribute to well-being, is a complex endeavour. Time provides a meaningful metric to compare experiences across different domains, and time use surveys are a critical tool for obtaining a comprehensive picture of people's lives. However, national time use surveys are rarely administered on a regular basis, and the definitions and methodologies differ between countries, hampering data comparability.

To improve statistical measurement in this domain, initiatives should be taken in the following fields:

- Efforts need to be made to harmonise time use measurement across countries, developing consistent methodologies and classifications for more internationally comparable data. These surveys should also be implemented at adequate frequency and over a full year, and should collect enough background information on respondents to analyse inequalities in time use among different demographic and socio-economic groups.[13]

- Time use surveys should also capture both the quantity and the quality of time spent in different activities. Activities can bring varying levels of enjoyment, depending on personal preferences and circumstances. Some OECD countries (France, the United States) have recently implemented specific modules or introduced special questions in their national time use surveys to elicit such evaluations from respondents (see Chapter 12 on subjective well-being). Other countries should consider extending such experiences based on approaches that would allow valid cross-country comparisons.

- Finally, it is also important to develop common questions to measure the time crunch experienced by individuals in general household surveys. For instance, the European Quality of Life Survey contains a menu of questions that widens the scope of work–life balance to include not only working time but also other aspects of work that might cause stress or tiredness and thus affect family life.[14] Such surveys can shed light not only on the impact of work on private life but also on the impact of family responsibilities on work. It would be important that questions of this type are regularly included in large sample surveys, covering all OECD countries through a harmonised questionnaire.

Developing and coordinating comprehensive and comparable measurement tools on the balance of work and life will require a great deal of investment by statistical agencies. However, this is an essential area for research on the quality of life, and one where there is currently wide scope for greater harmonisation and more consistent methodologies.

Conclusion

The balance of work and non-work activities has changed considerably in recent decades, with overall gains in leisure and overall reductions in hours worked. These broad trends however, conceal an increased complexity in our lives, with both men and women taking on a wider variety of tasks in the workplace and at home. The distribution of tasks within a family is still influenced by gender: men are more likely to work longer hours of paid work, while women spend longer hours in unpaid domestic work. While gender imbalances are to a large extent shaped by culture, policy makers can help to address the issue by encouraging supportive and flexible working practices, and thereby making it easier for parents to strike a better balance between work and home life.

Notes

1. Definition of the European Foundation for the Improvement of Living and Working Conditions (http://www.eurofound.europa.eu).

2. For example, in the European Union, 42% of self-employed workers regularly work over 48 hours per week (Eurofound, 2010).

3. Of course, the level of enjoyment can vary depending on the mode of transport. More active modes of travel such as walking and cycling tend to be more enjoyable than driving, which itself is more pleasurable than taking public transport (Turcotte, 2005; Páez and Whalen, 2010).

4. The European Quality of Life Survey also asks the question in a fifth area related to participation in voluntary work or political activities. While civic engagement is an important part of societal well-being, these data are not included here, in order to focus on more obvious areas of work-life conflict.

5. Similar, but non-comparable, questions on time crunches are also available for some non-European countries, as in the case of the General Social Survey regularly undertaken by Statistics Canada.

6. The EU Working Time Directive limits working time to no more than 48 hours per week on average, including overtime. It also creates the right for EU workers to a minimum number of holidays each year, paid breaks, and rest of at least 11 hours in any 24 hours of work, while restricting excessive night work.

7. In the time-use survey data used here, "leisure" refers to: sports activities; participating in and attending events; visiting or entertaining friends; watching TV or listening to radio at home; and other leisure activities. "Personal care" refers to: sleeping; eating and drinking; personal, household and medical services; and travel related to personal care.

8. Data for workers only are not available for Mexico; however, when looking at the population as a whole, Mexico is the country with the lowest combined personal care and leisure time.

9. Such differences may partly depend on different interpretations of what constitutes leisure and personal care between countries. One way of dealing with this is by taking a broader calculation of leisure, which includes any time devoted to personal care above a required minimum. The required minimum can be taken to be the lowest country rate (in this case, Canada at 10.1 hours); any personal care time above the lowest country rate is then added to leisure time to provide a "broad" leisure calculation. Using this broader definition of leisure raises the OECD average from 4.7 hours per day, for the narrower definition, to 5.5 hours per day. While this measure does not change the ranking of countries from the combined personal care and leisure measure, it does potentially give a more accurate picture of the time taken up by leisure in each country. (OECD, 2009)

10. While such findings may indicate that time stress is just a problem of the wealthy (Hamermesh and Lee, 2007), there is evidence to suggest that perceived levels of work-life conflict are higher in families where money is an issue (Duxbury and Higgins, 2001). Low-income families can face different types of stress, such as working irregular and unpredictable hours (Roy et al., 2005), and they are less able to purchase market services (*e.g.* childcare) which can alleviate work-life conflict.

11. Highly-educated workers are those with university/college or specialised vocational training, and low-educated workers with less than secondary education.

12. Only 12% of single-parent families in the OECD are headed by a man (OECD, 2011b).

13. An international task force under the aegis of the United Nations Economic Commission for Europe has been recently established to further the harmonisation of National Time Use surveys. See the Terms of Reference at: http://www.unece.org/stats/documents/ece/ces/bur/2010/2add.2-Terms%20of%20Reference_Time%20Use%20survey%20approved.pdf

14. The questions ask: how often the respondent has come home from work too tired to do some of the household jobs which need to be done?; how often has it been difficult for the respondent to fulfil family responsibilities because of the amount of time spent on the job?; and how often have they found it difficult to concentrate at work because of family responsibilities?

References

Aguiar, M. and E. Hurst (2006), "Measuring Trends in Leisure: The Allocation of Leisure Time over Five Decades", Federal Reserve Bank of Boston Working Papers.

Bowles, S. and Y. Park (2005), "Emulation, Inequality and Work Hours: Was Thorsten Veblen Right?", *The Economic Journal*, 115, pp. 397-412.

Burton, P. and S. Phipps (2007), "Families, Time and Money in Canada, Germany, Sweden, the United Kingdom and the United States", *Review of Income and Wealth*, Vol. 53, No. 3, pp. 460-483.

Duxbury, L. and C. Higgins (2001) "Work-Life Balance in the New Millennium: Where are we? Where do we need to go?" *Canadian Policy Research Networks Paper* No. 7314, Ottawa.

European Commission (2010a), *Gender Equality in the EU in 2009*, Special Eurobarometer 326, Brussels.

European Commission (2010b), *Report on Equality Between Women and Men 2010*, Brussels.

Eurofond (2010), "Changes over time – First findings from the fifth European Working Conditions Survey", European Foundation for the Improvement of Living and Working Conditions, Dublin. http://www.eurofound.europa.eu/publications/htmlfiles/ef1074.htm

Frase, P. and J. Gornick (2009), "The Time Divide in Cross-National Perspective: The Work Week, Gender and Education in 17 Countries", Luxembourg Income Survey Working Paper Series, No. 526.

Ganster, D. and J. Schaubroeck (1991), "Work Stress and Employee Health", *Journal of Management*, 17, pp. 235-271.

Gauthier, A. and T. Smeeding (2010), "Historical Trends in the Patterns of Time Use of Older Adults", *Ageing in Advanced Industrial States: International Studies in Population*, Vol. 8, No. 5, pp. 289-310.

Hamermesh, D. and J. Lee (2007), "Stressed out on four continents: Time crunch or yuppie kvetch?", *The Review of Economics and Statistics*, Vol. 89, No. 2, pp. 374–383.

Harvey, A. and A. Mukhopadhyay (2007), "When Twenty-Four Hours is Not Enough: Time Poverty of Working Parents", *Social Indicators Research*, 82, pp. 57-77.

Hill, J. (2005), "Work-Family Facilitation and Conflict, Working Fathers and Mothers, Work-Family Stressors and Support", *Journal of Family Issues*, Vol. 26, No. 6, pp. 793-819.

Krueger, A., D. Kahneman, D. Schkade, N. Schwarz, and A. Stone (2009), "National Time Accounting: The Currency of Life", in A.B. Krueger, ed., *Measuring the Subjective Well-Being of Nations: National Accounts of Time Use and Well-Being*, National Bureau of Economic Research, University of Chicago Press.

Major, V., K. Klein and M. Ehrhart (2002), "Work Time, Work Interference with Family, and Psychological Distress", *Journal of Applied Psychology*, Vol. 87, No. 3, pp. 427-436.

Miranda, V. (2011), "Cooking, Caring and Volunteering: Unpaid Work Around the World", OECD Social, Employment and Migration Working Papers, No. 116, OECD Publishing, Paris.

OECD (2008), *Economic Policy Reforms: Going for Growth 2008*, OECD Publishing, Paris.

OECD (2009), *Society at a Glance 2009: OECD Social Indicators*, OECD Publishing, Paris.

OECD (2011a), *Society at a Glance 2011: OECD Social Indicators*, OECD Publishing, Paris.

OECD (2011b), *Doing Better for Families*, OECD Publishing, Paris.

Páez, A. and K. Whalen, (2010), "Enjoyment of commute: A comparison of different transportation modes", *Transportation Research Part A: Policy and Practice*, Vol. 44, No. 7, pp. 537-549.

Putnam, R. (2000), *Bowling Alone: The Collapse and Revival of American Community*, Touchstone, New York.

Roy, K., C. Tubbs and L. Burton (2005), "Don't Have No Time: Daily Rhythms and the Organization of Time for Low-Income Families", *Family Relations: Interdisciplinary Journal of Applied Family Studies*, Vol. 53, No. 2, pp. 168-178.

Spurgeon, A., J. Harrington and C. Cooper (1997), "Health and safety problems associated with long working hours: A review of the current position", *Occupational and Environmental Medicine*, Vol. 54, No.6, pp. 367-375.

Stevenson, B. and J. Wolfers (2009), "The Paradox of Declining Female Happiness", *American Economic Journal: Economic Policy 2009*, Vol. 1, No. 2, pp. 190-225.

Stutzer, A. and B. Frey (2008), "Stress that Doesn't Pay: The Commuting Paradox", *Scandinavian Journal of Economics*, Vol. 110, No. 2, pp. 339-366.

Turcotte, M. (2005), "Like Commuting? Worker's Perceptions of their Daily Commute", Statistics Canada, Catalogue No. 11-008, Ottawa.

UNECE (2010), "In-Depth Review of Time Use Surveys in Different Countries", paper presented at the Conference of European Statisticians, 23 August, http://www.unece.org/stats/documents/ece/ces/2010/25.e.pdf

Vickery, C. (1977), "The Time Poor: A New Look at Poverty", *The Journal of Human Resources*, Vol. 12, No. 1, pp. 27-48.

Chapter 7

Education and skills

Education and skills have a strong influence on people's well-being. Education opens opportunities for people and brings a wide range of benefits to society, including higher economic growth, stronger social cohesion and less crime. By investing in education, families and governments can reach many economic and social goals at the same time. This chapter considers a few well-established educational indicators that provide a basic picture of both the current educational status of the adult population and selected skills of youth, skills needed to undertake the broad range of activities essential to life in modern society. This chapter finds that education has increased substantially over the past few decades, with countries converging towards a similar level of educational attainment. However, strong disparities remain in the quality of educational outcomes, as measured by the reading and civic skills of students. Despite the free availability of school services in many countries, educational attainment and students' skills are strongly influenced by the incomes and socio-economic backgrounds of their families, with educational disadvantage cumulating over the life course. This suggests that educational inequalities should be tackled as early as possible in life.

Why do education and skills matter for well-being?

Education and skills are key to the prosperity of nations and to better lives for people (OECD, 2011a). Developing skills is intrinsically valuable for humans as it responds to one of their most important aspirations: the basic need to learn. There are many types of skills, all of which matter for living a good life. In general, the capacity to understand and master the world opens considerable opportunities for people and enhances their control over their lives. In addition, education makes possible activities that bring intrinsic pleasure to individuals, such as reading a book, enjoying an art exhibition, etc.

Education not only has an intrinsic value but also influences well-being indirectly. Individuals benefit from education in a variety of ways: education has a strong positive impact on the material living conditions of people, as higher education leads to higher earnings and greater employability (OECD, 2010c; Boarini and Strauss, 2010; Sianesi and Van Reenen, 2003); more educated people generally have better health status, as they have a healthier life-style and an increased chance of doing a job in a working environment with fewer hazards (Miyamoto and Chevalier, 2010; La Fortune and Looper, 2009). Education also raises civic awareness and fosters political participation (Borgonovi and Miyamoto, 2010; OECD, 2010a). Finally, education provides individuals with the skills necessary to integrate more fully into their societies.

Education matters not only for those acquiring it but also at the wider, societal level. Education and skills bring important economic returns in the form of higher productivity and economic growth (Hanushek and Woessmann, 2010; Sianesi and Van Reenen, 2003), higher macro-economic and political stability, lower criminality and stronger social cohesion (OECD, 2010a; OECD, 2011a; Grossman, 2006). Furthermore, education has a major role to play in coping with the profound structural changes that modern society is undergoing: skills provide a powerful gateway to the future, empowering people and societies with great innovation potential (OECD, 2010b). Finally, improving the skills of those at the bottom of the income ladder plays a key role in countering the long-term trend of growing earnings and income inequality observed in many OECD countries (OECD, 2011a).

Research also shows that educational advantages tend to cumulate over time, starting from the first years of life, and that skills are not acquired solely through formal education (Box 7.1). Students' educational outcomes are largely affected by their family background and in particular by their parents' education (OECD, 2010f). This means that some children are already advantaged over others when they begin formal schooling, while in turn school results exert a strong influence on their university outcomes (Boarini *et al.*, 2008). Moreover, people with higher education and skills are more likely to undertake on-the-job training (OECD, 2010c). The way that inequalities are compounded means that educational deficiencies should be tackled as early as possible and that pupils from a lower socio-economic background should receive adequate support in schools to compensate for their initial disadvantage.

While many things make for a good life, education is perhaps the dimension most valued by parents for improving their children's future life chances. By investing in education, families and governments can reach many economic and social goals at the same time. Existing measures of educational outcomes are well-established and statistically sound. However, their scope is relatively narrow (*e.g.* most available indicators tend to focus on cognitive skills and on the education received in schools) and are usually limited to specific population groups (*e.g.* youth). Enhancing measures of education and skills will allow a better understanding of the potential impacts on other dimensions of people's lives. Such measures are also needed to design more effective policies.

Measuring education and skills

Education statistics are in general of good quality (Table 7.1), especially for OECD countries. However, while a wealth of information exists on education inputs (*e.g.* expenditures, teacher-to-student ratios, etc.) and outputs (educational attainment, completion rates, etc.), information on outcomes (which informs about the quality of education received and the effective skills that individuals have developed) has traditionally been less common. In the past twenty years, several instruments have been developed, notably the Programme for International Student Assessment (PISA), the Trends in International Mathematics and Science Surveys (TIMMS) and the Progress in International Reading Literacy Study (PIRLS). All these tools measure students' abilities in a broad range of tasks and, most importantly, make it possible to study the way educational systems influence people's abilities.

Despite the large amount of relevant evidence that these surveys have provided, they present three main limitations. Firstly, surveys tend to focus on cognitive abilities, such as literacy, numeracy and IT skills. Secondly, they have often been conducted on specific age groups of the population, *i.e.* youth during their school age. Thirdly, they measure individuals' acquired abilities, without informing about how these abilities are actually used in life. Some of these shortcomings are addressed by the OECD Programme for the International Assessment of Adult Competencies (PIAAC), which is discussed at the end of this chapter. It is important to put in place harmonised instruments that measure other types of skills, which are critical for innovation and economic growth but also for living a good life in general (*e.g.* social and emotional skills[1]; Almlund *et al.*, 2011). For the moment, these exist at national level only.

This chapter considers a few well-established educational indicators that provide a basic picture of both the current educational status of the adult population and selected cognitive skills of the youth. They inform about the competencies that help individuals undertake a broad range of the activities needed to live in modern societies.

Table 7.1. **The quality of environmental indicators**

	Target concept	INDICATORS							
		Relevance to measure and monitor well-being				Statistical quality			
		Face validity	Unambiguous interpretation (good/bad)	Amenable to policy changes	Can be disaggregated	Well-established instrument collected	Comparable definition	Country coverage	Recurrent data collection
Education and skills									
ES I Educational attainment	Quantity of education	√	√	√	√	√	√	√	√
es 1 Education expectancy		~	√	√	~	√	√	√	√
es 2 Lifelong learning		√	√	√	~	~	√	~	~
ES II Students' cognitive skills	Quality of education	√	√	√	√	√	√	√	~
es3 Civic skills		√	√	√	√	√	√	~	~

Note: The symbol √ shows that the indicator selected largely meets the considered criterion; the symbol ~ that the indicator meets the criterion to a large extent; the symbol x that the indicator does not meet the criterion or meets it only to a limited extent.

Box 7.1. **Spurring innovation and economic growth through skills:**

the OECD Innovation and Skills Strategies

Innovation covers a wide range of activities (*e.g.* invention and implementation, breakthroughs and minor improvements) and therefore requires a wide variety of skills. Among the most important ones are:

- *Basic skills and digital-age literacy.* These include reading, writing and numeracy as well as the skills needed to use digital technology and access and interpret information in a knowledge-based society.

- *Academic skills.* These are associated with disciplines found in educational institutions, such as humanities, mathematics, history, law and science. These skills are generally obtained through the education system and are transferable across situations.

- *Technical skills.* These are specific skills needed in an occupation and may include both academic and vocational skills and knowledge of certain tools or processes.

- *Generic skills.* Commonly mentioned skills in this category include problem-solving, critical and creative thinking, ability to learn, and ability to manage complexity.

- *"Soft" skills.* This category is sometimes grouped with (or classified as) generic skills. It includes working and interacting in teams and heterogeneous groups; communication; motivation; volition and initiative; ability to read and manage one's own and others' emotions and behaviours during social interactions; cultural openness; and receptiveness to innovation.

- *Leadership.* Similar in nature to "soft" skills, this includes team-building, steering, coaching and mentoring, lobbying and negotiating, co-ordination, ethics and charisma.

- *Managerial and entrepreneurial skills.* These skills and competencies relate to leadership, communication and self-confidence, as well as to relevant technical skills, and are readily transferable.

While measures of basic skills, digital skills, academic skills, technical skills and generic skills of youth are available from existing international assessment surveys, good measures of soft skills, leadership and managerial skills are available only at the national level.

The **OECD Innovation Strategy** recommends that public policies aim at equipping people with the foundations to learn and develop the broad range of skills needed for innovation in all of its forms, as well as with the flexibility to upgrade skills and adapt to changing market conditions.

To address the global dimensions of the supply and demand for skills, the OECD is preparing a global Skills Strategy. **The OECD Skills Strategy** seeks to help both OECD and non-member countries to improve: i) responsiveness – ensuring that education/training providers can adapt to changing demand; ii) quality and efficiency in learning provision – ensuring that the right skills are acquired at the right time, the right place and in the most effective mode; iii) flexibility in provision – allowing people to study/train in what they want, when they want and how they want; iv) transferability of skills – ensuring that skills gained at school are documented in a commonly accepted and understandable form and that the skills acquired over the course of the working life are recognised and certified; v) ease of access – *e.g.* by reducing barriers to entry, such as institutional rigidities, up-front fees and age restrictions, and by providing a variety of entry and re-entry pathways; and vi) lower the costs of re-entry – *e.g.* by granting credits for components of learning, and offering modular instruction, through credit accumulation and credit-transfer systems.

Source: OECD, 2010c; OECD, 2011a.

Selected indicators

Educational attainment (ES I)

Educational attainment gives a basic indication of the level of formal education attained by people in a given country. The definition chosen here focuses on the percentage of the population aged 25-64 who have completed at least an upper-secondary degree. This choice was made because, in OECD countries, the large majority of the population has already completed a lower educational degree (*i.e.* a primary degree); in addition, the economy of many of these countries increasingly needs high-skilled workers, requiring university training for which an upper-secondary credential is a necessary requisite. The chapter also discusses some specific evidence on tertiary educational attainment.

The data behind this indicator are collected through the annual OECD questionnaire on National Educational Attainment Categories (NEAC), which uses Labour Force Survey (LFS) data.[2] However, this indicator does not take into account people who have not completed a degree but might have learned useful skills outside school settings. In addition the indicator does not reflect the quality of education received, which may vary both within and across countries.

Education expectancy (es 1)

The educational attainment of the adult population is informative as a proxy of the stock of human capital accumulated in a country. It is, however, not informative about the educational opportunities available to today's youth. It may therefore be complemented by a measure of educational expectancy, which can be defined as the number of years of schooling that youth aged 15 today may expect to undertake while aged 15 to 29, based on the current enrolment of people aged 15-29. The threshold has been set at 15, the compulsory school age in many OECD countries, as the challenge is to extend education beyond that.

Data for this indicator are collected through the annual OECD data collection on the school-work transitions, which rely on Labour Force Surveys as the main source of information. The data usually refer to the first quarter of the calendar year, or the average of the first three months, thereby excluding summer employment. The indicator relies on the distribution of 15-29 year-olds in education, work or neither of the two. It is thus a good proxy of the numbers of years that an individual is likely to spend in education between age 15 and 29. However, this indicator may not reflect drop-out rates and temporary interruptions of study. Another limitation is that long study durations (*i.e.* beyond the prescribed time) will result in an overestimate of this indicator.

Lifelong learning (es 2)

Formal learning undertaken in schools and universities is the main pillar of the education received during people's life course. However, people improve their competencies and acquire new skills in other settings and times, notably in the labour market. Adult education and training increase people's productivity and earnings possibilities (OECD, 2005; OECD, 2004).

While measuring skills developed on the job is hard, existing indicators of participation in formal and non-formal education provide information on workers' learning opportunities. Formal education includes educational programmes for adults provided by schools, colleges, universities and other educational institutions; non-formal education is defined as an organised and sustained educational activity that does not correspond exactly to the above definition of formal education, and which may take place both within and outside educational institutions and cater to persons of all ages. Depending on the national context, it may cover educational programmes to impart adult literacy, basic education for out-of-school children, life skills, work skills and general culture.[3]

The source for this indicator is a specific OECD data collection. Data for non-EU countries were calculated from country-specific household surveys. Data for countries in the European Statistical System come from the pilot EU Adult Education Survey (AES). The EU AES surveys were carried out between 2005 and 2008 by 29 countries in the EU, EFTA and EU candidate countries. The EU AES is a pilot exercise which proposed a common framework for the first time, including a standard questionnaire, tools and quality reporting (OECD, 2010b).

Students' cognitive skills (ES II)

The measures presented so far provide information on countries' educational potential. They do not, however, indicate anything about the actual quality of the competences gained by people and therefore about how the qualifications earned contribute to individual well-being, *e.g.* by improving access to the labour market. Indicators that directly measure the skills of individuals are therefore needed. For this purpose, an indicator of reading skills of 15-year-old students is used here. This indicator captures reading literacy, defined as the "understanding, using, reflecting on and engaging with written tests, in order to achieve one's goals, to develop one's knowledge and potential, and to participate in society" (OECD, 2010c).

The indicator on reading skills was collected through the 2009 Programme on International Students Assessment (PISA) coordinated by the OECD. The 2009 wave of PISA tested 470 000 students, representing 26 million 15-year-olds in the schools of the 65 participating countries. The PISA student population is defined using stringent criteria to ensure a high level of coverage and full comparability of the assessment across countries (OECD, 2009b). The quality of the indicator is thus high. Despite the fact that reading literacy measures a relatively narrow set of competencies, there is strong evidence that reading literacy is strongly correlated with other cognitive and non-cognitive measures tested by PISA (*e.g.* mathematics, sciences, IT skills, etc. – OECD, 2011b). Finally, while this indicator covers only youth, cognitive skills at age 15 are strongly correlated with later educational outcomes and labour market performance (Juhn *et al.*, 1993).

Students' civic skills (es 3)

Standard cognitive skills are critical for doing well in the labour market and for performing many other activities that contribute to people's well-being, but they need to be complemented with other types of skills that make society strong and inclusive. Civic skills cover knowledge and understanding of civics and citizenship. Civic education focuses on people's knowledge and understanding of formal institutions and the processes of civic life (such as voting in elections), while citizenship education focuses on knowledge and understanding of opportunities for participation and engagement in both civics and civil society (*e.g.* ethical consumption), which are important for democracies. The indicator on civic skills shown here refers to both types of knowledge (*i.e.* civics and citizenship) of students aged around 14-15.[4]

The indicator is based on the International Civic and Citizenship Education Study (ICCS) carried out in 2009 on more than 140 000 Grade 8 (or equivalent) students in more than 5 300 schools from 38 countries. The participation rate required for each country was around 85% of the selected schools, and most of the countries sampled met this requirement. The ICCS is carried out by the International Educational Agency, which has a longstanding experience in international assessment surveys. Since not all OECD countries are covered, the indicator on civic skills is considered here as a secondary indicator.

Average patterns

Educational levels have increased in all countries

Today the large majority of the population aged 25-64 in OECD countries holds at least an upper secondary education degree, with a few remarkable exceptions, *e.g.* Portugal, Turkey and Mexico (Figure 7.1), where the share is around 30%. This share is notably lower than in Brazil, the only emerging country with available comparable information. About 30% of the population has completed a tertiary education programme in OECD countries, but tertiary educational attainment varies widely across countries, ranging between half of the population in Canada to around 10% of the population in Turkey (Figure 7.2).

With the exception of Denmark, where the share of the population with at least an upper-secondary degree has decreased in the last ten years, the average educational attainment has increased in all other OECD and non-OECD countries included in Figure 7.1, with a significant convergence in attainment levels across countries. In general, the stronger increase in educational attainment has been observed in countries starting from a lower stock of human capital, though education continued to rise also in some countries with already high educational attainment, as for instance in the Eastern European countries.

In all countries analysed most of the increase in educational attainment level can be attributed to an increasing number of tertiary graduates, while the number of upper-secondary graduates has remained broadly stable. In the past ten years the increase in the number of tertiary graduates has been high in Poland and Korea (Figure 7.2). A range of factors affecting educational attainment and the policy levers bearing on it are discussed in Box 7.2.

Figure 7.1. **Population that has attained at least an upper secondary education**

Percentage of the population aged 25 to 64

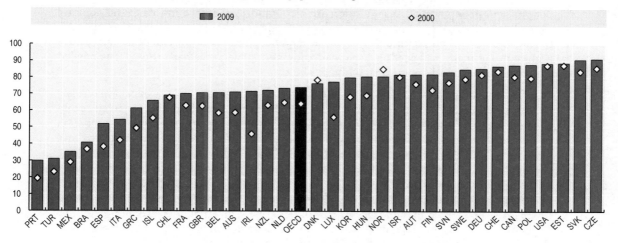

Note: The first available year is 2002 for Estonia, Israel and Slovenia; and 2007 for Chile and Brazil. Due to a change of the educational attainment classification, data before and after 2005 are not comparable for Norway. Starting from 2002, data on educational attainment below upper secondary school for Japan are no longer available. The OECD value is the simple average of the countries available in 2000 and 2009.

Source: OECD (2011), *Education at a Glance 2011: OECD Indicators*, Paris.

StatLink ⟪⟫ http://dx.doi.org/10.1787/888932492796

Figure 7.2. **Population that has attained a tertiary degree**

Percentage of the population aged 25-64

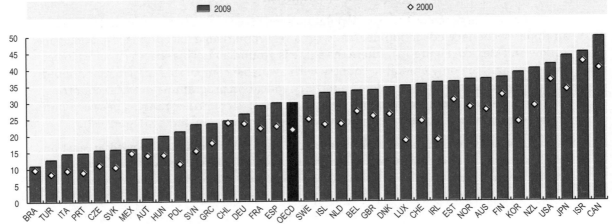

Note: The first available year is 2002 for Estonia, Israel and Slovenia; and 2007 for Chile and Brazil. Due to a change of educational attainment classification, data before and after 2005 are not comparable for Norway. The OECD value is the simple average of the countries available in 2000 and 2009.

Source: OECD (2011), *Education at a Glance 2011: OECD Indicators*, Paris.

StatLink ᴍⁱˢᴸ *http://dx.doi.org/10.1787/888932492815*

Box 7.2. **Factors influencing educational attainment**

Educational attainment results from the combination of: *i)* the demand for skills, as expressed by the economy and the labour market; and *ii)* the supply of skills, which itself depends on the demand of educational qualifications by individuals and households and the supply of these qualifications by the educational system. The structure of industry and the level of economic development play an important role in the former. Trade, migration openness and labour market regulation are also important determinants of the demand for skills (OECD, 2011a). In particular, over the recent past, there have been large changes in the structure of employment by industry and occupation. Employment in agriculture and manufacturing has declined, while employment in services has grown. This has led to growth in occupations requiring higher skills.

Many factors determine the supply of education and skills. These include expected returns to education (Becker, 1967; Freeman, 1986; Heckman *et al.*, 2005); liquidity constraints and financial market failures that prevent individuals from financing their studies through borrowing; a combination of cyclical, structural and demographic effects (Card and Lemieux, 2000; Heckman *et al.*, 2005); the disutility of school versus work (Card 2001); the quality of education, as a function of both peers' ability and resources directed to enhance school quality (Hoxby 2005; Epple and Sieg, 2006); and behavioural determinants of investment in education, including higher divorce rates, implying women's increased financial responsibility for children, girls' earlier maturity, and higher level of non-cognitive skills (Goldin *et al.*, 2006). Educational attainment also depends on the characteristics of the educational system, particularly its flexibility and its effectiveness.

OECD estimates of the impact of the various determinants of higher educational attainment show that graduation rates increase with individual returns to education and with the flexibility and accountability of tertiary education institutions (Oliveira *et al.*, 2007). This study also found that the availability of financial help for students increases graduation rates, as do universal financing systems, as opposed to family-based financing systems. Graduation rates are also higher in countries that have a higher PISA performance and a higher share of foreign students enrolled in universities.

Most youth may expect to study for six or seven years past age 15

In most OECD countries, today's 15-year-olds expect to pursue their studies for six or seven additional years (Figure 7.3). In Slovenia, Finland, Iceland and the Netherlands, youth aged 15 expect, on average, to continue to study for eight additional years or more, but in Mexico and Turkey for only five. Countries may differ in the transition patterns from education to work and, for a given number of additional expected years of education, whether youth alternate employment with studies or instead stay in education for the entire length of their studies may make a difference. However, no strong evidence suggests that uninterrupted spells of education are better than interrupted ones. Starker, more worrisome differences exist with respect to the expected years that youth will spend in neither education nor employment: in Mexico and Italy, 35% of youth aged 15 to 24 who are not in education are either unemployed or inactive. This contrasts with a level of only 10% in the Nordic countries and the Netherlands.

Over time, educational expectancy has increased substantially in most OECD countries, in particular beyond the upper-secondary educational level. In Spain, however, education expectancy has decreased. The highest increases in education expectancy have been observed in the Czech Republic and Slovak Republic, followed by Luxembourg, Turkey and Mexico.

Figure 7.3. **Additional expected years in education at age 15**

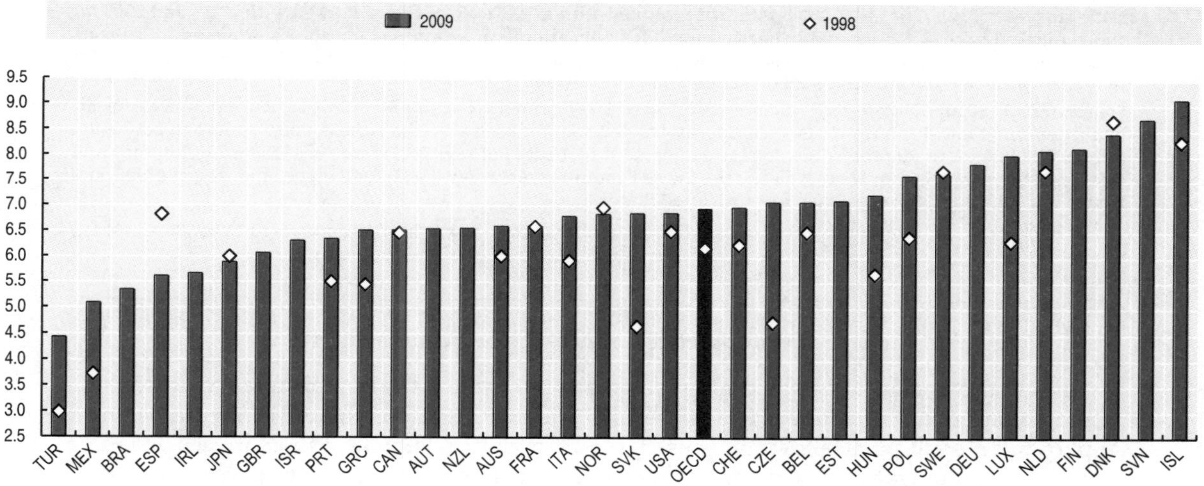

Note: Data refer to 15-24 years old for Japan. The OECD average excludes Chile, Estonia, Israel, Japan and Slovenia. Data for 1998 are not available for Austria, Estonia, Finland, Germany, Ireland, Israel, New Zealand, Slovenia, the United Kingdom and Brazil.
Source: OECD (2011), Education at a Glance 2011: OECD indicators, Paris.

StatLink ⟐ http://dx.doi.org/10.1787/888932492834

Lifelong learning

The Nordic countries and Switzerland are the countries where adults' participation in formal and non- formal education is the highest, with more than half of adults report having participated in some kind of lifelong learning activities during the year preceding the survey (Figure 7.4). Conversely, in Greece only around 10% of the population is involved in such activities. Participation in education beyond the age of schooling is, however, very much dependent on the individual's initial educational attainment, profession and industrial sector of employment, as adults with higher education and in white-collar occupations tend to update their skills more often than adults with lower education and in blue-collar occupations. This suggests that initial differences in educational attainment tend to reinforce over time. Box 7.3 discusses good practices in setting up adult learning systems.

Figure 7.4. Population that has participated in formal and non-formal further education

Percentage of the population aged 25 to 64, 2007

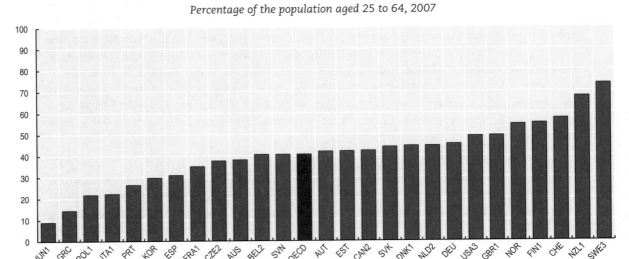

Note: The year of reference is 2008 for countries marked with a "1", 2006 for those marked with a "2", and 2005 for those marked with a "3". Formal education includes educational programmes for adults provided by various educational institutions; non-formal education is defined as an organised and sustained educational activity that may take place both within and outside educational institutions.

Source: OECD (2010), *Education at a Glance 2010*, Paris. Data drawn from the EU Adult Education Survey for EU countries; the Multi-Purpose Household Survey (2006-2007) for Australia; the Access and Support to Education Survey (2007) for Canada; the Educational Development Institute Survey (2007) for Korea; the Adult Literacy and Life Skills Survey (2006) for New Zealand; the Swiss Labour Force Survey (2007) for Switzerland; and the National Household Education Survey (2005) for the United States.

StatLink ⬛ℿ⬛ *http://dx.doi.org/10.1787/888932492853*

Box 7.3. Good practices of lifelong learning systems

The characteristics of adult learning systems partly explain the large differences in adult participation in formal and informal training and education highlighted by Figure 7.4. In particular, adult participation in these learning activities is highest in countries where education and training systems are more flexible, barriers to entry (*e.g.* institutional rigidities, high fees, age restrictions) are lower, where people needing a second chance or wanting to upgrade their skills have several choices in terms of entry and re-entry pathways and where the educational credentials acquired are well recognised through the accumulation and transfer of credits.

Another important determinant of adult learning at country level is the composition of the industrial and business sector, particularly in terms of firm size. The training supply is 50% lower in small and medium-size enterprises than in large firms (Martinez- Fernandez, 2008; Dalziel, 2010; Kubitz, 2011), due to a combination of lack of resources and time, red tape, lack of managerial skills and lack of customised training.

Source: OECD, 2011a.

Students' reading skills vary widely across countries

The average reading scores of 15 year-old pupils vary across countries (Figure 7.5). They are much lower than the OECD average in Mexico and Chile, as well as in other major economies, and much higher in Finland and Korea. The gap between the highest- and the lowest-performing OECD countries is 114 points on the PISA reading scale, the equivalent of the skills acquired in more than two school years. The gap between the highest- and lowest-performing emerging countries is even larger, at 242 score points, which is equivalent to more than five years of formal schooling. In many countries, including Mexico, Chile and Turkey, the highest reading proficiency achieved by most students was Level 2.[5] By contrast, 16% of students attained at least Level 5 in New Zealand, twice as high as the OECD average. Countries with similar levels of GDP per capita achieve very different results on this measure, with the correlation between GDP per capita and PISA reading performance predicting only 6% of the differences in average PISA scores across countries (OECD, 2010d). The determinants of reading skills are discussed more broadly in Box 7.4.

When looking at changes since 2000, Chile, Israel, Poland and Portugal recorded the largest improvements, while Ireland and Sweden experienced the biggest declines. These trends have led to a small fall in cross-country differences in student reading scores (OECD, 2010e). In emerging countries, reading scores are generally lower than in OECD countries, but have risen significantly in some of them, such as Brazil and Indonesia. In many countries, improvements in scores were largely driven by gains at the bottom end of the distribution of reading skills, suggesting greater equity in learning outcomes. The share of top performers (*i.e.* pupils attaining reading proficiency of 5 or 6) increased in Japan and Korea; these countries are now among the countries with the highest proportion of high-achieving students from all the countries participating in the 2009 assesment. New Zealand and Finland still have higher proportions of top performing students than Japan and Korea, but the share has declined in the former. Several countries that had a high share of top-performers in 2000, such as Ireland, recorded a fall.

Figure 7.5. **Reading skills of 15-year-old students**

PISA scores

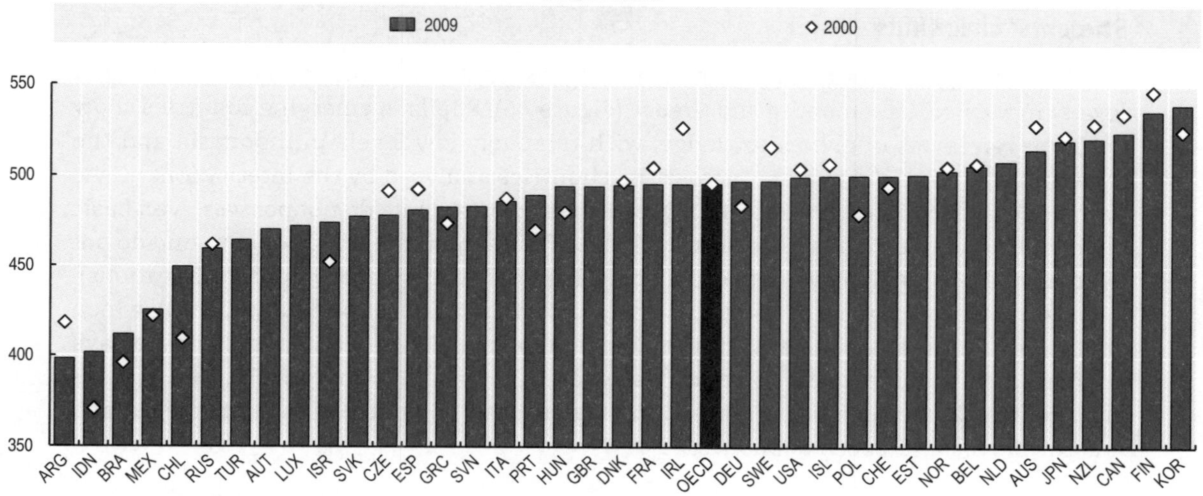

Note: PISA scores are measured on a scale which is normalised to be 500 for the OECD average. Data for 2000 are not available for Austria, Estonia, Luxembourg, the Netherlands, the Slovak Republic, Slovenia, Turkey and the United Kingdom.

Source: OECD (2010), *PISA 2009 at a Glance*, OECD, Paris

StatLink ⟶ http://dx.doi.org/10.1787/888932492872

Box 7.4. **Determinants of students' reading skills**

There is a large body of research on the determinants of learning outcomes as measured by PISA or other survey results (Fuchs and Woessmann, 2007; and Woessmann *et al.*, 2007, for a review). This research suggests that the main determinants of these learning outcomes are: *i)* pupils' socio-demographic characteristics; *ii)* pupils' learning strategies and attitudes to learning; *iii)* school policies and other features of the educational systems; and *iv)* characteristics of the countries, including their economies.

Family background generally has a strong, positive effect on student performance in all countries. The school system further reinforces this effect, through peer-selection and concentration of the best teachers in the best schools (OECD, 2010f). Pupils' learning strategies and attitudes towards learning also impact on learning outcomes, as students who know how to summarise large amounts of information and to make sense of what they have read tend to perform better on PISA scores (OECD, 2010g). In addition, students who enjoy reading and who are used to reading a variety of material tend to display higher reading skills.

Although generally less important than family background, features of the school system – both institutional characteristics such as accountability and autonomy as well as resource endowments – also matter for students performance. Many studies suggests that student outcomes respond to the incentives that schools have when the system is designed to be performance-oriented (Fuchs and Woessmann, 2007; OECD, 2007 and 2010h; Woesmann *et al.*, 2007; Boarini and Luedemann, 2009). Some studies also suggest that, in developed countries, the overall level of educational spending as well as the pupil/teacher ratio have no clear impact on student outcomes, with the exception of pupils from a difficult socio-economic background and pupils in the very early stage of education for whom resources do matter (Piketty and Valdenaire, 2006; Gufstafsson, 2003; OECD, 2004). By contrast, higher teachers' wages are associated with higher reading skills at the country level (Boarini and Luedemann, 2009; OECD, 2010h). Finally, factors such as the level of economic development and the existing stock of human capital influence pupils' cognitive skills, though this influence is weak (OECD, 2010d).

Students' civic skills

Civic competencies of 15 year-olds are highest in Korea, Finland and Denmark and lowest in Mexico, Luxembourg and Greece (Figure 7.6). Pupils in emerging countries show very uneven levels of civic knowledge, with relatively low levels in Indonesia and the Russian Federation. On average, across the countries analysed by the International Civic and Citizen Education Study (ICCS), 16% of 15 year-old students do not possess even basic civic proficiency (*i.e.* pupils have no knowledge of fundamental civic principles and do not even have a working knowledge of the operation of civic, civil and political institutions). Based on a special module of the ICCS survey (called Civic Education Study, CIVED), which was fielded for the first time in 1999, the civic content knowledge of students seems to have decreased on average in the 15 countries covered by both ICCS and CIVED. The average civic content knowledge has increased in Slovenia and fallen in Norway, Greece, Poland and the Slovak and Czech Republics.

Figure 7.6. **Civic competencies of students in selected countries**

Scores in civic knowledge, 2009

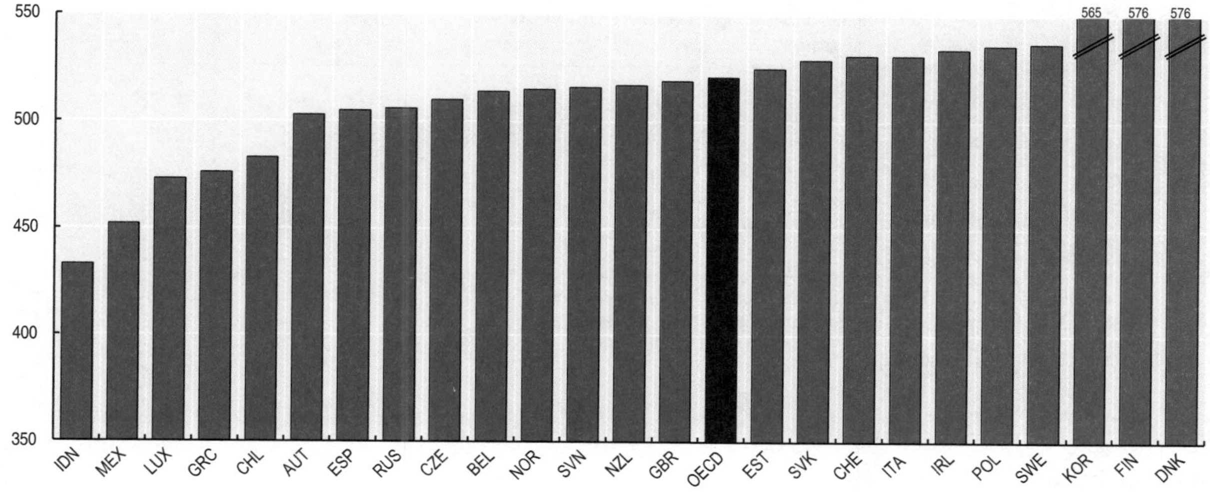

Note: Data are normalised to the ICCS average of 500. Data for Denmark, Switzerland, New Zealand, Norway, Belgium and the Czech Republic met guidelines for sampling participation rates only after schools that refused to participate in the study were replaced by others. Data for the United Kingdom nearly satisfied guidelines for sample participation only after replacement schools were included. Data for the United Kingdom refer to England only; data for Belgium refer to the Flemish region only.
Source: International Civic and Citizen Education Study, 2011

StatLink ⟨⟨⟨⟨ *http://dx.doi.org/10.1787/888932492891*

Indicators of education and skills are well correlated across countries

Almost all indicators analysed in this chapter are correlated with each other (Table 7.2), though this correlation is not perfect. This suggests that it is important to consider them all when assessing patterns of education and skills. In particular:

- Adult educational attainment is well correlated with reading skills, education expectancy and civic competencies.

- Reading skills are well correlated with civic competencies and educational attainment and correlated to a lesser extent with education expectancy.

- Education expectancy is well correlated with educational attainment, reading skills and civic competencies.

- Civic competencies are strongly correlated with reading skills and well correlated with educational attainment and education expectancy.

Table 7.2. **Correlation between different indicators of education and skills**

		ES I Educational attainment		es 1 Education expectancy		ES II Lifelong learning		es 2 Students'cognitive skills		es 3 Civic skills	
ES I	Educational attainment	1	(35)	0.58***	(33)	0.37	(27)	0.52***	(35)	0.50**	(23)
es 1	Education expectancy			1	(34)	0.18	(26)	0.44***	(34)	0.50**	(21)
es 2	Lifelong learning					1	(27)	0.28	(27)	0.26	(19)
ES II	Students'cognitive skills							1	(39)	0.84***	(25)
es 3	Civic skills									1	(25)

Note: Values in parenthesis refer to the number of observations. ** Indicates that correlations are significant at the 5% level; *** indicates that they are significant at the 1% level.

Source: OECD's calculations.

StatLink 🔗 *http://dx.doi.org/10.1787/888932494126*

Inequalities

Youth are more educated than the elderly

Educational attainment differs substantially across groups of the population. In particular, younger generations are more educated than older ones (Figure 7.7). For instance, in Portugal the number of people with at least an upper-secondary degree is three times higher in the age group 25-34 than among the 55-64 years old. Korea, Turkey, Mexico, Spain, Chile and Brazil also have much higher shares of young graduates, confirming the fast catch-up of these countries with respect to their stock of human capital only a few decades ago.

Figure 7.7. **Population that has attained at least an upper-secondary degree by age**

Percentage of various age groups, 2009

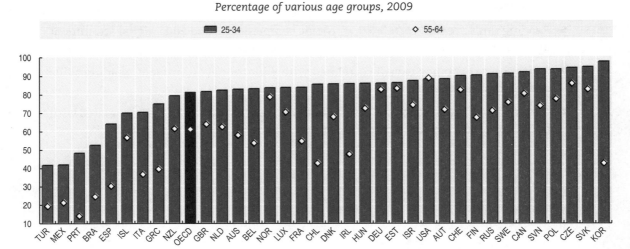

Note: Data for the Russian Federation refer to 2002. Data exclude the ISCED 3C short programmes.
Source: OECD (2011), *Education at a Glance 2011: OECD Indicators*, Paris.

StatLink 🔗 *http://dx.doi.org/10.1787/888932492910*

Among the young generations female graduates outnumber male graduates

A relatively recent trend in OECD countries is that women are achieving higher degrees than men are (Figure 7.8). On average there are more young women with a tertiary or upper-secondary degree than men, particularly so in Portugal, Spain, Iceland, Italy and Greece. There are more tertiary or upper-secondary educated men only in Switzerland, Austria and Turkey. In all countries for which information is available, women's educational attainment has increased significantly over the past 30 years: educational attainment of women has been multiplied by 9 in Korea and by more than 3 in Spain, Portugal and Mexico (OECD, 2011b). If these recent trends continue over the next two decades, women graduates will outnumber men graduates of all ages in most OECD countries.

Figure 7.8. **Population that has attained at least an upper secondary degree by gender**

Percentage of population aged 25 to 34, 2009

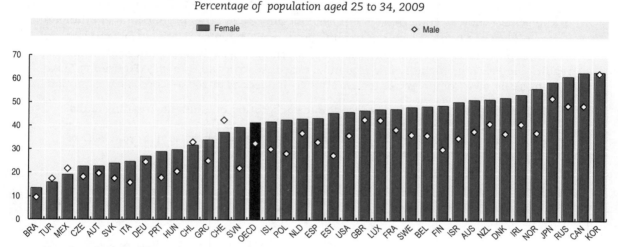

Note: Data for the Russian Federation refer to 2002.
Source: OECD (2011), *Education at a Glance 2011: OECD Indicators*, Paris.

StatLink ⬛⬛ *http://dx.doi.org/10.1787/888932492929*

Educational attainment also varies markedly between the native population and the foreign-born (OECD, 2010i). In Portugal, Ireland and Hungary, the number of tertiary graduates is higher among foreign-born than natives. In most other OECD countries, the shares of tertiary graduates among the foreign-born and native populations are comparable, with the exception of the United States where the native population are more educated than the foreign-born.

Individual educational attainment is also strongly related to parents' socio-economic background. Even though primary and secondary education is a universal right in many OECD countries, and in two-thirds of these countries tertiary education fees are low, the completion of higher education depends strongly on family income. This influence is very large in South European countries and in Luxembourg (Causa and Johansson, 2010). More generally, the correlation between parents' earnings and children's earnings attributable to educational attainment is very high in Italy, the United States and the United Kingdom and quite low in Nordic countries (D'Addio, 2007).

Reading skills are high among pupils from advantaged social-backgrounds, girls and native pupils

Educational outcomes, as measured by the cognitive skills of 15-year-olds, vary greatly for most countries, especially France, Luxembourg and United States (OECD 2010f). In Turkey, Chile and Estonia, by contrast, the skills of students are relatively homogenous. Skills inequalities can be decomposed into within-schools and between-schools differences. Most OECD countries present higher within-school variance than between-school variance (i.e. relatively homogeneous school performance across the country but strong variation across the students of the same school). Between-schools variation is however quite high in Turkey, Italy and Israel, indicating social stratification across schools (i.e. the concentration of students with the same socio-economic background in similar types of schools).

In general, the best-performing school systems manage to provide high-quality education to all students. Indeed, Canada, Finland, Japan and Korea perform well above the OECD mean performance and students tend to perform well regardless of their own background or the school they attend. These countries not only have large proportions of students performing at the highest levels of reading proficiency, but also relatively few students at the lower proficiency levels. Countries where the impact of socio-economic background on reading skills is high include New Zealand, France, Austria and Hungary (Figure 7.9).[6] Like reading skills, civic competencies too are strongly influenced by socio-economic background.

Figure 7.9. The impact of socio-economic background on students' reading skills

Point difference in the PISA reading-score associated with one unit increase in the PISA index of economic, social and cultural status, 2009

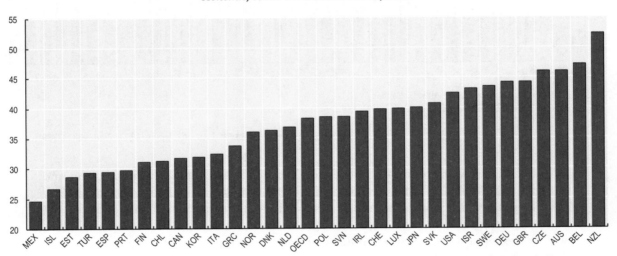

Source: OECD (2010), PISA 2009 Results: Overcoming Social Background. Equity in Learning Opportunities and Outcomes. Volume II, Paris.

StatLink ⇨ http://dx.doi.org/10.1787/888932492948

Girls outperformed boys in reading skills in all the countries participating in PISA 2009 (Figure 7.10), especially in Finland and Slovenia. Among OECD countries, the reading gap amounts to 39 score points, equivalent to more than half a proficiency level or one year of schooling. The gender gap did not narrow in any country between 2000 and 2009, while it widened in Israel, Korea, Portugal, France and Sweden. Factors such as predisposition, temperament, peer pressure and socialisation may contribute to boys having less interest in reading than girls. PISA results suggest that boys would catch up with girls in reading performance if they had higher levels of motivation and used more effective learning strategies.

Figure 7.10. **Gender differences in reading skills**

Point difference in PISA reading score, girls minus boys

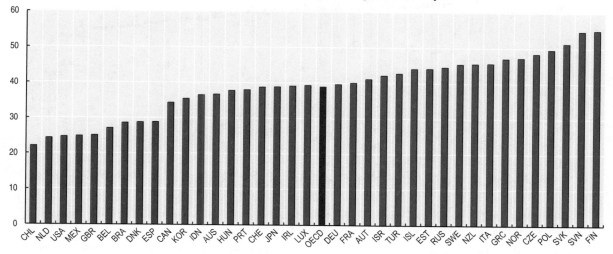

Source: OECD (2010), PISA 2009 Results: What Students Know and Can Do. Student performance in reading, mathematics and science, Paris

StatLink ⬛ꜜ⬛ http://dx.doi.org/10.1787/888932492967

The competencies of 15-year-old students also depend on the origin of the pupil and on the language spoken at home (Figure 7.11). First-generation students – those who were born outside the country of assessment and who have foreign-born parents score on average 52 points below students without an immigrant background. There is no positive association between the size of the immigrant student population and average performance at the country level, and there is also no relationship between the population of students with an immigrant background and the performance gap between native and immigrant students. Thus high levels of immigration do not lead to lower mean performance. Speaking a foreign language in the family is also a penalising factor for reading skills.

Figure 7.11. **The impact of immigration on reading skills**

PISA scores in reading

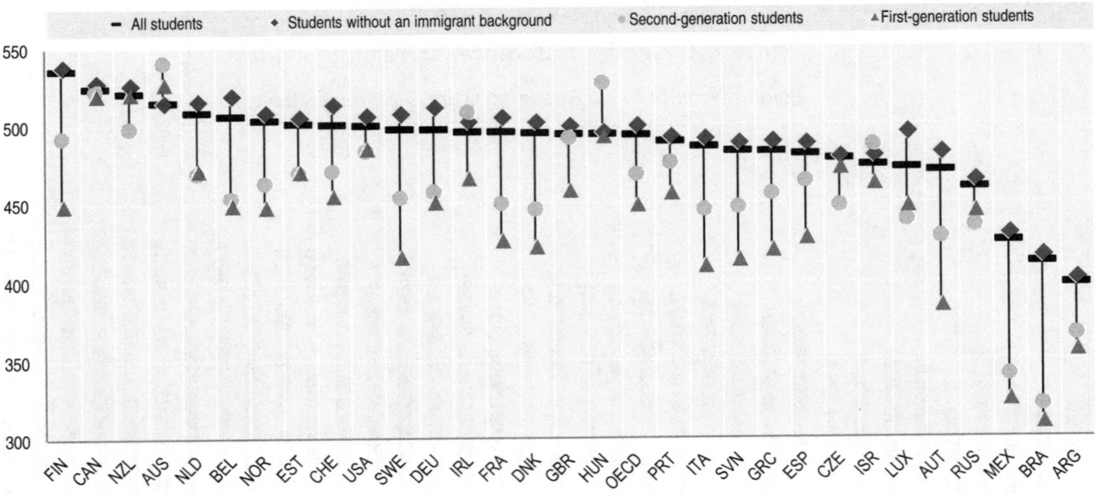

Source: OECD (2010), *PISA 2009 Results: Overcoming Social Background. Equity in Learning Opportunities and Outcomes.* Volume II, Paris.

StatLink ⎙ http://dx.doi.org/10.1787/888932492986

The statistical agenda ahead

As discussed in this chapter, some effort is required to extend the coverage of existing international assessment surveys to groups of the population other than the youth. This is notably the objective of the OECD Programme for the International Assessment of Adult Competencies (PIAAC), which was field-tested in 2010 and whose first results will be published in 2013. PIAAC will interview adults aged 15-65 years (5 000 per country) and assess their literacy and numeracy skills, as well as their ability to solve problems in technology-rich environments. This survey will also collect additional information on how skills are used at work and in other contexts such as at home and in community life.

While PIAAC expands the range of skills measured with respect to previous similar surveys, its first edition will not assess non-cognitive skills, such as social and personality skills. Personality skills can be defined as "relatively enduring patterns of thoughts, feelings and behaviours that reflect the tendency to respond in certain ways under certain circumstances" (Roberts, 2009). Personality skills are usually grouped under the "big five factors": openness to experience, conscientiousness, extraversion, agreeableness and neuroticism. Research shows that these factors are key to several important outcomes, such as individual labour market performance, health status and the propensity to commit crimes. While there are many existing national surveys that collect information on the "big five" factors (*e.g.* the German longitudinal survey SOEP), internationally comparable instruments are almost non-existent. The OECD is developing a project on Education and Social Progress which will aim, inter alia, at measuring personality skills through a common harmonised questionnaire. This exploratory work will be used to investigate the links between skills and measures of social progress (Box 7.5).

Box 7.5 **The OECD Project on Education and Social Progress**

The Education and Social Progress (ESP) project focuses on the role that individual's *cognitive and non-cognitive skills* play in fostering social progress in OECD countries. The project also looks at the role of *learning contexts*, such as family, school and community, in shaping these skills. The focus on skills is inspired by recent interdisciplinary research, which demonstrates that investment in skills is one of the most efficient ways to reduce educational, economic and social inequalities (*e.g.* Cunha and Heckman, 2008).

The project focuses on the following cognitive and non-cognitive skills: *cognitive ability*, which can be described as the mental capacity to acquire knowledge through thought, experience and the senses; and *personality traits*, which can be identified as "relatively enduring patterns of thoughts, feelings and behaviours that reflect the tendency to respond in certain ways under certain circumstance" (Roberts, 2009).

The project will investigate a variety of social progress measures as outcomes of skills, including *health* (*e.g.* health-related lifestyles and outcomes); *societal engagement* (*e.g.* civic and political participation); *family cohesion* (*e.g.* teenage pregnancy); *subjective well-being* (*e.g.* life satisfaction, happiness); *trust and tolerance* (*e.g.* interpersonal trust, tolerance); *public safety* (*e.g.* crime, bullying); and *the environment* (*e.g.* ecological behaviour).

It will be equally important to develop internationally comparable measures of skills and cognitive development of very young children, as the school-readiness of young children is a strong predictor of future learning outcomes, but also of adult health and other important social outcomes.[7] Interesting examples of such measures exist in Canada and Australia (Box 7.6).

Box 7.6. **Measuring childhood early development: The Canadian Early Development Instrument and the Australian Early Development Index**

The Canadian Early Development Instrument (EDI) provides an outcome measure of children's early development. It measures children's readiness to learn in the school environment in five general domains identified as relevant by research: physical health and well-being; social competence; emotional maturity; language and cognitive development; and communication skills and general knowledge in relation to developmental benchmarks rather than curriculum-based ones. The Early Development Instrument can be applied at either junior or senior kindergarten level, *i.e.* on either 4 or 5-year olds. A teacher completed the questionnaire based on her/his observations after several months of classroom/school interaction with the child.

The instrument provides information about groups of children in order to: *i)* report on areas of strength and deficit for populations of children; *ii)* monitor populations of children over time; and *iii)* predict how children will do in elementary school. The EDI was developed by the Offord Centre for Child Studies, McMaster University, Canada, and has now been completed on over 520 000 Canadian children. It is largely based on the National Longitudinal Survey of Children and Youth (NLSCY) and other existing developmental tests.

The Australian Early Development Index (AEDI) is a population measure of young children's development. Like the EDI, it provides information on the following five aspects of early childhood development: physical health and wellbeing; social competence; emotional maturity; language and cognitive skills (school-based); and communication skills and general knowledge.

> The AEDI is based on the Canadian EDI and has been adapted for use in Australia. The AEDI was first trialed in 2002-2003 and then piloted in 60 communities across Australia between 2004 and 2008. The first national implementation was carried out in 2009, and in 2010 follow-up data collection occurred in some small areas.

Other important future actions to develop further educational statistics and improve their quality include (UNESCO, 2011):

- Ensuring consistency in definitions and standards in collecting and compiling international education statistics, in particular with respect to human capital – understood as the skills used in the labour market (Box 7.7) – the inclusivity of education,[8] e-learning and early childhood education.

- Linking education data to other datasets to get a fuller picture of education pathways and transitions.

- Exploring the potential role of administrative data in supplementing survey data (using administrative data may reduce the burden of survey producers and provide additional information to be matched to longitudinal datasets on education).

- Developing better statistics on education outcomes of students, along with their determinants. While the OECD Assessment of Higher Education Learning Outcomes (AHELO) will assess learning outcomes of higher education students and the value-added of university, it will be important to develop instruments to determine the value-added of schools. In particular, there is a strong need to better measure teachers' skills, motivation and teaching strategies, extending the scope of studies such as the OECD Teaching and Learning International Survey (TALIS).

- Finally, developing satellite accounts for the education sector would be important to better understand the role played by education in economic growth. This would in particular help in the study of the productivity of the education sector and how educational services influence the material well-being of households.

Box 7.7. **The OECD Project on measuring the stock of human capital**

The purpose of the OECD human capital project is to identify common methodologies for measuring the stock of human capital for comparative analysis, both across countries and over time, and to implement these methodologies using OECD data. Estimates of the stock of human capital will notably help to assess the sustainability of current well-being over time. The method employed in this project is the lifetime income approach (Jorgenson and Fraumeni, 1989; Jorgenson and Fraumeni, 1992a; Jorgenson and Fraumeni, 1992b) that measures the value of the total stock of human capital embodied in individuals as the total discounted present value of the expected future incomes that could be generated over the lifetime of the people currently living.

Selected findings for the first phase of the project include:

- The estimated value of human capital is substantially larger than that of traditional physical capital by a factor ranging from around eight to over ten across the participating countries. These results are broadly in line with those reported in a number of national studies.

- The distributions of human capital by age, gender and education indicate that men have a higher stock of human capital than women. In addition, younger people have greater human capital than older people, although the detailed patterns vary across countries.

- Decomposition analysis demonstrates that in the past fifteen years or so, the observed increase in women's educational attainment has had little effect on the change in human capital per capita for all countries; population ageing has contributed negatively to the change in human capital per capita. The sensitivity analysis shows that estimates of the value of human capital depend on the choices of two parameters, *i.e.* the annual real income growth rate and the discount rate. But the within-country distribution of human capital and the trend in the human capital volume index in each country are less sensitive to these parameters.

Despite some deficiencies (such as the exclusion of the non-economic and social benefits of human capital investment, sensitivity to key exogenous parameters), the lifetime income approach, by bringing together the influence of a broad range of factors (demography, mortality, educational attainment and labour market aspects), allows comparing the relative importance of these factors and drawing useful policy implications.

Source: Liu, 2011.

Conclusion

This chapter has looked at education and skills in OECD countries and selected emerging countries. Education has increased substantially over the past decades, and countries have been converging towards a similar level of educational attainment. However, strong disparities remain in the quality of educational outcomes, as measured by reading and civic skills. Women are becoming more educated than men, reversing a historical gap. Finally, despite the free availability of school services in many countries, educational attainment and outcomes are strongly influenced by family income and socio-economic background. This suggests that special educational support should be granted to pupils with a disadvantaged economic and social background.

Notes

1.   See the OECD Education and Social Progress Project (Box 7.5).

2.   The INES Program provides methodological guidance on the development of internationally comparable data and indicators on education systems. The INES program has also contributed to assist in the revisions of the International Standard Classification of Education (ISCED), which is used for comparing educational attainment across countries.

3.   The Adult Education Survey (AES) uses an extensive list of possible non-formal educational activities, including courses, private lessons and guided on-the-job training, to prompt respondents to list all of their learning activities in the previous 12 months. Some of these learning activities might be of short duration.

4.   More precisely, the indicator covers the following domains: civic society and systems (40%), civic principles (30%), civic participation (20%) and civic identities (10%); and two cognitive domains: knowing (25%) and reasoning and analysing (75%).

5.   PISA 2009 provides an overall reading literacy scale for reading texts, drawing on all the questions in the reading assessment. The metric for the overall reading scale is based on the mean for the OECD countries, set at 500 in PISA 2000, with a standard deviation of 100. To help interpret what

students' scores mean in substantive terms, the scale is divided into levels, based on a set of statistical principles. Tasks are located within each level of proficiency and describe the kinds of skills and knowledge needed to complete them successfully, For PISA 2009, the range of task difficulty allows for the description of seven levels of reading proficiency (level 1a, 1b, 2, 3, 4, 5, 6). At level 2, students can locate one or more pieces of information in a text, recognise the main idea in the text, understand relationships, or infer meaning from a limited part of the text when the information is not prominent. Reflective tasks at this level require readers to make a comparison or several connections between the text and outside knowledge by drawing on personal experiences and attitudes.

6. In all countries covered by the ICCS, students whose parents worked in higher-status occupations reported higher civic knowledge scores. On average, the gap in civic scores between students with parents in the top six occupational status categories and students in the bottom six categories was 87 scale points, the equivalent of two standard deviations of the civic skills score. However, there are considerable differences among countries, with some countries having a more even distribution of achievement with regard to socio-economic background than others. Differences in the civic knowledge scores were also large between students from native families and those with an immigrant background, but this effect becomes smaller when the family background is controlled for. Students reporting that their parents were more interested in political and social issues display high civic skills. In most countries, this association is evident even after controlling for the effects of other student characteristics.

7. Existing indicators of early educational attainment may not be equally relevant for assessing young children's well-being, as there is ambiguous evidence on the impact of pre-school participation on children's later development (OECD, 2009a).

8. See the "Education for all" initiatives by the World Bank and UNESCO (http://www.unesco.org/education/efa/ed_for_all).

References

Almlund, M., A.L. Duckworth, J. J. Heckman and T. Kautz (2011), "Personality Psychology and Economics", IZA Working Paper No. 5500.

Becker, G.S. (1967), "Human Capital and the Personal Distribution of Income: An Analytical Approach", Woytinsky Lecture, No. 1, Ann Arbor: Institute of Public Administration.

Boarini, R. and E. Luedemann (2009), "The Role of Teacher Compensation and Selected Accountability Policies for Learning Outcomes: An Empirical Analysis for OECD Countries", OECD Journal of Economic Studies, Paris

Boarini, R. and H. Strauss (2010), "What is the Private Return to Tertiary Education? New Evidence from 21 OECD Countries", OECD Journal of Economic Studies, Volume 2010

Boarini R., J. Oliveira Martins., H. Strauss, C. de la Maisonneuve and G. Nicoletti (2008), "Investment in Tertiary Education: Main Determinants and Implications for Policy", CESifo Economic Studies, Vol. 54, 2/2008, pp. 277-312.

Borgonovi, F. and K. Miyamoto (2010), "Education and civic and social engagement", Chapter 3 of Improving Health and Social Cohesion through Education, OECD Publishing, 2010.

Card, D. (2001), "Estimating the Return to Schooling: Progress on Some Persistent Econometric Problems", Econometrica, Vol. 69 No. 5, pp. 1127-60.

Card, D. and T. Lemieux (2000), "Drop-out and Enrollment Trends in the Post-War Period: What Went Wrong in the 1970s?", NBER Working Paper No. 7658.

Causa, O. and A. Johansson (2010), "Intergenerational Social Mobility in OECD Countries", OECD Journal of Economic Studies, Volume 2010.

Cunha, F. and J.J. Heckman (2008), "Formulating, Identifying and Estimating the Technology of Cognitive and Noncognitive Skill Formation, The Journal of Human Resources, 43, 738-782.

D'Addio, A. (2007), "Intergenerational Transmission of Disadvantage: Mobility or Immobility Across Generations? A Review of the Evidence for OECD countries", OECD Social, Employment and Migration Working Papers, No. 52.

Dalziel, P. (2010), "Leveraging Training: Skills Development in SMEs – An Analysis of Canterbury Region, New Zealand", OECD Local Economic and Employment Development (LEED) Working Papers, No. 2010/03

Epple, D., R. Romano and H. Sieg (2006), "Admission, Tuition, and Financial Aid Policies in the Market for Higher Education", *Econometrica*, Vol. 74, No. 4, pp. 885-928

Freeman R. (1986), "Demand for Education", in O. Ashenfelter and R. Layard, eds, *Handbook of Labor Economics*, Vol. 1, Elsevier Publications, Netherlands, pp. 357-86.

Fuchs and Woesmann (2007), "What Accounts for International Differences in Student Performance? A Re-examination using PISA Data", *Empirical Economics*, Vol. 32, No. 2-3, pp. 433-464.

Goldin, C., Katz L.F. and I. Kuziemko (2006), "The Homecoming of American College Women: The Reversal of the College Gender Gap", NBER Working Paper No. 11544.

Grossman, M. (2006), "Education and Nonmarket Outcomes", in E. Hanushel and F. Welch, eds, *Handbook of the Economics of Education*, NorthHolland, Amsterdam.

Gufstafsson, J. (2003), "What do we know about effects of school resources on educational results", *Swedish Economic Policy Review*, 10, pp. 77-110.

Hanushek, E. A. and L. Woessmann (2010), *The High Cost of Low Educational Performance. The Long Run Impact of Improving PISA Outcomes*, OECD Publishing 2010.

Heckman, J.J., L.J. Lochner and P.E. Todd (2005), "Earnings Functions, Rates of Return, and Treatment Effects: The Mincer Equation and Beyond", NBER Working Paper, No. 12139.

Hoxby, C.M (2005), "The Effects of Geographic Integration and Increasing Competition in the Market for College Education", Mimeo, Department of Economics, Harvard University.

Kubitz, M. (2011), "Leveraging Training: Skills Development in SMEs: An Analysis of Zaglebie sub-region, Poland", OECD Local Economic and Employment Development (LEED) Working Papers, Paris.

Jorgenson, D.W. and B.M. Fraumeni (1989), "The Accumulation of Human and Non-Human Capital, 1948-1984", In *The Measurement of Savings, Investment, and Wealth*, R.E. Lipsey and H.S. Tice, eds. The University of Chicago Press, Chicago, pp. 227-82.

Jorgenson, D.W and B.M. Fraumeni (1992a), "The Output of the Education Sector", in Z. Griliches, ed, *Output Measurement in the Service Sectors*, The University of Chicago Press, Chicago.

Jorgenson, D.W and B.M. Fraumeni (1992b), "Investment in Education and U.S. Economic Growth", *Scandinavian Journal of Economics*, 94, Supplement, 51-70.

Juhn, C., K.M. Murphy and B. Pierce (1993), "Wage Inequality and the Rise in Returns to Skill", *Journal of Political Economy*, Vol. 101, No. 3, pp. 410-442.

La Fortune and Looper (2009), "Measuring Disparities in Health Status and in Access and Use of Health Care in OECD Countries", OECD Health Working Paper, No. 43, Paris.

Liu G. (2011), "Measuring the stock of human capital for comparative analysis: an application of the lifetime income approach to selected countries", OECD Statistics Working Papers, Paris.

Martinez-Fernandez, C. (2008), "Leveraging Training and Skills Development in SMEs", OECD/LEED 2008/6, Paris.

Miyamoto, K. and A. Chevalier (2010), "Education and health", Chapter 4 of *Improving Health and Social Cohesion through Education*, OECD Publishing.

OECD (2011a), "Towards an OECD Skills Strategy", Document Presented at the OECD Ministerial Council Meeting, Paris.

OECD (2011b), *Education at a Glance 2011*, forthcoming., OECD Publishing, Paris.

OECD (2010a), *Improving Health and Social Cohesion through Education*, OECD Publishing, Paris.

OECD (2010b), *Education at a Glance 2010*, OECD Publishing, Paris.

OECD (2010c), *The OECD Innovation Strategy. Getting a Head Start on Tomorrow*, OECD Publishing, Paris.

OECD (2010d), *PISA 2009 Results: What Students Know and Can Do. Student performance in reading, mathematics and science*, OECD Publishing, Paris.

OECD (2010e), *PISA 2009 Results: Learning Trends. Changes in Student Performance since 2000, Volume V*, OECD Publishing, Paris.

OECD (2010f), *PISA 2009 Results: Overcoming Social Background. Equity in Learning Opportunities and Outcomes, Volume II*, OECD Publishing., Paris.

OECD (2010g), *PISA 2009 Results: Learning to Learn. Student Engagement, Strategies and Practices, Volume III*, OECD Publishing, Paris.

OECD (2010h), *PISA 2009 Results: What makes a school successful. Resources, Policies and Practices, Volume IV*, OECD Publishing, Paris.

OECD (2010i), *Immigration Outlook*, OECD Publishing, Paris.

OECD (2009a), *Doing Better for Children*, OECD Publishing, Paris.

OECD (2009b), *PISA 2009 Technical Report*, forthcoming, OECD Publishing, Paris.

OECD (2007), *PISA 2006 Results, Volume I*, OECD Publishing, Paris.

OECD (2005), *Promoting Adult Learning*, OECD Publishing, Paris.

OECD (2004), *OECD Employment Outlook*, OECD Publishing, Paris.

OECD (2001), *The Wealth Of Nations*, OECD Publishing, Paris.

Oliveira Martins, J., R. Boarini, H. Strauss, C. de la Maisonneuve and C. Saadi et al. (2007), «The Policy Determinants of Investment in Tertiary Education,» OECD Economics Department Working Papers 576, OECD Publishing, Paris.

Piketty T. and M. Valdenaire (2006), «L'impact de la taille des classes sur la réussite scolaire dans les écoles, collèges, et lycées français: Estimations a partir du panel primaire 1997 et du panel secondaire 1995», Ministère de l'Éducation Nationale, Les Dossiers No. 173, Paris.

Roberts, B.W. (2009), "Back to the future: Personality and assessment and personality development", *Journal of Research in Personality*, 143, 137-145.

Sianesi B. and Van Reenen (2003), "The Returns to Education: Macroeconomics", *Journal of Economic Surveys*, Vol. 17, No. 2.

UNESCO - United Nations Economic and Social Council (2011), *Review of Education Statistics*.

Woesmann L., E. Luedemann, G. Schutz and M.R. West (2007), "School Accountability, Autonomy, Choice and the Equity of Student Achievement: International Evidence from PISA 2003", OECD Education Directorate Working Paper N. 14, Paris.

Chapter 8

Social connections

Beyond the intrinsic pleasure that people derive from spending time with others, social connections have positive spill-over effects for individual and societal well-being. People with extensive and supportive networks have better health, tend to live longer, and are more likely to be employed. At a society-wide level, social connections can generate shared values – such as trust in others and norms of reciprocity – which influence a range of outcomes, including economic growth, democratic participation and crime. The indicators used in this chapter to measure different aspects of social connections refer to social network support and to the frequency of social contact. Overall, personal social networks are relatively strong in OECD countries, with most people seeing friends and/or relatives on a regular basis and reporting that they have someone to count on in times of need. However, there are significant differences between different socio-economic and demographic groups, with the old, the poor and the less-educated having weaker social support networks. There are also wide cross-country differences in levels of interpersonal trust – one key indicator of the outcomes of social connections. Measuring social connections remains challenging, however, and more work is needed to develop comparable measures in this field.

Why do social connections matter for well-being?

Humans are social creatures. The frequency of contact with others and the quality of personal relationships are crucial determinants of people's well-being. People get pleasure from spending time with others – be it family, friends or colleagues – and activities are typically more satisfying when shared with others (Kahneman and Krueger, 2006). Furthermore, social networks provide material and emotional support in times of need, as well as access to jobs and other opportunities.

The way people interact with others also has implications beyond their immediate circles. Well-developed social connections can generate trust in other people, tolerance of diversity and norms of reciprocity as well as facilitating exchanges of information and collective action. Social networks, and the shared values and norms they generate, are foundational to social capital (see Box 8.1). Social capital is increasingly recognised as a driver of important well-being outcomes, including democratic participation, crime, health status and the strength of communities and economies (Putnam, 2000; Halpern, 2005).

This chapter looks at some indicators of social connections that have an impact on people's well-being. It covers measures of human contacts that are focused primarily on the well-being that people derive directly from contact with others, and also on broader measures of social capital that are thought to be important drivers of other social outcomes.

Measuring social connections

Measuring the complexity of human relationships and their contribution to individual and societal well-being is difficult. People's lives are made of countless social connections that vary in context and intensity: family, close friends, neighbours, colleagues, distant acquaintances – even a one-off interaction with a stranger in the street is a form of social contact. Such interactions may involve the physical presence of different parties in the same place, but also include interactions by mail, telephone and social media. Recent years have seen an increased focus on these issues, partly as a result of changes in patterns of living. More people are living alone than in the past, due to factors such as population ageing, family disruptions and higher geographical mobility; whether these changes in living patterns are a reflection of necessity or of choice, one implication is that people cannot always count on the support of their immediate family in case of need.

Despite the increasing recognition of the importance of these elements, official statistics on social connections are still scarce. Some of the most common approaches to measuring social connections have relied on indirect indicators, such as statistics on membership of associations (*e.g.* sporting clubs, community groups, religious or professional organisations) or on the density of voluntary organisations in a given area. However, such measures have been criticised on a number of levels. For example, several authors have argued that these measures capture participation only in formal networks, and do not describe informal connections such as those that people maintain with friends and relatives; also, formal membership in associations, and the importance of this, can differ over time and across countries, thereby hampering comparability; finally, such measures have also displayed poor predictive validity with respect to the range of outcomes that are usually associated with social connections, such as trust in others and civic engagement (Halpern, 2005). Today, it is increasingly recognised that meaningful indicators of social connections need to be based on surveys of people's actual behaviour (Stiglitz *et al.*, 2009).

Box 8.1. **What is social capital?**

In very general terms, social capital embodies the idea that social connections – friendship, family and other relationships – generate benefits above and beyond the intrinsic pleasure that comes from them. While definitions of social capital vary, most agree that social capital constitutes both social networks and the shared values, norms and understandings they generate, such as trust, tolerance of diversity, civic-mindedness, reciprocity, and mutual support. The OECD defines social capital as the "networks together with shared norms, values and understandings that facilitate co-operation within or among groups" (OECD, 2001). An often-cited example of social capital is that of New York diamond merchants who hand over bags of diamonds worth many thousands of dollars to other merchants in the community for pre-sale inspection, without contracts or insurance (Coleman, 1988). The high level of trust within the group means that there is no need to negotiate formal agreements between parties, thereby saving time and money for the participants and increasing the efficiency of doing business.

Social capital has been shown to influence a range of outcomes within a country or region, including democratic participation, governance, economic growth, labour market performance, crime rates and health (Putnam, 2000; Halpern, 2005). Social capital can also have a profound impact on individual well-being. People with extensive and supportive networks are more likely to be employed (Aguilera, 2002), to have better career progression (Podolny and Baron, 1997), to be paid more (Goldthorpe *et al.*, 1987), to have better mental health (Baum *et al.*, 2000; Veenstra, 2000), to be less affected by stress (Williams *et al.*, 1981), to successfully recover from health shocks, such as heart attacks (Case *et al.*, 1992) and to live longer in general (Berkman and Glass, 2000). Social capital can therefore be seen as both a public and a private good, with benefits for individuals as well as important spillover effects for society as a whole.

Governments are increasingly recognising the importance of social capital, but it remains a challenging area to measure. Some approaches focus on measuring key outcomes, such as levels of interpersonal trust (see indicator sc 3) as a proxy for social capital as a whole. However, this overlooks the fact that there can be different types of social capital – not all of which are necessarily good for society – that are generated by different types of relationships or social connections. For example, an important distinction is often made between "bridging" and "bonding" social capital, where bridging relationships bring people together from different backgrounds (for example through social movements), and bonding relationships reinforce links between people of similar background (for example, ethnic-based groups). Too much bonding in the absence of bridging social capital can lead to "in group/out-group" dynamics, leading to the exclusion of those outside the bonding group. Networks can also foster values that are detrimental for society, as is the case with mafia or terrorist organisations.

A meaningful set of social capital indicators will need to give sufficient detail about the different types of relationships and connections that make up people's social networks, as well as tracking society-level social capital outcomes over time.

Such surveys have been developed in a number of OECD countries; examples include dedicated surveys implemented by national statistical offices in the United Kingdom, Australia, Canada, Indonesia, Ireland, the Netherlands and, most recently, the United States. Relevant information on social connections is also provided by time use surveys, as diaries often include data on a range of social activities (such as attending cultural events) as well as on activities performed with others, providing information not just on their frequency but also on their duration. However comparability remains an issue, as no recognised standards or guidelines exist in this field. The only comparable information on this topic, covering a broad range of countries, is that provided by several small-scale unofficial surveys such as the Gallup World Poll, the World Values Survey and the International Social Survey Program. Officially produced comparable data are available for European countries through a 2006 special module of the EU Survey of Income and Living Conditions (EU-SILC).

This chapter relies on this range of sources to provide some comparative information on the breadth of social connections. It is important to note that social connections is an area where robust, comparable data is particularly lacking, and many of the indicators presented in this chapter should be seen as "placeholders" rather than definitive indicators. In particular, the use of Gallup World Poll data is less than ideal due to issues such as sampling size. One of the main purposes of this publication is to highlight areas where further development in official statistics is necessary. While significant advances in this area have been made by many national statistical offices, the data currently available from official sources is limited to a handful of countries.

Ideally, a set of indicators of social connections should describe a range of different relationships, as well as the quality of those relationships and the resulting outcomes for people (i.e. emotional and financial support, job opportunities, social isolation) and for society (i.e. trust in others, tolerance, democratic participation, civic engagement). The indicators used in this chapter have been selected based on their capacity to inform about both informal and formal types of social connections; the former aspect is represented by indicators on the frequency of socialising with friends and family members; and the latter aspect by measures of the time spent volunteering. In addition, two supplementary indicators are used to measure important individual and societal outcomes: respectively, social network support and trust in others. Table 8.1 assesses the statistical quality of these indicators.

Selected indicators

Social network support (SC I)

While close personal relationships bring intrinsic pleasure, they can also provide emotional and material support in times of need, and strengthen people's ability to deal with difficult times in their lives. Supportive relationships have been shown to protect against depression and to help in recovery after illness (Sherbourne et al., 1995; Seeman, 1996). Furthermore, they can also be instrumental in providing practical help, such as financial assistance. This indicator measures the proportion of people who respond positively to the question: "If you were in trouble, do you have relatives or friends you can count on to help you whenever you need them, or not?" While this question does not ask for more details on the types of support that might be expected, it provides a general measure of perceived social network support (Chan and Lee, 2006; Faber and Wasserman, 2002; Seeman and Berkman, 1988). Data for this indicator come from the Gallup World Poll. As noted in other chapters, while data from this poll are collected through the same questionnaire and rely on well-tested questions, the sample size is small This places considerable restrictions on the conclusions that can be drawn from these data. However, in the absence of data sources based on larger and better drawn samples and on the same type of question across countries, Gallup World Poll data is a second-best solution.

Frequency of social contact (sc 1)

The frequency of contact with others is an important determinant of people's well-being. Evidence from time use surveys has shown that socialising with friends is one of people's most enjoyable activities (Kahneman *et al.*, 2004. Kahneman and Krueger, 2006). This indicator measures the proportion of people who report socialising (*i.e.* meeting face-to-face) with friends and relatives living outside the household at least once a week. While the frequency of weekly contact is somewhat arbitrary, it provides the best picture of differences in the frequency of contact with others between countries, given the available data (daily/weekly/monthly). The data for this indicator come principally from the 2006 ad-hoc module of the EU Survey of Income and Living Conditions on Social Participation, which are limited to European countries. Additional data for Canada and New Zealand is included from their most recent General Social Surveys.

Table 8.1. **The quality of indicators of social connections**

		Target concept	INDICATORS								
			Relevance to measure and monitor well-being				Statistical quality			
			Face validity	Unambiguous interpretation	Amenable to policy changes	Can be disaggregated	Well-established instrument collected	Comparable definition	Country coverage	Recurrent data collection
Social Connections											
SC I	Social network support	Personal relationships	√	√	~	√	x	√	√	√
sc 1	Frequency of social contact	Community relationships	~	√	~	√	~	√	~	~
sc 2	Time spent volunteering		√	√	~	~	~	~	~	x
sc 3	Trust in others	Norms and values	√	√	~	√	x	√	√	√

Note: The symbol √ shows that the indicator selected largely meets the criteria shown in the table; the symbol ~ that the indicator meets the criteria to a large extent; the symbol x that the indicator does not meet the criterion or it meets it only to a limited extent

Time spent volunteering (sc 2)

People who volunteer tend to be happier and more satisfied with their lives than those who do not; this underscores the direct role that volunteering plays in contributing to people's overall well-being (Borgonovi, 2008). However, volunteering also delivers broader benefits to society, both in terms of the direct value of the volunteer's labour, and in terms of the contribution of volunteering to building a healthy civil society. While the economic value of non-market work – of which volunteering is an element – is discussed in Chapter 2 of this report ("Income and Wealth"), the focus here is on the broader impact of volunteering. Time use surveys provide data on the amount of time that people actually spend in volunteering activities. The data presented here are collected from various national time use surveys and have been harmonised by the OECD (see Miranda, 2011, and OECD, 2011). Definitions of volunteering activities in national time use surveys vary from country to country, however, sometimes significantly. The most common difference is whether only formal volunteering with an organisation is included, or whether more informal types of volunteering are also counted (such as someone helping an ill neighbour by preparing meals). Time use data on volunteering for some countries (*e.g.* Turkey) have been excluded, as they include religious activities that are performed alone, such as prayer, which do not fit into this chapter's focus on social connections.

Trust in others (sc 3)

Trust in others is also a key aspect of social connections and of social capital: many of the benefits of social capital flow from the way in which high levels of trust in other people living in the same community facilitate exchanges and enterprise. Indeed, some authors go so far as to define social capital as the level of interpersonal trust that prevails within a group or society, rather than just one of components of social capital (Paldam and Svendsen, 2000); other authors identify interpersonal trust as the best single proxy measure of social capital currently available (Halpern, 2005). The indicator shown here measures the proportion of people who agree with the statement that "most people can be trusted". This survey question leaves many aspects undefined (*e.g.* it does not specify who "most people" are, nor the type of action that they are expected to perform (see Morrone *et al.*, 2009). The data shown here come from the Gallup World Poll and are therefore subject to the same caveats as noted for the indicator on social network support.

Average patterns

Most people in OECD countries report having someone to count on in times of need

The capacity of social networks to provide support in case of emergency appears to be strong in most OECD countries. On average, more than 90% of people declare that they have someone to count on in times of need (Figure 8.1). According to this measure, among OECD countries support networks appear to be weakest in Turkey, Korea, Portugal and Estonia, and strongest in Iceland, Ireland, New Zealand and Denmark. When excluding OECD countries at both ends of the distribution, however, levels of social support are very similar across countries, ranging between 85 and 95%.

Figure 8.1. **Social network support**

*Percentage of people who have relatives or friends they can count on for help in times of need,
2010 or latest available year*

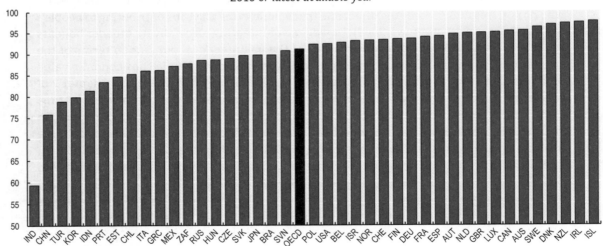

Note: Data refer to 2008 for Iceland and Norway; and to 2009 for Estonia, Israel, Switzerland and South Africa.
Source: Gallup World Poll.

StatLink ⟦⟧ *http://dx.doi.org/10.1787/888932493005*

Frequency of social contact varies widely in European countries

On average, across European countries, around 60% of people socialise with friends at least once a week. However, there is a wide degree of variation between countries, from around 40% of people in Poland to over 70% in Portugal and Greece (Figure 8.2). New Zealand and Canada, the only two non-EU countries included in this figure, tend to display above-average levels of social contacts.

In general, levels of social contact with friends and with family are correlated across countries. Countries where people socialise frequently with family members also tend to be those where people socialise more frequently with friends. However, there is a higher tendency to socialise with friends than with relatives on a weekly basis. Only in France, Hungary, the Slovak Republic, the Czech Republic, Belgium and Iceland is it more common to socialise with relatives than with friends. In the case of France and Hungary, this is also associated with a low absolute proportion of the population socialising with friends on a weekly basis. Box 8.2 provides more details on the drivers of social contact and trends over time.

Figure 8.2. **Frequency of social contact in selected OECD countries**

Percentage of people socialising with friends and relatives at least once a week during a usual year, 2006 or latest available year

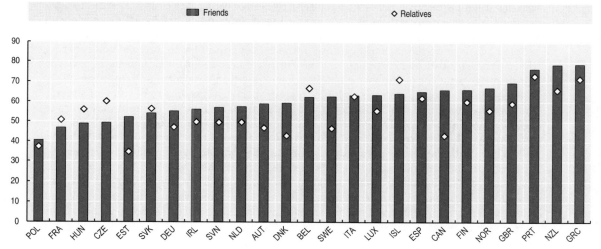

Note: Social contact refers here to "getting together" in the EU-SILC survey and face-to-face contact in the New Zealand and Canadian General Social Surveys, as opposed to other forms of distant contact such as exchanges by telephone or email. Data for Canada refers to "the past month" rather than a usual year.

Source: European Union Statistics on Income and Living Conditions (EU-SILC), 2006; Canada General Social Surveys, 2008; New Zealand General Social Surveys, 2008.

StatLink ⫘⫘ http://dx.doi.org/10.1787/888932493024

People in New Zealand, Ireland and the United States spend the most time volunteering

Figure 8.3 shows the amount of time that people spend volunteering per day in selected OECD countries. New Zealand has relatively high levels of volunteering based on this measure, followed by Ireland and the United States. These levels are double the OECD average. At the other end of the scale, many populations spend negligible time volunteering per day, including Hungary, India, Korea, South Africa, Poland, Slovenia, China, France, Estonia, Spain and Mexico. While time spent volunteering may seem low, it should be kept in mind that this indicator presents results for the whole population. People who do volunteer spend much more time per day – on average, over two hours per day across the OECD (Miranda, 2011).

Box 8.2. **What do we know about the drivers of social connections?**

Robert Putnam's seminal study of social capital in the United States, *Bowling Alone*, gained a great deal of attention when it was published in 2000. Not only did Putnam convincingly demonstrate that people's relationships and shared values are strongly linked to a range of issues related to societal well-being, but he also showed that social capital – including formal and informal social connections – was on the decline in the United States, a trend that seemed set to continue. Putnam explored different possible explanations for this decline, and identified four factors that seemed to be particularly important: generational change (with younger generations less socially engaged), television and electronic entertainment, work intensity and urban sprawl/commuting. In other words, people who watch more TV, work longer hours and commute longer distances tend to spend less time on building and maintaining their social capital. Commuting and urban sprawl also degrade social connections, as the proliferation of busy transport routes tends to divide and alienate. Halpern (1995) has shown that the more cars that pass along a street, the less likely it is that the residents will know their neighbours or describe them as friendly.

Subsequent research has shown that trends in social connections are not uniform across countries. For example, while Australia, and to a lesser extent, the United Kingdom, have shown similar patterns of decline (Leigh, 2010; Halpern, 2005), other countries seem to have experienced a rise in social connections, according to some indicators. Sweden experienced a rise in informal socialising between 1975 and 1995; in the Netherlands, the proportion of people having someone to count on rose in the 1990s; and in Japan, rates of volunteering tripled between 1976 and 1996 (Halpern, 2005). Furthermore, outside the United States patterns of declining social connections are not as universal within countries, and not necessarily generational: for example, in the United Kingdom social class seems to be more of a factor than age in determining social engagement (Halpern, 2005). Finally, different indicators of social connections do not always move in the same direction within countries; for example, in Germany, while informal socialising has increased, social trust has decreased (Halpern, 2005). These national divergences have highlighted the complexity of social connections and the need for a better understanding of their determinants. Alongside the factors proposed by Putnam, other possible drivers of social connections include residential mobility (Glaeser *et al.*, 2002); ethnic diversity (Fennema and Tillie, 1999); economic inequality (Knack and Keefer, 1997; Putnam, 1993); and education (Willms, 2001; see also the section on inequalities later in this chapter).

The question of how governments can foster social capital remains a challenging one, as establishing the direction of causality between many of the factors and trends involved in social connections is difficult, and the issue of policy intervention in people's social activities can be controversial. In terms of direct efforts to strengthen social capital, encouraging formal engagement in the voluntary sector is one area where governments can have an influence. For example, the United Kingdom government recently launched its "Big Society" initiative, with the goal of fostering a nation-wide culture of volunteerism at its core (UK Cabinet Office, 2010). In other areas related to social connections, such as urban planning and education policy, the importance of social connections should be taken into account when designing and implementing new projects.

Voluntary work can make an important material contribution to national economies. A tool for valuing volunteering is provided by the Handbook on Non-profit Institutions in the System of National Accounts, developed by the Johns Hopkins Center for Civic Society Studies in co-operation with the United Nations Statistics Division.

The Handbook recommends that countries regularly produce "satellite accounts" of the non-profit sector, providing a comprehensive picture of its size and operation. So far, eight OECD countries have implemented this Handbook, with data referring to a year between 1999 and 2004, and four additional countries have committed to do so in the future. Across the eight OECD countries that have implemented the UN Handbook, the non-profit sector (including volunteering) accounts for around 5% of GDP, with this share ranging from a little over 1% in the Czech Republic to over 7% in Canada and the United States (OECD, 2009).

Figure 8.3. **Time spent volunteering**

Minutes per day, latest available year

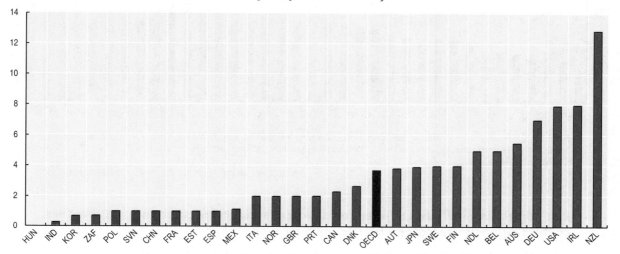

Note: Data refer to 1998-99 for France and New Zealand; 1999 for Portugal and India; 1999-2000 for Estonia, Finland and Hungary; 2000 for South Africa; 2000-01 for Norway, Slovenia, Sweden, and the United Kingdom; 2001 for Denmark; 2001-02 for Germany; 2002-03 for Italy and Spain; 2003-04 for Poland; 2005 for Belgium, Canada and Ireland; 2005-06 for the Netherlands; 2006 for Australia, Japan; 2008 for the United States and China; 2008-09 for Austria; 2009 for Korea and Mexico. The indicator refers to people aged 20-59 for Hungary and 30-59 for Korea. Data have been normalized to 1440 minutes per day. In other words, for those countries for which the time use did not sum up to 1440 minutes, the missing minutes were equally distributed across all activities.
Source: OECD Time Use Surveys database.

StatLink ᴹᴵˢᴸ *http://dx.doi.org/10.1787/888932493043*

There are striking variations in levels of in others trust across countries

Figure 8.4 shows how levels of interpersonal trust compare across OECD countries. People in Norway, Sweden and Denmark report the highest levels of trust in other people (with more than 50% of those interviewed answering that most people can be trusted), while Turkey, Portugal, Mexico, France and Poland are those with the lowest level of interpersonal trust (less than 20% think that most people can be trusted). On average, around one in three respondents in OECD countries report trusting others.

Figure 8.4. **Trust in others**

Percentage of people saying they most people can be trusted, 2009 or latest available year

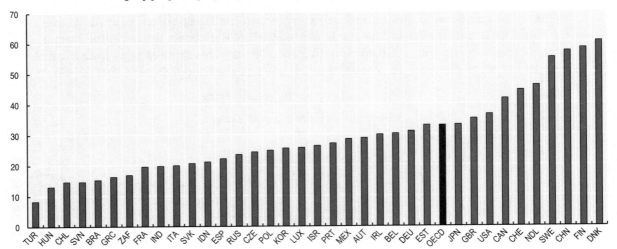

Note: Data refer to 2010 for Austria, Belgium, Chile, the Czech Republic, Denmark, Finland, Hungary, Luxembourg, Mexico, the Netherlands, Poland, Portugal, the Slovak Republic and Sweden.
Source: Gallup World Poll.

StatLink ⓘ http://dx.doi.org/10.1787/888932493062

Low correlations between different measures of social connections suggest that they capture different aspects of a broader phenomenon

Table 8.2 presents correlations among average measures of the different indicators of social connections presented in this chapter. None of the correlations are statistically significant at conventional levels. This may signify the importance of looking at a range of dimensions when monitoring social connections. However, one would expect there to be a higher degree of positive correlation between at least some of these indicators – for example, frequency of social contact and levels of social network support. The fact that these relationships seem absent may imply that there are underlying problems of data accuracy or validity in the indicators presented here. Nevertheless, some of the indicators on social connections used here are very well correlated with the other dimensions of well-being presented in this report (see chapter 1 of this report).

Table 8.2. **Correlation between different indicators of social connections**

	SCI Social network support	sc 1 Frequency social contact	sc 2 Time spent volunteering	sc 3 Trust in others
SC 1 Social network support	1 (24)	-0.11 (24)	0.15 30)	0.31 (37)
sc 1 Frequency social contact		1 (24)	0.13 19)	0.16 (22)
sc 2 Time spent volunteering			1 (30)	-0.08 (27)
sc 3 Trust in others				1 (37)

Note: Values in parenthesis refer to the number of observations.
Source: OECD calculations.

StatLink ⓘ http://dx.doi.org/10.1787/888932494164

Inequalities

The elderly and the poor face a higher risk of social isolation

Table 8.3 shows a breakdown for the frequency of socialising with friends and relatives by gender, age and poverty status in European countries. The table highlights several patterns:

- People 65 years of age and older are much less likely to report getting together with friends, *i.e.* slightly less than 20% of people aged 65 and over report having no contacts at all with friends, as compared to almost 7% of the working-age population and slightly above 2% of 16-17 year-olds. The share of elderly people who say they socialise with friends once a week is also much lower (only 40%) compared to people of working age (61%) and youth (92%). People's age has, however, much less of an impact on differences in the frequency of socialising with other relatives living outside the household.

- Gender has little influence on the frequency of socialising with friends. Women, however, report getting together with relatives from outside the household more frequently than do men. For example, almost 70% of all women have face-to-face contact with relatives at least once a week, as compared to around 59% of all men.

- Income status has a strong positive impact on the frequency of socialising. In European countries, the poor are twice as likely as the non-poor never get together with friends or family from outside the household. For example, just under 16% of the poor never see friends, compared to just under 8% of the non-poor; similarly, around 8% of the poor report never having contacts with relatives, compared to around 4% for the non-poor.

Table 8.3. Frequency of socialising with friends and family by gender, age and poverty status

European countries (EU 27), 2006

Friends								
		Gender		Age			Poverty statis	
	Total	Female	Male	16-17	18-64	65+	Non-poor	Poor
Never	9.0	8.7	9.4	2.2	6.7	19.1	7.8	15.8
At least once a week (not every day)	57.3	57.9	56.6	91.5	60.6	40.3	58.2	52.6
At least once a month (not every week)	27.9	28.0	27.8	5.6	27.9	31.1	28.4	24.8
At least once a year (less than once a month)	5.7	5.3	6.2	0.7	4.9	9.5	5.6	6.8
Family								
Never	4.7	3.5	5.9	6.4	4.0	6.5	3.9	8.4
At least once a week	64.6	69.9	58.7	53.2	65.1	64.0	65.5	59.4
At least once a month (not every week)	25.3	22.3	28.6	32.5	25.4	23.6	25.3	25.3
At least once a year (less than once a month)	5.5	4.3	6.9	7.9	5.3	5.9	5.2	6.9

Source: European Union Statistics on Income and Living Conditions (EU-SILC).

StatLink 🔗 *http://dx.doi.org/10.1787/888932494183*

The low-educated and the poor also have weaker social support networks

There is also a clear relationship between the availability of informal social support, on the one hand, and people's education and income, on the other (Figure 8.5). Around 72% of people with only primary education report having someone to count on for help in times of need, compared to over 90% of those with secondary and tertiary education. Similarly, while only 73% of respondents in the bottom income quintile report having someone to count on in case of need, this proportion increases progressively with income (*e.g.* more than 90% of those in the upper income quintile declare that they can count on someone in case of need).

While gender has little impact on social network support according to this measure, age has an influence. People's social support networks tend to weaken as they get older until late in their working life, but they strengthen again over the age of 65. This "U-shaped" pattern may reflect the supportive role played by parents, in the case of youth, and of grown-up children and younger spouses, for elderly people.

Figure 8.5. Social network support by gender, age, level of education and income quintile

Percentage of people reporting that they have someone to count on in times of need, 2010

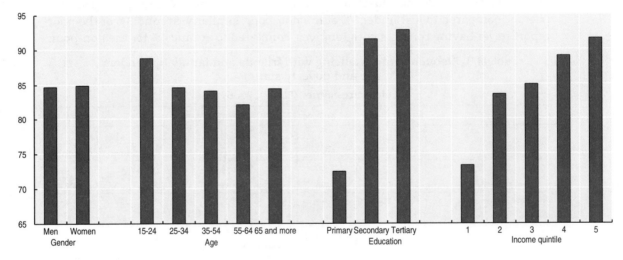

Source: Gallup World Poll.

StatLink ▬▬ *http://dx.doi.org/10.1787/888932493081*

Age, education and income also impact levels of trust in others

The probability of reporting high trust in others tends to increase with the age of the respondents but to drop off slightly after the age of 65 (Figure 8.6). A similar pattern can be observed with respect to income, with trust in others increasing with people's income up to a certain point, and then dropping off again in the two highest income quintiles. There is also a clear relationship between people's education and trust in others, with trust increasing continuously with the respondents' level of education. On average, among all the countries covered by the Gallup World Poll, men report a slightly higher level of trust in others than do women.

Figure 8.6. Trust in others by gender, age, level of education and income quintile

Percentage of people saying that most people can be trusted, 2010

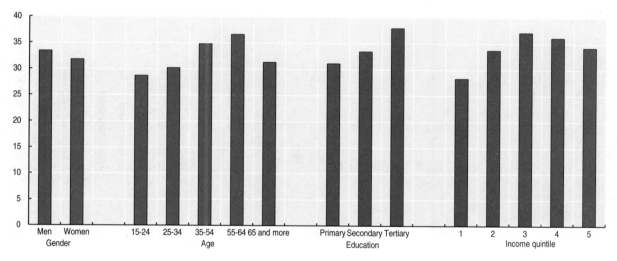

Source: Gallup World Poll.

StatLink ⟶ http://dx.doi.org/10.1787/888932493100

In most countries, older people volunteer more of their time

Older people tend to volunteer more of their time than do people of other ages (Figure 8.7). The difference is particularly clear in New Zealand, India and the United States. There has been an increasing trend for older people to use their free time after retirement for increased civic engagement (Sloan Center, 2010), and there is evidence that this leads to increased subjective well-being and improved health outcomes (Morrow-Howell *et al.*, 2003).

Figure 8.7. **Time spent volunteering by age and gender**

Latest available year

Gender

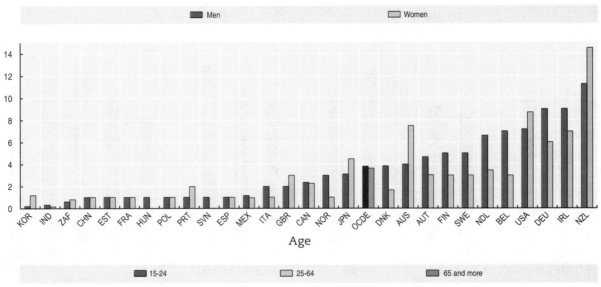

Age

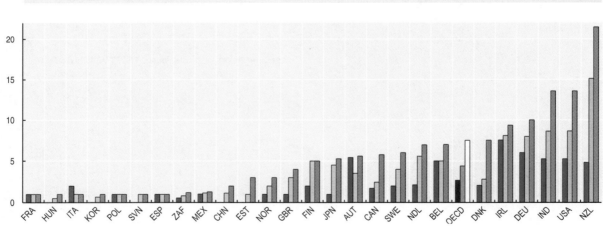

Note: Data refer to 1998-99 for France and New Zealand; 1999 for Portugal and India; 1999-2000 for Estonia, Finland and Hungary; 2000 for South Africa; 2000-01 for Norway, Slovenia, Sweden, and the United Kingdom; 2001 for Denmark; 2001-02 for Germany; 2002-03 for Italy and Spain; 2003-04 for Poland; 2005 for Belgium, Canada and Ireland; 2005-06 for the Netherlands; 2006 for Australia, Japan; 2008 for the United States and China; 2008-09 for Austria; 2009 for Korea and Mexico. The indicator refers to people aged 20-59 for Hungary and 30-59 for Korea. Data have been normalized to 1440 minutes per day. In other words, for those countries for which the time use did not sum up to 1440 minutes, the missing minutes were equally distributed across all activities.

Source: OECD Time Use Surveys Database.

StatLink 🔗 *http://dx.doi.org/10.1787/888932493119*

The statistical agenda ahead

The data on social connections available from official sources are currently sparse and lacking in terms of the availability of time-series, international comparability or both. The primary data source for two of the four indicators shown in this chapter is the Gallup World Poll, while for the two other indicators, which are based on official statistics, coverage is limited to European countries and time series information is unavailable. Given the importance of social connections both to people's subjective assessments of their well-being (Kahneman *et al.*, 2004; Helliwell, 2008) and to the productivity of the economy (Knack and Keefer, 1997), better measurement of social connections is essential to provide a more accurate picture of the quality of life. The statistical agenda ahead needs to encompass several strands of work.

- First, it is important to build a better understanding of how best to measure social connections. While there is some consensus around the importance of some aspects – such as measures of interpersonal trust as an indicator of social capital – many of the other measures used to describe social connections are not as well understood. The frequency of contact with friends and family, social isolation, social network support and friendship are key areas that need further research and testing. For example, providing more detail on the different sources (*e.g.* friends, neighbours, colleagues) and types of social network support (*e.g.* help finding a job, finding a place to live, financial support, emotional support, etc.) that people can count on.

- Second, it is important to ensure the standardisation and regular collection of official statistics for those measures for which there is a sufficient body of knowledge, in particular with respect to interpersonal trust.

- Third, another important issue is achieving greater standardisation of time use surveys in terms of providing more detailed information on episodes spent with others (*e.g.* volunteering) and a more consistent classification of activities. As noted in Chapter 6 ("Work and Life Balance"), there are huge margins for improving the international comparability of time use data, which underscores the importance of ongoing international initiatives in this field (*e.g.* the UNECE taskforce on time-use surveys).

Given the importance of this topic and the need for better measures in this area, the OECD will be undertaking a project to assess current measures of social capital and to identify best practices. This will lead to a report and to guidelines for social capital measurement in 2013.

Conclusion

Social connections play a role of central importance in people's lives, both on an individual and on a societal level. Overall, personal social networks are relatively strong in OECD countries, with the majority of people seeing friends and/or relatives on a regular basis and reporting that they have someone to count on in times of need. However, there are significant differences between different socio-economic and demographic groups, with the old, the poor and the less-educated tending to have weaker networks of social support. There are wide variations between countries in levels of interpersonal trust – one key indicator of the societal outcome of social connections. Measuring social connections remains, however, challenging, and more work is needed to develop comparable measures in this field.

Notes

1. Information on the accounts for non-profit institutions is provided in *Measuring Civil Society and Volunteering, Initial Findings from Implementation of the UN Handbook on Non-profit Institutions*, Johns Hopkins Center for Civil Society Studies. See also the information available at the *UN Non-profit Handbook Project* (www.jhu.edu/unhandbook/handbookdraft.html) and at the *Comparative Non-profit Sector Project* (www.jhu.edu/cnp/).

2. Levels of trust in others have changed over time, although the direction of this change varies across countries. According to analysis based on World Values Survey data spanning the last three decades (Morrone *et al.*, 2009), several countries recorded sharp falls in levels of trust in others. For example, Mexico, Portugal, Turkey, Poland, Spain and Hungary saw trust levels drop by one-third or more between the earliest and latest surveys. In Portugal and Mexico, levels of trust more than halved between 1990 and the early-2000s. However, trust in others increased by around 20% in Denmark, Switzerland, Sweden, Germany and Italy. The data from the study can give only a general idea of trends between countries, as the periods covered for each country vary. For example, the Mexican data cover 1990-2005 and the Portuguese data cover 1990-1999. The results are interesting, nonetheless, to indicate general trends. The data on interpersonal trust shown in this chapter, which are based on the Gallup World Poll, are strongly correlated ($R^2 = 0.79$, based on an analysis of 23 countries) with similar data from the World Values Survey (www.worldvaluessurvey.org) used in Morrone *et al.*, 2009 and other OECD reports (OECD, 2011).

References

Aguilera, M. (2002), "The impact of social capital on labour force participation: evidence from the 2000 Social Capital Benchmark Survey", *Social Science Quarterly*, 83: 3, pp. 853-74.

Baum, F., R.Bush, C.Modra, C.Murray, E.Cox, K.Alexander and R.Potter (2000), "Epidemiology of participation: an Australian community study", *Journal of Epidemiology and Community Health*, 54:6, pp. 414-423.

Berkman, L. and T.Glass (2000), "Social integration, social networks, social support, and health", in Berkman, L. and I.Kawachi, eds. *Social Epidemiology*, Oxford University Press; Oxford.

Borgonovi, F. (2008), "Doing well by doing good: The relationship between formal volunteering and self-reported health and happiness", *Social Science & Medicine*, 66: 11, pp. 2321-2334.

Case, R., A.Moss, N.Case, M.McDermott and S.Eberly (1992), "Living alone after myocardial infarction: impact on prognosis", *Journal of the American Medical Association*, 267:4, pp. 515-519.

Chan, Y. and R.Lee (2006), "Network Size, Social Support and Happiness in Later Life: A Comparative Study of Beijing and Hong Kong", *Journal of Happiness Studies*, 7, pp. 87-112.

Coleman, J. (1988), "Social Capital in the Creation of Human Capital", *American Journal of Sociology*, 94 Supplement: S95-S120.

Faber, A.D. and S. Wasserman (2002), "Social support and social networks: Synthesis and review", in J.A. Levy and B.A. Pescosolido eds., *Social Networks and Health*, Elsevier Science, Amsterdam, pp. 29 -72.

Fennema, M. and J.Tillie (1999), "Political participation and political trust in Amsterdam: civic communities and ethnic networks", *Journal of Ethnic and Migration Studies*, 25:4, 703-26.

Glaeser, E., D.Laibson and B.Sacerdote (2002), "An Economic Approach to Social Capital", *Economics Journal*, 112:483, 437-458.

Goldthorpe, J., C.Llewellyn and C.Payne (1987), *Social mobility and Class Structure in modern Britain* (2nd Edition), Clarendon Press: Oxford.

Halpern, D. (1995), *Mental Health and the Built Environment: More than bricks and mortar?*, London: Taylor and Francis.

Halpern, D. (2005), *Social Capital*, Polity Press, Cambridge.

Helliwell, J. (2008), "Life Satisfaction and Quality of Development", NBER Working Paper Series No. 14507, http://www.nber.org/papers/w14507.

Kahneman, D., A. Krueger, D. Schkade, N. Schwarz, and A. Stone (2004), "A Method for Characterizing Daily Life Experience: The Day Reconstruction Method", *Science*, 306: 5702, pp. 1776-1780.

Kahneman, D and A.Krueger (2006), "Developments in the Measurement of Subjective Well-Being", *Journal of Economic Perspectives*, 20:1, pp. 3-24.

Knack, S. and P.Keefer (1997), "Does social capital have an economic payoff? A cross-country investigation", *Quarterly Journal of Economics*, 112: 4, pp. 1251-88.

Leigh, A. (2010), *Disconnected*, University of New South Wales Press: Sydney.

Miranda, V. (2011), "Cooking, Caring and Volunteering: Unpaid Work Around the World", OECD Social, Employment and Migration Working Papers No. 116, Paris.

Morrone, A., N.Tontoranelli and G.Ranuzzi (2009), "How Good is Trust? Measuring Trust and its Role for the Progress of Societies", OECD Statistics Working Paper, Paris.

Morrow-Howell, N., Hinterlong, J., Rozario, P.A., Tang, F.(2003), "Effects of volunteering on the well-being of older adults", *The Journals of Gerentology Series B: Psychological Sciences and Social Sciences*, 58:3, 137-45.

OECD, (2001), *The Well-Being of Nations*, OECD Publishing, Paris.

OECD (2009), *OECD Factbook 2009: Economic, Environmental and Social Statistics*, OECD Publishing, Paris.

OECD (2011), *Society at a Glance 2011: OECD Social Indicators*, OECD Publishing, Paris.

Paldam, M. and G.Svendsen (2000), "An Essay on Social Capital: Looking for the Fire Behind the Smoke", *European Journal of Political Economy*, 16: 2, pp. 339-366.

Podolny, J. and J.Baron (1997), "Resources and relationships: social networks and mobility in the workplace", *American Sociological Review*, 62, pp. 673-693.

Putnam, R. (1993), *Making Democracy Work: Civic Traditions in Modern Italy*, Princeton University Press, Princeton.

Putnam, R. (2000), *Bowling Alone: The Collapse and Revival of America's Community*, Simon and Schuster, New York.

Seeman, T.E. and L.F. Berkman: 1988, "Structural characteristics of social networks and their relationship with social support in the elderly: Who provides support", *Social Science and Medicine*, 26: 7, pp. 737-749.

Seeman, T. (1996), "Social ties and health: The benefits of social integration", *Annals of Epidemiology*, 6:5, pp. 442-451.

Sherbourne, C., R.Hayes and K.Wells (1995), "Personal and psychological risk factors for physical and mental health outcomes and course of depression amongst depressed patients", *Journal of Consulting and Clinical Psychology*, 63 (3): 345-55.

Sloan Center on Aging & Work (2010), "Trends in Volunteerism among Older Adults", *Fact Sheet 03* (January), Boston College, http://www.bc.edu/ageingandwork

Stiglitz, J.E., A. Sen and J.-P. Fitoussi (2009), *Report by the Commission on the Measurement of Economic Performance and Social Progress*, http://www.stiglitz-sen-fitoussi.fr/documents/rapport_anglais.pdf

UK Cabinet Office (2010), http://www.cabinetoffice.gov.uk/big-society

Veenstra, G. (2000), "Social capital, SES and health: an individual level analysis", *Social Science and Medicine*, 50:5, pp. 619-29.

Williams, A., J.Ware and C.Donald (1981), "A model of mental health, life events, and social supports applicable to general populations", *Journal of Health and Social Behaviour*, 22, pp. 324-336.

Willms, J., (2001), "Three Hypotheses about Community Effects", in J.F. Helliwell (ed.), *The Contribution of Human and Social Capital to Sustained Economic Growth and Well-being: International Symposium Report*, Human Resources Development Canada and OECD.

Chapter 9

Civic engagement and governance

Civic engagement allows people to express their voice and to contribute to the political functioning of their society. In turn, in well-functioning democracies, civic engagement shapes the institutions that govern people's lives. While civic engagement and governance are essential for democracies, they are also very difficult to measure. This chapter presents some limited evidence, and emphasises the need for a better conceptual foundation for these concepts and for their measurement. The indicators included provide information about the possibility for citizens to express their voices in political processes, on some aspects of the quality of governance, and on people's satisfaction with public institutions. Even if these indicators are far from ideal, this chapter identifies some important patterns. First, while levels of voter turnout vary across countries, most OECD countries experienced declining participation rates over the last few decades. Second, the shift towards greater transparency and consultation in rule-making has not translated into higher civic engagement. Third, even if all OECD citizens enjoy fundamental civic rights, they do not necessarily exercise them effectively, particularly in the case of the poor, the less educated and the youth. Overall, these patterns are important as they point to shortcomings in democratic institutions, and to a gap between how citizens and elites perceive the functioning of democratic systems.

Why do civic engagement and governance matter for well-being?

Civic engagement, which refers to the various activities that people perform to express their political voice and contribute to the political functioning of society, is essential to individual well-being. Political voice is one of the basic freedoms and rights that are worthwhile to all humans and that people have reason to value (Sen, 1999). Furthermore, people who are given the opportunity to participate in a decision are more likely to endorse the decision as they consider it fair (Frey and Stutzer, 2006). Civic engagement may also increase people's sense of personal efficacy and control over their lives (Barber, 1984). Finally, civic engagement allows individuals to develop a sense of belonging to their community, trust in others and a feeling of social inclusion.[1]

Beyond its intrinsic value, civic engagement also enhances the effectiveness of public policy (Knack, 2002). By engaging in political activities, people openly express their preferences and needs; this in turn can inform policy, thereby influencing people's well-being. Political voice may also reduce the potential for conflicts and enhance the prospect of building consensus on key policies, leading to more effective policy implementation and strengthening the relationship between citizens and government. Finally, political voice increases the accountability of policy-makers, leading to better governance and thus better policies.

Governance relates to the institutions by which authority in a country is exercised.[2] The quality of these institutions strongly conditions people's quality of life, by setting regulations, defining and implementing public policies and establishing the rule of law. Good, effective public governance also deepens confidence in government and public administration, and thus increases well-being (OECD, 2001b). Good governance may hence be seen as a mutually supportive relationship between governments, on one side, and citizens, on the other: governments' legitimate authority stems from the consent of the governed and, through political and civic activities, citizens in turn shape the functioning of governments and public institutions.

The concepts of civic engagement and governance involve a number of aspects that are difficult to conceptualise and measure. Both concepts have been proxied through a wide range of indicators. However, none of the existing measures are really satisfactory. Improving indicators of governance and civic engagement is paramount to understanding whether people are satisfied as citizens and whether they believe that public policies and institutions promote the common good, and benefit ordinary citizens.

Measuring civic engagement and governance

Ideal indicators of civic engagement would measure whether citizens are involved in a range of important civic and political activities that enable them to effectively shape the society where they live. Similarly, indicators of the quality of governance should measure whether public policy is effective and transparent in achieving its stated goals, and whether individuals trust the government and the institutions of the country where they live.

In practice, measuring civic engagement and governance is a considerable challenge. First, the quality of governance encompasses a large number of factors, including the efficiency and the transparency of the various institutions, their range of action, and their openness and accessibility to all citizens, regardless of their educational and social background. Second, people can engage in society in various ways, *e.g.* by volunteering or participating in other types of associations that benefit society at large. Common expressions of civic engagement include voting, signing petitions and using social networks to share political ideas and values. Finally, another challenge for measuring civic engagement involves distinguishing between the processes that allow freedom of choice and action, on one side, and whether people actually take avail of these opportunities, on the other side.

The indicators of governance and civic engagement in use today meet this ideal set of principles only to a limited extent. First, despite the plethora of existing indicators of governance, these indicators lack a recognised statistical standard and are affected by insufficient quality, a small scope, low coverage and over-reliance on information from institutional sources and experts.[3] Second, while civic engagement indicators are potentially available for many dimensions of participation, they very often rely either on official surveys that are not harmonised across countries, or on surveys carried out outside the boundaries of the official statistical system.

The evidence discussed in this chapter therefore focuses on voter turnout as the main proxy for political participation, complemented by indicators of self-reported participation in other political activities. Regarding governance, this chapter mainly relies on an indicator developed by the OECD that measures one aspect of the quality of governance, namely the existence of formal and open consultation procedures on rule-making. This indicator informs about both the quality of regulation and the opportunities for citizens to express their views in the regulatory process. Because this indicator covers only one particular aspect of the quality of governance, it is accompanied by one other subjective indicator on people's perception of the quality of governance: the people's confidence in various institutions.[4] Table 9.1 summarises the main quality features of the selected indicators.

Selected indicators

Voter turnout (CEG I)

Political participation is crucial for democratic institutions, because it ensures the accountability of governments and public institutions and increases the chance that the decisions taken by the political system reflect the will of a large number of individuals. Voter turnout is the best available indicator for measuring individual participation in an election. This indicator captures peoples' opportunities for expressing their voices, but it is also an outcome measure that looks at the final choices expressed by citizens. Voting can be seen as a resource that is transformed into well-being by citizens: they vote in order to affect the actions of government in ways that are meaningful to them.

Voter turnout can be measured in two ways: either as the number of total votes cast over the voting-age population or as the number of total votes cast over the population registered to vote. The voting-age population is the population aged 18 or more in most countries, while the registered population refers to the number of people listed on the voters' register. The total number of votes cast is gathered from national statistics offices and electoral management bodies. The indicator shown here is compiled by the International Institute for Democracy and Electoral Assistance (IDEA). The voting-age population tends to overstate the size of the electorate in countries where a large share of the population is not eligible to vote (e.g. non-citizen residents who are not eligible to vote).[5] The indicator showing the number of votes cast over the population registered to vote is a better measure of the political participation of nationals. Both indicators relate to major national elections, i.e. those that attract the largest number of voters.[6] The main limitation of these indicators is that differences across countries in institutional features of the voting systems might affect cross-country comparisons (Box 9.1).

Box 9.1. **The impact of some institutional features of electoral systems on voter turnout**

A plurality of factors may give people an incentive to participate in elections. Two potentially important determinants of voting are the nature of voting (compulsory or not) and the registration process. With respect to the first factor, all democratic countries consider participation in national elections as a right of citizens. Some countries also consider voting as a duty of citizens and make voting legally compulsory. It is important to distinguish between countries where voting is compulsory in principle and in practice (i.e. non-voting brings sanctions) and those where voting is only compulsory in principle (i.e. countries have compulsory voting laws but do not enforce them). Among the 34 OECD member countries, only three countries (Australia, Belgium and to a lesser extent Chile) enforce voting in principle and in practice, while seven more countries have a few elements of compulsion.

While the impact of compulsory voting on turnout is potentially important, in practice this impact depends on several factors, such as the age of the democracy and the type of electoral systems in place (plurality/majority, proportional representation or mixed systems). For example, Norris (2002) found that while compulsion is associated with higher levels of turnout in established democracies, this is not the case in new democratic regimes. This suggests that comparing countries on the basis of the compulsory character of voting is not sufficient to explain the observed cross-country variation in voter turnout and that the variation reflects genuine differences in political participation across countries.

Registration procedures may also affect voter turnout. Registration conditions the exercise of voting rights: in some countries, citizens - and sometimes residents - are required to take active steps with some central registry specifically to be allowed to vote in elections. Registration may be compulsory or voluntary, continuous or periodic, and initiated by citizens or undertaken by a responsible agency. Complicated registration procedures may discourage people from registering and thus depress voting participation.

In addition, by limiting registration to citizens only, a varying part of the population in OECD countries may be politically disenfranchised. Using the voting-age population as the denominator in the voter turnout indicator provides a partial estimation of those who are disenfranchised.

Sources: López Pintor and Gratschev (2002) and Norris (2002).

Participation in other types of political activities (ceg 1)

Voter turnout provides only a partial picture of political participation. Citizens can express their political voices in other ways, such as by signing a petition, joining a political organisation or participating in a political rally or demonstration. These activities are important instrumentally, as they can provide a corrective to public policy by revealing people's needs (Stiglitz *et al.*, 2009); maintain political vigilance among citizens (Benn, 1979); and improve the quality of a democracy (Almond and Verba, 1963; Paxton, 2002). These activities also intrinsically matter for people because they are a way of socialising with others, which is an essential determinant of individual well-being (Helliwell and Putnam, 2004; Owen *et al.*, 2008).

The propensity of people to engage in political activities other than voting may be measured through survey questions. One such question is: "During the last 12 months, have you done any of the following: contacted a politician, government or local government official, worked in a political party or action group, worked in another organisation or association, worn or displayed a campaign badge/sticker, signed a petition, taken part in a lawful public demonstration, boycotted certain products?".[7] The indicator shown in this chapter refers to the number of people who responded "yes" to at least one of the previous propositions. Data are limited to European countries and based on Round Four (2008) of the European Social Survey, a survey conducted outside the official statistical system of European countries.[8] This indicator is therefore presented here as a secondary indicator.

Consultation on rule-making (CEG II)

Good governance is generally characterised by accessibility, accountability, predictability and transparency (Morita and Zaelke, 2005). Improving transparency in the access to regulations is thus a key element for fostering good governance. Further, promoting access to the consultation process is one way to improve confidence in the authorities, as people's confidence is influenced by the degree of contact with institutions (Hudson, 2006). The indicator on consultation on rule-making used in this chapter relates to the efforts made by governments to engage citizens in social life and it captures the possibility given to individuals to have a say in the framing of new policies.

The indicator on consultation on rule-making measures the extent to which formal and open consultation processes are built in at key stages of the design of policy proposals, and the mechanisms that exist for the outcome of that consultation to influence the preparation of primary laws and subordinate regulations.[9] The indicator does not inform about effective citizen participation in the consultation processes or about how this actually impacts the policies that are finally adopted. Nevertheless, the existence of such consultation processes may positively affect the quality of life of citizens by increasing their trust in existing regulations and institutions.[10] The indicator presented here has been developed by the OECD in consultation with member countries. It is a composite index combining information on the openness and transparency of the consultation process when designing policies (Box 9.2.).

Box 9.2. The characteristics of formal and open consultation processes

The indicator on consultation on rule-making draws upon country responses to the OECD's survey of regulatory management systems, where the respondents are government officials in OECD countries. Three waves of surveys on countries' regulatory management systems have been carried out, starting in 1998, with a second round in 2005 and a third round in 2008. Data for 2005 and 2008 are shown in this report. This box presents information about the content of the consultation on the rule-making indicator for 2008, which contains more individual indicators than the 2005 indicator. The full set of questions and the weighting are provided in Annex 9.A.

The 2008 survey contains 19 questions about the core policy areas covered by the OECD Principles for Regulatory Quality and Performance. The indicator on "consultation and rule-making" relates to question 9 of the survey, which has several sub-items focusing on consultation processes. In most cases, answers are dichotomous (i.e. "yes or no"), with the weight attached to positive answers depending on the sub-item considered. The sub-items relate to:

- Whether public consultation with parties affected by regulations is a routine part of developing draft new legislation (with follow-up questions on when the consultation is conducted and whether this is mandatory).

- Whether public consultation is based on guidelines, what form this consultation takes (circulation of proposals, public notice, public meetings, internet, advisory groups, public commissions) and whether any citizen can participate.

- The length of the period for comments inside the government and for consultation by the public.

- Whether the views of participants in the consultation are made public and included in regulatory impact analysis; whether regulators are required to respond in writing to the authors of these comments; whether there are processes to monitor the quality of the consultation; and whether guidance is available on how to conduct effective consultation.

From these answers, a composite index is constructed by the OECD based on the OECD quality framework for statistics and the OECD "Handbook on Constructing Composite Indicators". The robustness of the composite index is tested with statistical techniques and by sensitivity analysis for alternative weights. A peer review process aims to enhance data quality, temporal consistency and cross-country comparability (OECD, 2009b). The responsibility for countries' responses remains with member countries.

Source: OECD (2009b).

Caution is needed when interpreting this indicator. First, countries that undertake extensive consultation of large social groups – such as trade unions, employers associations, representatives of communities and consumer organisations – may not necessarily score well on this index (*e.g.* Belgium and Germany, OECD, 2009b). Second, the indicator on formal and open consultation processes is also *de jure* and does not provide information on whether a system works well, which depends on the specific context and requires in-depth analysis and country reviews (OECD, 2009a and 2009b). Finally, different consultation methods might be more appropriate in different countries, depending on their cultural, institutional and historical contexts. This might affect the cross-country comparability of the index.

Trust in institutions (ceg 2)

Political efforts to achieve greater transparency of governance may be hampered by people's lack of confidence in various institutions (the national government, the judicial system and courts, and the media) of the country where they live. Confidence in these institutions is essential for social stability and the functioning of democracy (Morrone *et al.*, 2009) and for economic growth (Knack and Keefer, 1997; Knack and Zak, 2001; Glaeser *et al.*, 2004). The national government is charged with putting into effect a country's laws and administering its functions; a fair and accessible justice system guarantees that every citizen is equal before the law; finally, the media plays an important role in informing people and in making democracy work. Trust may be hampered by high levels of perceived corruption in institutions (Box. 9.3).

The empirical literature on the role of trust in institutions has been limited, principally due to data limitations.[11] The indicator presented here is based on a non-official survey, the *Gallup World Poll*, because no harmonised official survey across countries exist at the moment for measuring people's confidence in institutions. This survey covers all OECD member countries and some emerging countries. The indicator relies on people's self-reporting, as assessed using the following question: "Do you have confidence in the national government/the judicial system and courts/the media?" with answers grouped into two categories (yes/no). Because of the small samples and other methodological limitations of this survey, caution is warranted when interpreting the indicator. It is presented here as a secondary indicator for illustrative purposes.

Box 9.3. **The importance of trust and perceived corruption in institutions**

Declining levels of trust in institutions are a concern for the functioning of democratic systems. A growing body of research suggests that trust in institutions influences a wide range of economic and social phenomena and that it is both a prerequisite and a consequence of effective public policy (Putnam, 1994). La Porta *et al.* (1997) show that, across countries, the effects of institutional trust on governance performance are large and statistically significant. While many studies suggest that people's trust in institutions "causes" government effectiveness, others suggest that causality works in the opposite direction (*i.e.* people are more willing to trust more effective governments) (Morrone *et al.*, 2009).

Since the direction of causality is ambiguous, governments need to build up their credibility. Blinder (2000) defines government credibility as "living up to its word". The credibility of political action is directly related to trust in institutions: as successive governments implement policies that consistently produce successful results, trust develops over time; conversely, if policies are ineffective, governments will lack credibility, distrust will follow and be likely to persist over time. Every policy thus contributes to building the trustworthiness of governments: as a result, good governance and credible policies have a significant impact on trust in institutions.

Corruption (*i.e.* the misuse of public office for private gain) can stifle institutional trust through a variety of channels and then endanger the relationship of government and citizens. First, corruption undermines the efficiency and effectiveness of legal guarantees. Second, by their actions, corrupt elected politicians show that they do not care for citizens. Third, corrupt elected politicians are not reliable, as citizens will not know which policy outcomes to expect.

Figure 9.1 suggests that there is a strong negative relationship across countries between the share of people expressing high trust in the national government and the share of people thinking that corruption in the government is widespread.[1] The direction of causality between the two variables is unclear, but understanding this direction is essential from a policy-perspective. Uslaner (2002) suggests that trust and corruption have similar consequences: societies where institutional trust is strong and corruption is low have better governance, stronger economic growth and greater respect for the law among the citizenry. Some cross-sectional results have found that the effect of corruption on trust is greater than the opposite causal link (Uslaner, 2002), suggesting that reducing the level of corruption may improve the level of trust.

Corruption is difficult to measure because it is hidden and can take a wide range of forms. Perceptions of corruption, however matter in themselves, as they indicate that citizens do not trust their governments and institutions. It is not enough for political leaders to fight corruption; they also have to avoid appearing as corrupt (Warren, 2006). However, subjective measures are not sufficient and have to be complemented with objective indicators aimed at assessing the level of corruption.

The OECD plays a pivotal role in developing policy instruments and practical tools to fight corruption and build integrity in the public sector. Four major instruments may be singled out. First, the OECD Integrity Framework promotes integrity in public procurement by mapping out good practices and developing principles, guidelines and tools focusing on areas vulnerable to misconduct, fraud and corruption. Second, the OECD has developed Guidelines for Managing Conflict of Interest in the Public Service. Third, the OECD Recommendation on Principles for Transparency and Integrity in Lobbying is the first international instrument providing guidance to policy-makers on how to promote good governance principles in lobbying. Finally, the OECD Convention on Combating Bribery of Foreign Public Officials in International Business Transactions establishes legally binding standards to criminalise

---

bribery of foreign public officials in international business transactions and foresees a host of related measures to make this effective.

Figure 9.1. **Correlation between trust in institutions and perceived corruption in government**

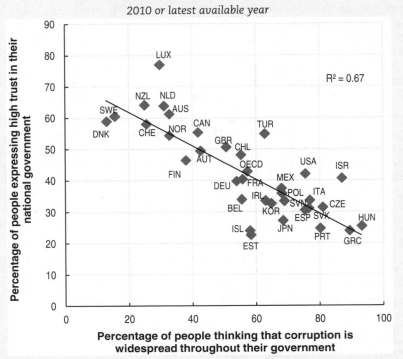

2010 or latest available year

Note: Data refer to 2009 for Estonia, Israel, Switzerland and South Africa; and to 2008 for Iceland and Norway. Data on perceived corruption are based on a question asking respondents whether they think that corruption in widespread throughout their government, with responses grouped into two categories (yes/no). The value for the OECD is an average of OECD countries for which data are available in the latest wave of the survey.
Source: Gallup World Poll.

StatLink ⟨ᴍꜱ⟩ *http://dx.doi.org/10.1787/888932493138*

Table 9.1. **The quality of civic engagement and governance indicators**

		INDICATORS							
	Target concept	Relevance to measure and monitor well-being				Statistical quality			
		Face validity	Unambiguous interpretation (good/bad)	Amenable to policy changes	Can be disaggregated	Well-established instrument collected	Comparable definition	Country coverage	Recurrent data collection
Civic engagement and governance									
CEG I Voter turnout	Civic engagement	~	√	√	x	~	√	√	~
ceg 1 Participation in political activities		√	~	√	√	~	√	√	~
CEG II Consultation on rule-making	Quality of governance	~	√	√	x	√	√	√	~
ceg 2 Confidence in national government, judicial system and courts and media	People's confidence in their public institutions	√	√	√	√	x	√	√	~

Note: The symbol √ shows that the indicator selected largely meets the criteria shown in the table; the symbol ~ that the indicator meets the criteria to a large extent; the symbol x that the indicator does not meet the criterion or it meets it only to a limited extent.

Average patterns

Many OECD countries show declining levels of voter turnout

Voter turnout rates vary substantially across countries: Denmark's voter turnout rate is more than double Switzerland's (Figure 9.2), whatever the definition of voter turnout considered.[12] Voter turnout is generally high in Nordic countries and low in Eastern European countries. As for the emerging countries, Brazil and Indonesia display higher levels of voter turnout than India or the Russian Federation.

Beside differences in levels, which may partly reflect differences in electoral systems, many OECD countries experienced declining levels of voter participation in the last two decades, following a prolonged period of increase in previous decades (OECD, 2007 and 2011). This decreasing participation is less visible in the emerging countries included in Figure 9.2, with the exception of South Africa, where voter turnout has declined sharply since the mid-1990s. In Indonesia and India, electoral participation has remained stable, while the Russian Federation experienced a rise. High turnout countries are neither consistently new democracies nor long-established ones. However, it seems that electoral participation has declined faster in countries where the voter turnout was already low.

Comparing the two measures of voter turnout shown in Figure 9.2 provides some information about the proportion of residents who lack political voice in national elections. This information is useful because the number of regular residents without citizenship has been rising in many countries due to greater international migration. In general, electoral participation is higher when considering the registered population than the voting-age population. However, country rankings are little affected by the exact definition used, with the important exception of the United States, where electoral participation is close to 90% when considering the registered voting-age population but falls below 60% when considering the voting-age population (see Box 9.1 for possible explanations of turnout drivers).

Other forms of political participation differs widely among European countries and across political activities

Participation in political activities other than voting varies substantially among European countries. It is the highest in Norway and Finland and the lowest in Turkey and Portugal (Figure 9.3). The above-average level of political participation in Switzerland contrasts with the low level of voter turnout. Turkey displays an opposite pattern, combining low levels of other forms of political participation and high levels of voter turnout. This suggests that elections are not the only means of expressing political opinions, feelings and interests and that measures of people's involvement in other political activities provide useful complementary information. Participation in political activities also depends on the activity considered (Table 9.2). Overall, around 22% of surveyed people in Europe declared having signed a petition in the last 12 months, while less than 4% declared having worked in a political party or action group.

Figure 9.2. **Lower voter turnout in most OECD countries and other major economies**

Percentage of people who casted a ballot as a share of the registered population

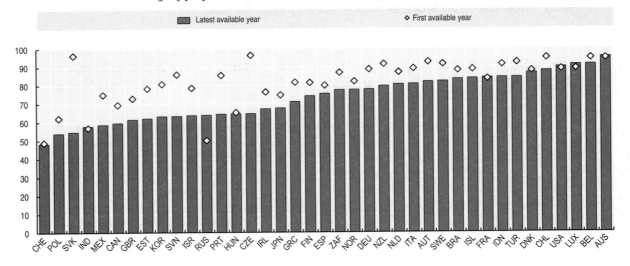

Percentage of people who casted a ballot as a share of the voting age population

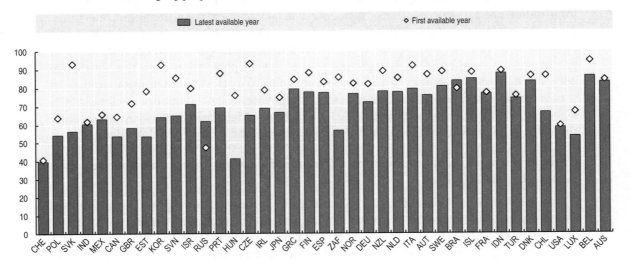

Note: The latest available year is 2004 for India and Indonesia; 2005 for Chile, Germany, Japan, Norway, Portugal and the United Kingdom; 2006 for the Czech Republic, Finland, Hungary, Israel, Mexico, the Netherlands, the Slovak Republic, Sweden and Brazil; 2007 for Australia, Belgium, Denmark, Estonia, France, Iceland, Ireland, Korea, Poland, Switzerland, Turkey and the Russian Federation; 2008 for Austria, Canada, Italy, New Zealand, Slovenia, Spain and the United States; and 2009 for Greece, Luxembourg and South Africa. The first available year is 1980 for Australia, Canada, Germany, Japan, Portugal, the United States and India; 1981 for Belgium, Denmark, France, Greece, Ireland, Israel, Netherlands, New Zealand, Norway; 1982 for Finland, Mexico, Spain, Sweden and Indonesia; 1983 for Austria, Iceland, Italy, Switzerland, Turkey and the the United Kingdom; 1984 for Luxembourg; 1989 for Chile, Poland and Brazil; 1990 for the Czech Republic, Estonia, Hungary and the Slovak Republic; 1992 for Slovenia; 1993 for the Russian Federation; 1994 for South Africa; and 1997 for Korea. Presidential elections are considered for Brazil, Finland, France, Korea, Mexico and the United States; parliamentary and legislative elections for other countries.
Source: International Institute for Democracy and Electoral Assistance, Stockholm.

StatLink 𝄜 *http://dx.doi.org/10.1787/888932493157*

Figure 9.3. **Participation in political activities other than voting in European countries**

Percentage, 2008

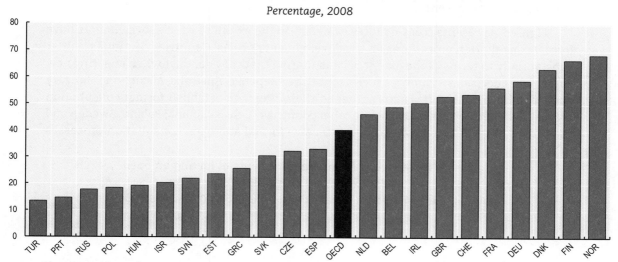

Note: Data refer to the percentage of people responding "yes" to questions whether they had done one of the following actions: contacted a politician, government or local government official; worked in a political party or action group; worked in another organisation or association; worn or displayed a campaign badge/sticker; signed a petition; taken part in a lawful public demonstration; and boycotted certain products.
Source: European Social Survey.

StatLink ⬛⬛⬛ http://dx.doi.org/10.1787/888932493176

Table 9.2. **Prevalence of different types of political activities in European countries**

Percentage of people indicating they have done one of the following activities during the last 12 months, 2008

	Contacted a politician, government or local government official	Worked in a political party or action group	Worked in another organisation or association	Worn or displayed a campaign badge/sticker	Signed a petition	Taken part in a lawful public demonstration	Boycotted certain products
Belgium	15.3	4.3	21.1	7.0	27.6	7.4	11.2
Czech Republic	15.5	2.3	9.1	3.7	15.2	4.5	7.4
Denmark	18.7	4.5	24.7	10.6	33.9	9.3	21.5
Estonia	11.1	3.0	5.3	5.3	8.0	2.1	5.6
Finland	21.1	4.1	34.1	15.3	32.3	2.5	30.3
France	15.4	3.8	15.2	11.2	33.6	15.3	27.7
Germany	16.8	3.8	25.9	5.2	30.8	8.1	31.1
Greece	10.6	4.2	4.0	3.2	4.3	6.1	14.4
Hungary	8.6	0.8	5.1	0.8	6.8	1.8	5.9
Ireland	23.0	4.7	16.5	9.8	24.1	9.8	13.6
Israel	7.6	4.7	4.5	5.5	10.7	6.9	5.9
Netherlands	14.1	3.4	26.2	5.1	23.5	3.3	9.4
Norway	21.5	6.1	27.9	26.0	37.8	7.2	22.5
Poland	7.2	2.6	5.9	4.2	7.5	1.6	4.5
Portugal	6.7	1.3	2.7	2.7	4.9	3.7	3.2
Slovak Republic	7.1	1.9	5.7	2.2	22.1	1.7	6.9
Slovenia	11.4	3.3	1.6	3.7	8.7	1.6	5.1
Spain	10.0	2.9	9.5	4.7	17.0	16.0	7.9
Sweden	14.8	4.4	27.0	18.4	47.2	6.5	37.3
Switzerland	12.0	4.9	13.1	6.9	37.7	7.7	25.0
Turkey	6.1	2.7	1.9	3.0	4.5	4.2	6.7
United Kingdom	16.9	2.2	6.6	5.6	38.2	3.8	24.2
OECD	13.1	3.4	13.3	7.1	21.6	6.2	15.2
Russian Federation	6.4	3.6	4.4	2.9	5.8	6.0	4.1

Source: European Social Survey.

StatLink ⬛⬛⬛ http://dx.doi.org/10.1787/888932494221

Consultation on rule-making has become more formalised and open but cross-country differences remain

Figure 9.4 presents cross-country evidence on the extent to which governments have formal consultation procedures on the development of rules. Countries continue to differ substantially in terms of the extent of consultation that they conduct when enacting new government decisions. Countries such as the Czech Republic, Australia, Mexico and Hungary appear to have considerably strengthened their efforts to establish formal consultation process between 2005 and 2008, while other countries such as Canada, Poland, Sweden and the United Kingdom already recorded extensive formal and open consultation processes in 2005.

Figure 9.4. Existence of formal requirements of having an open consultation on rule - making

Formal and open consultation processes on rule-making, 2005 and 2008/2009

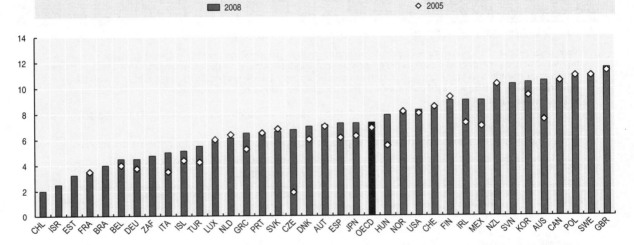

Note: The composite indicator rises with the number of key elements of open and formal consultation processes. However, it does not gauge whether these processes have been effective. The characteristics of the consultation processes are detailed in Box 9.2. Annex 9.A enumerates the items underling the composite and the weights assigned to each component. Data for Brazil, Chile, Estonia, Israel, Slovenia and South Africa refer to 2009. For more information on the new OECD member countries as well as Brazil and South Africa, see the country notes at www.oecd.org/regreform/indicators.

Source: OECD Regulatory Management Systems' Indicators Survey 2005 and 2008/2009, www.oecd.org/regreform/indicators

StatLink ⟨⟨⟨⟩ *http://dx.doi.org/10.1787/888932493195*

Confidence in various institutions differs widely across countries

On average, people's trust is higher in the judicial system and courts than in national governments and the media. This holds true even when trust in the judicial system is compared with other public institutions, such as parliament and the civil service, based on different data sources (Morrone *et al.*, 2009). On average, 51% of surveyed individuals across OECD countries reported a high trust in the judicial system and courts of their country (Figure 9.5, left-hand panel). Cross-country differences are, however, sizeable: the Czech Republic, Portugal and the Slovak Republic report levels of trust in the judicial system and courts of around 30% or less, while Luxembourg, Norway and Switzerland have levels above 70% (and above 80% in the case of Denmark).

Cross-country differences are also large regarding reported trust in the national government (Figure 9.5, middle panel): Estonia and Greece have levels of confidence barely above 20% while the Nordic countries as well as India and Indonesia display levels above

60%. The media appear to be a less-trusted institution, with only 40% of surveyed individuals across OECD countries expressing high trust in it. All the emerging countries exhibit levels of confidence in the national government and in the media above the OECD average (with the exception of respondents in the Russian Federation with respect to the media), while results are more varied when considering self-reported confidence in the judicial system and courts.

Figure 9.5. **Trust in institutions**

Percentage of respondents reporting high levels of trust in institutions, 2010

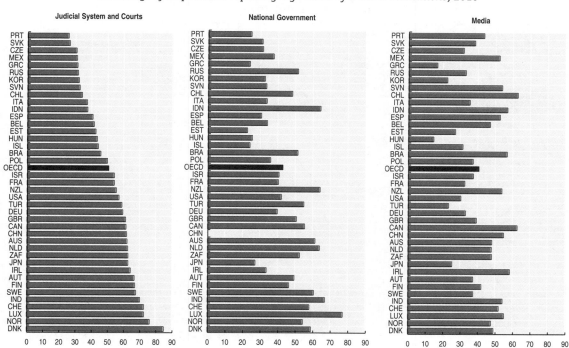

Note: Data refer to 2009 for Estonia, Israel, Switzerland and South Africa; and to 2008 for Iceland and Norway. Data regarding trust in the national government are not available for China. The value for the OECD is an average of OECD countries for which data are available in the latest wave of the survey.
Source: Gallup World Poll.

StatLink ⬛ http://dx.doi.org/10.1787/888932493214

The various indicators of civic engagement and governance are closely linked

The indicators presented in this chapter are based on various sources and capture different aspects of civic engagement and governance. For this reason, it is important to assess whether they convey a consistent picture. Table 9.3, which reports correlation between the indicators presented in this chapter across countries, highlights several patterns:

- Regarding civic engagement, both measures of voter turnout are strongly correlated (at the 1% level).[13] The indicator relating to other forms of political participation correlates well with the voter turnout rates irrespective of the definition of turnout considered. The lack of full correlation underscores the need for looking at a range of measures to get a good appreciation of people's civic engagement.[14]

- Various components of institutional trust are also correlated with each other. In particular, the correlation between confidence in the government and confidence in the judicial system and in the media is strong and significant. However, indicators of people's trust in institutions and the index for consultation on rule-making are not correlated across countries. A lack of knowledge about the possibility of comments by citizens, or worse, an indication about the ineffectiveness of consultation procedures to take into account all views in the regulatory process could explain the gap between subjective indicators of governance and objective ones.

● The indicator for non-voting political participation correlates strongly with indicators of institutional trust, suggesting that civic engagement is closely linked with subjective appreciations of institutions.

Table 9.3. **Correlation between different indicators of civic engagement and governance**

	CEG I Voter turnout		ceg 1 Participation in other types of political activities	CEG II Consultation on rule-making	ceg 2 Confidence in institutions		
	Percentage of the registered population	Percentage of the voting age population			Judicial system and courts	National government	Media
CEG I Voter turnout							
Percentage of the registered population	1 (39)	0.75*** (39)	0.43** (23)	-0.29 (35)	0.14 (39)	0.16 (39)	0.02 (39)
Percentage of the voting age population		1 (39)	0.40 (23)	-0.22 (35)	0.02 (39)	0.11 (39)	0.12 (39)
ceg 1 Participation in other types of political activities			1(24)	0.22 (23)	0.73*** (24)	0.54*** (24)	0.41** (24)
CEG II Consultation on rule-making				1 (36)	0.21 (36)	0.20 (36)	0.11 (36)
ceg 2 Confidence in institutions							
Judicial system and courts					1 (41)	0.62*** (40)	0.23 (41)
National government						1 (40)	0.54*** (40)
Media							1 (41)

Note: Values in parenthesis refer to the number of observations. ** Indicates that correlations are significant at the 5% level; *** indicates that they are significant at the 1% level.

Source: OECD's calculations.

StatLink ⟳ http://dx.doi.org/10.1787/888932494240

Inequalities

While the indicators on consultation on rule-making, which pertain to government processes, do not allow disaggregation across individuals (*i.e.* all citizens are assumed to benefit equally from opportunities to express their political voice), those pertaining to civic participation can be used to describe inequalities in political voice among people with different characteristics.

Age, education and income have an important bearing on the probability of voting...

Even if the right to vote is universal in all OECD countries, not everyone exercises this right. Table 9.4 presents some information about the socio-economic characteristics of voters. These data refer to surveys that ask respondents whether they cast a ballot during the last election, and are compiled by the Comparative Study of Electoral Systems (CSES), an international research programme that collects comparable data on elections. The table presents ratios of self-reported voter turnout between different subgroups of the population. These results have to be interpreted with some caution, as self-reported rates of turnout may be quite different from official voter turnouts.[15]

While on average there are few differences between men and women concerning the probability of participation in elections, the differences are more significant with respect to age: participation in election increases monotonically with age, with youth voter turnout being, on average, 28 percentage points lower than that of individuals aged 65 and more. Differences are also large when looking at the breakdown of voters according to their educational attainment.[16] Across OECD countries, voter turnout is 12 percentage points higher for people with tertiary education than for those with less than secondary education, with larger gaps for Poland, Hungary, the Czech Republic and the United States. Education seems to play an even larger role for electoral participation in Brazil and the Russian Federation. The relationship between educational attainment and political interest generally remains evident even when comparing people with the same income (OECD, 2010). In general, income has a strong influence on voter turnout. People in the lower quintile of the income distribution report rates of participation 14 percentage points lower than those in the top, with a gap of more than 30 percentage points in the United States, Poland and Chile. Voter turnout increases with individual income, although this effect seems to taper off at the top of at the distribution.

Table 9.4. **People who are younger, less educated, and with lower income are less likely to participate in elections**

Self-reported voter turnout by selected socio-economic characteristics,
ratios relative to different groups

	Year of election	Gender	Age				Educational attainment		Self reported employment status				Income			
		Women relative to Men	Persons aged 65 and over relative to:				Persons with tertiary education relative to:		Employed relative to:				Top income quintile relative to:			
			15-24	25-34	35-54	55-64	Less than secondary	Secondary	Unemployed	Retirees	Students	Housewives and others	Bottom quintile	Second quintile	Third quintile	Fourth quintile
Australia	2007	1.00	1.00	0.99	0.99	1.00	1.01	1.01		1.01	0.99	0.99	1.02	1.01	1.01	1.00
Belgium	2003	0.84	1.04	0.91	0.93	0.93	1.08	1.02		1.06	1.28	1.05				
Canada	2004	0.95	1.27	1.12	1.06	1.01	1.07	1.06	0.96	0.95	1.07	0.99	1.11	1.05	1.02	1.01
Chile	2005	0.98	1.03	1.04	1.00	0.98	0.98	1.00	0.95	0.98	0.99	0.99	1.05	1.05	1.03	1.06
Czech Republic	2002	1.01	1.33	1.16	1.03	1.04	1.28	1.15	0.93	0.96	1.17	1.64	1.23	1.06	1.02	1.07
Denmark	2001	0.91	1.17	1.06	1.02	1.00	1.07	1.02					1.06	1.04	1.02	1.02
Estonia	2004	1.12	1.09	1.07	0.97	0.96	1.03	1.03	1.00	0.97	0.92	0.94	0.99	0.97	0.98	0.95
Finland	2007	0.98	1.56	1.19	1.10	1.02	1.28	1.11	1.31	0.95	1.16	1.17	1.25	1.12	1.12	1.13
France	2002	1.00	1.26	1.22	1.00	0.96	1.08	1.06					1.13	1.11	1.11	1.04
Germany	2005	1.01	1.02	1.00	0.97	0.97	1.06	1.02	1.12	1.02	0.98	1.05	1.11	1.05	1.03	1.00
Hungary	2002	1.03	1.03	1.00	0.92	0.88	1.28	1.08	0.93	1.05	1.04	1.34	1.32	1.19	1.11	1.10
Iceland	2003	0.96	0.96	0.98	0.95	0.93	1.02	1.10	0.97	1.05	1.02	1.06	1.06	1.09	1.02	1.02
Ireland	2002	0.99	1.26	1.08	0.96	0.94	0.96	0.98	1.04	0.98	1.23	0.96	0.96	0.97	0.96	0.95
Israel	2006	0.99	1.47	1.24	1.09	1.04	1.11	1.13	1.32	0.92	1.23	1.23	1.12	1.18	1.06	1.12
Italy	2006	1.01	0.93	0.91	0.85	0.80	1.07	1.00	0.96	1.12	1.13	1.04	1.10	1.12	1.04	1.04
Japan	2007	1.03	1.47	1.29	1.14	0.97	0.99	1.01	0.94	0.88	1.29	0.91	1.00	0.98	0.97	0.93
Korea	2008	0.95	1.42	1.34	1.04	0.93	0.88	0.87	1.12	0.72	1.21	0.99	1.55	1.43	1.41	1.44
Mexico	2003	0.97	1.31	1.04	1.01	0.92	1.01	1.07	0.94	0.95	1.16	1.08	1.12	1.15	1.12	1.11
Netherlands	2002	0.95	1.02	1.01	1.00	0.99	1.03	0.99	0.98	1.00	0.97	1.00	1.05	1.02	0.99	1.00
New Zealand	2002	1.00	1.27	1.24	1.08	1.03	1.07	1.03	1.11	0.92	1.03	1.08	0.91	0.88	0.90	0.88
Norway	2005	0.95	1.27	1.08	1.01	1.00	1.14	1.11	1.25	0.99	1.17	1.04	1.17	1.10	1.10	1.01
Poland	2001	0.96	1.46	1.52	1.08	0.95	1.46	1.19	0.92	0.85	1.00	1.20	1.29	1.08	1.15	0.96
Portugal	2005	0.98	1.43	1.17	1.01	0.94	1.07	1.07	0.91	0.92	1.35	1.01	1.14	1.16	1.08	1.05
Slovenia	2004	0.95	1.42	1.22	1.03	0.93	1.15	1.11	0.89	0.89	1.30	1.08	1.18	1.07	1.07	1.00
Sweden	2006	1.00	1.06	1.04	1.03	1.02	1.07	1.04	1.13	0.97	0.99	0.92	1.07	1.09	1.08	1.00
Switzerland	2007	1.05	1.48	1.36	1.19	1.02	1.34	1.15	1.46	0.86	1.14	1.14	1.01	0.95	0.89	0.81
United Kingdom	2005	0.99	2.50	1.67	1.22	1.15	1.07	1.01	0.96	0.83	2.51	1.14	1.24	1.00	1.01	0.97
United States	2004	1.03	1.32	1.08	1.02	0.98	1.65	1.20	0.91	0.99	1.32	1.03	1.41	1.21	1.07	1.00
OECD		0.98	1.28	1.14	1.03	0.97	1.12	1.06	1.04	0.95	1.18	1.08	1.14	1.07	1.05	1.02
Russian Federation	2004	0.99	1.51	1.33	1.13	1.06	1.03	1.16	0.95	0.90	1.41	1.19	1.01	1.07	1.01	1.03
Brazil	2006	1.04	1.00	0.79	0.77	0.78	1.14	1.03					1.04	0.99	0.95	0.91

Note: Less than secondary education refers to category 1-4 in CSES (from none to incomplete secondary); secondary education refers to category 5-6 (from complete secondary to post-secondary); and tertiary education refers to category 7-8 (university level).
Source: Module 2 and 3 of the Comparative Study of Electoral Systems (CSES).

StatLink ᴍᴵˢᴾ *http://dx.doi.org/10.1787/888932494259*

... and on trust in institutions

As in the case of voter turnout, age, education and income significantly affect the degree of people's trust in institutions (Table 9.5). The impact is, however, generally lower than in the case of voting, with the possible exception of income. In OECD countries, women and men tend to express similar levels of trust in institutions, while in emerging countries women are significantly less confident in institutions than are men. In general, confidence grows with age, though this effect is not monotonic. In OECD countries, trust in the judicial systems and in the national government also tends to rise with the level of education, while confidence in the media declines with the level of education. In emerging countries, higher education is generally associated with lower trust in institutions. The relationship between income and trust is very similar to that between education and trust.

Table 9.5. **Income and age are important determinants of people's trust in institutions**

Percentage of people expressing high levels of trust by selected socio-economic characteristics, ratios relative to different groups, 2010

	Countries	Gender	Age						Educational attainment		Income
		Women relative to men	Persons aged 65 and over relative to:						Persons having attained tertiary education relative to:		Highest income quintile relative to bottom quintile
			15-24	25-34	35-44	45-54	55-64		Less than secondary	Secondary	
Confidence in the judicial system and courts	OECD	1.00	0.89	1.02	0.99	1.02	1.01		1.2	1.1	1.15
	Other major economies	0.93	0.91	0.96	0.94	0.97	0.94		0.81	1.11	0.91
Confidence in the national government	OECD	0.96	1.00	1.17	1.12	1.13	1.07		1.1	1.1	1.10
	Other major economies	0.93	1.04	1.12	1.04	1.18	1.04		0.87	1.05	0.93
Confidence in the media	OECD	0.94	0.89	1.02	1.04	1.13	1.05		0.83	0.88	0.87
	Other major economies	0.93	0.84	0.95	0.89	0.93	0.88		0.87	0.95	1.04

Note: Other major economies include the Russian Federation, Brazil, China, India, Indonesia and South Africa. Data refer to 2009 for Estonia, Israel, Switzerland and South Africa; and to 2008 for Iceland and Norway. The value for the OECD is an average of OECD countries for which data are available in the latest wave of the survey.
Source: Gallup World Poll.

StatLink *http://dx.doi.org/10.1787/888932494278*

The statistical agenda ahead

While civic engagement and governance are essential domains for individual and societal well-being – and several initiatives are aiming to provide better indicators in this field – identifying solid and reliable indicators remains challenging. This reflects the many aspects encompassed by the broad notions of civic engagement and governance as well as the difficulties of measuring each of them.[17] Further, most of the indicators available in this domain are based on experts' views, which raises questions about the legitimacy of the measures and their consistency both over time and across countries. Consequently, the picture of civic engagement and governance provided in this chapter remains limited in important ways. A number of actions aimed at improving the notions of civic engagement and governance should be pursued in the future:

● First, the very concepts of civic engagement and governance need a better conceptual foundation. Civic engagement takes many forms, while governance pertains to different institutions, each characterised by its own practices. Statistics regarding these aspects have been typically developed outside the boundaries of official statistics, combining expert views about complex concepts (*e.g.* rule of law, transparency), data derived from administrative processes (*e.g.* on the functioning of the judiciary system) and self-perception data based on surveys. OECD (2009a) proposed a framework to deconstruct the concept of "governance" into manageable components and suggested a strategy to collect data on both inputs and outputs in this area. However, more work needs to be done to develop a similar framework for "civic engagement" and to provide guidelines on the best way of measuring it.[18]

- Second, data based on expert assessments and on the existence of specific practices within the public sector, such as the indicator on the consultation in rule-making used in this chapter, need to be extended to other aspects of governance, so as to provide a more holistic perspective on the quality of various institutions and democratic practices. Comparative measures also need to be developed for specific sectors that impact directly on people's lives, such as the justice system.

- Third, better measures are required to assess how people perceive the quality of the democratic institutions in the country where they live. While many unofficial surveys contain questions for measuring civic engagement and governance, they typically have a narrow geographic coverage, small sample size and inadequate sampling procedures.[21] Steps should be taken to include questions on civic participation and trust in institutions in large-scale official surveys, through a combination of a few recurrent questions in regular surveys and more detailed questions in (less frequent) dedicated modules, as is already done in some OECD countries (*e.g.* special modules of the Current Population Survey on voting and civic engagement in the United States).

- Finally, better data are needed to assess the existence of causal relationships. While the cross-sectional surveys used in this chapter allow describing associations between individuals' behaviour (*e.g.* voting or trusting) and other socio-demographic variables, only longitudinal data would make it possible to identify causations.

Conclusion

This chapter has presented evidence on civic engagement and governance in OECD and other major countries. This evidence is limited principally due to the paucity of reliable and relevant data for measuring the concepts of civic engagement and governance. The chapter highlights that most of these countries have expanded the use of practices of good governance in recent years, such as public consultation on rule-making. Nevertheless, this shift towards greater effective transparency has not translated into higher levels of trust expressed by citizens in how various institutions function, nor in higher rates of voter turnout.

In all the countries covered by this chapter, people enjoy rights that are intrinsically important but they do not necessarily exercise them effectively. This is particularly relevant for specific socio-economic groups of the population, especially the poor, the less educated and young people. Low trust in public institutions and declining levels of civic engagement point to a growing gap between how citizens and elites perceive the functioning of democratic systems. Identifying reliable indicators that can account for this gap, and understanding what type of policies and practices may help to reduce it, are some of the biggest challenges confronting communities and official statistics.

Notes

1. According to Knack (1992), participation in political life (through voting or engaging in associations) is influenced by "solidarity incentives" that are "intangible costs and benefits of a social nature deriving, for example, from friendship, camaraderie, recreational activity, status, social pressure, or a sense of belonging".

2. Kaufmann *et al.* (1999) include in this definition of governance "the process by which governments are selected, monitored and replaced, the capacity of the government to effectively formulate and implement sound policies, and the respect of citizens and the state for the institutions that govern economic and social interactions among them".

3. Several international initiatives aim at measuring selected aspects of governance. These initiatives include: the International Country Risk Guide (ICRG); the annual ratings provided by Freedom House; the World Bank Institute governance indicators; Transparency International's Corruption Perception Index; the Global Integrity Index; the Rule of Law Index developed by the World Justice Project; and the Bertelsmann Stiftung Sustainable Governance Indicators. All these initiatives generally aggregate multiple sources of information on various aspects of governance based on experts' assessments. Also these composite measures generally combine evaluations relating to both the "inputs" and "outputs" of government decisions (Arndt and Oman, 2006). However, these measures have been criticised for poorly measuring the concept they are intended to measure (Glaeser *et al.*, 2004).

4. Kaufmann *et al.* (2005) argued that objective measures of governance provide only an incomplete picture of governance and that perceptions-based data provide valuable insights into this objective data.

5. The voting-age population is not an exact measure of the number of citizens entitled to vote, because it does not take into account the legal or systemic barriers to voting that confront some members of the population. The voting-age population includes those who may not be eligible to vote at national elections (*i.e.* non-citizens, convicted criminals and some prison inmates) and excludes a part of the eligible population (*i.e.* the military personnel and civilians living outside the country considered). The voting-eligible population (defined as the voting-age population minus disenfranchised criminals and non-citizens plus eligible overseas citizens) would capture these discrepancies, but it is hard to collect the necessary data. McDonald and Popkin (2001) estimated that, in the United States, the population ineligible to vote constituted nearly 10% of the voting-age population in 2004, as compared to 2% in 1972. To some degree, the decline in the voter turnout rate observed in the United States over the last 30 years can be attributed to the increased number of ineligible people.

6. Presidential elections in Brazil, Finland, France, Mexico, Poland and the United States, and parliamentary elections for other countries. Criteria for being entitled to vote are typically more restrictive for national elections than for local ones.

7. This indicator does not cover other important political activities, such as the citizen's right to promote new political initiatives, vote in referendums and participate in social networks. Hence, this indicator may underestimate political participation in European countries where these activities are widespread.

8. The European Social Survey is an academically-driven household survey designed to explain the interaction between Europe's institutions and the attitudes, beliefs and behaviours of its populations. Currently in its fifth round and preparing for a sixth, the survey covers more than 30 nations and employs rigorous methodologies. It takes the form of a repeat cross-sectional survey, with data often collected by national statistical offices. The survey has been funded through the European Commission's Framework Programmes, the European Science Foundation and national bodies in each country.

9. The indicator on consultation has been selected because it allows for a partial measurement of whether people can express their views in the regulatory process, even though it does not measure actual consultation. Hence, this indicator measures only one precise aspect of governance. In consequence, other indicators are needed for a broader assessment of the quality of governance.

10. According to Sen (1999), processes that allow freedom of actions and decisions are intrinsically valuable for people and shape their individual quality of life by offering them the opportunity to exercise their agency. A number of studies (Frey and Stutzer, 2005 and 2006; Weitz-Shapiro and Winters, 2008) have shown that people value the political process in its own right, independently of policy outcomes. The simple existence of consultation processes may thus positively affect the quality of life of citizens, even when they do not use them substantially, because it increases the feeling of trust in existing regulations and institutions. Knack and Zak (2001) have shown that policies (particularly policies aimed at improving the quality of governance and civil liberties) induce higher levels of trust. Similarly, Mishler and Rose (2001) have argued that political trust is largely endogenous and influenced by the quality of institutions.

11. See for instance Beugelsdijk *et al.* (2004), who concluded that the empirical literature on trust is more plagued by data limitations than by econometric problems (such as omitted variable biases that may drive the correlations). This is also in line with Knack and Zak (2001).

12. Voters may become more reluctant to participate when they are required to vote too often. This "voter fatigue" may depress turnouts at national elections, as experienced in the case of Switzerland, where up to four electoral consultations are held each year on various aspects of policy and law-making.

13. The compulsory character of the vote may influence electoral results. It is thus of interest to consider the proportion of informal votes (*e.g.* blank ballots) in elections (especially for countries where voting is strongly enforced), because these votes are a way for citizens to voice their discontent. For this reason, *Measures of Australia's Progress* (http://www.abs.gov.au/AUSSTATS/abs@.nsf/mf/1370.0?opendocument#from-banner=LN) includes the proportion of informal votes in federal elections as a measure of civic engagement. In reality, Australian citizens rarely spoil their vote by voting informally (the proportion of informal votes fluctuated between 4% and 5% for the House of Representatives between 1998 and 2007 and was slightly lower for the Senate), which is a valid indication of their feeling of trust regarding political campaigners.

14. Non-linear correlations also give significant results: the Spearman's rank correlation coefficient is 0.7565 while the Kendall rank coefficient (which is more sensitive to outliers) is 0.6064.

15. Further, various measures of political participation for European countries (based on the European Social Survey) provide a coherent picture of political participation, with most of the correlations (between responses to questions on "having contacted a politician, government or local government", "having worked in a political party of action group", "having worn or displayed a campaign badge/sticker", "having signed a petition", "having taken part in a lawful demonstration" and "having boycotted certain products") being statistically significant.

16. While self-reported turnouts are a poor way to measure the absolute value of turnout rates, their use is less problematic to analyze the correlates of voting (Brady, 1999; Katosh and Traugott, 1981). Indeed, no clear pattern emerges for misreported voters (Katosh and Traugott, 1981). Abramson *et al.* (1986) showed that among non-voters, the highly educated and those most supportive of civic norms are the most likely to overreport their vote; as those groups have relatively few non-voters, their overreporting does not distort the overall results. In general, overreporting results from a desire to look good before the interviewer, with better educated and higher status non-voters overreporting more often because they are more aware that voting is the response most likely to create a good impression (Bernstein *et al.*, 2001).

17. OECD (2007, 2011); see Tenn (2007) for a literature review.

18. For instance, the ABS report *Measures of Australia's Progress* (http://www.abs.gov.au/AUSSTATS/abs@.nsf/mf/1370.0?opendocument#from-banner=LN) includes the "democracy, governance and citizenship" among its dimensions of progress but presents no headline indicators since "it is difficult to find a single indicator that adequately captures the wide range of aspects that this dimension includes". Similarly, the United Nations Indicators of Sustainable Development (United Nations, 2007) cover the governance dimension with two indicators: one relating to the number of recorded homicides per 100 000 population (a similar indicator is included in Chapter "Personal Security" of this report) while the other indicator relates to the number of people having been asked to pay a bribe by a government official.

19. OECD, 2009a divides government activities into inputs, processes, outputs and outcomes. Processes focus on how decisions are made and implemented, covering such topics as integrity, openness, e-government, budgeting, regulatory governance and human resource management.

20. The European Social Survey, the European Quality of Life Survey and the US Citizenship Survey include a menu of questions regarding political interest and political participation at large.

References

Abramson, P. R., B. A. Anderson and B. D. Silver (1986), "Who Overreports Voting?", *The American Political Science Review*, Vol. 80, No. 2, pp. 613-624.

Almond, G.A. and S. Verba (1963), *The Civic Culture: Political Attitudes and Democracy in Five Nations*. Princeton, N.J.: Princeton University Press.

Arndt, C. and C. Oman (2006), "Uses and Abuses of Governance Indicators", *Development Centre Studies*, OECD Publishing.

Barber, B. R. (1984), *Strong Democracy: Participatory Politics for a New Age*, University of California Press.

Benn, S. (1979), "The Problematic Rationality of Political Participation", in P. Laslett and J. Fishkin, eds., *Philosophy, Politics, and Society*. New Haven: Yale University Press.

Bernstein R., A. Chadha and R. Montjoy (2001), "Overreporting Voting: Why It Happens and Why It Matters", *The Public Opinion Quarterly*, Vol. 65, No. 1 (Spring, 2001), pp. 22-44

Beugelsdijk, S., H. L.F. de Groot and A.B.T.M. van Schaik (2004), "Trust and economic growth: A robustness analysis", *Oxford Economic Papers*, Oxford University Press, Vol. 56, No. 1, pp. 118-134.

Blinder, A. S. (2000), "Central Bank Credibility: Why Do We Care? How Do We Build It?", *American Economic Review*, Vol. 90, No.5, pp. 1421-1431.

Brady, H. E. (199), "Political participation", in *Measures of Political Attitudes*, ed. John P. Robinson, Phillip R. Shaver and Lawrence S. Wrightsman, pp. 737-801. San Diego, CA: Academic Press.

Frey, B. S. and A. Stutzer (2005), "Beyond Outcomes: Measuring procedural utility", *Oxford Economic Papers*, Oxford University Press, Vol. 57, No. 1, pp. 90-111.

Frey, B.S. and A. Stutzer (2006), "Political Participation and Procedural Utility: An Empirical Study". *European Journal of Political Research*, Vol. 45, No. 3, pp. 391-418.

Glaeser, E., R. La Porta, F. Lopez-de-Silanes and A. Shleifer (2004), "Do Institutions Cause Growth?" *Journal of Economic Growth*, Vol. 9, pp. 271-303.

Helliwell, J. F. and R. D. Putnam (2004), "The social context of well-being", Phil Trans R. Soc Lon, B359: 1435-46. Reprinted in Huppert F.A., Kaverne B., Baylis N., (eds.), *The Science of Well-Being*, Oxford University Press, London.

Hudson, J. (2006), "Institutional Trust and Subjective Well-Being across the EU", Kyklos, Blackwell Publishing, Vol. 59(1), pp. 43-62, No. 1.

Katosh, J. P. and M. W. Traugott (1981), "The Consequences of Validated and Self-Reported Voting Measures", *The Public Opinion Quarterly*, Vol. 45, No. 4, pp. 519-535.

Kaufmann, D., A. Kraay and M. Mastruzzi (2005). "Measuring Governance Using Cross-Country Perceptions Data," MPRA Paper 8219, University Library of Munich, Germany.

Kaufmann, D., A. Kraay and P. Poido-Lobaton (1999), "Governance matters," Policy Research Working Paper Series 2196, The World Bank.

Knack, S. (2002), "Social capital and the quality of government: Evidence from the States", *American Journal of Political Science*, Vol. 46, pp. 772-785.

Knack, S. and P. J. Zak, (2001). "Building trust: Public policy, interpersonal trust and economic development," MPRA Paper 25055, University Library of Munich, Germany.

Knack, S and P. Keefer (1997), "Does Social Capital Have a Payoff? A Cross-Country Investigation", *The Quarterly Journal of Economics*, Vol. 112, No. 4, pp. 1251-88, November, MIT Press.

Knack, S. (1992). "Civic Norms, Social Sanctions, and Voter Turnout". *Rationality and Society*, Vol. 4, pp. 133-156.

La Porta, R., F. Lopez-de-Silanes, A. Schleifer and R. W. Vishny (1997), "Trust in Large Organizations," *American Economic Review*, American Economic Association, vol. 87(2), pp. 333-38.

López Pintor, R. and M. Gratschev (2002), "Voter Turnout since 1945 – A Global Report", International Institute for Democracy and Electoral Assistance (IDEA), Stockholm.

McDonald, M. and S. Popkin (2001), "The Myth of the Vanishing Voter", *American Political Science Review*, Vol. 95, No. 4.

Mishler, W. and R. Rose (2001), "What are the Origins of Political Trust? Testing Institutional and Cultural Theories in Post-Communist Societies", *Comparative Political Studies*. 34: 1, pp. 30-62.

Morita, S. and D. Zaelke (2005), "Rule of Law, good governance, and sustainable development", presented in the Seventh International Conference on Environmental Compliance and Enforcement, Morocco.

Morrone, A., N. Tontoranelli and G. Ranuzzi (2009), "How Good is Trust?: Measuring Trust and its Role for the Progress of Societies", OECD Statistics Working Papers, No. 2009/03.

Newton, K. (2001), "Trust, Social Capital, Civil Society, and Democracy", *International Political Science*, Vol. 22, pp. 201-214.

Norris, P. (2002), *Democratic Phoenix: Reinventing Political Activism*. New York: Cambridge University Press, pp. 290.

OECD (2011), *Society at a Glance 2011: OECD Social Indicators*, OECD Publishing, Paris.

OECD (2010), "What are the social outcomes of education?", in OECD, *Education at a Glance 2010: OECD Indicators*, OECD Publishing, Paris.

OECD (2009a), *Government at a Glance 2009*, OECD Publishing, Paris.

OECD (2009b), Indicators of Regulatory Management Systems, 2009 Report, *Regulatory Policy Committee*, OECD Publishing, Paris.

OECD (2008), Regulatory Management Systems' Indicators Survey, www.oecd.org/regreform/indicators

OECD (2007), *Society at a Glance 2006: OECD Social Indicators*, OECD Publishing, Paris.

OECD (2001a), *Citizens as Partners: Information, Consultation and Public Participation in Policy-Making*, OECD Publishing, Paris.

OECD (2001b), *The Well-being of Nations: The Role of Human and Social Capital*, OECD Publishing, Paris.

Owen, A. L, J. Videras and C. Willemsen (2008), "Democracy, Participation, and Life Satisfaction," *Social Science Quarterly*, The Southwestern Social Science Association, Vol. 89, No. 4, pp. 987-1005.

Paxton, P. (2002). "Social capital and democracy: An interdependent relationship". *American Sociological Review*, 67 (2): 254-277.

Putnam, R. D. (1994), "Social Capital and Public Affairs", *Bulletin of the American Academy of Arts and Science*, Vol 47, No. 8, May, American Academy of Arts & Sciences.

Putnam, R. (1993). *Making democracy work: Civic traditions in modern Italy*. Princeton: Princeton University Press.

Sen, A, (1999), *Development as Freedom*, Oxford: Oxford University Press.

Stiglitz, J.E., A. Sen and J.-P. Fitoussi (2009), *Report by the Commission on the Measurement of Economic Performance and Social Progress*, http://www.stiglitz-sen-fitoussi.fr/documents/rapport_anglais.pdf

Tenn, S. (2007), "The Effect of Education on Voter Turnout", Political Analysis 15 (4): 446-464.

United Nations (2007), *Indicators of Sustainable Development: Guidelines and Methodologies* (Third Edition), United Nations publication, New York.

Uslaner, E. M. (2002), "Trust and Corruption", Paper presented at the annual meeting of the American Political Science Association, Boston Marriott Copley Place, Sheraton Boston & Hynes Convention Center, Boston, Massachusetts, available at http://www.allacademic.com/meta/p65251_index.html

Warren, M.E. (2006), "Democracy and Deceit. Regulating Appearances of Corruption", *American Journal of Political Science*, Vol. 50, No. 1, pp. 160-74.

Weitz-Shapiro, R. and M. S. Winters (2008), "Political participation and Quality of Life", Working Paper No. 638, Inter-American Development Bank.

ANNEX 9.A

Formal and open consultation processes

The indicator on consultation on rule-making draws upon country responses to the OECD's survey of regulatory management systems conducted in 2005 and 2008. Table 9.A.1 presents the full set of questions and weights used to derive the composite index on consultation on rule-making used in this chapter.

Table 9.A.1 **The construction of the composite indicator on rule-making**
2008

Questions	Weights	Scores
a) Is public consultation with parties affected by regulations a part of developing new draft primary laws?	1/12.25	No=0, In some cases=0.5, Yes=1
b) Is public consultation with parties affected by regulations a part of developing new draft subordinate regulations?	1/12.25	No=0, In some cases=0.5, Yes=1
b(iv) Primary laws: Is consultation mandatory?	0.5/12.25	No=0, Yes=1
b(iv) Subordinate regulations: Is consultation mandatory?	0.5/12.25	No=0, Yes=1
b(vii-1) Primary laws: What forms of public consultation are routinely used (tick all that apply):		
- Broad circulation of proposals for comment?	0.25/12.25	No=0, Yes=1
- Public notice and calling for comment?	0.5/12.25	No=0, Yes=1
- Public meeting?	0.25/12.25	No=0, Yes=1
- Simply posting proposals on the internet?	0.25/12.25	No=0, Yes=1
- Advisory group?	0.25/12.25	No=0, Yes=1
- Preparatory public commission/committee?	0.25/12.25	No=0, Yes=1
b(vii-2) Subordinate regulations: What forms of public consultation are routinely used (tick all that apply):		
- Broad circulation of proposals for comment?	0.25/12.25	No=0, Yes=1
- Public notice and calling for comment?	0.5/12.25	No=0, Yes=1
- Public meeting?	0.25/12.25	No=0, Yes=1
- Simply posting proposals on the internet?	0.25/12.25	No=0, Yes=1
- Advisory group?	0.25/12.25	No=0, Yes=1
- Preparatory public commission/committee?	0.25/12.25	No=0, Yes=1
b(viii) Primary laws: Can any member of the public choose to participate in the consultation?	0.5/12.25	No=0, Yes=1
b(viii) Subordinate regulations: Can any member of the public choose to participate in the consultation?	0.5/12.25	No=0, Yes=1
c) Where there is a formal requirement for public consultation with parties affected by regulations, what is the minimum period for consultation that is specified? In number of weeks from 1 to 25 weeks.		
c(i-1) What is the minimum period for allowing consultation comments inside government?	0.5/12.25	0, 0.125, 0.25, 0.375, 0.5 (0, 1, 2, 3, 4 or more weeks)
"c(ii-1) What is the minimum period for allowing consultation comments by the public, including citizens, business and civil society organisations?"	0.75/12.25	0, 0.125, 0.25, 0.375, 0.5, 0.75 (0, 2, 4, 6, 8, 12 or more weeks)
d(i-1) Primary laws: Are the views of participants in the consultation process made public?	0.5/12.25	No=0, Yes=1
d(i-2) Subordinate regulations: Are the views of participants in the consultation process made public?	0.5/12.25	No=0, Yes=1
d(ii-1) Primary laws: Are regulators required to respond in writing to the authors of consultation comments?	0.25/12.25	No=0, Yes=1
d(ii-2) Primary laws: Are regulators required to respond in writing to the authors of consultation comments?	0.25/12.25	No=0, Yes=1
d(iii-1) Primary laws: Are the views expressed in the consultation process included in the regulatory impact analysis?	0.5/12.25	No=0, Yes=1
d(iii-2) Subordinate regulations: Are the views expressed in the consultation process included in the regulatory impact analysis?	0.5/12.25	No=0, Yes=1
d(iv-1) Primary laws: Is there a process to monitor the quality of the consultation process (*e.g.* surveys or other methods)?	0.5/12.25	No=0, Yes=1
d(iv-2) Subordinate regulations: Is there a process to monitor the quality of the consultation process (*e.g.* surveys or other methods)?	0.5/12.25	No=0, Yes=1

Source: OECD (2008), OECD Regulatory Management Systems' Indicators Survey 2008, Question 9, www.oecd.org/regreform/indicators

StatLink ᐧᐧᔌᔎ *http://dx.doi.org/10.1787/888932494297*

Chapter 10

Environmental quality

People's lives are strongly affected by the healthiness of their physical environment. The impact of pollutants, hazardous substances and noise on people's health is sizeable. Environmental quality also matters intrinsically, as most people value the beauty and healthiness of the place where they live, and care about the degradation of the planet and the depletion of its natural resources. Preserving environmental and natural resources is also one of the most important challenges for ensuring the sustainability of well-being over time. This chapter shows that in OECD countries the concentrations of particulate matters in the air have dropped in the last twenty years, although in many countries they remain above target levels. People in other major economies, in addition to being exposed to high pollutant concentrations, often lack access to basic environmental services such as safe drinking water and sanitation. For the world as a whole, around one-fourth of the total burden of disease, or 13 million premature deaths, could be prevented every year through environmental improvements. Environmental policies have a critical role to play in dealing with global health priorities and in improving people's lives.

Why does environmental quality matter for well-being?

Environmental quality is a key dimension of people's well-being, as quality of life is strongly affected by a healthy physical environment (Khan, 2002; Holman and Coan, 2008). The impact of environmental pollutants, hazardous substances and noise on people's health is sizeable: environmental factors play a role in more than 80% of the major diseases, and worldwide around one-fourth of diseases and overall deaths are due to poor environmental conditions (Prüss-Üstün and Corvalán, 2006). Environmental factors of a more extreme nature, such as natural disasters (earthquakes, cyclones, floods, drought, volcanic eruptions and epidemic outbreaks) may also cause deaths, injury and disease in significant proportions.[1] In the long term, drastic changes in the environment may also impair human health through climate change, transformations in the carbon and water cycles and biodiversity loss.

Besides affecting people's health, the environment also matters intrinsically as many people attach importance to the beauty and the healthiness of the place where they live, and because they care about the degradation of the planet and the depletion of natural resources (Balestra and Dottori, 2011). People also directly benefit from environmental assets and services, such as water, sanitation services, clear air, lands, forests, and access to green spaces, as they allow them to satisfy basic needs and to enjoy free time and the company of others.

Preserving environmental and natural resources is also one of the most important challenges for ensuring the sustainability of well-being over time. However, measuring environmental sustainability is difficult; first, because the size of the impacts of current environmental trends on future well-being is uncertain; second, because there are few comparable indicators that meet agreed standards. For these reasons, this chapter mainly looks at the importance of the environment for people's current well-being. Selected measures of environmental sustainability based on some of the OECD Green Growth Indicators (OECD, 2011b) are presented in Annex 10.A.

Measuring environmental quality

The concept of "environmental quality" is a broad one, and an ideal set of indicators would inform on a number of environmental media (soil, water, air), on people's access to environmental services and amenities, as well as on the impact of environmental hazards on human health. Unfortunately, available data are scattered and not comparable across countries. For these reasons, the objective indicators presented in this chapter are limited to only a subset of the relevant conditions.

Objective indicators, such as the concentrations and emissions of various pollutants, are combined here with indicators based on people's subjective perceptions of the quality of the environment where they live. These subjective indicators are useful as they: i) summarise in one indicator a multidimensional phenomenon; ii) offer information about the environmental hazards that individuals may experience due to their own specific circumstances (e.g. people suffering from asthma will report, ceteris paribus, lower satisfaction with air quality, a type of information that is not provided by objective indicators); and iii) may capture the intrinsic value that people give to the environment (e.g. people attaching greater importance to nature are more likely to report lower satisfaction with the quality of the environment, due to their higher standards). As in the case of other subjective data, indicators of satisfaction with environmental quality may suffer from cultural biases and other limits that may affect cross-country comparisons.

Selected indicators

Air quality (EN I)

Air quality is measured through population-weighted average annual concentrations of fine particles in the air (measured in micro grams per cubic meter). The data refer to residential areas of cities larger than 100 000 inhabitants. Particulate matters (PM) consist of small liquid and solid particles floating in the air, and include sulphate, nitrate, elemental carbon, organic carbon matter, sodium and ammonium ions in varying concentrations. Of greatest concern to public health are the particles small enough to be inhaled into the deepest parts of the lung: these particles are less than 10 microns in diameter (PM_{10}). Looking at concentrations rather than at emissions allows assessing the effective impacts of air pollution on people's health (Box 10.1).

Ideally, several measures of air quality should be grouped together in a composite air quality index. However, constructing a composite indicator is difficult, as it involves contentious challenges in terms of gathering and weighting data (given that pollutants mixed together can have additive, synergistic, or antagonistic effects on human health). PM pollution is regularly monitored in most OECD countries and has been consistently associated with serious effects on human health.[2] This indicator is based on good-quality time-series data that allow comparisons across countries and over time. Improvements in pollution monitoring and statistical techniques during the last decades have enhanced the ability to measure air pollution and provided a broad picture of how pollution affects urban spaces and the people within them. However, these data are limited in several respects. First, they relate to annual levels, and they may obscure important variations at smaller time scales (*e.g.* hours or months). Second, air pollution data assume that everyone living in an urban area is equally exposed; in practice, personal exposure varies substantially, depending on where people live and work, their occupations, lifestyles and behaviours.

Box 10.1. **Impact of air pollution on health**

The particulate matter levels that are most relevant to human health are commonly less than 10 micrometers across and are known as PM_{10} (particle ten micrometers = 10µm). The fraction of the PM_{10} which are thought to be the most poisonous are less than 2.5 micrometers across and are called $PM_{2.5}$. Epidemiological studies conducted over the past twenty years have reported significant associations between short-term and long-term exposure to increased ambient PM concentrations and increased morbidity (*e.g.* cardiovascular and respiratory diseases) and (premature) mortality. PM_{10} are readily inhalable and because of their small size are not filtered and reach the upper part of the airways and lungs. Those smaller than 2.5 µm penetrate deep into the bottom of the lung, where they can move to the blood stream, thus allowing many chemicals harmful to human health to reach many internal organs and causing a wide range of illness and mortality including cancer, brain damage and damage to the fetus.

Although it is commonly assumed that there is no threshold below which health effects of PM are unlikely to occur, the recent update of the WHO Air Quality Guidelines for PM proposed that guidelines should be set to minimise the risk of adverse effects of both short- and long-term exposure to PM. These values are set at 20 µg/m3 as an annual mean and 50 µg/m3 as a daily mean for PM_{10}, with corresponding values of 10 µg/m3 and 25 µg/m3 for

---

PM$_{2.5}$. The WHO also suggests using as indicators of health risks the mass concentrations of PM$_{10}$ and PM$_{2.5}$. The health outcomes of air pollution depend upon the sensitivity and the exposure of the susceptible population to a specific pollutant. Pollutant exposure levels may be difficult to estimate because of individual time-activity patterns. As a result, health impacts are generally based on the population-weighted average ambient concentration of the pollutants measured at fixed monitoring sites located in different parts of cities.

Environmental burden of disease (en 1)

The environmental burden of disease (EBD) quantifies the disease burden that could be avoided by modifying the environment as a whole. Health effects relate to pollution of air, water and soil, radiations, noise, occupational risks, land use patterns, agricultural methods and irrigation schemes, as well as man-made changes to the climate and ecosystems (Prüss-Üstün and Corvalán, 2006). Measures of the environmental burden of disease at the country level are made by the World Health Organisation (WHO) according to an exposure approach, and supported by a comprehensive analysis of the evidence for the given health risks. Exposure-response relationships for a given risk factor are obtained from epidemiological studies, and the derived attributable fractions are then applied to disease burden, expressed in terms of either premature deaths or DALYs (Disability-Adjusted Life Years), a measure that combines information on deaths and disabilities.[3]

Conceptually, the overall EBD estimate has some limitations. First, people are exposed to a complex mix of environmental factors, yet EBD estimates often treat each environmental hazard individually, thus simplifying the underlying causal processes. Second, EBD does not account for benefits other than health gain, while environmental modifications may deliver other types of social benefits. Third, the population-based approach allows estimating total national impacts, but does not allow identifying impacts on specific population groups, e.g. people who are highly exposed or especially vulnerable due to worse health conditions. For these reasons, EBD is presented here as a secondary indicator. This indicator covers all OECD and emerging countries, although time trends at the national level are hard to establish since data are not collected regularly.

Satisfaction with the quality of local environment (en 2)

In addition to the objective measures presented above, subjective data on environmental quality also provide critical information on environmental conditions. The indicator considered here is informative about people's subjective appreciation of the environment where they live. The indicator is based on the following two questions: "In the city or area where you live, are you satisfied or dissatisfied with the quality of air?"; and "In the city or area where you live, are you satisfied or dissatisfied with the quality of water?" Answers are grouped into two categories (yes/no). Data are based on the World Gallup Poll, with all OECD and emerging countries covered in the Poll.[4]

Since the samples are small and the dataset suffers from other methodological limitations, the evidence from this indicator has to be taken with caution. In addition, self-reported satisfaction with the quality of the local environment may reflect cultural biases or other individual influences. For these reasons, this indicator is shown here as a secondary indicator.

Access to green spaces (en 3)

This indicator refers to the share of people who have "very many reasons" or "many reasons" to complain about the lack of access to recreational or green zones, as measured on a four-item scale. Access to green spaces is essential for quality of life, as an unspoiled environment is a source of satisfaction (World Bank, 1992), improves mental well-being (Pretty *et al.*, 2005, Brown and Grant, 2007), allows people to recover from the stress of everyday life (Mace *et al.*, 1999) and to perform physical activity. Cross-sectional studies find that levels of physical activity are higher and obesity is lower in areas with higher levels of greenery (Ellaway *et al.*, 2005). Natural resources also play an important role in building social ties and reducing physical violence. Several studies show that green spaces in urban areas encourage social interaction, alleviate crime and aggression and generate a sense of place (Ward Thompson, 2002; Armstrong, 2000; Milligan *et al.*, 2004).

This indicator is based on data from the European Quality of Life Survey, a non-official household survey limited to European countries. This survey is based on small samples and is conducted with low frequency. This implies that small differences between countries may not be statistically significant. Given these shortcomings, the indicator is presented here as a secondary indicator.

A summary of the quality of the indicators used in this chapter is provided in Table 10.1.

Table 10.1. **The quality of environmental indicators**

	Target concept	INDICATORS							
		Relevance to measure and monitor well-being				Statistical quality			
		Face validity	Unambiguous interpretation (good/bad)	Policy amenable outcomes	Can be disaggregated	Well-established instrument collected	Comparable definition	Country coverage	Recurrent data collection
Environmental quality									
EN I Air quality	Quality of environment	~	√	√	x	√	√	√	~
en 1 Environmental burden of disease	Impact of environmental hazards on human health	√	√	√	x	√	√	√	~
en 2 Satisfaction with local environment	Subjective perceptions of environment	√	~	~	√	x	√	√	√
en 3 Access to green spaces		√	√	√	√	x	√	~	~

Note: The symbol √ shows that the indicator selected largely meets the criterion shown in the table; the symbol ~ that the indicator meets the criterion to a large extent; the symbol X that the indicator does not meet the criterion or it meets it only to a limited extent.

Average patterns

Air pollution remains above dangerous levels

In 2008, PM_{10} concentrations in many OECD countries were above the mean annual WHO target level of 20 μg/m3 (Figure 10.1). Within the OECD region, the highest concentration levels were found in Chile, Turkey and Poland. Over time, PM concentrations have dropped steadily – due to improvements in technology and structural shifts in economies, especially in Eastern Europe (*i.e.* the Czech Republic, Estonia, the Slovak Republic), though not as much as other pollutants. While this trend is visible in all regions, air pollution still shows high concentrations in urban areas in parts of Africa and Asia (Figure 10.2). All emerging countries except Brazil and South Africa have concentration levels well above the OECD average. Since air pollution by particulate matter is linked to a range of anthropogenic activities such as industrial production and traffic (Box 10.2), the recent economic and financial crisis might have contributed to a further decline (Arruti *et al.*, 2011). However, the OECD projects a further increase of PM concentrations by 2030 in the most polluted regions of the world, where 50-90% of the urban population will be exposed to concentrations above 70 μg/m3 (OECD, 2008)

Figure 10.1 **Air concentrations of particulate matter**

PM_{10} concentrations, micrograms per cubic meter

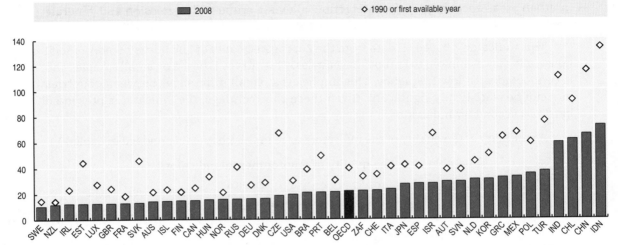

Note: Data are urban-population weighted PM10 levels in residential areas of cities with more than 100 000 residents. The first available year is 1994 for Slovenia.
Source: World Bank; OECD (2008), *OECD Environmental Outlook to 2030*, Paris.

StatLink http://dx.doi.org/10.1787/888932493233

Figure 10.2. **Air concentrations of particulate matter by region**

PM_{10} concentrations, micrograms per cubic meter

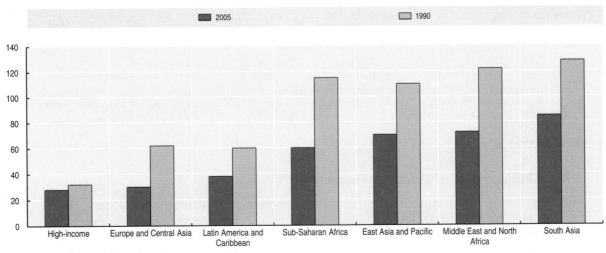

Source: World Bank (2009), *Atlas of Global Development: Second Edition*, Glasgow.

StatLink http://dx.doi.org/10.1787/888932493252

Box 10.2. **Drivers of air pollution**

In 2008, for the first time in history, more than half of the world's population lived in towns and cities. By 2030 this number will swell to almost 5 billion (UNFPA, 2008). Rapid urbanisation presents challenges that may threaten the environment and quality of life. One of the main problems facing burgeoning towns is outdoor air pollution from a range of anthropogenic sources:

- **Road transport.** In many countries, air pollution from motor vehicles has replaced coal smoke as the major cause for concern; the continuing growth in the use of motor vehicle means that efforts to reduce emissions from individual vehicles are in danger of being overtaken by increases in the volume of traffic. In many developing countries the use of old vehicles, which do not meet modern pollution control requirements, makes efforts to control pollution from this source increasingly difficult.

- **Power generation.** Generating power produces more pollution (in particular, sulphur dioxide and nitrogen oxides) than any other single industry. Better dispersion of pollutants emitted by tall chimneys brings better dilution in the air and lowers local concentrations of pollutants. This, however, leads to pollution being dispersed more widely and to transboundary air pollution. Stricter operating practices and the use of modern abatement techniques have resulted in a sizeable reduction in the amount of pollutants emitted from power stations. High concentrations still occur in many developing countries, particularly from older power stations and from the use of high sulphur lignite or coal.

- **Waste disposal.** Landfill and incineration are the most common methods of waste disposal. If not properly managed, landfill sites can cause a number of problems, such as the production of methane gas, dangerous levels of carbon dioxide, and trace concentrations of a range of organic gases and vapors. Poorly managed incineration can result in the production of poisonous chemicals such as hydrochloric acid, dioxins, furans and heavy metals. Hydrochloric acid produced by the burning of plastics contributes locally to acid rain. The burning at low temperature of organic matter and plastics can also lead to emissions of dioxins.

Source: Adapted from EEA, 2010; 2011 and EEA website

The environmental burden of disease is substantial in emerging countries

According to the WHO, 24% of the total burden of disease at the world level, or 13 million premature deaths, could be prevented through environmental improvements (Prüss-Üstün and Corvalán, 2006). While the EBD ranges between 13% and 20% in many OECD countries (Figure 10.3), it reaches higher levels in Eastern Europe, Korea and Turkey, where up to one-third of the disease burden could be prevented through better environmental conditions. Emerging economies suffer the most from poor environmental factors, losing up to 6 times more healthy years of life per person per year than high-income countries (Box 10.3).

Figure 10.3. **Environmental Burden of Disease**

DALYs per 1000 people, 2006

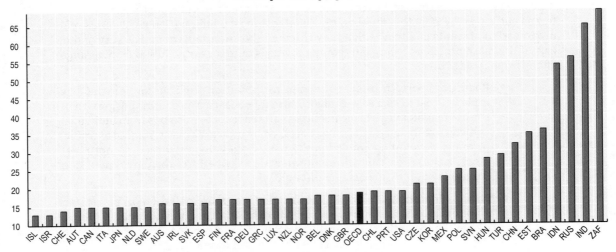

Source: WHO (2004), Water, Sanitation and Hygiene Links to Health: Facts and Figures updated March 2004, Geneva.

StatLink ᷄ᡟ᪥ᡅ᧭ *http://dx.doi.org/10.1787/888932493271*

Box 10.3. **Drivers of the environmental burden of disease**

Results of international studies on the environmental burden of disease (EBD) differ significantly across countries: estimates of the total disease burden caused by environmental exposure range from about 2 to 20%. These differences may in part reflect differences in methodologies, in data quality (information on environment and health is often scattered across many institutions and gathered in a non-standardised format), and in the range of risk factors considered by different studies. However, most of the variation in estimates is likely to reflect actual differences in environmental conditions.

WHO recent profiles of EBD for 192 countries refer to a selected set of the known environmental risk factors for which quantification of health impacts is possible. In particular, the core set of environmental risks considered by the WHO includes: *i)* water, sanitation and hygiene; *ii)* indoor air; and *iii)* outdoor air. These environmental factors display a clear socio-economic pattern: while in developed countries the environmental component of the disease burden operates mainly through non-communicable diseases (*e.g.* lung cancer and cardiovascular diseases) related to outdoor air pollution, developing countries suffer most from indoor air pollution from solid fuel use and communicable diseases due to unsafe water, scarce hygiene and sanitation (*e.g.* diarrhea and malaria).

Although richer countries are not immune to environmental risks, the environmental burden of disease per capita falls as per capita GDP increases (Figure 10.4). People in poorer countries typically live in less healthy areas and are more vulnerable to the effects of environmental hazards due to their lower health status and poorer access to basic services. In richer countries (where the greatest environmental burden relates to outdoor air pollution) deaths caused by environmental hazards generally occur later in life, leading to high premature death rates but low DALY rates.

Countries with similar GDP per capita may also perform differently in terms of environmental health impacts. For countries with GDP per capita below 10 000 USD, the environmental burden can vary by a factor of two (*e.g.* China and Brazil perform considerably better than India, Indonesia and South Africa). These differences are explained mainly by differences in terms of unsafe water, poor hygiene and sanitation; in India, Indonesia and South Africa a sizeable share of EBD is caused by these environmental hazards, while in China and Brazil this share is much lower. Differences in DALY rates are magnified by the fact that most of the mortality from malnutrition, diarrhoea and other communicable diseases concern children under the age of five.Box 10.3.

Figure 10.4. **The relationship between the environmental burden of diseases and GDP per capita**

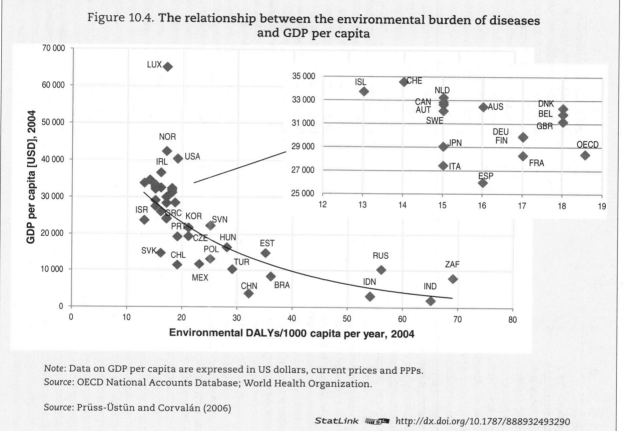

Note: Data on GDP per capita are expressed in US dollars, current prices and PPPs.
Source: OECD National Accounts Database; World Health Organization.

Source: Prüss-Üstün and Corvalán (2006)

StatLink *http://dx.doi.org/10.1787/888932493290*

Satisfaction with the quality of the local environment varies considerably across OECD countries

The majority of respondents in OECD countries report being satisfied with the air quality of the surrounding area. In Denmark, New Zealand, Australia and Ireland, more than 90% of the population expresses contentment over the quality of local air. However in Brazil, Greece and the Czech Republic, one individual in three declare being dissatisfied with air quality. In the Russian Federation and Israel, the share of dissatisfied people is close to 50% (Figure 10.5).

A larger share of the population declares being satisfied with the quality of the water. However, in some countries such as Turkey, Israel, Greece, Estonia and Mexico, the proportion of those not satisfied with water quality is high. In India only 60% of the population is satisfied with the quality of the local water, while in the Russian Federation this percentage falls to 40% (Figure 10.6).

Figure 10.5. **Satisfaction with air quality**

Percentage of satisfied people, 2010 or latest available year

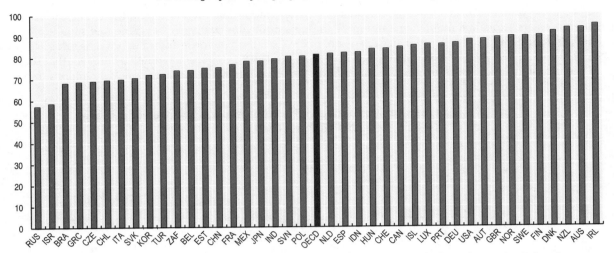

Note: Data refer to 2008 for Iceland and Norway; and to 2009 for Estonia, Israel, Switzerland, the Russian Federation and South Africa.
Source: Gallup World Poll.

StatLink ᵃᵍˢᴸ http://dx.doi.org/10.1787/888932493309

Figure 10.6. **Satisfaction with water quality**

Percentage of satisfied people, 2010 or latest available year

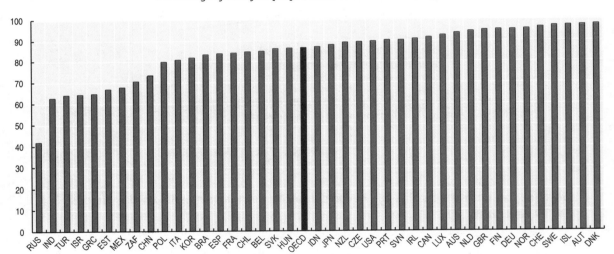

Note: Data refer to 2008 for Iceland and Norway; and to 2009 for Estonia, Israel, Switzerland, the Russian Federation and South Africa.
Source: Gallup World Poll.

StatLink ᵃᵍˢᴸ http://dx.doi.org/10.1787/888932493328

A large share of the European population report having very limited access to green spaces

The available data on the access to green spaces show that there are large differences across European countries in terms of the share of population who declare that they have access to green space. In Italy and Turkey, almost one person in three declares having very many or many reasons to complain about the lack of green space. In the Nordic countries, less than 5% of the population is dissatisfied with their access to green spaces (Figure 10.7).

Besides green space, access to other types of environmental services is also critical for people's well-being, especially for the population of emerging countries who may lack access to important basic amenities (Box 10.4).

Figure 10.7. **Access to green spaces in European countries**

Percentage of population having reasons to complain about the lack of access to recreational and green spaces, 2000

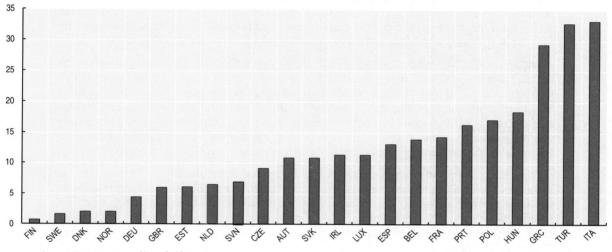

Source: European Quality of Life Survey.

StatLink ⚙ *http://dx.doi.org/10.1787/888932493347*

Box 10.4. **Access to basic environmental services**

While in industrialised countries, most people have access to basic environmental services such as fresh water, basic sanitation facilities and wastewater treatment, in developing countries a large share of the population remains without these basic services. A poor water supply and poor hygiene practices cause 1.8 million deaths every year from diarrheal diseases, 90% of whom are children under the age of 5 (WHO, 2004). Access to these basic environmental services is also essential to ensure human dignity, reduce poverty and social exclusion and promote economic development (OECD, 2011a)

The data presented here refer to the share of the population who have access to: *i*) safe drinking water sources; *ii*) improved sanitation facilities; and *iii*) wastewater treatment. Safe drinking water sources include several types of water supply for drinking: *i*) piped water into the dwelling, plot or yard; *ii*) public tap/standpipe; *iii*) borehole/tube well; *iv*) protected dug well; *v*) protected spring; *vi*) rainwater collection; and *vii*) bottled water (if a secondary available source is also available). Improved sanitation facilities refer to: *i*) flush/pour flush toilets or latrines connected to a sewer; *ii*) ventilated improved pit latrines; and *iii*) pit latrines with a slab or platform of any material that covers the pit entirely. As for access to wastewater treatment, the indicator takes into account several systems, ranging from the most basic (primary system) to the most sophisticated, effective and safest (tertiary system).

With respect to water sources and sanitation, most people in OECD countries have access to these services, although there are some disparities across urban and rural areas. However, in India, Indonesia and China a relatively large share of the population does not have adequate access to safe water and sanitation facilities. Over time, access to improved water and sanitation has increased in all the countries considered, particularly in those countries where the access to these amenities was particularly low (*e.g.* Turkey, India, China). In Estonia, Poland and Russia, however, access to sanitation has not improved much (Figure 10.8).

Connection to wastewater treatment has increased substantially in Turkey, Greece, Iceland, Korea and Spain in the last 30 years (Figure 10.9, Panel a). A large majority of OECD countries have either secondary or tertiary waste water treatment. Exceptions are Iceland, where more than the half of the population is connected to primary wastewater treatment, and Turkey, Greece and Hungary where the access to tertiary treatment is limited (Figure 10.9, Panel b).

Box 10.4. **Access to basic environmental services** (cont.)

Figure 10.8. **Access to water and sanitation**

Percentage of population

Panel a: Access to improved water source

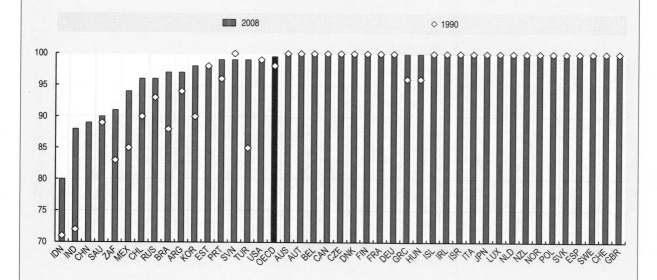

Panel b: Access to improved sanitation facilities

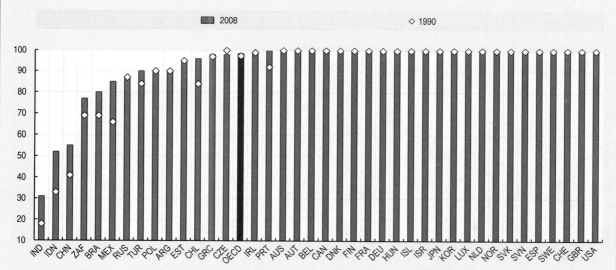

Notes: Panel a: Data refer to 1995 and 2008 for Korea; and to 2000 and 2008 for the Slovak Republic. Panel b: Data refer to 2000 and 2008 for Poland; and to 1995 and 2008 for Estonia. Data are not available for Italy and New Zealand.
Source: WHO/UNICEF Joint Monitoring Programme.

StatLink ⫘⫘⫘ *http://dx.doi.org/10.1787/888932493366*

Box 10.4. **Access to basic environmental services** (*cont.*)

Figure 10.9. **Access to different types of wastewater treatment**

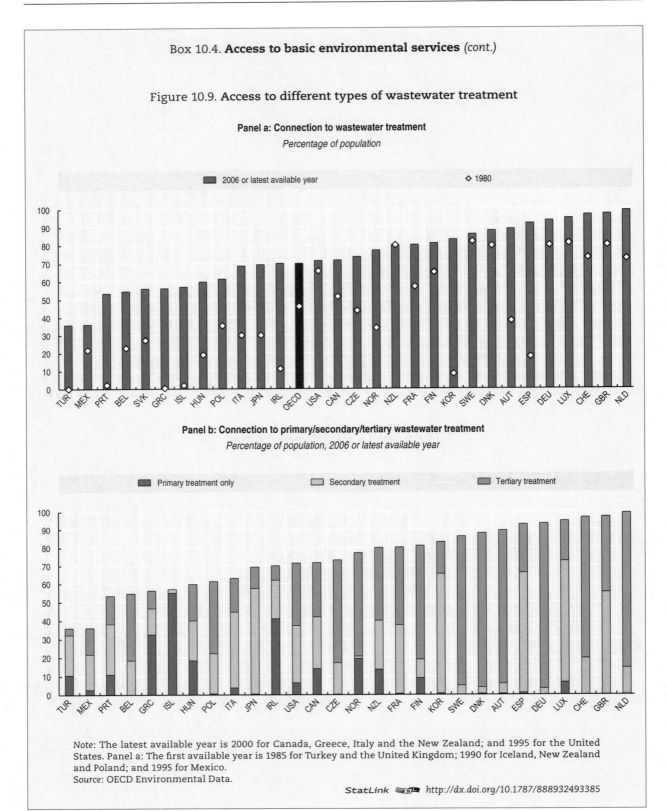

Panel a: Connection to wastewater treatment
Percentage of population

Panel b: Connection to primary/secondary/tertiary wastewater treatment
Percentage of population, 2006 or latest available year

Note: The latest available year is 2000 for Canada, Greece, Italy and the New Zealand; and 1995 for the United States. Panel a: The first available year is 1985 for Turkey and the United Kingdom; 1990 for Iceland, New Zealand and Poland; and 1995 for Mexico.
Source: OECD Environmental Data.

StatLink ⟦ᵐˢᴸ⟧ http://dx.doi.org/10.1787/888932493385

The various indicators capture different dimensions of environmental quality

The set of indicators presented in this chapter summarises information about major dimensions of environmental quality and how environmental hazards impact on human health. It is important to assess whether and how these indicators are interlinked (Table 10.2). In general:

- At a given point in time, the relation between the objective indicator of air quality (*i.e.* PM_{10} concentrations) and people's subjective judgement on air quality in the surroundings is quite weak. In countries with high PM_{10} concentrations (*e.g.* Poland and Turkey), people do not seem much more dissatisfied with air quality than people in countries where PM_{10} concentrations are significantly lower. This might reflect several factors.

- First, the objective measure of air quality used here takes into account PM_{10} concentrations only, while tropospheric air pollution – as perceived by individuals – may refer to a complex mixture of single pollutants. Second, people's perception of the local environment is also shaped by additional factors, such as cultural values, media exposure and local economic development. Third, people's environmental satisfaction may be influenced by relative changes in air quality rather than absolute values. People living in clean areas become accustomed to a high environmental quality, but are not content with this and request an even higher quality. By contrast, when the quality of local natural resources is poor, even small improvements make people contented, as they feel that the environment has become better (Zheng, 2010).

- In terms of subjective appreciations of environmental quality in general, measured as perceived air and water quality and lack of access to green spaces, the correlation is pretty strong, suggesting that these indicators are consistent with the level of subjective satisfaction with the local environment.

- Measures of the environmental burden of disease display a significant correlation with PM_{10} concentrations.

Table 10.2. **Correlation between different indicators of environmental quality**

		EN I Air quality	en 1 Environmental burden of disease	en 2 Satisfaction with local environment				en 3 Lack of access to green spaces	
				air		water			
EN I	Air quality	1	0.42*** (41)	-0.27	(41)	-0.31	(41)	0.57**	(23)
en 1	Environmental burden of disease		1 (41)	-0.33**	(41)	-0.60***	(41)	0	(23)
en 2	Satisfaction with local environment								
	Satisfaction with local air			1	(41)	0.75***	(41)	-0.63***	(23)
	Satisfaction with local water					1	(41)	-0.73***	(23)
en 3	Lack of access to green spaces							1	(23)

Note: Values in parenthesis refer to the number of observations. ** Indicates that correlations are significant at the 5% level; *** indicates that they are significant at the 1% level.

Source: OECD's calculations.

StatLink ⬛⬛ *http://dx.doi.org/10.1787/888932494335*

Inequalities

Youth, elderly and people from poor socio-economic backgrounds are the most vulnerable to pollution

The association between fine-particle pollution and heart and respiratory diseases is mediated by many factors, including occupational exposure, age, gender, underlying disease, smoking, health habits, body mass, education and income (Hill, 2004). Studies have shown that some groups of the population are especially vulnerable to air pollution and other environmental hazards. The very young (Box 10.5) and the very old are more at risk than the remainder of the population (Pope and Dockery, 1992; Schwarz, 1994). People with pre-existing cardiovascular and respiratory disease are also more susceptible to ambient PM (Goldberg et al., 2001; Dockery et al. 2001). Short-term effects of PM appear to be restricted largely to people with low socio-economic status (Gwynn and Thurston, 2001). Moreover, attributes of poor education (*e.g.* nutritional status, increased exposure, lack of access to good-quality medical care) may modify people's susceptibility to fine-particle pollution (Dockery et al., 2001). Most of these studies of air-pollution-related adverse health effects are based on national or local samples.

Box 10.5. **The effects of air pollution on children's health**

According to the WHO Task Force on the Protection of Children's Environmental Health, respiratory infections account for 20% of mortality in children under the age of five. Many OECD countries also report asthma epidemics that have been shown to be aggravated by air pollution: for example, in the United States approximately 4.8 million school-age children have asthma. It has been estimated that 43% of the global environmental burden of disease falls on children under five, and that 80% of the burden of disease for infants and young children has an environmental origin.

Much of the existing literature on the impact of the environment on human health has focused on adults. Even though the current knowledge of children's vulnerability is not sufficient, epidemiological evidence suggests that there are differences between children and adults with respect to air pollution and environmental toxicity. In many cases, children do not have the capacity to metabolise and detoxify toxic compounds. Moreover, their developing organisms require a higher rate of energy consumption and thus of food, air and water intake (*e.g.* when children are exercising during sport events, they may take in 20 to 50% more air – and thus air pollution – than adults in comparable activities). Different behavioural patterns may also play a role in the special vulnerability of children to environmental degradation: children spend more time outside than adults, and are often outdoors during times when air pollution is at its highest. Children also have more time to develop diseases that take a long time to develop, such as cancer, cardiovascular and neurodegenerative disease. Moreover, they may be exposed to a specific agent throughout their life, as compared to shorter periods of exposure by adults to chemicals that have only recently appeared on the market. Despite a large number of actions undertaken in OECD countries to protect children's health from environmental degradation, most existing legislation does not take into account children's special vulnerability to environmental risks.

Source: OECD (2006a); OECD (2008).

Satisfaction with the local environment varies according to social and geographical conditions

From an analytic and policy perspective, it is important to know how social and geographical influences may affect perceptions of how pollution is experienced (King and Stedman, 2000; Day, 2007). Early works explored some possibilities, with mixed results; some authors suggested that habituation could occur following higher or longer exposure, though others did not. Some studies reported that environmental concerns were higher among people with a higher socio-economic status, while others found mixed results. For example, Bickerstaff and Walker (2001) reported an inverse relationship between socio-economic status and concern for air quality, suggesting that this reflect differences in environmental quality and a reluctance to recognise negative conditions in localities where satisfaction is high. Elliot *et al.* (1999) found that the presence of other social problems in the neighbourhood could lead to a lower relative importance being ascribed to air pollution.

Table 10.3 below reports the results of a multivariate analysis based on a selection of socio-economic variables available in the Gallup World Poll (see Balestra and Sultan, 2012 for more details). The results are shown separately for both OECD and other major countries. Some of the main patterns are:

- The area where people live is the strongest predictor of perceptions of local environmental quality. In OECD countries, populations living in large cities or in their suburbs are significantly less satisfied with the quality of local air than people living in rural areas or small towns. The effect of the living area on the satisfaction with the quality of local water is however milder

- More educated people are less satisfied with the quality of the local environment, a pattern that holds in both OECD and emerging countries. This result is in line with the existing research, which suggests that more educated people appreciate more the consequences of certain human effects on the environment, and that they can make a stronger connection between social welfare and the environment (Van Liere and Dunlap, 1980; Thalmann, 2004; Kahn and Matsusaka, 1997).

- Access to the Internet (a proxy for media exposure) has an ambiguous effect on satisfaction with the local environmental quality. In emerging countries, people who potentially have access to a larger set of scientific information on environmental hazards and their harmful effects on human health, are less satisfied with the quality of local air and water. By contrast, in OECD countries the access to the Internet has a positive and significant effect on people's perception of the quality of local water.[5]

- Age also affects perceived environmental quality, although its effect is not strong. In OECD countries, older people are less satisfied with air and water quality, possibly because they are likely to suffer from pre-existing respiratory or cardiovascular diseases and spend more time outdoors.

- Similarly, gender seems to play a role in satisfaction with the local environment, with women significantly more dissatisfied than men, but only in OECD countries.

- Unemployed people living in emerging countries are on average less satisfied with the environment than their employed counterparts.

Table 10.3. **The determinants of satisfaction with environmental quality**

Marginal effects of explanatory variables on satisfaction with air and water quality

Explanatory variables	Satisfaction with air quality		Satisfaction with water quality	
	OECD countries only	Other major economies only	OECD countries only	Other major economies only
Female	-0.03***	0.01	-0.02**	0.01
Age	-0.01*	0.01	-0.01***	-0.01
Age squared	0.01**	-0.01	0.01***	0.01
Household income	0.01	0.01	0.01*	0.02***
Unemployed	0.01	-0.11***	-0.03	-0.09***
Secondary education	-0.03*	-0.05**	-0.03***	-0.04***
Tertiary education	-0.03*	-0.05***	-0.02*	-0.05**
Small town	-0.06***	-0.05***	-0.02	-0.03**
Big city	-0.20***	-0.14***	-0.06***	0.01
Suburb of a big city	-0.14***	-0.11***	-0.01	0.01
Children	-0.01*	-0.01	-0.01	-0.02*
Access to the Internet	0.01	-0.06***	0.03***	-0.05**

Note: Probit analysis includes all OECD countries, Brazil, China, India, Indonesia, the Russian Federation and South Africa. * indicates that values are significant at 10% confidence level; ** indicates that they are significant at 5% confidence level; and *** indicates that they are significant at 1% confidence level. The variable "household income" refers to the base-2 logarithm of the household disposable income. The variable "children" refers to having at least one child under 15 years old living at home. The number of observations is 28 432 for OECD countries and 11 830 for other major economies. *Source:* OECD's calculations based on Gallup World Poll., 2009 and 2010.

StatLink ᴬᴵˢᴸ *http://dx.doi.org/10.1787/888932494354*

The statistical agenda ahead

Comparing environmental quality across countries is difficult because of several reasons:

- First, objective data on local environmental conditions are typically collected by different public agencies in the context of programmes to monitor public health and environmental conditions. The quality of such measures depends on the number of monitoring stations, their distribution on the territory, and the type of pollutants that they monitor. While monitoring systems are generally well developed for air quality, this is less the case for many other environmental media. Further, most of these statistics are developed outside the framework of official statistics and with little concerns for international comparability. The statistical community agrees that it is timely to further develop environmental-economic accounting and related statistics within the national statistical system, in order to respond to increasing policy demands. To this end, the United Nations Statistical Commission issued the Handbook of National Accounting: Integrated Environmental and Economic Accounting (SEEA) (United Nations et al., 2003), which enables environmental statistics to be compared to economic statistics and shows different patterns of sustainability for production and consumption.

- Second, a variety of pollutants will affect the quality of a given environmental media, and each of them may be monitored in different ways.[6] Even with respect to air, while the monitoring of concentrations of particulate matter below 10 microns in diameter is relatively well established, this is not the case for the particles that are the most harmful to human health, *i.e.* those below 2.5 microns.[7]

- Third, it is difficult to move from data on the concentration of various pollutants to information on the number of people exposed to them. Traditionally, data on air pollution are assigned to populations in an area of interest by assuming that everyone in the population is equally exposed. However, personal exposure may vary substantially, depending on several factors (*e.g.*, daily movements, work activities, lifestyle or behaviours). Further, environmental media tend to be affected by site-specific factors: environmental quality is a local public good, rather than a national one. Better-quality data on personal exposure are needed, and the Geographical Information System (GIS) could provide a better insight into topical environmental pressures and generate new environmental indicators at the local level.

- The need to better relate data on exposure to people's susceptibility to its consequences is particularly important for measuring health effects better. More research is needed to disentangle the impact of different air pollutants on the health of children as well as the pollutants' interactions with other environmental hazards and with genetic factors affecting susceptibility. Existing measures of the environmental burden of disease may underestimate the magnitude of these effects, as research suggests that official health statistics (deaths, illnesses, hospitalisations, etc.) represent only a portion of the environmental impact on human health. Many health effects (*e.g.*, sub-clinical toxicity, neuropsychiatric disorders, fertility impairment, intellectual impairment, etc.) often escape detection, are not reported, or are attributed to non-environmental factors. Further research on the environmental burden of disease should extend the range of health effects attributed to environmental conditions and focus more on vulnerable populations (*e.g.*, children, women, low-income populations).

- Finally, objective data on environmental quality need to be combined with data on people's subjective perceptions of local environmental quality, so as to provide a more detailed picture of both the determinants of satisfaction with the quality of natural assets and the socio-economic distribution of environmental impacts. While specific surveys on these issues are undertaken in some countries as part of their official statistical systems (*e.g.* Canada, the United Kingdom, Switzerland), and some comparative information is available from a few non-official surveys (*e.g.* the Gallup World Poll and, at the European level, the European Quality of Life Survey), more could be achieved by developing and coordinating activities in this field.

Conclusion

This chapter has provided a general picture of the impacts of environmental quality on public health and well-being. The concept of environmental quality is a broad one, encompassing a number of environmental media (*e.g.* soil, water, air). However, due to the lack of relevant data for some of these media and the evidence of sizeable effects of air pollutants on human health, this chapter paid great attention to air pollution. The chapter has used measures covering: i) people's exposure to air pollutants and the associated health effects; ii) people's exposure to environmental risks; and iii) subjective perceptions of the quality of the environment where people live.

In OECD countries the concentrations of PM_{10} have dropped in the last twenty years, although in many OECD countries they remain well above the WHO annual target. In major non-OECD countries, in addition to being exposed to high pollutant concentrations, a large share of the population remains without basic services, such as access to safe drinking water and sanitation. For the world as a whole, 24% of the total burden of disease, or 13 million premature deaths, could be prevented through environmental improvements. Environmental policies could be of great importance in dealing with existing global health priorities.

Notes

1. Natural disasters may also cause malnutrition and associated disorders through the failure of crops; diarrhoeal diseases via contaminated water; and food poisoning. These side effects are more likely to affect people in developing countries due to their lower capacity to cope with natural disasters.

2. Time-series studies have established that the effects of PM on health were not attenuated after other gaseous pollutants were considered (Samet *et al.* 2000; Katsouyanni, 2001), thus suggesting that PM may be serving as a general proxy for the overall air pollution mixture.

3. The DALY is a health gap measure, which extends the concept of potential years of life lost due to premature death to include equivalent years of healthy life lost by virtue of individuals being in states of poor health or disability. One DALY can be thought of as one lost year of healthy life and the burden of disease as the measure of the gap between current health status and an ideal situation where everyone lives into old age free from disease and disability (World Bank, 2006).

4. Surveys on public attitudes and behaviours towards the environment have been carried out in many countries (*e.g.* the United Kingdom, Canada, Australia and Switzerland) in the past few years. However, data from national surveys are difficult to compare, as they rely on different methodologies and questionnaires. Comparative results on households attitudes and environmental behaviours, limited to 10 OECD countries, are presented in OECD (2011d).

5. The variable "access to the Internet" is based on the following question: "Does your home have access to the Internet?"

6. There is a wealth of air quality indices and even countries that share the same legislation or cities within the same country may have different indicators. This hampers the comparison of air quality at the international level. The CITEAIR project started in March 2004, proposes a single common index (CAQI) aimed at comparing the air quality of European cities, http://www.airqualitynow.eu. At the moment, about 60 European cities and regions are taking part in the project.

7. In the quest for concise information, a large set of indicators that refer to each individual pollutant can prove too cumbersome and not suitable for cross- and within-country comparisons. One way to deal with this information overload is to develop aggregate indices that summarise the information from many environmental pollutants affecting the same environmental media. However, summarising different data into a single value is difficul, and the scientific community is still divided between different types of approaches, such as providing either aggregate indicators or indicator "profiles" (matrices). Both approaches have positive and negative aspects, and there is no perfect solution. While the scientific debate centres on the amount of information lost in the simplification made possible by the aggregate index, and on the potential misinterpretation of the data to which the aggregation can lead, it is critical for better reporting and comparability to respond to this demand for concise measures.

References

Ahmad, N and N. Yamano (2011), "Carbon Dioxide Emissions Embodied in Goods and Services: Domestic Consumption versus Production", *OECD Statistics Directorate Working Papers*, forthcoming, OECD, Paris

Armstrong, D. (2000), "A survey of community gardens in upstate New York: Implications for health promotion and community development", *Health & Place*, Vol. 6, No. 4, pp. 319-327.

Arruti, A., I. Fernández-Olmo and A. Irabien (2010), "Impact of the global economic crisis on metal levels in particulate matter (PM) at an urban area in the Cantabria Region (Northern Spain)", *Journal of Environmental Monitoring*, Vol. 7, No. 12, pp. 1451-1458.

Balestra, C. and D. Dottori (2011), "Ageing Society, Health and the Environment", *Journal of Population Economics,* http://dx.doi.org/10.1007/s00148-011-0380-x.

Balestra, C. and J. Sultan (2012), "Home sweet home: The determinants of residential satisfaction and its relation with well-being", OECD Statistics Directorate Working Papers (forthcoming), OECD, Paris.

Bickerstaff, K. and G. Walker (2001), "Public understandings of air pollution: The 'localisation' of environmental risk", *Global Environmental Change*, 11, pp. 133-145.

Brown, C. and M. Grant (2007), "Natural medicine for planners", *Town and Country Planning*, Vol. 76, No. 2, pp. 67-68.

Day, R. (2007), "Place and the experience of air quality", *Health & Place*, vol 13, pp. 249-260.

Dockery, D.W. (2001), "Epidemiologic evidence of cardiovascular effects of particulate air pollution", *Environmental health perspectives*, Vol. 109, pp. 483–486.

EEA (2010), *The European Environment. State and Outlook 2010: Air Pollution*, European Environmental Agency, Copenhagen.

Ellaway, A., S. Macintyre and X. Bonnefoy (2005), "Graffiti, greenery, and obesity in adults: Secondary analysis of European cross-sectional survey", *British Medical Journal*, Vol. 331, 17 September, pp. 611-613.

Elliot, S., D. Cole, P. Krueger, N. Voorberg and S. Wakefield (1999), "The power of perception: Health risk attributed to air pollution in an urban industrial neighbourhood", *Risk analysis*, Vol. 19, pp. 621-634.

European Commission (2010), *Green Paper on Forest Protection and Information in the EU: Preparing forests for climate change*, http://ec.europa.eu/environment/forests/pdf/green_paper.pdf.

Goldberg, M.S., R.T. Burnett, J.C. Bailar, R. Tamblyn, P. Ernst, K. Flegel, J. Brook, Y. Bonvalot, R. Singh, M.F. Valois and R. Vincent (2001), "Identification of persons with cardio-respiratory conditions who are at risk of dying from the acute effects of ambient air particles", *American Journal of Epidemiology*, Vol. 109, pp. 487–494.

Gwynn, R.C. and G.D. Thurston (2001), "The burden of air pollution: Impacts among racial minorities", *Environmental Health Perspectives*, Vol. 109, pp. 501–506.

Hill, M.K. (2004), *Understanding Environmental Pollution*, Cambridge University Press, New York.

Holman, M.R. and T. G. Coan (2008), "Voting Green", *Social Science Quarterly*, Vol. 89, pp. 1121–1135.

Kahn, M.E. and J.G. Matsusaka (1997), "Demand for Environmental Goods: Evidence from Voting Patterns on California Initiatives" *Journal of Law & Economics*, Vol. 40, No. 1, pp. 137–173.

Kahn, M.E. (2002), "Demographic change and the demand for environmental regulation", *Journal of Policy Analysis and Management*, Vol. 21, No. 1, pp. 45–62.

Katsouyanni, K., G. Touloumi, E. Samoli, A. Gryparis, A. Le Tertre, Y. Monopolis, G. Rossi, D. Zmirou, F. Ballester, A. Boumghar, H.R. Anderson, B. Wojtyniak, A. Paldy, R. Braunstein, J. Pekkanen, C. Schindler and J. Schwartz (2001), "Confounding and effect modification in the short-term effects of ambient particles on total mortality: Results from 29 European cities within the APHEA2 project", *Epidemiology*, Vol. 12, pp. 521-531.

King, K. and J. Stedman (2000), *Analysis of air pollution and social deprivation*, AEA Technology Environment report AEAT/R/ENV/0241.

Mace, B., P. Bell and R. Loomis (1999), "Aesthetic, affective, and cognitive effects of noise on natural landscape assessment", *Social and Natural Resources*, Vol. 12, No. 3, pp. 225-242.

Milligan, C., A. Gatrell and A. Bingley (2004), "Cultivating health. Therapeutic landscapes and older people in Northern England", *Social Science and Medicine*, Vol. 58, No. 9, pp. 1781-1793.

OECD (2006a), *Economic Valuation on Environmental Health Risks to Children*, OECD Publishing, Paris.

OECD (2006b). *OECD Environmental Data. Compendium 2006-2008*, OECD Publishing, Paris.

OECD (2008), *OECD Environmental Outlook to 2030*, OECD Publishing, Paris.

OECD (2010), *OECD Factbook 2010*, OECD Publishing, Paris.

OECD (2011a), *Benefits of Investing in Water and Sanitation: An OECD Perspective*, OECD Publishing, Paris.

OECD (2011b), *Towards green growth: Monitoring Progress – OECD Indicators*, OECD Publishing, Paris.

OECD (2011c), *Towards Green Growth*, OECD Publishing, Paris.

OECD (2011d), *Greening Household Behaviour - The Role of Public Policy*, OECD Publishing, Paris.

Pope, C.A. and D.W. Dockery (1992), "Acute effects of PM10 pollution on symptomatic and asymptomatic children", *American Review of Respirratory Disease*, Vol. 145, pp. 1123-8.

Pretty, J., J. Peacock, M. Sellens and M. Griffin (2005), "The mental and physical health outcomes of green exercise", *International Journal of Environmental Health Research*, Vol. 15, No. 5, pp. 319-337.

Prüss-Üstün, A. and C. Corvalán (2006), *Preventing disease through healthy environments: Towards an estimate of the environmental burden of disease*. World Health Organization, Geneva.

Samet, J.M., F. Dominici, F.C. Curriero, I. Coursac and S.L. Zeger (2000), "Fine Particulate Air Pollution and Mortality in 20 U.S. Cities, 1987-1994", *The New England Journal of Medicine*, Vol. 343, No. 24, pp. 1742-1749.

Schwartz, J. (1994), "What are people dying of on high air pollution days?", *Environmental research*, Vol. 64, pp. 26–35.

Stiglitz, J.E., A. Sen and J.-P. Fitoussi (2009), Report by the Commission on the Measurement of Economic Performance and Social Progress, http://www.stiglitz-sen-fitoussi.fr/documents/rapport_anglais.pdf

Thalmann, P. (2004), "The Public Acceptance of Green Taxes: 2 Million Voters Express Their Opinion", *Public Choice*, Vol. 119, No. 4, pp. 179–217.

UNECE (2009), *Measuring sustainable development*, United Nation Economic Commission for Europe, United Nations Publication, New York and Geneva.

UNFPA (2008), *State of the World Population 2008. Reaching Common Ground: Culture, Gender and Human Rights*, United Nations Population Fund, New York.

United Nations (2008), *Measuring Sustainable Development. Report of the Joint UNECE/OECD/Eurostat Working Group on Statistics for Sustainable Development*, New York and Geneva, http://www.oecd.org/dataoecd/30/20/41414440.pdf

United Nations, European Commission, IMF (International Monetary Fund), OECD and World Bank (2003), *Handbook of National Accounting – Integrated Environmental and Economic Accounting*, ST/ESA/STAT/SER.F/Rev.1 (final draft).

Van Liere, K.D. and R.E. Dunlap (1980), "The social bases of environmental concern: A review of hypotheses, explanations, and empirical evidence", *Public Opinion Quarterly*, Vol. 44, No. 2, pp. 181–197.

Ward Thompson, C. (2002), "Urban open space in the 21st century", *Landscape & Urban Planning*, Vol. 60, pp. 59-72.

WHO (2004), Water, *Sanitation and Hygiene Links to Health: Facts and Figures updated March 2004*, WHO Library Cataloguing-in-Publication Data, Geneva.

World Bank (1992), *World Bank Report: Development and the Environment*, Oxford University Press, New York.

World Bank (2006), *Global burden of disease and risk factors*, World Bank, Washington D.C.

World Bank (2009), *Atlas of Global Development: Second Edition*, World Bank, Washington D.C.

Zheng, Y. (2010), "Association Analysis on Pro-environmental Behaviors and Environmental Consciousness in Main Cities of East Asia", *Behaviormetrika*, Vol. 37, No. 1, pp. 55-69.

ANNEX 10.A

Measuring environmental sustainability

This chapter has focused on the effects of environmental quality for the well-being of the present generation. However, measuring sustainability is also critical. The well-being of a generation is determined by the stock of resources that is inherited from previous generations and by the choices that each generation makes. Hence, many policy decisions taken today – by influencing the stock of tangible or intangible resources that will be available in the future – impact on future well-being. In some cases, actions taken today, such as investing in clean technologies, will increase the stock of resources available tomorrow; in other cases, policy decisions that increase current well-being will use up some of that stock.

The Commission on the Measurement of Economic Performance and Social Progress (Stiglitz *et al.*, 2009) recommends measuring environmental sustainability through indicators that inform about changes in the quantities of some key stocks and that forewarn about the proximity to dangerous levels of environmental risk. In practice, few such benchmarks exist or are easily applicable in an international context. This often reflects the fact that critical levels of environmental assets may vary locally, making national averages not very meaningful, and that there is often scientific uncertainty about where critical limits lie.

Several international initiatives to build sustainable development dashboards are being pursued. In 2008, the Joint UNECE/Eurostat/OECD Working Group on Measuring Sustainable Development produced a report that advocated a stock-based approach to address the inter-temporal dimension of sustainability as the best way of structuring a set of sustainability indicators that combines both stock and flow variables (United Nations, 2008). This report also suggested a distinction between capital measures of "economic" well-being (amenable to monetary evaluation) and measures of "foundational" well-being (requiring physical measures for various stocks and flows of environmental capital).

In 2009, following a mandate from Ministers, the OECD started to develop a Green Growth Strategy, with the intent of "fostering economic growth and development while ensuring that the quality and quantity of natural assets can continue to provide the environmental services on which our well-being relies" (OECD, 2011c). The set of indicators incorporated in the OECD Green Growth Strategy released in May 2011 mainly focuses on the concept of decoupling environmental pressures from economic growth (*i.e.* indicators on environmental intensities), although some of these indicators refer to the total pressures on the natural asset base (as affected by both environmental intensities and by the scale of economic activities). In a perspective of assessing environmental sustainability, this annex considers some of the Green Growth Strategy indicators as well as additional indicators whose development is still in progress:

- **Change in production- and demand-based CO_2 emissions.** CO_2 emissions have detrimental impacts not only on global temperatures and on the Earth's climate, but also for ecosystems, human settlements and socio-economic activities. It is now generally accepted that policies are needed to stabilise concentrations of CO_2 in the atmosphere at levels that would prevent dangerous anthropogenic interference with the climate system. Many of these policies target those activities that directly result in the use of fossil fuels, either through pricing mechanisms that increase the cost of these activities, or through the adoption of cleaner technologies that result in lower CO_2 emissions. The mechanisms therefore typically focus on reducing emissions on the production side of the economy. However such policies might encourage companies to offshore carbon intensive activities or push up the costs of goods such that the same goods are imported from countries subject to lower environmental costs. As a result, focusing purely on production-based figures may not tell the whole story. Therefore, there is a need for complementary consumption- or demand-based figures that reflect the impact of an economy's demand on global emissions, both to put production figures in an explanatory light and, potentially, to develop demand-based policy measures. Figure 10.A.1 shows the annual rate of change in production- and demand-based CO_2 emissions for OECD and other emerging countries at the aggregate level. Production-based estimates include emissions from domestic economic activities due to the use of oil, natural gas and coal, as well as emissions from natural gas flaring, but exclude emissions from land use and deforestation. Demand-based figures allocate the CO_2 emitted in producing a product to the final purchaser of that product, irrespective of how many intermediate processes and countries the product passes through before arriving to its final purchaser. The comparison of production and demand-based estimates shows that the contribution of OECD countries to overall global emissions has a strong demand component, that, in recent years, has been growing at a faster pace than production based emissions, as OECD economies increasingly source products from emerging economies (see Ahmad and Yamano, 2011 for more details).

Figure 10.A.1. Production-based and demand-based CO_2 emissions

Rate of change per year, 1995-2005

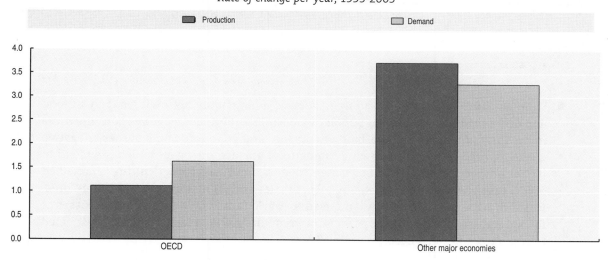

Source: OECD (2011b), *Towards Green Growth: Monitoring Progress* – OECD Indicators, OECD Publishing, Paris.

StatLink ⧉ *http://dx.doi.org/10.1787/888932493423*

- **Intensity of forest resource use**. This indicator, which relates fellings to annual gross increment, allows understanding how sustainable is the forest resource management, including for biodiversity (forests hold the vast majority of the world's terrestrial species). Deforestation, along with habitat fragmentation and degradation, is one of the biggest threats for forest biodiversity. Forests also play a key role for the climate, as they act as sinks that remove carbon dioxide from the air and help keep global warming below 2°C (European Commission, 2010). At national levels, most OECD countries make a sustainable use of their forest resources, but with significant variations within countries. From 1990 to 2009 the volume of felled trees as a percentage of annual productive capacity have decreased in Japan, Luxembourg, Hungary, Norway and Slovenia; while it has increased in other countries, notably in the Slovak Republic, Germany, Sweden, Switzerland and Austria (Figure 10.A.2). Over the past 50 years, the area of forests and wooded land has remained broadly stable (or has slightly increased) in most OECD countries, but has been declining at the world level due to the deforestation of tropical forests (OECD, 2008).

Figure 10.A.2. **Intensity of use of forest resources**

Fellings as percentage of annual gross increment

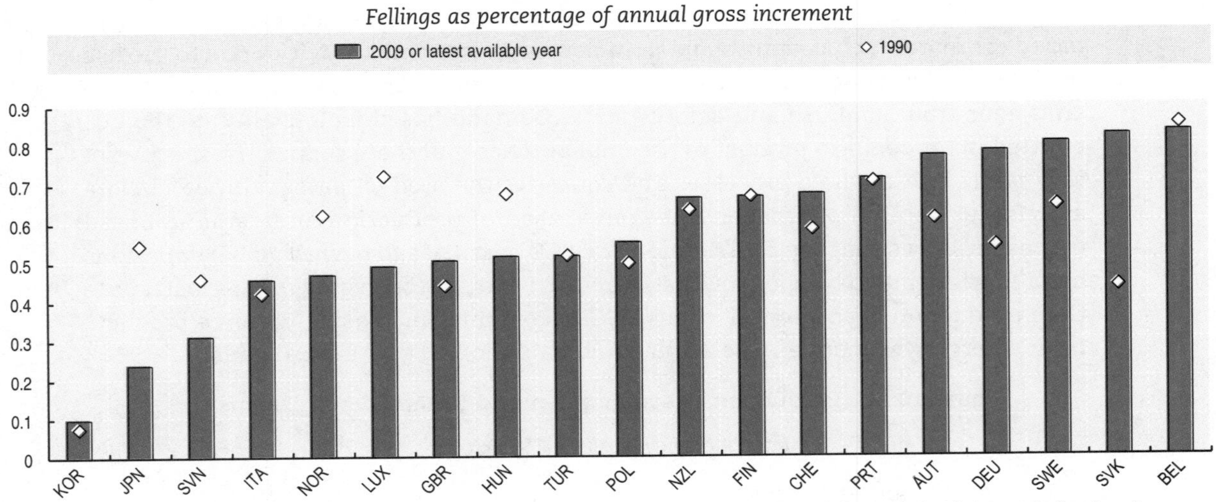

Note: The latest available year is 2007 for Luxembourg; and 2005 for Austria, Belgium, Finland, Japan, Poland and Portugal. The first available year is 1993 for Germany.

Source: OECD Environmental Database.

StatLink http://dx.doi.org/10.1787/888932493442

- **Land used for agriculture.** Land management must ensure a growing supply of food and other resources to human populations, while minimising negative consequences in the form of climate change, biodiversity loss and pollution. Some of these negative consequences reflect the growing intensity of surface nitrogen, which may lead to higher nitrogen levels of drinking water. The total land used for agriculture is projected to increase over the next 20 years in all countries and regions except Japan and Korea. In South Asia, this increase in land used for agriculture could imply further losses of forests and scrublands. In Europe, most of the additional land for agriculture is expected to come from Eastern Europe (Table 10.A.1).

Table 10.A.1 **Changes in land used for agriculture by 2030**

2005=100

North America	Europe	Japan Korea	Australia New Zealand	Brazil	The Russian Federation	South Asia	China	Middle East	South East Asia	Caucasus and Other Central Asia	Other Latin America	Africa	World
104	105	83	104	108	115	124	101	100	127	104	109	118	110

Source: OECD (2008), OECD Environmental Outlook to 2030, OECD Publishing, Paris.

StatLink http://dx.doi.org/10.1787/888932494373

- **Nitrogen surplus**. This indicator is calculated as the difference between the total quantity of nitrogen entering an agricultural system (mainly fertilisers and livestock manure) and the quantity of nutrient leaving the system (mainly uptake of nutrients by crops and grassland). It is a good indication of the level of environmental pressures from nutrients on natural assets, in particular soil and water. Elevated levels of nitrogen contribute to algal blooms in freshwater habitats and coastal areas, thus depriving other species of oxygen and reducing plant diversity. Nitrogen surplus is driven by different factors: agricultural land use, methods of farm management and nitrogen surplus intensities. Nitrogen surplus intensity per unit of agricultural output has decreased between 1900 and 2008, although with large differences between countries (nitrogen surplus intensity has considerably declined in the Netherlands, Belgium, Luxembourg and Denmark but increased in Canada, the Czech Republic, New Zealand and Poland, Figure 10A.3). Due to the combined effect of changes in nitrogen surplus intensities and of land used for agriculture, the total nitrogen surplus from agriculture is projected to increase significantly in India and China, while it may decrease in the United States and Europe. By 2030, most of the projected global increase of 0.8% will be occurring in non-OECD economies (OECD, 2008).

Figure 10.A.3. **Nitrogen surplus intensities**

Kg per hectare of agricultural land, 1990/92 and 2006/08

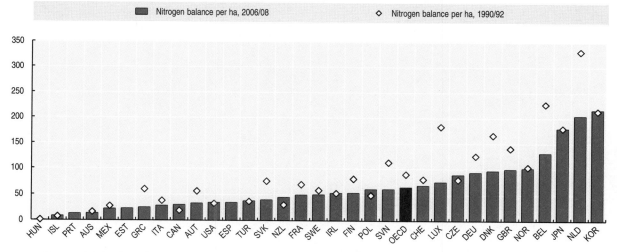

Source: OECD (2011), *Towards Green Growth: Monitoring Progress* – OECD Indicators, OECD Publishing, Paris.

StatLink ᘉᘔᕵ *http://dx.doi.org/10.1787/888932493461*

- **Freshwater abstractions**. This indicator refers to freshwater taken from ground or surface water sources, either temporarily or permanently, and conveyed to the place of use. Mine water and drainage are included, while water used for hydroelectricity generation is excluded. In the OECD area, the greatest demands for water come from irrigation (43%), electrical cooling and industry (42%), and public water supplies (15%) (OECD, 2008). Since the 1980s, most OECD countries have stabilised total water abstraction thanks to more efficient irrigation techniques, shrinking water-intensive industries (*e.g.* mining, steel), increased use of cleaner production technologies and reduced losses in pipe networks (Figure 10.A.4). Over the next twenty years, pressures on water use are projected to grow much more in developing countries than in OECD countries, due to population growth and a sharp increase in agricultural production.

Figure 10.A.4. **Freshwater abstraction in OECD countries (1980=100)**

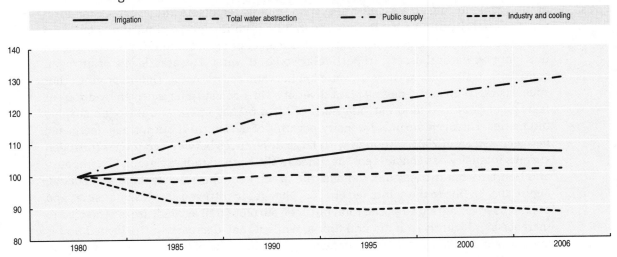

Source: OECD (2010), *OECD Factbook 2010 - Economic, Environmental and Social Statistics*, OECD Publishing, Paris.

StatLink ⧉ *http://dx.doi.org/10.1787/888932493404*

Chapter 11

Personal security

Personal security is a key component of people's well-being. Although many factors influence personal security, crime is one of the most common ones. Crime may lead to the loss of life and property, physical pain, post-traumatic stress and anxiety, both in the short and in the long run. Living in safe communities is essential to people's well-being, as feelings of insecurity will limit people's daily activities and functionings. The indicators considered in this chapter provide a general picture of the nature and extent of crime, and of its effects on people's well-being. This chapter shows that intentional homicide rates are low in most OECD countries, although there is significant variation across countries. Self-reported victimisation rates for assaults and muggings are below 5% in most OECD countries, but higher in other major economies. Similarly, most people living in OECD countries declare that they feel safe when walking alone in their neighbourhood at night, while this proportion is much lower in some of the other major economies. Evidence on other threats to personal security, such as domestic violence, remains scattered and suffers from cultural biases and methodological limitations that hamper international comparability.

Why does personal security matter for well-being?

Physical security is a broad concept, as the range of threats to people's lives includes wars, political and ethnic conflicts, terrorism, environmental and natural hazards, industrial accidents and occupational injuries. Some of these threats are rare, while indicators pertaining to more common ones (e.g. occupational injuries) have been presented in other parts of this report. This chapter deals with crime, as one of the most common threats to personal security in developed and emerging countries. Crime encompasses a large number of criminal offences, such as murders, crimes against property (e.g. car theft, burglary in one's own home), contact crimes (e.g. assault, mugging) and non-conventional crimes (e.g. consumer fraud, corruption). This chapter focuses mainly on violent and contact crimes for two reasons. First, data available at international level on other types of conventional crimes are outdated, while evidence on non-conventional crimes is still sparse. Second, personal harm and contact crimes have severe and long-lasting effects on people's well-being.

While the media pay great attention to sensational crimes, less visible but far more widespread forms of violence permeate the lives of many people around the world. Some crimes may lead to loss of life, while others have a strong impact on the victims' mental and physical health, both in the short and long term (Michalos and Zumbo, 2000; Hanson et al., 2010). Crime has also large indirect impacts on the well-being of non-victims, through the increase in worry and anxiety and the hampering of daily activities and functioning to which fear of crime may lead (Amerio and Roccato, 2007).[1] Living in safe communities is then intrinsically important to people's well-being, but it is also – and perhaps equally – important that people *perceive* that they live in a safe place (Hanson et al., 2010). Freedom from crime is also instrumental to the achievement of well-being more generally, as safer communities tend to be richer in many other dimensions, for example, by fostering closer inter-personal relationships in an area (Detotto and Otranto, 2010).

Policies need to evaluate the social costs of crime and the benefits of higher personal security. Crime imposes direct costs on affected people – such as stolen and damaged property, personal spending on security measures, pain and suffering, lost lives – and on society, in the form of public spending to prevent crime or to remedy its consequences (OECD, 2009a). Anderson (1999) estimated that the total annual cost of criminal activity (including, for instance, medical care, mental health services, police interventions and judiciary investigations) accounted for 12% of GDP in the United States. However, these estimates do not include the costs incurred by people due to their *fear of crime*, and so understate the true cost of crime (Dolan and Peasgood, 2007).[2] Estimating such costs can help to inform policy-makers about the scale of the intervention needed.

Measuring personal security, even when limited to people's experience of crime, is particularly challenging. As the chapter will show, the available statistics often point to ambiguous conclusions, and it is sometimes hard to know whether this reflects the limitations of existing measures or the fact that indicators capture different facets of personal security. While the evidence presented in this chapter is not conclusive, it highlights the need to improve existing data and indicators.

Measuring personal security

A set of ideal indicators of personal security would inform about the various crimes and offenses experienced by individuals, weighting these crimes by their seriousness. This set would also provide information on the various risks and dangers that condition people's beings and doings (*e.g.* terrorism, war, etc.). To put in place preventive policies against crime, it would be equally important that the indicators on personal security report detailed information on the victims, their background and the circumstances in which they have been attacked. Finally, a set of ideal indicators on personal security would include information on fear of crime, which may strongly affect people's lives and well-being even when not corroborated by objective danger.

Current indicators of personal security meet these ideal requirements only in part (Table 11.1). For instance, data on the total number of crimes reported to the police are not ideal as a statistical tool, because they are sensitive to changes in legislation (as new offences are introduced), and because they are not informative about the severity of each offence.[3] In addition, official police-based statistics tell only a part of the story, as a large portion of crimes are neither reported nor recorded (the so-called "dark figure", Box 11.1). Moreover, official records of crime may not be comparable across countries due to differences in what is counted as crime in various countries, and the comparability over time of these data may be limited due to changes in recording practices.[4] Police discretion in the recording of crime is a further element that affects the reliability of measures of crime based on police records (Burrows *et al.*, 2000; Nickels, 2007; Boivin and Cordeau, 2011). As the potential for overcoming these difficulties is limited, it is important to supplement the information gathered through police statistics with evidence from crime victimisation surveys, so as to have a more comprehensive picture of the scope, prevalence and incidence of crime.

Due to methodological constraints, victimisation surveys cannot provide a definitive measure of the volume of illegal acts that occur in society either. First of all, there may be cultural variations in sensitivity to crimes and in the willingness of the person interviewed to speak out; and some crimes may be underestimated or overestimated due to the subjective interpretation of what constitutes a crime by respondents.[5] Similarly, some victims may be reluctant to disclose information on incidents of a sensitive nature, such as sexual assault. Moreover, the accuracy of victimisation surveys is influenced by people's ability to recall past crimes. The longer the elapsed period, the less likely it is that a victimisation will be recalled accurately, and the respondent may tend to report incidents that occurred before the time period covered by the survey (so-called "telescoping"), thus inflating the results (United Nations, 2010). Despite these methodological drawbacks, victimisation surveys bring into focus the extent of crime problems that affect ordinary citizens most often and – if conducted at regular intervals and with the same methodology – have the capacity to provide measures of changes in levels of crime over time.

While in most developed countries detailed information is available for property and contact crimes, data on other types of crime such as consumer fraud, offences against computer data and systems, money-laundering, hate crimes and corruption is scattered. Many countries are not able to provide relevant information, and agreed standards for such crimes do not yet exist.

Table 11.1. **The quality of personal security indicators**

	Target concept	INDICATORS							
		Relevance to measure and monitor well-being				Statistical quality			
		Face validity	Unambiguous interpretation (good/bad)	Amenable to policy changes	Can be disaggregated	Well-established instrument collected	Comparable definition	Country coverage	Recurrent data collection
Personal security									
PS I Intentional homicides	Opportunities to live in a safe environment	~	√	√	x	√	√	√	~
PS II Self-reported victimization		√	√	√	√	x	√	√	√
ps 1 Domestic violence on children		~	√	√	x	√	√	√	~
ps 2 Feeling of security	Fear of crime	~	~	√	√	x	√	√	√

Note: The symbol √ shows that the indicator selected largely meets the criteria shown in the table; the symbol ~ that the indicator meets the criteria to a large extent; the symbol x that the indicator does not meet the criterion or it meets it only to a limited extent.

Selected indicators

Homicide rate (PS I)

This indicator refers to victims of *intentional* homicide, defined as an unlawful death deliberately inflicted on one person by another person.[6] Police homicide records suffer less from the above-mentioned problems of cross-country comparability, under-reporting and under-recording, as in all countries the police is required to intervene. Hence, homicide is one of the few crimes for which recorded crime figures provide a reasonably accurate measure of crime levels. However, differences in definitions and procedures in statistics production may hinder cross-country comparison. Homicide is widely considered as the most important indicator of violent crime, as many other types of crimes with lesser impacts on victims (*e.g.* robbery) are associated with it. However, it should be stressed that homicide is a very rare crime, especially when compared to contact or property crimes such as mugging and theft.

The data shown here are collected by the United Nations Office on Crime and Drugs (UNODC) and show the number of reported intentional homicides (male and female victims) annually per 100 000 population. The United Nations Survey of Crime Trends (UN-CTS) conducted by the UNODC collects national data on crime and criminal justice from law enforcement institutions, prosecutor offices, and ministries of interior and justice. Other international organisations that collect information in the area of crime and criminal justice include Interpol, Eurostat, and regional crime prevention and violence observatories.

Self-reported victimisation (PS II)

The indicator shown here represents the percentage of people aged 15 and over who declare having been the victim of assault or mugging in the preceding calendar year. It excludes crimes against property that do not involve physical contact between the victim and the offender. This indicator refers to data drawn from the Gallup World Poll [7] based on the following question: "Within the past 12 months, have you been assaulted or mugged?"[8]

Although the data are deemed to be of adequate quality, the sample sizes are small, a limit that is especially important for measuring events that typically affect only a small proportion of the entire population. Due to this and other methodological limitations, the evidence from this indicator ought to be taken with caution. National crime victimisation surveys exist in some countries but are not based on common standards and methodologies.

Box 11.1. **The "dark figure"**

A large number of crimes are never reported to the police (Taylor, 2003). In the United States, only 40% of property crimes and 49% of violent crimes were reported to the police in 2009 (Bureau of Justice Statistics, 2010). Although in some countries crime-reporting has increased in recent years (Van Djik *et al.*, 2008), too many crimes still do not get the attention of the police, a phenomenon called "dark figure" according to the term popularised by Biederman and Reiss, 1967. Some of the key factors influencing reporting behaviour are:

- *Demographic and Socio-economic characteristics.* Research has shown that women are more likely than men to report crime to the police (Skogan, 1984). However, this crime-reporting behaviour differs by the type of crime and the relationship between the victim and the offender. When the offender is known to them, women are less likely than men to report assaults to the police, while the reverse is true for property crimes (Carcach, 1997). Also, comparing age groups, crime-reporting rates are highest among older people and lowest among young people (Tanton and Jones, 2003). Ethnicity is not a strong predictor of crime-reporting behaviour (Davis and Henderson, 2003), although it is an important factor when taking into account police behaviour and attitudes towards the police.

- *Attitudes to the police.* Victims who perceive the police to be ineffectual in dealing with crime, or who have had a negative experience with the police in the past, are less likely than others to contact the police about an incident (Skogan, 1984). Victimisation surveys have shown that certain groups within inner cities are far more likely to experience burglary, but also that this experience tends to reduce their reporting inclinations due to lower expectations about the outcome (Maguire, 1997). Fear of the police is a strong determinant of crime-reporting behaviour, especially in developing countries (Marenin, 1997). Victims may also be less willing to contact the police if they believe that they are in some way responsible for the incident (Skogan, 1984).

- *Incident-specific factors.* The type and seriousness of the crime, the relationship between the victim and the offender, and the loss or damage involved with the incident also affect crime-reporting behaviour. In general, property crimes are more likely to be reported by higher-income people, while lower-income groups are more likely to report violent crimes; this suggests that the link between crime-reporting behaviour and socio-economic status is explained more by the consequences of crime than by its seriousness (*e.g.* reporting property crimes to the police may be done mainly for insurance purposes, Lewis, 1989; Goudriaan, 2006).

Beyond under-reporting, the size of the "dark figure" also depends on a number of institutional factors such as the legal system in use, the definitions applied to different crimes, the efficiency of the law enforcement and criminal justice system in controlling crime, and the capacity of the criminal justice system to discover, record and investigate crimes.

Source: Adapted from MacDonald (2001; 2002).

Violence against children (ps 1)

Children have a right to a childhood free of abuse and neglect. Although is likely that in all OECD countries only a minority of children suffer from maltreatment, abuse and neglect, violence against children has serious and long-lasting effects on child well-being. Often representing the endpoint of a continuum of violence, the killing of a child or infant (through a combination of a single violent incident and of deliberate neglect) has been referred to as a "sentinel" event in society: no matter how small in absolute numbers, each such event attains a special significance and attracts great attention from people and the media (Jenny and Isaac, 2006).

The indicator shown here measures the annual number of deaths of children under the age of 20 from acts of commission (assault and maltreatment) and acts of omission (neglect). Data are normally averaged over a two year period and expressed per 100 000 children in the age group. Deaths can take place in the home or outside. Data are based on an OECD analysis of official statistical records submitted by national governments to the World Health Organisation (WHO) for inclusion in the Mortality Database. The underlying cause of death is defined in accordance with the rules of the International Classification of Diseases. This indicator covers most OECD countries, although data are not collected regularly.

The statistics shown here need to be interpreted with great caution, as the cause or process by which child deaths are reported, the rigour with which they are investigated and the criteria by which they are classified can vary widely and hamper international comparability. Moreover, data on intentional child deaths suffer from major methodological limits. First, data refer to cases of child deaths as registered in governmental vital statistics, where a police investigation has concluded that the deaths stemmed from negligence, maltreatment or assault; it is generally acknowledged that the recorded cases of child (and especially infant) deaths are an underestimate of the actual number of deaths due to these reasons (Brookman and Nolan, 2006; Creighton, 2001; Lundstrom and Sharpe, 1991; Wilczynski, 1994; UNICEF, 2003).[9] Moreover, child homicides may be missed in countries with less advanced systems for registering and prosecuting these incidents. Finally, child deaths are the *most extreme form* of domestic violence, and they do not necessarily reflect the true scale of the overall violence on children (Box 11.2; OECD, 2011a). As data on child maltreatment are not fully comparable across countries, it must be left to individual national examples to suggest the scale of the issue. According to an Australian survey, for instance, in 1999-2000 for every death from child maltreatment there were 150 cases of physical abuse supported by proof or evidence and 600 cases if neglect and sexual and emotional abuse were included. In France, a study suggested around 300 cases of child abuse and neglect for every death (UNICEF, 2003).[10] Due to these drawbacks, it must be emphasised that child death rates from maltreatment, assault and neglect are used here as an imperfect proxy for child maltreatment. For this reason, this indicator is shown here as a secondary indicator. Data on attitudes towards corporal punishment and emotional violence towards children and on their prevalence are not shown here due to differences across countries in the way these types of behaviour are viewed.

Feeling of security (ps 2)

Fear of crime is as important as crime itself due to the depth and breadth of its consequences on people's lives (Adams and Serpe, 2000). However, defining and measuring fear of crime is a complex task (Gabriel and Greve, 2003). Fear of crime includes many dimensions, ranging from fear of physical violence to fear of loss or damage to property (Amerio and Roccato, 2007).[11] While, in some circumstances, fear may be a beneficial, even life-saving, emotion, in most cases fear due to perceived personal insecurity will constrain behaviour, restrict freedom and threaten the foundation of communities (Warr, 2000). The indicator shown here is the percentage of the population who declare that they feel safe walking alone at night in their neighbourhood. The indicator is based on the data drawn from the Gallup World Poll based on the following question: "Do you feel safe walking alone at night in the city or area where you live?"

While the regular collection of survey data on this item permits comparison over time, small sample sizes and other limitations suggest that caution is needed when interpreting changes in this indicator.[12] Moreover, as fear of crime is partially dependent on how it is measured and acknowledged, the indicator shown here is an imperfect proxy for the prevalence of fear of crime (Farrall and Gadd, 2003). Nevertheless, the measured feeling of security obtained through this survey question is not radically different from that measured in other national surveys (Warr, 2000). It is presented here as a secondary indicator.

Average patterns

Homicide rates are low in most OECD countries

In most OECD countries homicide rates are low (below the OECD average of 2.2 homicides per 100 000 people). They are, however, more than twice as high in the United States (5.2) and even higher in Chile, Mexico, Russia and, especially, South Africa.[13] Between 2003 and 2008, homicide rates have declined in all countries except Brazil, with an especially large decline in countries with high homicide levels in the early 2000s (Figure 11.1). In the last 50 years, despite the proliferation of increasingly dangerous weapons, the lethality of criminal assaults has dropped sharply due in part to developments in medical support services (Aebi, 2004; Harris et al., 2002).

Figure 11.1. **Intentional homicides**

Rate per 100,000 population

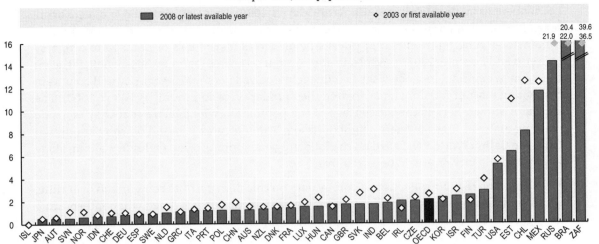

Note: The latest available year is 2007 for Austria, Denmark, Ireland, Italy, Netherlands, Norway, the United Kingdom, China and India; and 2004 for Indonesia. The first available year is 2007 for Brazil; 2006 for Luxembourg; 2005 for New Zealand and Spain; and 2004 for South Africa. Data for the United Kingdom are collected by three different jurisdictions (England and Wales, Scotland and Northern Ireland); the value shown is an unweighted average of the values for the three jurisdictions. Numerical values are shown for countries whose homicide rate exceeds the vertical scale.

Source: UNODC; Eurostat; Crime and Criminal Justice Statistics for Austria, Denmark, Ireland and Netherlands.

StatLink ⟐⟐⟐ *http://dx.doi.org/10.1787/888932493480*

Assault and mugging rates are low in most OECD countries

In 2010, only a small minority of people in OECD countries reported that they had been victim of an assault or mugging over the preceding 12 months; however, there is major variation in rates within the OECD region. The rates for Canada, Japan, the United States, Poland, Israel and the United Kingdom are below 2%, but they are significantly higher in Chile and especially in Mexico. Self-reported assault and mugging victimisation rates are also higher in emerging countries, especially in Brazil, South Africa and India (Figure 11.2).

Figure 11.2. **Self-reported victimisation**

Percentage of people declaring having been assaulted or mugged over the previous 12 months, 2010

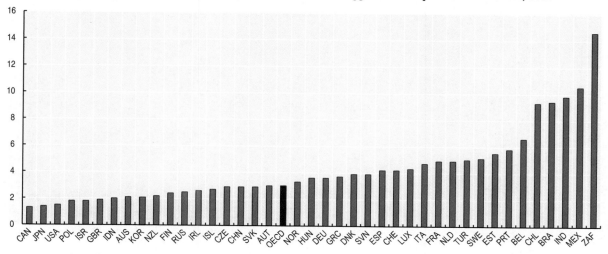

Note: Data refer to 2008 for Iceland and Norway; and to 2009 for Estonia, Israel, Switzerland, the Russian Federation and South Africa.

Source: Gallup World Poll.

StatLink ⬛ *http://dx.doi.org/10.1787/888932493499*

The number of child deaths is high in the United States and Mexico

Child death rates due to negligence, maltreatment or physical assault vary widely across OECD countries. The United States has the highest child death rate, followed by Mexico, while Switzerland, Estonia, Korea, Luxembourg and the Slovak Republic have virtually nil child death rates (Figure 11.3). The high rate of child deaths due to negligence, maltreatment or physical assault in the United States partly reflects the higher quality of the US system used to identify the cause of death (Friedman *et al.*, 2005). However, other factors, such as "easy" access to firearms, may also influence this high rate. On average, one in three child deaths takes place at home; however, no information about child deaths occurring at home is available for the Nordic countries (Figure 11.3).

Figure 11.3. **Child deaths due to negligence, maltreatment or physical assault**

Children 0-19 years old, rate per 100 000 people, 2006-2008 or latest available years

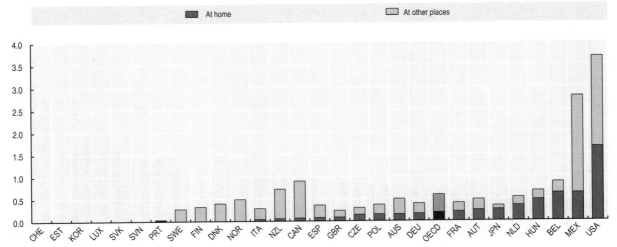

Note: Data sorted in ascending order of child death rates occurring at home. Data are averaged over the period 2006-2008 for Austria, the Czech Republic, Estonia, Finland, Japan, the Netherlands and Slovenia; 2005-2007 for France, Norway, Poland, Sweden, Switzerland and the United Kingdom; 2004-2006 for Denmark, Germany, Korea, Luxembourg, Mexico and New Zealand; 2003-2005 for Australia, Hungary, the Slovak Republic, Spain and the United States; 2002-2004 for Canada; 2003,2006,2007 for Italy; and 2004 for Belgium. Data for Iceland have been excluded due to the small number of children in the relevant age group.

Source: OECD's calculations based on the WHO mortality database.

StatLink http://dx.doi.org/10.1787/888932493518

Box 11.2. **The consequences of child abuse**

Deaths represent the "tip of the iceberg" as far as child abuse and maltreatment is concerned. For every child who is killed, many more are physically injured or psychologically damaged. Although there has been great progress in recent years in acknowledging the importance and severity of child abuse, we are still a long way from understanding the overall impact this has on society.

One of the major consequences of child abuse is poor health. While some of the health impacts of child abuse have been extensively researched (*e.g.* bruises, bumps, wounds), others have only recently been given attention, including psychiatric disorders and suicidal behaviour (Fergusson *et al.*, 2008; Trowell *et al.*, 1999). Importantly, there is now evidence that some major forms of illness in adult life, such as ischemic heart disease, cancer, chronic lung disease, fibromyalgia and infertility are related to experiences of abuse during childhood (WHO, 2002). The mechanism likely to explain the transmission of child abuse into adult life is the adoption of behaviours that are damaging to people's health, such as smoking, drugs and alcohol abuse, poor diet and lack of exercise (Felitti *et al.*, 1998; Springer *et al.*, 2007). Similarly, many studies have documented short-term and long-term psychological consequences of child abuse, in the form of anxiety, violence, depression, shame or cognitive impairments (Putnam, 2003).

Children who witness violence between parents or who are victims of family violence are also at higher risk of bullying other children, of achieving poor school performance, and of experiencing other negative outcomes (Gilbert *et al.*, 2009; Bowes *et al.*, 2009, 2010). They also tend to replicate these patterns with their partners and/or their own children, leading to an intergenerational transmission of family violence (Laing and Bobic, 2002).

> The consequences of child abuse vary among individuals, depending on the age at onset of the abuse, the relationship with the abuser, the frequency of abuse, and the severity of the assault. They also differ between girls and boys, with boys tending to react outwardly on other people and girls tending to react inwardly. The consequences also depend on the socio-economic status of the family, support structures at school and in the community, and the response received when the child reports the maltreatment.
>
> *Source* : WHO (2002), World Report on Violence and Health, Geneva.

There is substantial variation in the feeling of security across countries

In Canada, New Zealand and the Slovak Republic, around 80% or more of the population declare that they feel safe when walking alone at night. This proportion is close to 50% in Portugal, Greece, Hungary and Luxembourg. In South Africa only one person in five feels safe when walking alone at night in their neighbourhood (Figure 11.4).

Figure 11.4. **Feeling of security**

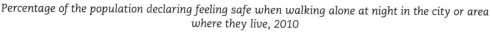

Percentage of the population declaring feeling safe when walking alone at night in the city or area where they live, 2010

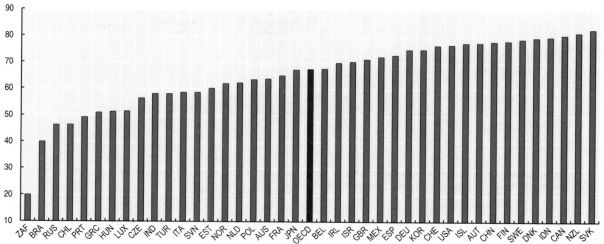

Note: Data refer to 2008 for Iceland and Norway; and to 2009 for Estonia, Israel, Switzerland, the Russian Federation and South Africa.
Source: Gallup World Poll.

StatLink ⟨img⟩ *http://dx.doi.org/10.1787/888932493537*

The various indicators convey a consistent picture of personal security

Personal security captures a variety of dimensions, and the indicators shown here measure various aspects of crime. Correlations between the different indicators used in this chapter highlight a number of patterns (Table 11.2):

● There is a strong correlation between the number of intentional homicides and the percentage of people who declare having been assaulted. The indicator measuring the number of intentional homicides also correlates well with the child death rate due to negligence, maltreatment or physical assault, which is in turn correlated with self-reported victimisation (even though in this case the correlation is weaker). On average, OECD countries with high homicide rates also experience high levels of physical assault, both inside and outside the household. This suggests that we can talk about an "overall level of crime/insecurity" experienced by society.

- Self-reported victimisation is also negatively correlated with people's feeling of security (ps 2). On average, countries characterised by a higher share of people having experienced assault and mugging tend to feature stronger fears of crime. This is in line with both previous research and the results of multivariate analysis summarised in Table 11.4. However, the weak correlation indicates that the links between victimisation rates and the feeling of security are complex, with many factors at work (Box 11.3).

- The feeling of security and violence against children are not correlated. This is not surprising, for several reasons. First, while violence against children takes place mostly at home, the feeling of security is related to the outdoor environment. Second, the samples from which data are drawn are remarkably different: while violence against children is experienced mostly by very young children and teenagers, only individuals aged 15 and over are represented in the survey measuring feelings of security.

Table 11.2. **Correlation between different indicators of personal security**

		PS I Intentional homicides		PS II Self-reported victimisation (assaults)		ps 1 Child deaths due to maltreatment		ps 2 Feeling of security	
PS I	Intentional homicides	1	(41)	0.7154***	(41)	0.7303***	(29)	-0.3442**	(41)
PS II	Self-reported victimsation (assaults)			1	(41)	0.3971**	(29)	-0.3247**	(41)
ps 1	Child deaths due to maltreatment					1	(29)	0.0866	(29)
ps 2	Feeling of security							1	(41)

Note: Values in parenthesis refer to the number of observations. ** Indicates that correlations are significant at the 5% level; *** indicates that they are significant at the 1% level.

Source: OECD's calculations.

StatLink *mls* http://dx.doi.org/10.1787/888932494411

Box 11.3. **Does self-reported victimisation reflect the fear of crime?**

Despite a general reduction in assault victimisation rates in the past five years, according to the data used in this report, in many OECD countries feelings of security have declined. In Norway, Portugal, Poland and France, for instance, despite a decrease in self-reported victimisation rates, the feeling of security has dropped by between 11 and 25 percentage points. Conversely, in Korea and the Slovak Republic, the feeling of security has risen strongly despite small changes in the number of self-reported assaults (Figure 11.5). These changes need however to be interpreted with caution due to the small sample size of the Gallop World Poll, and to the possibility that this survey may understate self-reported victimisation and exaggerate fear of crime (at least in some population groups).

Figure 11.5. **Do self-reported victimisation and the feeling of security evolve in the same direction?**

Percentage change, 2005-2010

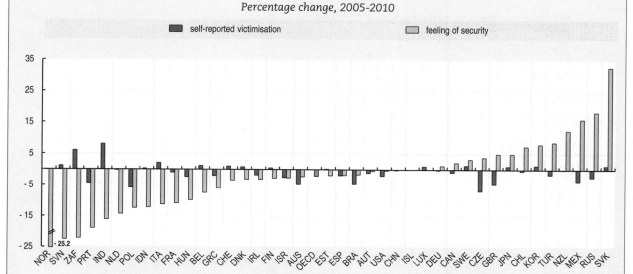

Note: Countries are sorted in ascending order of the change in the feeling of security. For Norway the percentage change for self-reported victimisation is - 0.1
Source: Gallup World Poll.

StatLink ⟨⟩ *http://dx.doi.org/10.1787/888932493556*

Different factors can explain why victimisation rates and the feeling of security do not always move in the same direction:

- First, due to lack of comparable data, this chapter has considered only one type of conventional crime (*i.e.* assault), while several other crimes (*e.g.* theft, burglary, robbery, etc.) may affect feelings of security.

- Second, perceptions of crime may far exceed crime rates due to the influence of the media. Research has acknowledged the role of the media in overemphasizing violent crime, misleading reports in crime statistics and feeding people's feeling of insecurity. A few noteworthy crimes reported in the media can increase the public's fears and alter their behaviour, despite no increase in the probability of being victimised.

- Third, irrespectively of the actual level of crime, neighbourhood structural characteristics have an impact on feelings of security (Pain, 1997). Unruly gatherings of young men or visual clues of disorder, such as smashed bus shelter windows or the presence of graffiti appearing overnight on public buildings, are seldom recorded as crimes but play into a wider feeling among the public that levels of law and order are declining. These factors may induce a fear of crime in some people and be viewed as an invitation to crime by others.

Inequalities

Homicide rates for men are usually four or five times larger than for women

Data from various sources – which are not directly comparable with the data shown in this chapter – indicate that homicide rates for men are usually far greater than those affecting women (Geneva Declaration, 2008). Moreover, the lower the overall rates of homicide victims, the higher is the share of women in the total.

Figure 11.6. **Homicides by gender and age, 2008**

Rate per 100 000, World estimates

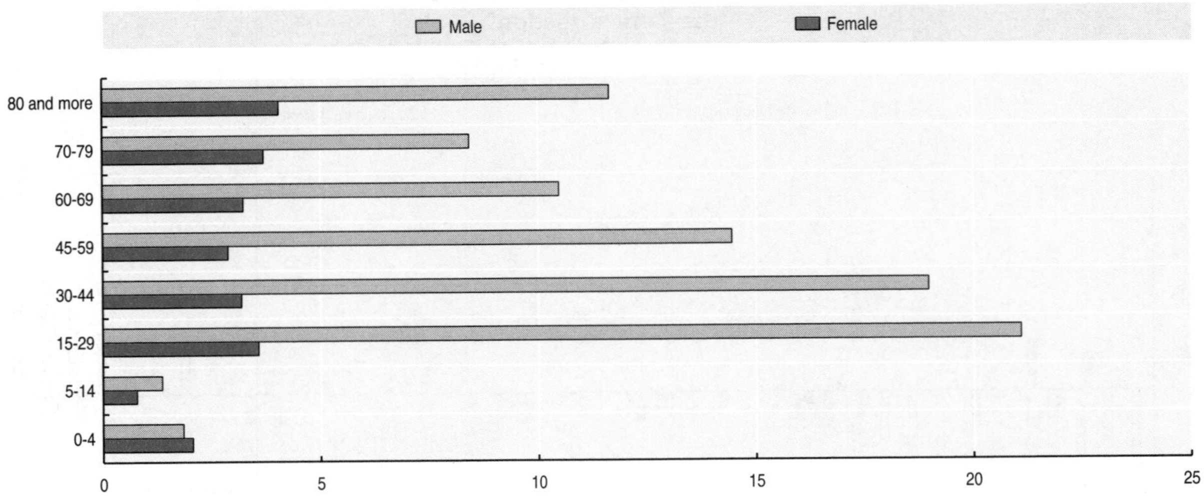

Note: World estimates include WHO Member Countries.

Source: OECD estimates based on WHO Global Burden of Disease project.

StatLink http://dx.doi.org/10.1787/888932493575

Figure 11.6 shows that the population group most at risk of being victims of homicide are men between the ages of 15 and 29 (reflecting patterns of criminal activity, such as youth gangs and drug smuggling). The risk then declines monotonically with age, before rising among the very elderly (aged 80 and above). There are fewer differences in the risk of homicide according to age in the case of women. Females are more vulnerable than males to homicide in the very first years of life; this might reflect practices of female infanticide in some developing and emerging countries, and the general neglect of baby girls in many societies.[14] Beyond the first years of life, female risk of being a victim of homicide is little affected by age.

Average data on child deaths mask large differences between groups

Child and juvenile homicide is unevenly distributed, with certain groups of the population experiencing the overwhelming burden of the problem. Although the statistics presented here do not allow a breakdown by population subgroup, many national studies suggest a U-shaped pattern of child homicide by age (UNICEF, 2003). While infants are disproportionally affected, middle childhood seems to be a time when children are relatively immune from the risk of homicide and death due to maltreatment or neglect.[15] Physical vulnerability plays a role in shaping this pattern: older children have outgrown some of the physical factors that make very young children vulnerable to lethal force. An additional factor may relate to the routine activities of children: relative to their younger counterparts, those over five years of age spend more time away from their parents and other adult caregivers, who are the primary perpetrators of early childhood homicide (Crittenden and Craig 1990).[16] With the onset of adolescence, juvenile death rates begin to rise again. However, unlike homicides of young children, relatively few homicides of teenagers are committed by family members. Most of these incidents consist of murders of teens by other teens (WHO, 2002; OECD, 2009b).

In most countries, over the very first years of life face higher probability of violent deaths than do girls, while girls are at a higher risk of sexual abuse, neglect and being forced into prostitution (Finkelhor, 1994; National Research Council, 1993). Research also suggests that child deaths and abuse are strongly related to depressed or substance-abusing parents, single parenthood, poverty and parents' lack of social relations (Coulton *et al.*, 1999; OECD, 2011a; Runyan *et al.*, 1998). These factors often overlap and interact and, to the extent they raise the risk of child death or maltreatment, they do so by complex pathways. This makes it difficult to know how, for example, poverty per se affects the likelihood of physical abuse. Young and older women are also disproportionately exposed to acts of violence perpetrated by their partners (Box 11.4)

Box 11.4. **Intimate partner violence**

Women are more likely than men to be the target of violence by an intimate partner. The WHO suggests that between 40% and 70% per cent of all women homicides are committed by an intimate partner (Krug *et al.*, 2002). Such violence, including rape, domestic violence, murder and sexual abuse, is a significant cause of mortality and a leading cause of injury for women aged 15 to 44 (Geneva Declaration, 2008).

Data on violence against women are scattered and unsystematic, and some forms of violence against women (*e.g.* intimidation, emotional violence, etc.) are difficult to measure accurately and robustly in quantitative form. The data shown in Figure 11.7 come from the International Crime Victims Survey (ICVS) and the European Crime and Safety Survey (2005) and refer to prevalence rates for physical assaults, threats and sexual offences (rape, attempted rape or indecent assault) committed by current or former partner. While the large majority of intimate partner violence is perpetrated by men against women and girls, women can also be perpetrators of partner violence (with men as the victims). Partner violence can also affect gays, lesbians, transgender and transsexual people. Physical violence is defined here as incidents where respondents were attacked or threatened in a frightening way, as well as sexual acts carried out in an offensive way.

Figure 11.7. **Physical or sexual assault committed by current or former partner**

Percentage of population, women and men, 2005

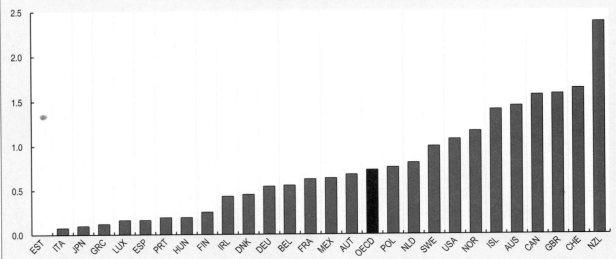

Note: Data refer to 2004 for Australia, Canada, Estonia, Japan, Mexico, New Zealand, Norway, Poland and the United States.
Source: International Crime and Victim Survey (2004-2005) and European Crime and Safety Survey (2005).

StatLink ⟨ms⟩ *http://dx.doi.org/10.1787/888932493594*

Intimate partner violence is in general low in OECD countries, with less than 2% of the population reporting such incidents. There are however large cross-national differences. English-speaking and Nordic countries seem to experience higher rates of partner violence compared to Southern European countries (Figure 11.7). However, these comparisons should be made with great caution, due to cultural biases and differences in views of what constitutes violence and in the willingness to speak out.

Drivers of crime victimisation and the feeling of security

Individuals differ in their exposure to crime and in their feelings of security. Some important determinants of victimisation and fear of crime are whether people lead a risky lifestyle, including how much they go out at night, how attractive they are as a target (*e.g.* whether they are perceived as vulnerable or they simply own valuable objects) and the extent of guardianship (*e.g.* the absence of a capable guardian or security measures that can deter crime), (Carrabine *et al.*, 2009). Other determinants of victimisation and fear of crime include:

- *Age*. Young people are more exposed to risks of being a victim of some crimes than adults, irrespectively of gender, class and location. While people's physical resiliency declines with age, increasing their vulnerability, younger people face a higher risk of some criminal aggressions because of their lifestyle (*e.g.* because they go out more often). Evidence is mixed on the impact of people's age on their fear of crime, with some research suggesting that elderly people are the most fearful and others highlighting the opposite pattern (Moore and Shepherd, 2007)[17]

- *Gender*. Both police records and victimisation surveys show that men are at greater risk of being victims of assaults and violent crimes (Carrabine *et al.*, 2009). However, despite being less victimised, women report lower feelings of security than men, due to a combination of greater fears of sexual attacks (Ferraro, 1995), feeling that they must protect not only themselves but also their children or that they may be perceived as partially responsible (e.g. due to routine activities, clothing, etc.) if they are the victim of crime (Schafer *et al.*, 2006).

- *Ethnicity*. Ethnic minority groups generally suffer higher victimisation rates than other groups in society, although it is difficult to isolate this effect as other socio-economic factors related to ethnicity may be at work (*e.g.* ethnic minority groups are more likely to live in socially disadvantaged areas, Modood *et al.*, 1997).

- *Living area*. Crime is concentrated spatially, with higher crimes in urban areas (as opposed to rural areas) and in poor areas (as opposed to wealthy areas). Urban dwellers may live closer to high offending populations, and their daily routines bring them into contact with others in more anonymous settings (Lee, 2000; OECD, 2011b). People living in major cities or their suburbs are also more concerned about crime than people living in smaller settlements (Van Dijck and Smit, 2008).

- *Social status*. People with higher incomes and higher education usually report higher feelings of security and face lower risks of crime (especially property crime), as they can afford better security and are less likely to associate with people whose likelihood of being an offender is higher (Kelly, 2000).

- *Marital status*. Being married reduces the risk of being assaulted and increases the feeling of security, due to the effect of marriage in lowering risk-taking behaviour (*e.g.* going out at night, using public transport), strengthening social control (Umberson, 1987; Cheung; 1998) and reducing the sense of vulnerability (Mesch, 2000).

- *Physical impairments*. People with physical impairments or who are psychologically distressed are more likely to be victimised and to fear crime, as these conditions make them less capable of deterring crime and easier targets (Nosek *et al.*, 2001; Marley and Buila, 2001, Stiles *et al.*, 2003).

● *Social network.* Social ties may reduce concerns about crime, as they provide a support structure for coping with crime and a sense of familiarity and control in the neighbourhood where people live (Carrabine *et al.*, 2009).

Following the empirical approach taken by these various studies, an analysis of the main determinants of victimisation and feelings of security has been carried out based on the indicators from the Gallup World Poll (Box 11.5). Most of the findings of this analysis are consistent with those from the research discussed above, although a few are not fully in line with the literature, thus suggesting the need for further research.

Box 11.5. **Determinants of assault victimisation and the feeling of security**

Table 11.3 reports the results of a regression analysis for a selection of socio-economic variables on self-reported assault and mugging victimisation and the feeling of security (see Balestra and Sultan, 2012 for more details). The sample includes both OECD and emerging countries (Brazil, the Russian Federation, India, Indonesia and China). The results of this analysis have to be taken with caution, as the underlying data suffer from some methodological shortcomings.

Table 11.3. **The determinants of self-reported assault and the feeling of security**

Marginal effects of explanatory variables on self-reported victimisation and feeling of security

Explanatory variables	Self-reported victimisation	Feeling of security
Female	-0.01***	-0.13***
Age 25-34	-0.01***	0.02**
Age 35-54	-0.02***	0.03***
Age 55-64	-0.02***	0.04***
Age 65+	-0.02***	-0.01
Married	-0.01***	0.02***
Household income	-0.01***	-0.01
Secondary education	-0.01***	-0.01
Tertiary education	-0.01***	0.03***
Small town	0.01***	-0.10***
Big city	0.03***	-0.15***
Suburb of a big city	0.01**	-0.09***
Poor health status	0.02***	-0.04***
Social network support	-0.01**	0.04***
Previous victimisation		-0.22***

Note: Probit analysis includes all OECD countries, Brazil, China, India, Indonesia, the Russian Federation and South Africa. * indicates that values are significant at 10% confidence level; ** indicates that they are significant at 5% confidence level; and *** that they are significant at 1% confidence level. A positive value in the left column means that the explanatory variable increases the likelihood of being victim of an assault, while a negative value in the right column means that the explanatory variable increases the likelihood of feeling safe when walking at night in the neighbourhood. The variable "household income" refers to the natural logarithm of the household disposable income. The number of observations is 124 027.

Source: OECD's calculations based on data from the Gallup World Poll, 2005 to 2010.

StatLink ᴹˢ⁼ *http://dx.doi.org/10.1787/888932494430*

The results shown in the left column of Table 11.3 refer to self-reported assault and mugging victimisation. In line with previous research, people living in large conurbations and people reporting health problems (as measured by the following question "Do you have any problems that prevent you from doing any of the things people of your age normally do?") experience higher levels of self-reported victimisation. Men and young people between the age of 16 and 24 face a higher risk of assault, while being married reduces that risk. In line with previous studies, higher levels of education or income seem to lower the risk of being assaulted. Social ties (as measured by the question: "If you were in trouble, do you have relatives or friends you can count on to help you whenever you need them, or not?") are associated with lower victimisation.

The right column of Table 11.3 shows the effect of the explanatory variables on the feeling of security. Previous victimisation is the strongest negative determinant. Moreover, in line with previous research, women report lower feelings of security than man, despite being less likely to be victimised (see left column of Table 11.3). One possible explanation of this seemingly paradoxical relationship is that the fear of crime leads women to change their routines, thus avoiding certain areas and people. Young people are more fearful (and more likely to be assaulted, see left column of Table 11.3) than those between 25 and 64 years old. The effect of age on the feeling of security of the elderly is negative, albeit not statistically significant. Married people and those who have relatives or friends they can count on in case of trouble (as proxied by the variable "perceived social network") feel safer when walking alone at night in their neighbourhood. People living in cities and their suburbs are significantly more fearful than their counterparts living in rural settlements. People with a higher education credential report higher feelings of security than individuals with lower education levels. Contrary to previous research, income does not seem to influence the feeling of security.

This analysis needs to be corroborated by further research. In particular, the analysis would benefit from the consideration of more detailed individual and risk-related variables (*e.g.* risky lifestyle, ethnicity, satisfaction with the neighbourhood and the police).

The statistical agenda ahead

Indentifying reliable indicators for personal security is challenging. Despite a number of initiatives to improve crime and criminal justice statistics in recent years, including the emergence of observatories and task forces on crime, violence and delinquency, statistics on crime and criminal justice are still scarce and not very comparable. Given the importance of personal security to people's life, better measures are essential to provide a more accurate picture of the scale and trends of crime across countries. For the purpose of international comparability, an agreement should be reached on which indicators to use, as well as on shared concepts and definitions. Some of the priorities for future work in this field include the following:

- While most developed countries are able to provide police statistics on general categories such as homicide, robbery, assault and theft, these may fail to meet the requirements for international reporting when more details on the circumstances are requested.[18] Furthermore, other major countries still face significant challenges in compiling, processing and disseminating crime and criminal justice statistics in a systematic way.

- Victimisation surveys are critical for the development of internationally comparable indicators. Many countries have undertaken household surveys and collected data on crimes experienced by the victims, their reactions (including reporting the incident to the police), their view about police performance and their attitudes to crime (*e.g.* fear of crime). However, data from national surveys are difficult to compare, as they rely on different methodologies, categories of crimes and questionnaires. In the attempt to improve cross-country comparability, the United Nations recently released the UN *Manual on Victimisation Surveys*. The *Manual* highlights a number of key topics for inclusion and will be particularly useful for countries that want to implement a survey of this type for the first time or have limited experience in this field. In response to the lack of comparable information on crime highlighted in the 2009 Stockholm Programme, Eurostat has developed, together with the Member States, the methodology for an EU Safety Survey (SASU), which will be conducted by the European Statistical System in 2013.

- More work needs to be done to develop reliable indicators on violence against children and women. The UN recommends both the development of specific surveys and the use of administrative records – depending on the form of violence experienced – to measure the prevalence and severity of the type of violence.

- Finally, further efforts should be promoted to develop measures applicable to non-conventional crimes (such as trafficking of persons, smuggling of immigrants, corruption, bribery, consumer fraud) and new kinds of crimes (e-crime, identity thief, cyber attacks).

Conclusion

This chapter has provided a general picture of the level and extent of crime, and of its impacts on people's personal security. The concept of crime is a broad one, encompassing a number of conventional and non-conventional activities. However, due to the lack of comparable or recent data for some of these activities, as well as evidence of large effects of contact crimes on people's well-being, this chapter has focussed on violent crimes and assaults, based on measures covering: i) intentional homicides reported to the police; ii) self-reported prevalence of assault and mugging; and iii) violence against children and women. This indicator set has been supplemented with subjective measures, of people's feeling of security in the area where they live.

In OECD countries the number of homicides is low, although remarkable variations are reported across countries. Assaults are rare in most OECD countries, while they are still common in some emerging countries. The large majority of people living in OECD countries declare that they feel safe when walking alone in their neighbourhood at night, even though there is significant variation across countries. Available data on domestic abuse fail to provide satisfactory evidence, as they are sparse and suffer from cultural bias and methodological limitations that hamper international comparability.

Notes

1. According to Dolan and Peasgood (2007), nearly one-fourth of UK respondents identified fear of crime as an important factor affecting their well-being in 2001. Crime was the third most frequently cited factor affecting quality of life following money and physical health.

2. Costs associated with the fear of crime are both intangible (*e.g.* emotional distress) and tangible (*e.g.* people may prefer to use their car or take a taxi rather than walk or use public transport out of fear).

3. In 2009, Canada introduced the "Severity Crime Index", which makes it possible to track changes in the severity of police-reported crime by accounting for both the amount of crime reported by the police in a given jurisdiction and the relative seriousness of these crimes.

4. According to the rules regulating the way in which data are recorded, countries can be classified into: i) those with input statistics; ii) those with output statistics; and iii) those with intermediate statistics. In countries using input statistics, data are recorded for statistical purposes when the offence is reported to the police. In countries using output statistics, data are recorded when the police have completed the investigation. In between these extremes, some countries record data at some point in time between the input and the output. It is likely that, all other things being equal (*e.g.* the definition of offences, the actual level of crime, the propensity to report and to record offences as well as all other statistical, legal and substantive factors), countries using input statistics will report higher rates of recorded crime than countries using output statistics (Aebi, 2003).

5. Comparability problems arise especially for non-conventional crimes (fraud, bribe, corruption), and sexual crimes (*e.g.* due to differences across countries in the perception of what is unacceptable sexual behaviour).

6. According to UNODC, "intentional homicide" captures a wide range of acts, including domestic disputes that end in a killing, interpersonal violence, violent conflicts over land resources, inter-gang violence over turf or control, and predatory violence and killing by armed groups. Whilst the term is broad, however, it does not capture all intentional killing. In particular, deaths arising from armed conflict are usually considered separately: individuals or small groups usually commit homicide, whereas killing in armed conflict is usually committed by groups of up to several hundred members.

7. Currently available data from existing international surveys on the subject (the International Crime Victim Survey, (ICVS) have the advantage (relative to the Gallup World Poll) of relying on a broader suite of questions to assess the extent and nature of crime. However, they do not include all OECD and emerging countries, they refer to the mid-2000s; and they are also based on small samples. More over, self-reported victimisation rates based on the Gallup World Poll correlate better than ICVS self-reported victimisation rates with other objective indicators of crime presented in this chapter.

8. As the Gallup question does not consider assault and mugging as separate offences, in the case of a victim who experienced both assault and mugging over the previous 12 months only one offence will be counted, thus leading to an underestimation of the self-reported level of crime.

9. Herman-Giddens *et al.* (1999) suggest that child deaths are under-recorded by between 16 and 59%.

10. As for Australia, data on child maltreatment cited by UNICEF (2003) are from the study "Child Protection Australia 1999-00" (Australian Institute of Health and Welfare, 2001). The proportion of physical abuse cases has been imputed from the proportion among all children aged up to 17. French data come from the "Rapport au parlement sur l'enfance maltraitée" (Ministère du Travail, 2000).

11. Fear of crime has also been identified as distinct from general concern about crime. While fear of crime refers to the anticipation of personal victimisation, concerns about crime reflect the perception of crime as a social problem (Amerio and Roccato, 2007).

12. Some of the limits of the Gallup question on the feeling of security are that it does not mention the type of crime considered nor the intensity and the frequency of crime, that it refers to a hypothetical situation, and that the evaluation is limited to night-time (Ferraro, 1995). Moreover, the wording of this question can exaggerate and overestimate fear of crime, as it evokes an atmosphere of foreboding, which can lead respondents to presume that they should be afraid (Farrall and Gadd, 2003).

13. Homicide rates in OECD countries are far lower than in Africa (with the exception of North Africa), and Central and South American countries, where they are in the range 20-30 homicides per 100 000 population.

14. While data on the male-to-female homicide ratio are fairly reliable in developed countries, this is not the case in many developing countries where many female deaths are concealed as accidents or attributed to natural or unknown causes (Geneva Declaration, 2008). In places where deaths of babies and women are not routinely investigated or where autopsies are not carried out, cases may be wrongly attributed to illness or other natural causes.

15. Among all the categories of homicide, infanticide is one of the most susceptible to under-reporting and misclassification. Many infant homicides may be undetected when maltreatment is misdiagnosed, as some other cause of death (e.g. sudden infant death syndrome, SIDS, and the reluctance of pathologists to cite possible cases of abuse). For example, although US death certificate data show that one infant (younger than 1 year of age) is killed every day, it has been suggested that the actual prevalence may be twice that level (Herman-Giddens et al., 1999; McClain et al., 1993). Similar claims have been made in the United Kingdom (Marks and Kumar, 1993).

16. In several cases children were not the primary, or even intended, victim of the attack, which was instead usually targeted at the mother.

17. Recent research has recognised that fear of crime may differ depending on different types of crime. According to Moore and Shepherd (2007), fear of personal victimisation was highest among those aged 16 to 25; by contrast, fear of property victimisation was associated with the middle-age years and was highest among those aged 40 to 60.

18. For instance, while more than 90% of countries reporting to the United Nations Survey of Crime Trends and the Operations of Criminal Justice Systems (UN-CTS) provide data on homicides, only two-thirds can provide information on homicides committed with firearms.

References

Adams, R.E. and R.T. Serpe (2000), "Social integration, fear of crime and life satisfaction", *Sociological Perspectives*, Vol. 43, No. 4, pp. 605-629.

Aebi, M.F. (2003), *Methodological Issues in International Comparisons of Recorded Crime: The Role of Statistical Counting Rules*, www.istat.it/istat/eventi/2003/perunasocieta/relazioni/Aebi_abs.pdf

Aebi, M.F. (2004), "Crime Trends in Western Europe from 1990 to 2000", *European Journal on Criminal Policy and Research*, Vol. 10, Nos. 2-3, pp. 163-186.

Amerio, P. and M. Roccato (2007), "Psychological reactions to crime in Italy: 2002-2004", *Journal of Community Psychology*, Vol. 35, No. 1, pp. 91-102.

Anderson, D.A. (1999), "The Aggregate Burden of Crime", *Journal of Law and Economics*, Vol. 42, No. 2, pp. 611-642.

Australian Institute of Health and Welfare (2001), "Child Protection Australia 1999-00", *Child Welfare Series No. 27*, Camberra.

Balestra, C. and J. Sultan (2012), "Home sweet home: The determinants of residential satisfaction and its relation with well-being", OECD Statistics Directorate Working Papers (forthcoming), OECD, Paris.

Biederman A.D. and A.Jr.Reiss (1967), "On exploring the 'dark figure' of crime", *The Annals*, Vol 374, No. 1, pp. 1-15.

Boivin, R. and G. Cordeau (2011), "Measuring the Impact of Police Discretion on Official Crime Statistics: A Research Note", *Police Quarterly*, Vol. 14, No. 2, pp. 186-203.

Bowes, L., B. Maughan, A. Caspi, T.E. Moffitt and L. Arseneault (2010), "Families promote emotional and behavioural resilience to bullying: Evidence of an environmental effect", *The Journal of Child Psychology and Psychiatry*, Vol. 51, No. 7, pp. 809-817.

Bowes, L., L. Arseneault, B. Maughan, A. Taylor, A. Caspi and T.E. Moffitt (2009), "School, neighborhood, and family factors are associated with children's bullying involvement: A nationally representative longitudinal study", *Journal of the American Academy of Child and Adolescent Psychiatry*, Vol. 48, No. 5, pp. 545-553.

Brookman, F. and J. Nolan (2006), "The Dark Figure of Infanticide in England and Wales - Complexities of Diagnosis", *Journal of Interpersonal Violence*, Vol. 21, No. 7, pp. 869-889.

Bureau of Justice Statistics (2010), *Criminal Victimization 2009*, Washington, DC: U.S. Department of Justice.

Burrows, J., R. Tarling, A. Mackie, R. Lewis and G. Taylor (2000), *Review of the Police Forces' Crime Recording Practices*, Home Office Research Study No. 204, Home Office, London.

Carrabine, E., P. Iganski, L. Maggy, K. Plummer and N. South (2009), *Criminology: A Sociological Introduction*, Routledge, New York.

Carcach, C. (1997), *Reporting crime to the police*, Australian Institute of Criminology, Australia.

Cheung, Y.-B. (1998), "Accidents, Assaults, and Marital Status", *Social Science & Medicine.*, Vol. 47, No. 9, pp. 1325-1329.

Coulton, C.J., J.E. Korbin and M. Su (1999), "Neighborhoods and child maltreatment: A multi-level study", *Child Abuse & Neglect*, Vol. 23, pp. 1019-1040.

Creighton, S.J. (2001), "Childhood deaths reported to coroners: An investigation of the contribution of abuse and neglect", in *Out of sight: NSPCC report on child deaths from abuse 1973 to 2000* (2nd ed., pp. 39-69), National Society for the Prevention of Cruelty to Children, London.

Crittenden, P. and S. Craig (1990), "Trends in child homicide", *Journal of Interpersonal Violence*, Vol. 5, No. 2, pp. 202-16.

Davis, R.C. and N.J. Henderson (2003), "Willingness to report crime: The role of ethnic group members and community efficacy", *Crime & Delinquency*, Vol. 49, No. 4, pp. 564-580.

Detotto, C. and E. Otranto (2010), "Does Crime Affect Economic Growth?", *Kyklos*, Vol. 63, No. 3, pp. 330-345.

Dolan, P. and T. Peasgood (2007) "Estimating the economic and social costs of the fear of crime", *British Journal of Criminology*, Vol. 46, pp. 505-518.

Farrall, S. and D. Gadd (2003), *Fear Today, Gone Tomorrow: Do Surveys Overstate Fear Levels?*, www.istat.it/istat/eventi/perunasocieta/relazioni/Farral_abs.pdf

Felitti, V.J., R.F. Anda, D. Nordenberg, D.F. Williamson, A.M. Spitz, V. Edwards, M.P. Koss and J.S. Marks (1998), "Relationship of childhood abuse and household dysfunction to many of the leading causes of death in adults", *American Journal of Preventive Medicine*, Vol. 14, pp. 245-258.

Fergusson, D.M, J.M. Boden and L.J. Horwood (2008), "Exposure to childhood sexual and physical abuse and adjustment in early adulthood", *Child Abuse & Neglect,* Vol. 32, pp. 607-619.

Ferraro, K.F. (1995), *Fear of Crime: Interpreting Victimisation Risk*, State University of New York Press, Albany.

Finkelhor, D. (1994), "The international epidemiology of child sexual abuse", *Child Abuse & Neglect*, No. 18, pp. 409–417.

Friedman, S.H., S.M. Horowitz and P.J. Resnick (2005), "Child Murder by Mothers: A Critical Analysis of the Current State of Knowledge and a Research Agenda", *American Journal of Psychiatry*, 162, pp. 1578-1587.

Gabriel, G. and W. Greve (2003), "The Psychology of Fear of Crime", *British Journal of Criminology*, Vol. 43, pp. 600-614.

Geneva Declaration (2008), *Global Burden of Armed Violence*, Geneva Declaration Secretariat, Geneva.

Gilbert, R., C. Spatz Widom, K. Browne, D. Fergusson, E. Webb and S. Janson (2009), "Burden and consequences of child maltreatment in high-income countries", *Lancet*, Vol. 373, pp. 68-81.

Goudriaan, H. (2006), *Reporting crime: Effects of social context on the decision of victims to notify the police*, University Press, Veenendaal.

Hanson, R.F., G.K. Sawyer, A.G. Begle and G.S. Hubel (2010), "The Impact of Crime Victimisation on Quality of Life", *Journal of Traumatic Stress*, Vo. 23, No. 2, pp. 189-197.

Harris, A.P., S.H. Thomas, G.A. Fisher and D.H. Hirsch (2002), "Murder and Medicine: The Lethality of Criminal Assault 1960-1999", *Homicide Studies*, Vol. 6, No. 2, pp. 128-166.

Herman-Giddens, M.E., *G.Brown, S.Verbiest, P.J. Carlson, E.G. Hooten, E.Howell and J.D.Butts* (1999), "Under-ascertainment of child abuse mortality in the United States", *Journal of the American Medical Association*, Vol. 282, No. 5, pp. 463-467.

Jenny, C. and R. Isaac (2006), "The relation between child death and child maltreatment", *Archives of Disease in Childhood*, Vol. 91, No. 3, pp. 265-269.

Kelly, M. (2000), "Inequality and crime", *The Review of Economics and Statistics*, Vol. 82, No. 4, pp. 530-539.

Krug, E.G., J.A. Mercy, L.L. Dahlberg and A.B. Zwi (2002), "The world report on violence and health", *Lancet*, Vol. 5, pp. 1083-1088.

Laing, L. and N. Bobic (2002), *Economic Costs of Domestic Violence: Literature Review*, Australian Domestic & Family Violence Clearinghouse, University of New South Wales, Sydney.

Lee, M.R. (2000), "Community Cohesion and Violent Preparatory Victimization: A Theoretical Extension and Cross-National Test of Opportunity Theory", *Social Forces*, Vol. 79, pp. 683-706.

Lewis, H. (1989), *Insuring against Burglary Losses*, Home Office Research and Planning Unit Paper 52, Home Office, London.

Lundstrom, M. and R. Sharpe (1991), "Getting away with murder", *Public Welfare*, Vol. 49, pp. 18-29.

MacDonald, Z. (2001), "Revisiting the Dark Figure: A Microeconometric Analysis of the Under-reporting of Property Crime and Its Implications", *British Journal of Criminology*, Vol. 41, pp. 127-149.

MacDonald, Z. (2002), "Official Crime Statistics: Their Use and Interpretation", *The Economic Journal*, Vol. 112, pp. 85-106.

Maguire, M. (1997), "Crime statistics, patterns and trends: Changing perceptions and their implications", in M. Maguire, R. Morgan and R. Reiner (eds.), *The Oxford Handbook of Criminology*, pp. 135-88, Clarendon Press, Oxford.

Marley, J. A. and S. Buila (2001), "Crimes against people with mental illness: Types, perpetrators, and influencing factors", *Social Work*, Vol. 46, No. 2, pp. 115-124.

Marenin, O. (1997), "Victimisation Surveys and the Accuracy and Reliability of Official Crime Data in Developing Countries", *Journal of Criminal Justice*, Vol. 25, No. 6, pp. 463-475.

Marks, M.N. and R. Kumar (1993), "Infanticide in England and Wales", *Medicine, Science and the Law*, Vol. 33, No. 4, pp. 329-339.

McClain, P., J. Sacks, R. Froehlke and B. Ewigman, (1993), "Estimates of fatal child abuse and neglect, United States, 1979-88", *Pediatrics*, Vol. 91, pp. 338-343.

Mesch, G.S (2000), "Perceptions of risk, lifestyle activities, and fear of crime", *Deviant Behavior*, Vol. 21, pp. 47-62.

Michalos, A.C. and B.D. Zumbo (2000), "Criminal Victimization and the quality of life", *Social Indicators Research*, Vol. 50, pp. 245-295.

Ministère du Travail, des relations sociales et de la solidarité (2000), *Rapport au parlement sur l'enfance maltraitée*, Paris.

Modood, T., R. Berthoud, J. Lakey, J. Nazroo, P. Smith, S. Virdee and S. Beishon (1997), *Ethnic Minorities in Britain: Diversity and Disadvantage - Fourth National Survey of Ethnic Minorities*, Policy Studies Institute, London.

Moore, S. and J. Shepherd (2007), "The Elements and Prevalence of Fear", *The British Journal of Criminology*, Vol. 47, No. 1, pp. 154-162.

National Research Council (1993), *Understanding child abuse and neglect*, National Academy of Sciences Press, Washington, DC.

Nickels, E.L. (2007), "A note on the status of discretion in police research", *Journal of Criminal Justice*, Vol. 35, pp. 570-578.

Nosek, M., C. Clubb Foley, R.B. Hughes and C.A. Howland (2001), "Vulnerabilities for abuse among women with disabilities", *Sexuality and Disability*, Vol. 19, No. 3, pp. 177-189.

OECD (2009a), *Armed Violence Reduction: Enabling Development*, OECD Publishing, Paris.

OECD (2009b), *Society at a Glance 2009: OECD Social Indicators*, OECD Publishing, Paris.

OECD (20011a), *Doing Better for Families*, OECD Publishing, Paris.

OECD (2011b), *Preventing and Reducing Armed Violence in Urban Areas: Programming Note*, Conflict and Fragility, OECD Publishing, Paris.

Pain, R. (1997), "Social geographies of women's fear of crime", *Transactions, Institute of British Geographers*, Vol. 22, pp. 231-244.

Putnam, F.W. (2003), "Ten-year research update review: Child sexual abuse", *Journal of American Academy of Child & Adolescent Psychiatry*, Vol. 42, No. 3, pp. 269-278.

Runyan, D.K., W.M. Hunter, R.R. Socolar, L. Amaya-Jackson, D. English, J. Landsverk, H. Dubowitz, D.H. Browne, S.I. Bangdiwala and R.M. Mathew (1998), "Children who prosper in unfavorable environments: The relationship to social capital", *Pediatrics*, Vol. 101, pp.112-118.

Schafer, J.A., B.M. Huebner and T.S. Bynum (2006), "Fear of crime and criminal victimisation: Gender-based contrasts", *Journal of Criminal Justice*, Vol. 34, pp. 285-301.

Skogan, W.G. (1984), "Reporting crime to the police: The status of world research", *Journal of Research in Crime and Delinquency*, Vol. 21, No. 2, pp. 113-137.

Skogan, W.G. (1987), "The Impact of Victimization on Fear", *Crime and Delinquency*, Vol. 33, No. 1, pp. 135-154.

Stiles, B.L., S. Halim and H.B. Kaplan (2003), "Fear of Crime among Individuals with Physical Limitations", *Criminal Justice Review*, Vol. 28, pp. 232-253.

Tanton, R. and R. Jones (2003), *Australian victims' propensity to report assault and break and enter to police*, Paper Presented at the Evaluation in Crime and Justice: Trends and Methods Conference, Canberra, Australia.

Taylor, N. (2003), "Under-reported crime against small business: Attitude toward police and reporting practices", *Police and Society*, Vol. 13, pp. 79-89.

Trowell, J., B. Ugarde, I. Koldim, M. Berelowitz, H. Sadowski and A. Le Couteur (1999), "Behavioural psychopathology of child sexual abuse in schoolgirls referred to a tertiary centre: A North London study", *European Child and Adolescent Psychiatry*, Vol.8, pp. 107-116.

Umberson, D. (1987), "Family status and health behaviors: Social control as a dimension of social integration", *Journal of Health and Social Behavior*, Vol. 28, pp. 306-319.

UNICEF (2003), *A league table of child maltreatment deaths in rich nations*, Innocenti Report Card, Issue No. 5, United Nations Children's Fund, Florence.

United Nations (2010), *Manual on Victimization Surveys*, United Nations, Geneva.

Van Djik, J., J. van Kesteren and P. Smit (2008), "Criminal Victimisation in International Perspective: Key Findings from the 2004-2005 International Crime Victims Survey and European Survey on Crime and Safety", *WODC Publication*, No. 257.

Warr, M. (2000), "Fear of crime in the United States: Avenues for research and policy", *Journal of Criminal Justice*, Vol. 4, pp. 451-483.

WHO (2002), *World Report on Violence and Health*, World Health Organisation, Geneva.

Wilczynski, A. (1994), "The incidence of child homicide: How accurate are the official statistics?", *Journal of Clinical Forensic Medicine*, No. 1, pp. 61-66.

Chapter 12

Subjective Well-Being

Subjective well-being reflects the notion that how people experience a set of circumstances is as important as the circumstances themselves, and that people are the best judges of how their own lives are going. This chapter uses two measures of subjective well-being: an average measure of how people evaluate their lives as a whole, and a measure of the share of the population experiencing more positive than negative emotions. The chapter finds that, for most OECD countries, levels of subjective well-being are high, regardless of the measure used. However, there is much variation across countries, and some OECD countries have levels of subjective well-being that are lower than those experienced by some middle-income or developing nations. Although only limited information is available on changes over time, average life satisfaction appears to have increased over the past thirty years in some countries and stagnated in others. As the limited evidence on subjective well-being that is currently available is based on small scale unofficial surveys, the chapter draws attention to the importance of building on ongoing initiatives to establish more robust and comparable measures and to forge a better understanding of its drivers.

Why does subjective well-being matter for well-being?

Notions of "happiness", "utility" and "welfare" have a long tradition of use as part of conceptions of a good life. They capture the notion that what matters to a good life is the impact of a specific set of circumstances on how people feel about their life, and rely on the view that people are the best judges of how their life is going. This chapter measures overall well-being as perceived by individuals. Research has identified three main components of subjective well-being.[1] These are life satisfaction, positive affect and negative affect. These measures capture distinct elements of subjective experience and it is important to consider them all.

Life satisfaction captures a reflective assessment of how things are going in one's own life. Measures of life satisfaction are a useful complement to more traditional indicators based on objective conditions because they present an overall picture of well-being that is grounded in people's preferences rather than in a-priori judgements about what are the important drivers of individuals' well-being.

Positive and negative affect measure emotions at a point in time. Positive affect captures experiences of feelings such as happiness, joy, excitement or love. Similarly, negative affect describes people's experience of feelings such as anger, pain or sadness. In addition to representing an important aspect of well-being in their own right, such measures are useful in circumstances where measures of life satisfaction are less informative. For example, affect measures can be used to identify the impact of specific daily activities (such as commuting or socialising with friends) on people's feelings for which measures of life satisfaction provide little information.

There are two key challenges associated with the use of subjective well-being indicators. The first is that what drives people's life satisfaction may be ethically objectionable or affected by personal circumstances to which individuals adapt, even if that is not objectively good (Sen, 1970, 1976, 1979). Therefore information from subjective well-being measures has to be used alongside indicators focusing on objective features of people's life (Stiglitz *et al.*, 2008). The second challenge is whether subjective views are truly measurable, in the sense that: i) all individuals understand the question in the same terms and tend to answer according to the same standard; and ii) answers are not affected by external transient factors. A large body of recent research has shown that these shortcomings have a limited effect on subjective measures of well-being and that it is indeed possible to make valid comparisons between different groups of people (Box 12.1). After having long been relegated to academic research, these measures are today increasingly accepted more widely.

Box 12.1. Can we really measure subjective well-being?

Only a few years ago, meaningful measurement of well-being was considered challenging or out of reach. However, over the last decade an increasing body of evidence has supported the view that it is possible to gather valid measures of subjective well-being based on surveys.

At a very general level, questions on subjective well-being have a degree of intuitive plausibility in that concepts such as "satisfaction" and "happiness" are subjects that people can easily relate to. In support of this, there is much evidence that people find it easy to respond to questions on subjective well-being. For example, subjective questions have lower non-response rates than in the case of many objective measures such as income or consumption expenditure (Rässler and Riphahn, 2006). Similarly, people generally give similar answers to questions if they are repeated at another time (Krueger and Schkade,

---

2007). Studies also show that subjective well-being questions are understood in a similar way across cultures (Diener and Tov, 2005), although there is some debate about the degree to which it is possible to directly compare results between different cultures (Angelini, Cavapozzi and Paccagnella, 2008).

Subjective measures of well-being have been tested against a wide range of indirect measures of well-being, and generally show the expected relationships. For example, subjective measures of well-being correlate well with frequency of expression of positive emotions and with frequency of smiles – particularly "unfakeable" or "Duchenne" smiles (where the skin around the subject's eyes "crinkles" in response to automatic and largely involuntary muscle contractions). Biological measurements, including left/right brain activity, and levels of the stress hormone cortisol show a consistent relationship with self-ratings of well-being. In addition, both ratings made by friends and ratings made by strangers correlate well with self-assessments (Diener and Tov, 2005; Kahneman and Krueger, 2006).

Finally, there is good evidence to suggest that subjective well-being predicts behaviour in a meaningful way. Subjective well-being measures predict risks of suicide, sociability, extroversion, quality of sleep and the happiness of close relatives (Diener and Tov, 2005). There is also evidence that these measures change in response to changed circumstances. For example, it has been shown that becoming disabled has a large and lasting impact on life satisfaction, and that the severity of this impact increases with the severity of the disability (Lucas, 2006).

Measuring subjective well-being

A comprehensive approach to measuring subjective well-being would require measures of how people evaluate their life and of how they feel. In other words, it would comprise both measures of life satisfaction and measures of affect. Ideally, the measures used would be both highly reliable and able to be linked to a wide range of variables known to affect subjective well-being. This would imply relying on robust measures based on responses to multiple questions, and drawn from large, high-quality surveys.[2]

Unfortunately, there is currently no well-established programme of official reporting on subjective well-being in OECD countries. Consequently, for both life satisfaction and affect, the chapter relies primarily on data drawn from an unofficial survey, the Gallup World Poll. These measures are collected in a comparable way across different countries, and are based on well tested questions. However, the sample size for the Gallup World Poll is relatively small, and this places some restrictions on the conclusions that can be drawn from these data. These indicators are thus considered as placeholders and their use is experimental. They will be replaced with indicators relying on better data sources, as the information becomes available in the future.

Selected indicators

Life Satisfaction (SW I)

Life satisfaction is a measure of how people evaluate their life as a whole. It is a cognitive assessment rather than a statement of a person's current emotional state. Only few countries currently collect life satisfaction data as part of their official statistics (notably Canada since 1985, but also more recently New Zealand, France and Italy) and these measures are hardly comparable across countries.[3] For these reasons, the data presented here come from an unofficial survey that, while limited in several aspects, has the advantage of using the same methodology and questionnaire in all countries. The indicator is based on the Cantril Ladder, which asks people to rate their current life relative to the best and worst possible lives for them on a scale from 0 to 10, and is computed as the weighted-sum of different response categories.[4]

While the Cantril Ladder represents the best available scale for overall life satisfaction for which there is extensive comparable data, it does have limitations. How people respond to the Cantril Ladder can be affected by personality, mood, cultural norms and relative judgements. Some of these effects, such as personality and mood, can largely be ignored for the purposes of comparisons between countries, since these will average out in a sufficiently large sample. Other factors, such as the impact of cultural factors on response styles, may be more significant and suggest some caution in international comparisons.[5]

The Gallup World Poll only provides information on life satisfaction for the period since 2005. This is insufficient to identify trends in life satisfaction, which tends to change only at a slow rate. For this reason, data from Eurobarometer are also used to describe trends in major European countries since 1973. However, this source provides no information for other OECD countries, and is based on a slightly different life satisfaction question, which uses only four categories compared to the eleven categories in the Cantril Ladder.

In the following analysis, average life satisfaction scores are computed as if life satisfaction were a cardinal variable (i.e. as if the number reported has a quantitative meaning, not simply an ordinal one). Although whether well-being is best conceived of as cardinal or ordinal in nature can be debated, there is strong evidence that in practice the assumption of cardinality does not unduly bias the results of analysis of subjective well-being data (Ferrer-i-Carbonell and Frijters, 2004).

Affect balance (SW II)

In contrast to life satisfaction, which requires an evaluative judgement from people, positive and negative affect focus on how people are feeling at a specific point in time. They capture experienced well-being rather than evaluated well-being. Ideally, affect should be calculated using data from Time Use Surveys, allowing the analysis of affect in relation to specific activities and at a particular point in time. Data of this sort have been used to calculate the so-called "U-index", i.e. the proportion of time in the previous day during which negative affect is the dominant emotion (Kahneman and Krueger, 2006). In the absence of affect measures linked to detailed time use data for all OECD nations, the measure of affect used here is computed as the share of respondents who report having experienced more positive than negative emotions on the previous day.[6] This is referred to as the affect balance, and is derived from data from the Gallup World Poll.[7]

Because measures of affect are less influenced by memories and evaluations, they are less subject to systematic biases in the respondent's recall of events. Affect balance is also thought to be less subject to biases due to individual differences in how survey questions are interpreted because any idiosyncrasies in the individual's response style will affect both the positive and negative sides of the calculation and thus cancel out to some degree. Because affect measures are less subject to biases in recall and response style (Kahneman, Diener and Schwarz, 1999), they potentially provide a useful point of comparison for evaluative measures such as life satisfaction. In particular, the affect balance might be expected to be less subject to cultural differences in reporting style than life satisfaction. Table 12.1 provides an assessment of the two indicators relative to the quality criteria used in this report.

Table 12.1. **The quality of subjective well-being indicators**

| | | Target concept | INDICATORS | | | | | | | |
| | | | Relevance to measure and monitor well-being | | | | Statistical quality | | | |
			Face validity	Unambiguous interpretation (good/bad)	Policy amenable outcomes	Can be disaggregated	Well-established instrument collected	Comparable definition	Country coverage	Recurrent data collection
	Subjective well-being									
SW I	Life Satisfaction	Evaluation of life	√	√	~	√	x	√	√	√
SW II	Affect Balance	Positive and negative feelings	√	√	~	√	x	√	√	√

Note. The symbol √ shows that the indicator selected largely meets the criteria shown in the table; the symbol ~ that the indicator meets the criteria to a large extent; the symbol x that the indicator does not meet the criterion or it meets it only to a limited extent.

Average patterns

There is large variation in average life satisfaction across countries

Across OECD and large emerging countries, the gap between countries with the highest life satisfaction and those with the lowest is approximately 3 points on an 11 point scale. In broad terms, countries fall into three groups (Figure 12.1). The first group of countries has relatively low level of average life satisfaction compared to other countries, with average scores of less than 5.5. This group includes some OECD countries (Hungary, Portugal, Estonia and Turkey) and some emerging economies (China, South Africa and Indonesia). A second group of countries comprises much of the OECD and Brazil, and records average life satisfaction scores below 7. Finally, the highest achieving group comprises only OECD member countries, predominantly Nordic European and some Anglophone countries. Average life satisfaction scores for this latter group are above 7. Countries with a higher average level of life-evaluations tend to feature a higher GDP per capita but the association is weak and tapers off at higher GDP levels (Box 12.2).

Some East Asian countries have lower levels of life satisfaction than might be expected given their economic development. Both Japan and Korea report an average life satisfaction score half a point below the OECD average, and China has the lowest reported average life satisfaction among all the countries included in Figure 12.1, despite being considerably wealthier (in GDP terms) than either India or Indonesia. By way of contrast, a number of Latin American countries, including Chile, Brazil and Mexico, have high average levels of life satisfaction given their economic development. Two main explanations have been advanced to explain this "Latin American" paradox. The first refers to differences in cultural patterns of response, with people from East-Asian societies less likely to record extreme scores compared to Latin Americans. The second possibility is that non-economic factors might account for this difference in life satisfaction.

Figure 12.1. **Life satisfaction**

Cantril Ladder, mean value in 2010

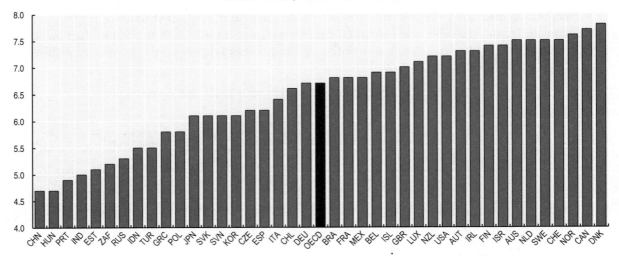

Note: The Cantil ladder is measured on a scale from 0 to 10. Data refer to 2008 for Iceland and Norway; and to 2009 for Estonia, Israel, Switzerland and South Africa.
Source: Gallup World Poll.

StatLink ᵐᵐᵖ *http://dx.doi.org/10.1787/888932493613*

Levels of life satisfaction tend to change over time, in contrast to a widespread view that they do not. However, the direction and the speed of this change is not even across European countries for which comparable evidence exists. Figure 12.2 illustrates that both Denmark and Italy experienced gains in measured life satisfaction over the period between 1975 and 2000. France also experienced an increase in average levels of life satisfaction since 1978. Life satisfaction in Ireland seems to have declined between 1975 and 1987, but improved thereafter. In Belgium, however, life satisfaction declined from 1975 to 1985, and has fluctuated around this lower level subsequently. The United Kingdom, Germany and the Netherlands experienced no consistent change over this period. Very little information is available on the impact of the recent financial crisis on life satisfaction

Figure 12.2. **Life satisfaction in selected OECD countries**

Cantril ladder, mean value in 1973-2007

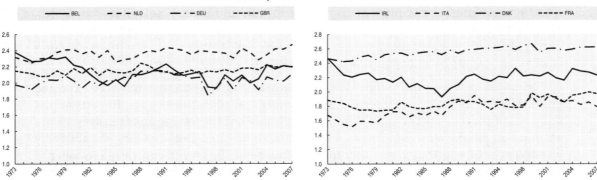

Note: The Cantril ladder is measured on a scale from 0 to 10.
Source: Eurobarometer.

StatLink ᵐᵐᵖ *http://dx.doi.org/10.1787/888932493632*

Box 12.2. **The Easterlin Paradox**

An interesting feature of the distribution of life satisfaction among developed countries is that it has only a weak relationship to the ranking of per capita income (Figure 12.3). Although the cross-country correlation between income and life satisfaction improves as low income countries are included in the sample, the correlation over time remains weak.

The lack of a strong time-series correlation between changes in average income and changes in measures of subjective well-being in wealthy countries, combined with the existence of a strong correlation between the same two measures at the individual level was noted by Richard Easterlin (1974), and is generally referred to as the so-called "Easterlin paradox". The Easterlin paradox argues that a higher rise in personal income leads to higher subjective well-being for that person, but that a rise in average incomes for a country does not give rise to a corresponding increase in the country's average subjective well-being.

Figure 12.3. **Life satisfaction and GDP per capita**

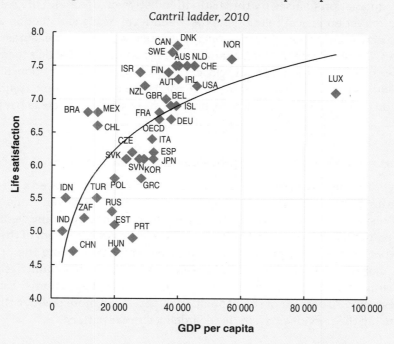

Cantril ladder, 2010

Note: The Cantril ladder is measured on a scale from 0 to 10. GDP per capita values are in current prices and PPPs. Data refer to 2009 for Iceland and Norway; and to 2009 for Estonia, Israel, Switzerland and South Africa. The value of GDP per capita refers to 2009, instead of 2010, for Australia, Canada, Chile, Japan, Mexico, New Zealand, Turkey, the United States, the Russian Federation and China.
Source. GDP per capita: OECD National Accounts and International Monetary Fund databases. Life Satisfaction: Gallup World Poll.

StatLink ᵐˢᴸ *http://dx.doi.org/10.1787/888932493651*

Among the explanations put forward to account for the Easterlin paradox are the following:

- The fact that relative, rather than absolute, income matters the most for individuals' life-evaluations; people are happier or more satisfied if they are better off than those to whom they compare themselves.

- The fact that people adapt to a change in their circumstances over time; this effect leads to the so-called "adaptive treadmill", where an increase in income initially increases subjective well-being but this gain is eroded over time as people adapt to their new situation.

- Factors other than income may drive differences in subjective well-being, and changes in these may account for the lack of the expected correlation with income over time. Among OECD countries, there are only small differences across countries in the relationship between subjective well-being and its objective determinants (Helliwell, 2008), suggesting broad cross-cultural comparability in at least some aspects of subjective well-being. However, there are significant differences in levels of unemployment, crime and health status.

- Because most of the countries for which time series information on subjective well-being is available are relatively wealthy, the effect of income growth may be too small to be observed in existing data. In this case, a stronger relationship between trends in income and subjective well-being for developing nations may become apparent as longer time series become available for these countries over the next decade.

- One last explanation focuses on the distinction between affect and life satisfaction. While there is a robust empirical relationship between level of life satisfaction and level of GDP per capita across countries, this relationship is much weaker for measures of affect (Diener, Kahneman, Tov and Arora, 2010). Richard Easterlin's original 1974 article focused on measures of happiness, which are conceptually closer to affect than life satisfaction. Similarly, much of the subsequent literature has used measures of happiness to examine trends over time. Life satisfaction may increase with income, but measures of affect such as happiness may not.

People report more positive than negative emotion in all countries

The majority of people in OECD and emerging economies experienced a preponderance of positive affect over negative affect (Figure 12.4). There is, however, some variation in the share of respondents experiencing a positive affect balance. For some OECD countries, including Denmark, Iceland, Japan, Norway and Sweden, over 85 percent of the population reported experiencing more positive than negative emotions during the previous day. This was also observed for China and Indonesia. However, in other countries the balance between positive and negative affect was more even. In Turkey, Estonia, Hungary, Italy and Israel less than 70 percent of the population experienced more positive than negative emotions during the previous day. India recorded a similar pattern.

Figure 12.4. **Positive affect balance**

Percentage of the population with positive affect balance, 2010

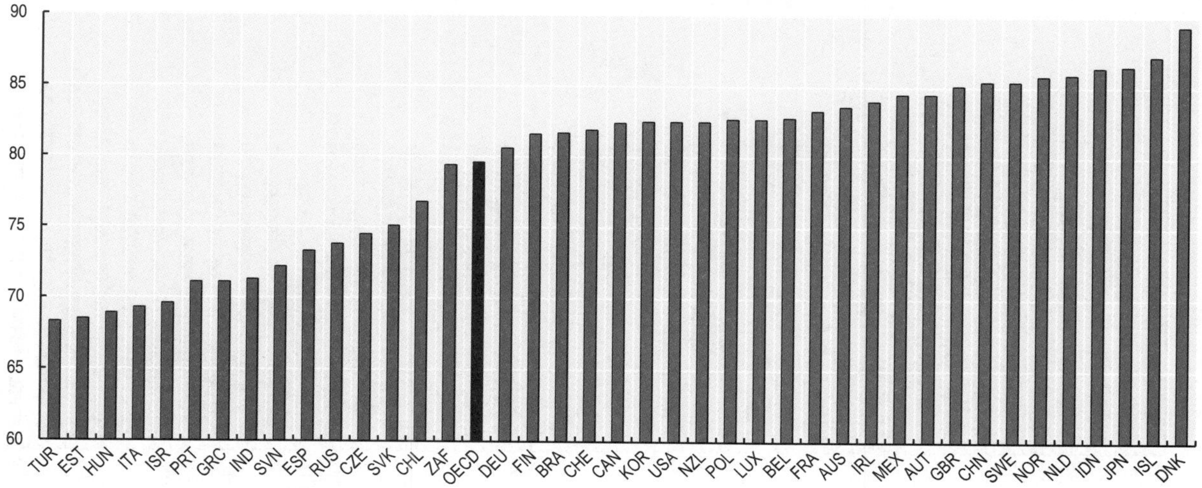

Note: Data refer to 2008 for Iceland and Norway; and to 2009 for Estonia, Israel, Switzerland and South Africa.
Source: OECD's calculations based on data from The Gallup World Poll.

StatLink http://dx.doi.org/10.1787/888932493670

Affect and life satisfaction show different patterns for some countries

In some countries, there are differences in the picture offered by the affect balance, on one side, and life satisfaction, on the other. All Asian countries included in Figure 12.4 rank higher using affect balance than using life satisfaction. This is particularly striking for China, Indonesia and Japan which all move from near the bottom of the hierarchy to near the top. By way of contrast, a number of countries such as Israel, Italy, Finland, Switzerland and Canada rank significantly lower in terms of affect balance than life satisfaction. The differences in country ranking between measured life satisfaction and affect balance can be explained by the fact that the two measures are influenced in different ways by objective circumstances (*e.g.* levels of income have a stronger impact on life satisfaction than on affect) and by the fact that affect balance may be less affected by differing cultural response styles than measures of life satisfaction.

Inequalities

There is substantial variation in subjective well-being within countries

The average level of subjective well-being in a country provides important information about the subjective well-being of the population, but it is also important to know whether that average represents the experience of most people, or whether there is a wide variation in subjective well-being within the country. Figure 12.5 shows the difference between the life-satisfaction scores of the person at the bottom of the population's most satisfied decile and the one at the top of the least satisfied decile. While some countries have a relatively equal distribution of life satisfaction (*e.g.* much of Western Europe, Israel, Japan and New Zealand), others countries display a much greater variance. The difference in inequality between the most equal country (the Netherlands) and the least equal ones (Chile, Slovenia, Portugal and Brazil) is equal in size to the gap in average life satisfaction between the highest and lowest country in the OECD.

Figure 12.5. **Inequality in life satisfaction**

Point difference between the 90th percentile and 10th percentile of the Cantril ladder scores, 2010

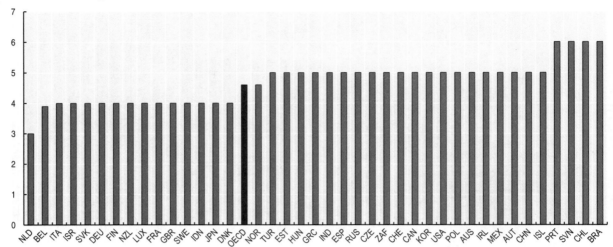

Note: The Cantril ladder is measured on a scale from 0 to 10. Data refer to 2008 for Iceland and Norway; and to 2009 for Estonia, Israel, Switzerland and South Africa.
Source: OECD's calculations based on data from The Gallup World Poll.

StatLink ᴍᴎ𝙨᠍ᴇ *http://dx.doi.org/10.1787/888932493689*

Many factors may account for the variation of subjective well-being across the population. The rest of this chapter discusses the main demographic and socio-economic drivers of this variation, while Box 12.3 summarises the results of an empirical exercise aimed at assessing the relative impact of these drivers. Confirming previous studies in this field, the analysis finds that standard demographic and socio-economic characteristics, such as gender, age, education, income and unemployment status account for a large share of the explained variance. In addition, other aspects such as the health status and the frequency of human contacts also drive life satisfaction to a large extent.

Women report lower positive affect balance compared to men

In a small majority of the countries covered, women report higher average levels of life satisfaction than do men (Figure 12.6). However, the picture changes for the affect balance where, in more than two-thirds of the countries analysed, more men report a positive affect balance than women. Despite these differences in averages, there is, on the whole, a high degree of consistency in the gender gap in both life satisfaction and affect balance. For instance, in the United States, Japan and Finland, women have both higher average levels of life-satisfaction and higher affect balance. Among emerging countries, this same pattern is observed for China and Indonesia. By way of contrast, men are both more satisfied and more likely to report positive affect balance in Eastern and Southern European countries, in Latin American countries and in the Russian Federation.

Figure 12.6. **Gender gap in life satisfaction and affect balance for OECD and emerging countries, 2010**

Ratio of men to women , 2010

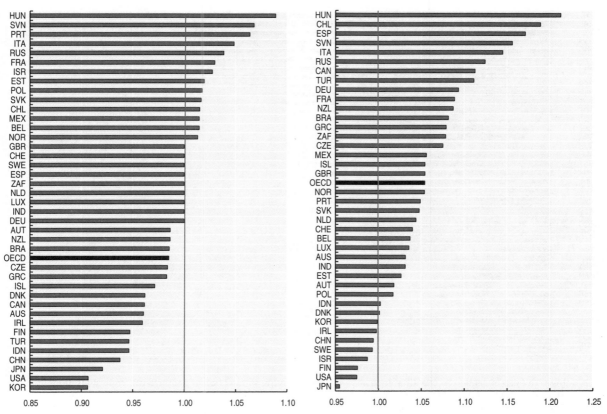

Life satisfaction   **Affect balance**

Note: For life satisfaction, the gender gap is defined as the ratio of the mean life satisfaction of men to that of women. For positive affect balance, the gender gap is defined as the ratio of the share of men reporting positive affect balance to the share of women reporting positive affect balance. Data refer to 2008 for Iceland and Norway; to 2009 for Estonia, Israel, Switzerland and South Africa.

Source: OECD's calculations based on data from The Gallup World Poll.

StatLink ⟪ᵐˢ⟫ *http://dx.doi.org/10.1787/888932493708*

Poor education is associated with lower levels of life satisfaction

Low levels of education are associated with lower levels of life satisfaction (Figure 12.6). This effect is particularly strong for countries with lower GDP per capita. Among countries shown here, Portugal, Spain, Slovenia and Hungary have particularly large gaps in life satisfaction between people with and without tertiary education. This is also true in many of the non-OECD countries observed, and in particular in South Africa and Indonesia. In contrast, Ireland, Sweden, Denmark and Norway have small education-related gaps. Although there is a direct relationship between life satisfaction and education, this correlation weakens when analysed alongside measures of income and health status (Box 12.3). This suggests that education may contribute to subjective well-being primarily via its impact on other life outcomes.

Figure 12.7. **Gap in life satisfaction by level of education**

Cantril ladder, 2010

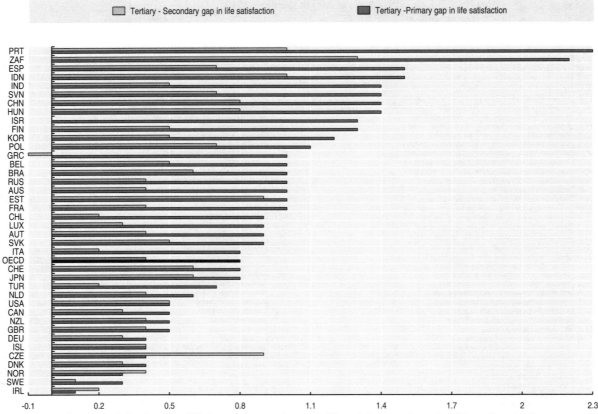

Note: The gap is defined as the difference between the mean life satisfaction of people with tertiary attainment and the mean life satisfaction of people with primary (secondary) education.

Source: OECD's calculations based on data from The Gallup World Poll.

StatLink 🔗 *http://dx.doi.org/10.1787/888932493727*

Box 12.3. **The determinants of life satisfaction**

Subjective measures of well-being are particularly valuable because they provide a metric that enables the empirical evaluation of the relative importance of different life domains. Over the past decade an extensive literature on the drivers of life satisfaction has emerged. The key points emerging from this literature can be summarised as follows:

- There is a non-linear relationship between income and life satisfaction (Box 12.2). This relationship holds across individuals and across countries (Sacks, Stevenson and Wolfers, 2010), although the evidence is weaker for changes in average income within a country. Measures of affect also show a relationship with income, but this tails off once a threshold income level is reached (Kahneman and Deaton, 2010).

- Health status has a major impact on life satisfaction, with this effect generally being stronger for measures of mental health than physical health (Dolan, Peasgood and White, 2008). Disability has a large permanent negative impact on life satisfaction (Lucas, 2007).

- Becoming unemployed has a strong negative lasting impact on life satisfaction and affect. This effect is many times larger than that due to the income loss associated with unemployment (Winkelman and Winkelman, 1998). On average, a one percentage point change in the unemployment rate has a negative effect on life satisfaction within countries at least twice as high as that of a one percentage point change in inflation (Dolan , Peasgood and White, 2008).

- Social contact is strongly correlated with higher life satisfaction and affect. Living in a stable relationship has an effect between half and a third as large as that of being unemployed, although in the opposite direction. Other measures of social support and trust are also positively associated with life satisfaction (Helliwell, 2008).

- Across countries higher trust in government and lower levels of perceived corruption are correlated with high levels of life satisfaction (Helliwell, 2008). The level of democratic engagement has also been found to be positively correlated with life satisfaction (Frey and Stutzer, 2000).

- Commuting negatively affects both affect and life satisfaction (Frey and Stutzer, 2008). Evidence from time use studies shows that commuting is the activity with the highest incidence of negative emotions (Kahneman and Krueger, 2006). For life satisfaction the effect appears to be about half the size of that associated with having a partner.

- There is weaker evidence on the impact of the state of the environment and crime levels on subjective wellbeing, reflecting the limited availability of comparable data in these areas.

Table 12.2 reports the results of a regression analysis for a selection of indicators used in this report on life satisfaction, for OECD countries. The coefficients listed are grouped under the domains used in *How's Life?* (even though, owing to the need for individual-level data for the regression analysis, the variables used to proxy these domains come from the World Gallup Poll and not from the indicators used in this report). The results are consistent with what is known from the international literature, and generally indicate a positive correlation between the *How's Life?* domains and life satisfaction, providing empirical support to the fact that the domains in *How's Life?* relate to aspects that are of direct importance to well-being. The indicators for income and wealth, health, jobs and earnings, education and skills and human contact each have a large and independent impact on life satisfaction; safety, governance and the environment have weaker but still positive effects on life satisfaction. Results are also consistent with what is known about the demographic correlates of life satisfaction: women have a slightly higher average life satisfaction than men, and there is a "U-shaped" relationship between life satisfaction and age, although the age at which life satisfaction is lowest (65) is somewhat higher than has been found elsewhere. The regression analysis in based on individual level data from the Gallup World Poll, pulling together three waves of the survey (2008-2010). The estimation relies on a standard technique for analysing the determinants of life satisfaction (*e.g.* Stevenson and Wolfers, 2008), namely a weighted least square (WLS) model controlling for country and year fixed effects, (although the results do not differ much when using an ordinal probit model). A full account of the regression model can be found in Boarini *et al.*, (2011).

It is somewhat difficult to directly compare the size of coefficients from a regression such as that reported in Table 12.2 since each indicator is measured in different units. In particular, income is a continuous variable, while many other measures are dichotomous. One way to address this difficulty is reported in the second column of the table. This column shows the relative size of the impact on life satisfaction from a change in the status of each measure compared to the effect of doubling income. It is readily apparent that the impact of being unemployed, in poor health, and having friends to count on is very large relative both to changes in income and other variables. For example, to offset the negative impact of becoming unemployed, income would have to increase more than eight-fold (equivalent to doubling 3.1 times, i.e. increasing income by a factor of 23.1), while being married rather than unmarried is roughly equivalent to the impact of income tripling (doubling 1.6 times).

Table 12.2. **The determinants of life satisfaction in OECD countries**

Determinants	Coefficient	Effect size relative to doubling of income
Demographics		
Female	0.0850*	0.6
Age	-0.0524***	-0.4
Age squared	0.0004***	0.003
Born abroad	-0.2891***	-2
Income and Wealth		
Income	0.1475***	1
Not enough money for food	-0.9288***	-6.3
Jobs and Earnings		
Unemployed	-0.4662***	-3.1
Health Status		
Health problems	-0.4599***	-3.1
Education and skills		
With secondary education	0.2192***	1.5
With tertiary education	0.4399***	3
Personal Security		
Feel safe walking alone in the night	0.1710***	1.2
Report having money or property been stolen	-0.1471**	-1
Human Contact		
Married	0.2432***	1.6
Number of children	-0.004	0
Have friends to count on	0.7658***	5.2
Volunteering	0.3756***	2.5
Environmental Quality		
Satisfied with air quality	0.163**	1.1
Satisfied with water quality	-0.035	-0.2
Governance		
Confident in the judicial system	0.1605***	1.1
Proportion of the population afraid to express political views	-0.062	-0.4
Aggregate level of social trust	0.0453***	0.3

N = 12 736 observations. R2 = 0.346

Note: The number of observations is N = 12,736 and the R2 = 0.346. * indicates that values are significant at 10% confidence level; ** Indicates that they are significant at 5% confidence level and *** indicates that they are significant at 1% confidence level. The variable "household income" refers to the base-2 logarithm of the household disposable income.

Source: OECD's calculations based on data from the Gallup World Poll.

StatLink ᵐˢᵖ *http://dx.doi.org/10.1787/888932494468*

There is a "U-shaped" relationship between age and subjective well-being

Measures of subjective well-being are consistently higher among youths and older people than they are during the middle of life (Box 12.3). Typically, average levels of subjective well-being are lowest for people aged 35 to 55. This "U-shaped" relationship between age and subjective well-being does not change when controlling for other factors, such as income and health status.

The statistical agenda ahead

The picture of subjective well-being provided in this chapter is necessarily limited. It is only in the last decade that the evidence underpinning the validity of such measures has been widely accepted, and consequently there is short tradition of their use. The available data sources are relatively limited in terms of the consistency of the measure used, the time-series for which these measures are available, and the range of countries covered.[8] In addition, the literature on subjective well-being is still developing, and there are a wide range of important research questions that still lack definitive answers. Many of these research questions will not be resolved without access to large national datasets containing both measures of life evaluation and affect and a range of information on other aspects of quality of life.

The key priority for statistical developments in the area of subjective well-being is to establish a robustly collected set of consistent measures across countries. Standards are needed because subjective well-being measures are strongly affected by question structure and context, and the results from differently worded questions (or even a different ordering of similar questions) are likely to affect comparability. The OECD is working with a range of national statistical agencies and researchers to prepare a set of guidelines on the collection and use of measures of subjective well-being. It is envisaged that the guidelines will comprise both a handbook on measuring subjective well-being and a set of prototype question modules that can be used by producers of measures of subjective well-being. These guidelines are expected to be published in mid-2012.

Despite these limits, measures of subjective well-being are starting to find their way in the world of official statistics. In Canada, Statistics Canada has collected information on subjective well-being in the General Social Survey since 1985, and published this information as part of data releases from the survey for some time; Canada probably has the longest record of continuous official statistical releases on life satisfaction among major national statistical agencies. New Zealand also collects data on life satisfaction through the New Zealand General Social Survey, and this forms a core component of the data release. In Australia, the Australian Bureau of Statistics included subjective measures of well-being in the 2009 version of *Measures of Australia's Progress*.

Further, in recent months, a number of important initiatives have been launched by several official statistical agencies. These include the UK initiative (launched in the spring of 2010) to develop a new set of measures of national well-being (combining both subjective and objective measures), and the steps taken by Eurostat to develop a module on subjective well-being for the 2013 wave of EU-SILC. Similarly, the French national statistical office developed a subjective well-being module for the national component of EU-SILC and has collected information on affect in the Enquete Emploi du Temps 2009-10 as part of the follow-up to the recommendations of the Sen-Stiglitz-Fitoussi Commission. A module on affect has also been included in the most recent wave of the American Time Use Survey. In Italy, the national statistical office has recently published first official measures of life satisfaction as part of their general social survey (*Indagine Multiscopo*). In Poland, a new multi-dimensionsal social cohesion survey was implemented in 2011 that contained a number of subjective measures of well-being. Finally, in the Netherlands, the national statistical office is currently scoping a module on subjective well-being for one of their surveys to go into the field (if approved) in late 2011/2012.

Conclusion

Subjective measures of well-being capture information about aspects of quality of life that conventional measures omit. For most countries, regardless of the measure used, average levels of subjective well-being are high. However, there is significant variation across OECD countries, and the few countries at the bottom of the OECD league have average levels of subjective well-being lower than many middle income and developing nations, a result that holds regardless of the measure used. While there is only limited information available on how levels of subjective well-being have evolved over time, they appear to have increased (over the past thirty years) in some countries and stagnated in others. Although there is an increasing body of knowledge about the drivers of subjective well-being at an individual level, there is much less information about what causes changes over time at the country level. Current initiatives contributing towards more robust comparable measures are essential in order to build a better understanding of the drivers of subjective well-being.

Notes

1. Diener (1984); Kahneman *et al.* (1999); Stiglitz *et al.* (2008).

2. Multi-item measures of subjective well-being are less sensitive to mood and personality differences than answers to a single question.

3. Efforts have been made to homogenise the limited official data on subjective well-being that are available through the World Database on Happiness. However, it is not yet possible to obtain from this database a set of measures covering all OECD countries and based on similar questions asked over the same time period.

4. This measure is more properly known as the "Self-Anchoring Striving Scale", which is the title Cantril originally gave to his question.

5. One approach to addressing cultural differences in response styles involves the use of illustrative vignettes to help calibrate scales between countries (Angelini, Cavapozzi and Paccagnella, 2009). There is not currently a sufficiently large body of results from such work to allow the normalisation of scales across OECD countries, but this may be a promising approach for the future. The approach taken in this report has been to supplement measures of life satisfaction with a measure of affect balance that is unlikely to be subject to the same biases.

6. Unlike the measure of life satisfaction used above, the affect balance is an ordinal measure that does not assume that subjective scales are comparable between people, even in aggregate (i.e. the data are interpreted as an ordinal ranking rather than as cardinal scores).

7. This is not the only way to calculate affect balance. It is, for example, possible to calculate a cardinal measure of affect balance by subtracting the sum of reported negative emotions from the sum of reported positive emotions. The measure of affect balance used in this report is binary, both because this is likely to minimise reporting biases across countries, and to complement the measure of life satisfaction, which in this chapter is effectively treated as being cardinal.

8. Two datasets achieve two of these outcomes (the Gallup World Poll and the World Values Survey), but not all three.

References

Albouy V., P. Godefroy and S. Lollivier (2010), "Une mesure de la qualité de vie", in INSEE, *France, Portrait Social, edition 2010*, pp. 99-114, Paris.

Angelini V., L. Cavapozzi and O. Paccagnella (2008), "Do Danes and Italians Rate Life Satisfaction in the Same Way? Using Vignettes to Correct for Individual-Specific Scale Biases", *Marco Fanno Working Paper 90*, Dipartimento di Scienze Economiche Marco Fanno.

Bjornskov C. (2010), "How Comparable are the Gallup World Poll Life Satisfaction Data?", *Journal of Happiness Studies*, Vol. 11, pp. 41-60.

Blanchflower D. G. and A. J. Oswald, (2004) "Money, Sex and Happiness: An Empirical Study", *Scandinavian Journal of Economics,* Vol. 106 (3), pp. 393-415.

Boarini R., M. Comola, F. De Keulenauer, R. Manchin and C. Smith (2011) "The Determinants of Well-being in OECD Countries", OECD Statistics Directorate Working Paper, forthcoming, Paris.

Clark A. and C. Senik (2010) "Will GDP growth increase happiness in developing countries?", *Paris School of Economics Working Paper* No 2010-43.

Diener E. and W. Tov (2006), "National Accounts of Well-being", K. Land (ed), *Encyclopedia of Quality of Life*.

Diener E. (1984), "Subjective Well-Being", *Psychological Bulletin*, No. 93, pag. 542-575.

Diener E., J. F. Helliwell and D. Kahneman (2010), *International Differences in Well-Being*, Oxford University Press, New York.

Dolan P., T. Peasgood and M. White (2008), "Do we really know what makes us happy? A review of the economic literature on the factors associated with subjective well-being", *Journal of Economic Psychology*, Vol. 29, pp. 94-122.

Easterlin R. (1974) "Does Economic Growth Improve the Human Lot? Some Empirical Evidence", in David, P. A. and M. W. Reder, *Nations and Households in Economic Growth: Essays in Honour of Moses Abramovitz*, New York, Academic Press Inc, pp. 89-125.

Ferrer-i-Carbonell A. and P. Frijters (2004), "How important is methodology for the estimates of the determinants of happiness?", *The Economic Journal*, Vol. 114, pp. 641-659.

Frey B. S. and A. Stutzer, (2000), "Happiness, Economy and Institutions", *The Economic Journal*, Vol. 110. (466), pp. 918-938.

Frey B. S. and A. Stutzer (2008), "Stress that Doesn't Pay: The Commuting Paradox", *Scandinavian Journal of Economics*, Vol. 110 (2), pp. 339-366.

Helliwell J. F. and C. P. Barrington-Leigh (2010), "Measuring and Understanding Subjective Well-being", NBER Working Paper 15887, National Bureau of Economic Research,

Helliwell J. F. (2008) "Life Satisfaction and the Quality of Development", NBER Working Paper 14507, National Bureau of Economic Research.

Kahneman D. and A. Deaton (2010), "High income improves life evaluation but not emotional well-being", Proceedings of the National Academy of Sciences, Vol. 107 (38), pp. 16489-16493.

Kahneman D. and A. B. Krueger (2006), "Developments in the Measurement of Subjective Well-Being" *Journal of Economic Perspectives,* Vol. 20 (1), pp. 19-20.

Kahneman D., E. Diener and N. Schwarz (1999), *Well-Being. The Foundations of Hedonic Psychology*, Russel Sage Foundation, New York.

Krueger A. B. and D. A. Schkade (2007), "The Reliability of Subjective Well-Being Measures", NBER Working Paper 13027, National Bureau of Economic Research.

Larson R. J. and B. L. Fredrickson (1999), "Measurement Issues in Emotion Research", in D. Kahneman, E. Diener and N. Schwarz (eds), *Well-Being. The Foundations of Hedonic Psychology*, Russel Sage Foundation, pp. 40-60, New York.

Lucas R. R. (2007), "Long-Term Disability Is Associated With Lasting Changes in Subjective Well-Being: Evidence From Two Nationally Representative Longitudinal Studies", *Journal of Personality and Social Psychology*, Vol. 92, (4), pp. 717-730.

Rässler S. and R. T. Riphahn (2006), "Survey item nonresponse and its treatment", *Allgemeines Statistisches Archi,v* 90, pp. 217-232.

Sacks W. D., B. Stevenson and J. Wolfers (2010), "Subjective Well-being, Income, Economic Development and Growth", NBER Working Paper 16441,National Bureau of Economic Research.

Sen A. (1979), "Personal utilities and public judgements: or what's wrong with welfare economics", *Economic Journal*, No. 89, pag. 537-558

Sen A. (1976), "Liberty, unanimity and rights", *Economica*, No. 43, pag. 217-245

Sen A. (1970), "The impossibility of a paretian liberal", *Journal of Political Economy*, No. 78, pag. 152-157

Stevenson B. and J. Wolfers, (2008) "Economic Growth and Subjective Wellbeing: Reassessing the Easterlin Paradox", NBER Working Paper No. 14282, National Bureau of Economic Research.

Stiglitz J.E., A. Sen and J.-P. Fitoussi (2009), Report by the Commission on the Measurement of Economic Performance and Social Progress, http://www.stiglitz-sen-fitoussi.fr/documents/rapport_anglais.pdf.

Winkelman L. and R. Winkelman (1998), "Why Are The Unemployed So Unhappy? Evidence From Panel Data?", *Economica*, Vol. 65. pp. 1- 15.

ORGANISATION FOR ECONOMIC CO-OPERATION AND DEVELOPMENT

The OECD is a unique forum where governments work together to address the economic, social and environmental challenges of globalisation. The OECD is also at the forefront of efforts to understand and to help governments respond to new developments and concerns, such as corporate governance, the information economy and the challenges of an ageing population. The Organisation provides a setting where governments can compare policy experiences, seek answers to common problems, identify good practice and work to co-ordinate domestic and international policies.

The OECD member countries are: Australia, Austria, Belgium, Canada, Chile, the Czech Republic, Denmark, Estonia, Finland, France, Germany, Greece, Hungary, Iceland, Ireland, Israel, Italy, Japan, Korea, Luxembourg, Mexico, the Netherlands, New Zealand, Norway, Poland, Portugal, the Slovak Republic, Slovenia, Spain, Sweden, Switzerland, Turkey, the United Kingdom and the United States. The European Union takes part in the work of the OECD.

OECD Publishing disseminates widely the results of the Organisation's statistics gathering and research on economic, social and environmental issues, as well as the conventions, guidelines and standards agreed by its members.

OECD PUBLISHING, 2, rue André-Pascal, 75775 PARIS CEDEX 16
(30 2011 06 1 P) ISBN 978-92-64-11161-5 – No. 59005 2011-02